SILENT DANCE

MATTEO CASALI
writer

GRAZIA LOBACCARO
ALESSANDRO DeANGELIS
artists

GABRIELE DELL'OTTO
with Grazia Lobaccaro
cover art

D1149607

SILENT DANCE

written by **Matteo Casali**

art by **Grazia Lobaccaro** and **Alessandro DeAngelis**

lettering and design by **Innocent Victim**

cover by **Gabriele Dell'Otto** with **Grazia Lobaccaro**

Published by **SLG Publishing**

President & Publisher
Dan Vado

Editor-in-Chief
Jennifer de Guzman

Director of Sales
Deb Moskyok

Production Assistant
Eleanor Lawson

SLG Publishing
P.O. Box 26427
San Jose, CA 95159-6427

www.slavelabor.com
www.innocentvictim.com

Silent Dance is ™ and © **Matteo Casali**, **Grazia Lobaccaro**
and **Alessandro DeAngelis**, 2005, all rights reserved.
No part of this publication may be reproduce without the permission of the
authors and SLG Publishing, except for purposes of review.
Printed in Canada.

First Printing: July 2005
ISBN 1-59362-019-5

LEEDS LIBRARY AND INFORMATION SERVICE	
32653034	
S004955	
	£9.99

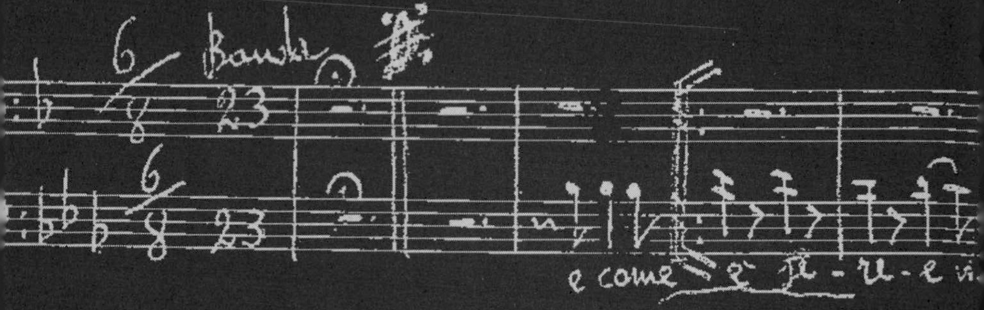
e come

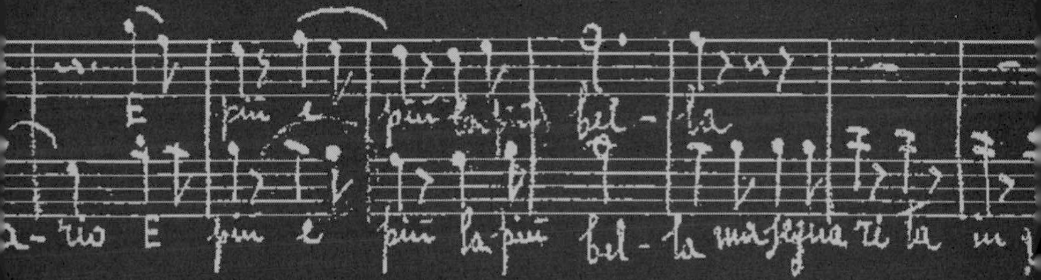
più è più la più bel- la

prologue

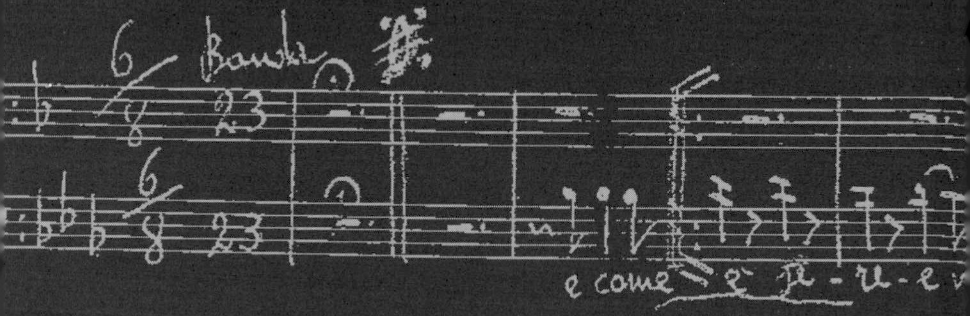
e come

Story
MATTEO CASALI

Art
GRAZIA LOBACCARO

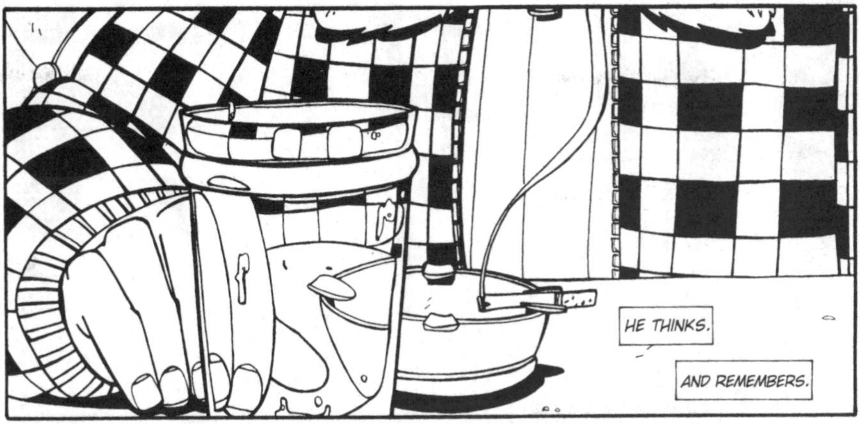
HE THINKS.
AND REMEMBERS.

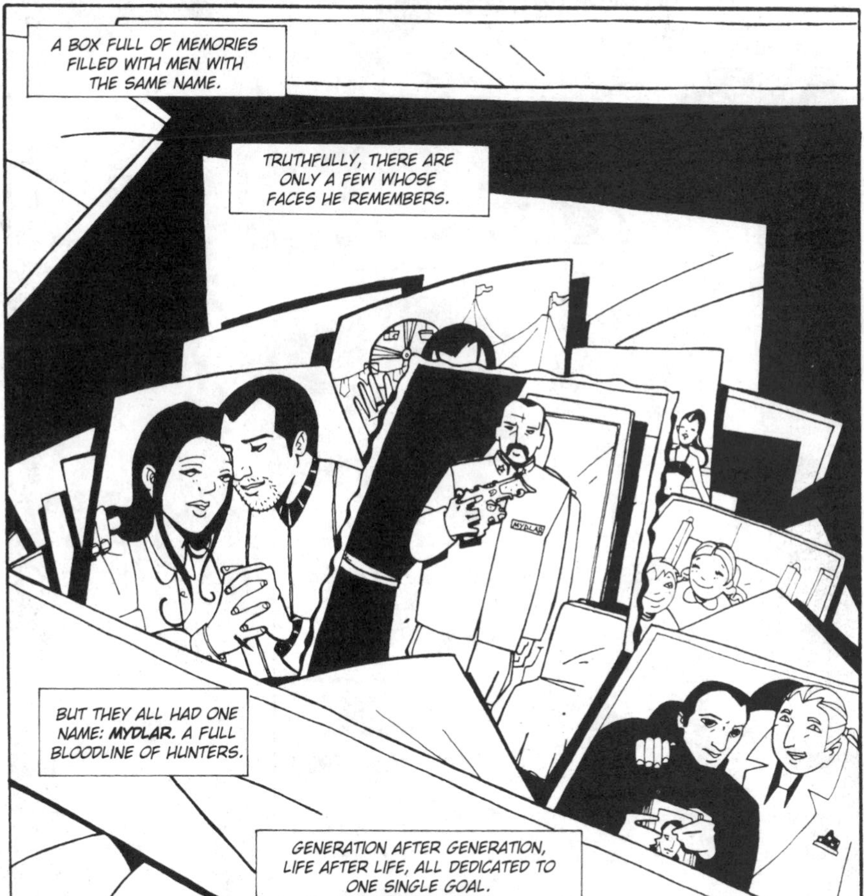
A BOX FULL OF MEMORIES FILLED WITH MEN WITH THE SAME NAME.
TRUTHFULLY, THERE ARE ONLY A FEW WHOSE FACES HE REMEMBERS.
MYDLAR
BUT THEY ALL HAD ONE NAME: **MYDLAR.** A FULL BLOODLINE OF HUNTERS.
GENERATION AFTER GENERATION, LIFE AFTER LIFE, ALL DEDICATED TO ONE SINGLE GOAL.

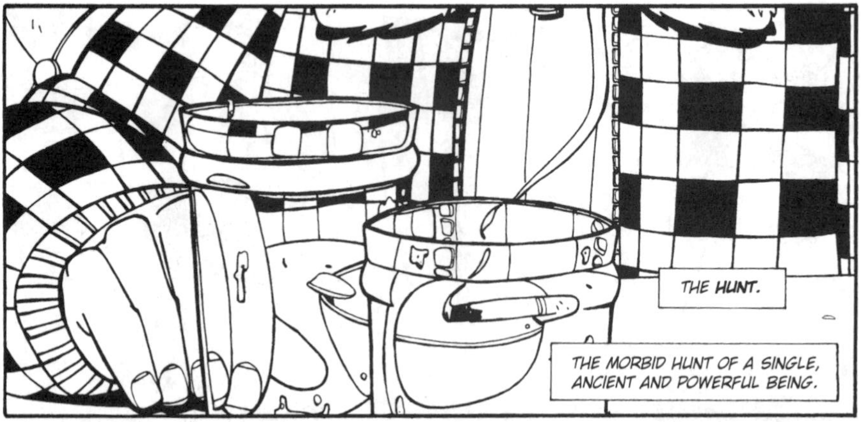
THE HUNT.
THE MORBID HUNT OF A SINGLE, ANCIENT AND POWERFUL BEING.

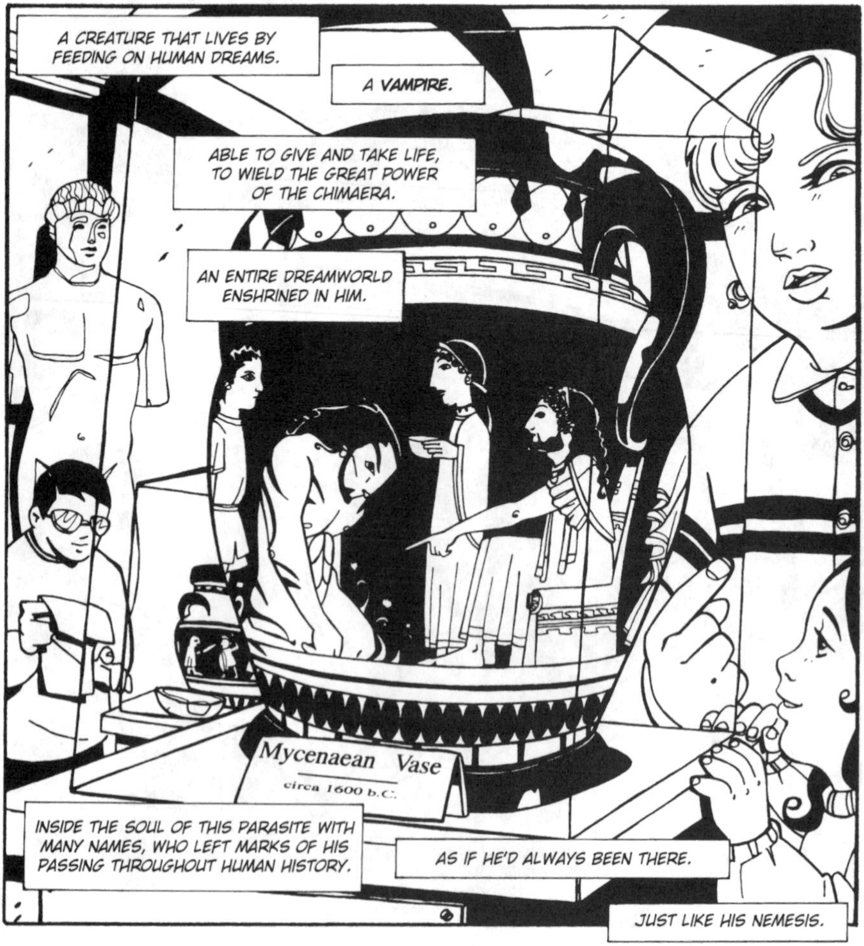
A CREATURE THAT LIVES BY FEEDING ON HUMAN DREAMS.
A VAMPIRE.
ABLE TO GIVE AND TAKE LIFE, TO WIELD THE GREAT POWER OF THE CHIMAERA.
AN ENTIRE DREAMWORLD ENSHRINED IN HIM.
Mycenaean Vase
circa 1600 b.C.
INSIDE THE SOUL OF THIS PARASITE WITH MANY NAMES, WHO LEFT MARKS OF HIS PASSING THROUGHOUT HUMAN HISTORY.
AS IF HE'D ALWAYS BEEN THERE.
JUST LIKE HIS NEMESIS.

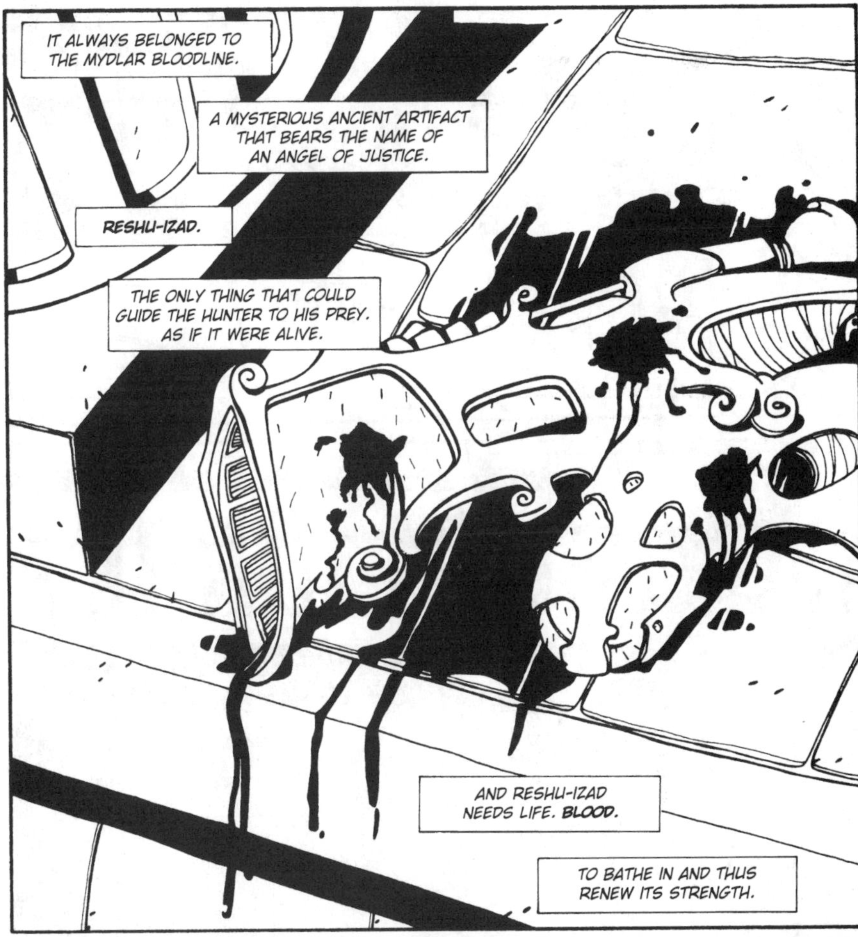
IT ALWAYS BELONGED TO THE MYDLAR BLOODLINE.
A MYSTERIOUS ANCIENT ARTIFACT THAT BEARS THE NAME OF AN ANGEL OF JUSTICE.
RESHU-IZAD.
THE ONLY THING THAT COULD GUIDE THE HUNTER TO HIS PREY. AS IF IT WERE ALIVE.
AND RESHU-IZAD NEEDS LIFE. BLOOD.
TO BATHE IN AND THUS RENEW ITS STRENGTH.
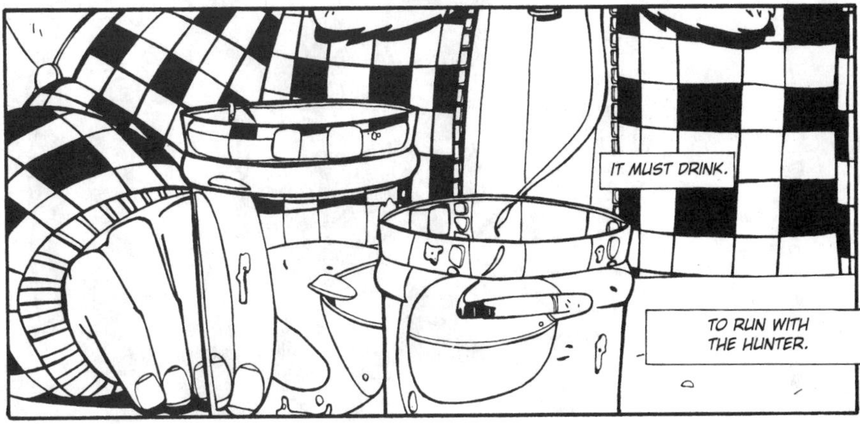
IT MUST DRINK.
TO RUN WITH THE HUNTER.

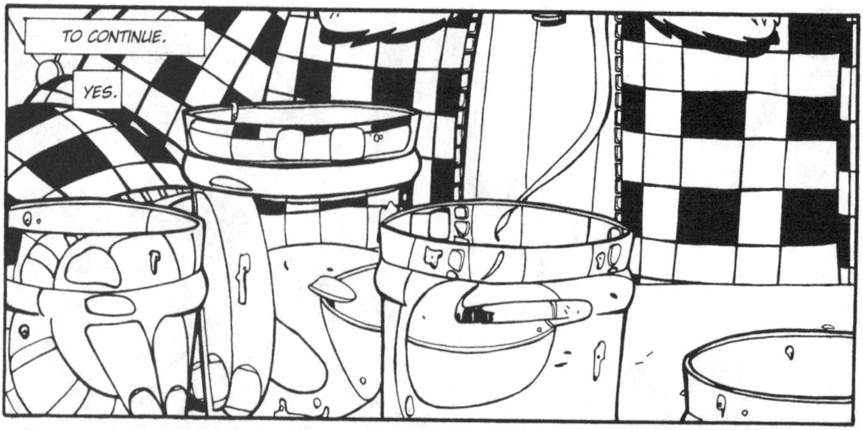
TO CONTINUE.
YES.

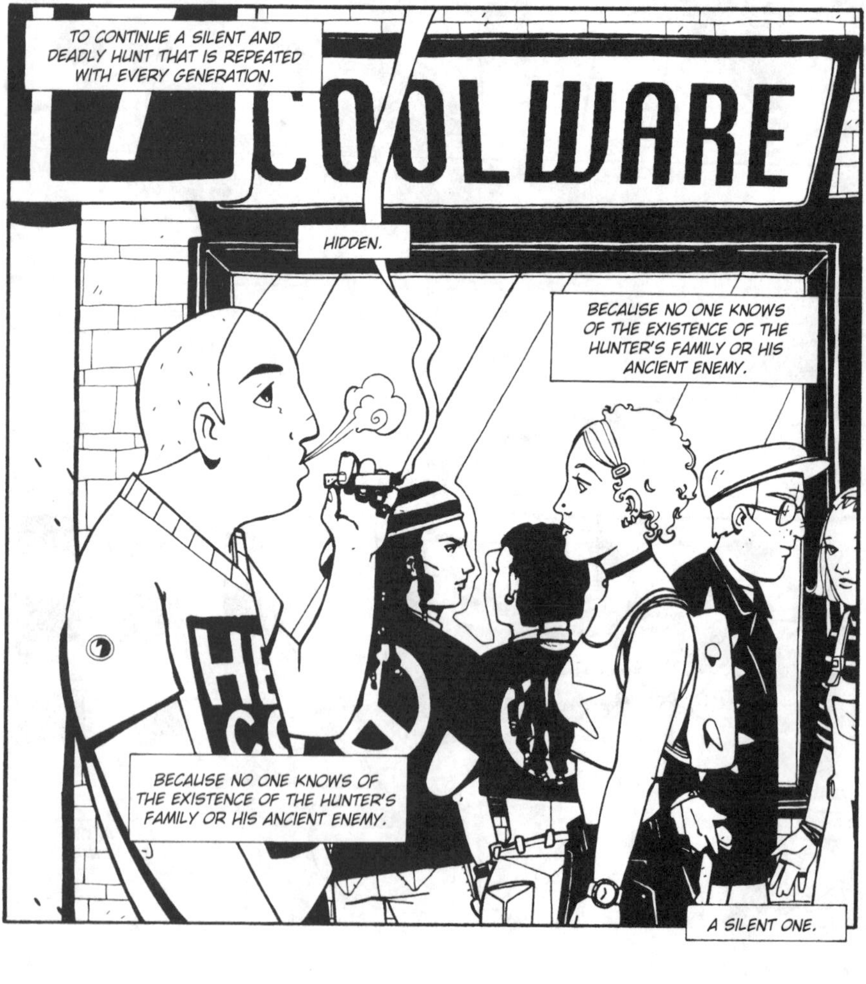
TO CONTINUE A SILENT AND DEADLY HUNT THAT IS REPEATED WITH EVERY GENERATION.
COOLWARE
HIDDEN.
BECAUSE NO ONE KNOWS OF THE EXISTENCE OF THE HUNTER'S FAMILY OR HIS ANCIENT ENEMY.
BECAUSE NO ONE KNOWS OF THE EXISTENCE OF THE HUNTER'S FAMILY OR HIS ANCIENT ENEMY.
A SILENT ONE.

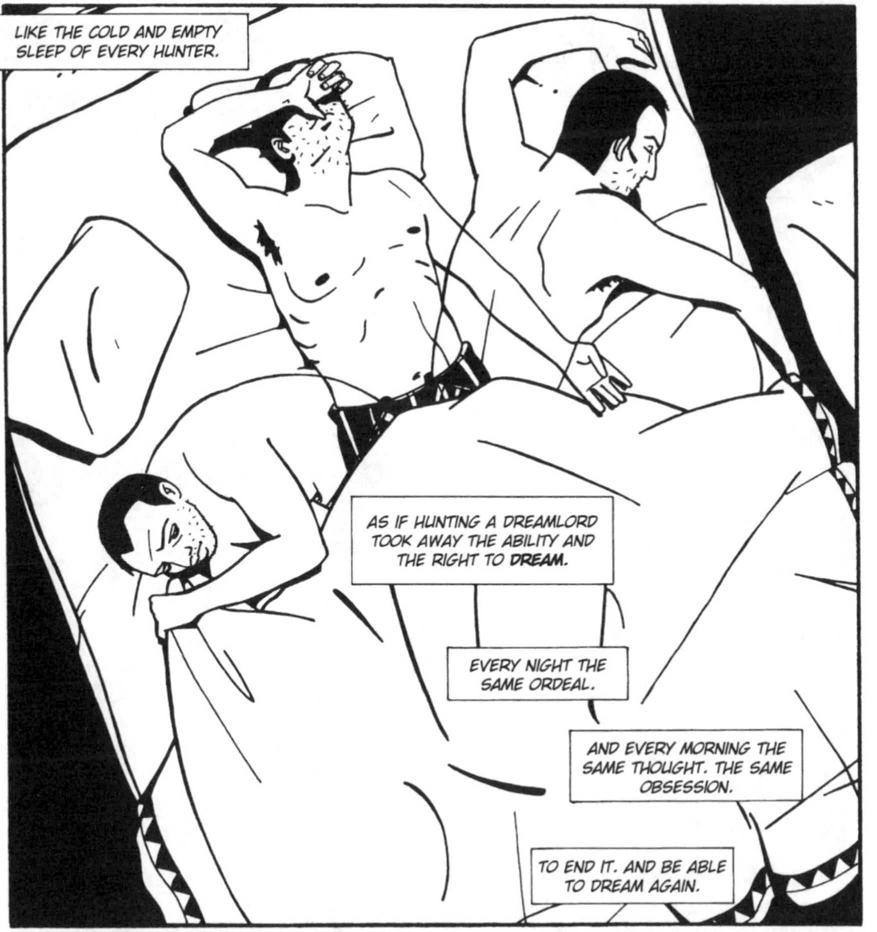
LIKE THE COLD AND EMPTY SLEEP OF EVERY HUNTER.
AS IF HUNTING A DREAMLORD TOOK AWAY THE ABILITY AND THE RIGHT TO **DREAM.**
EVERY NIGHT THE SAME ORDEAL.
AND EVERY MORNING THE SAME THOUGHT. THE SAME OBSESSION.
TO END IT. AND BE ABLE TO DREAM AGAIN.
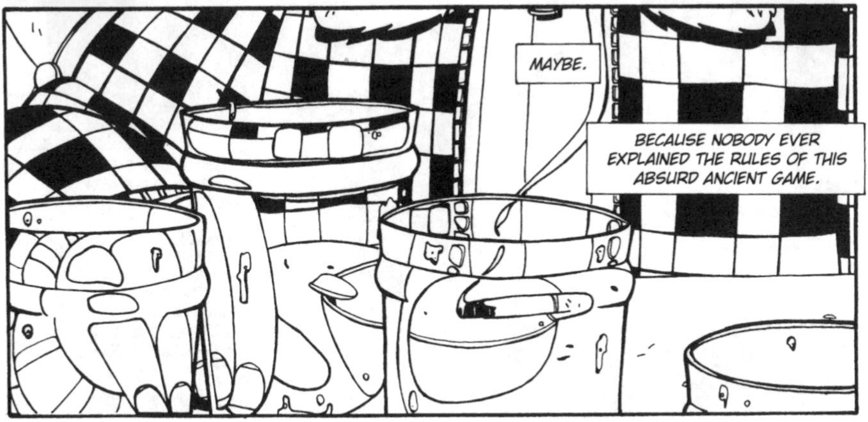
MAYBE.
BECAUSE NOBODY EVER EXPLAINED THE RULES OF THIS ABSURD ANCIENT GAME.

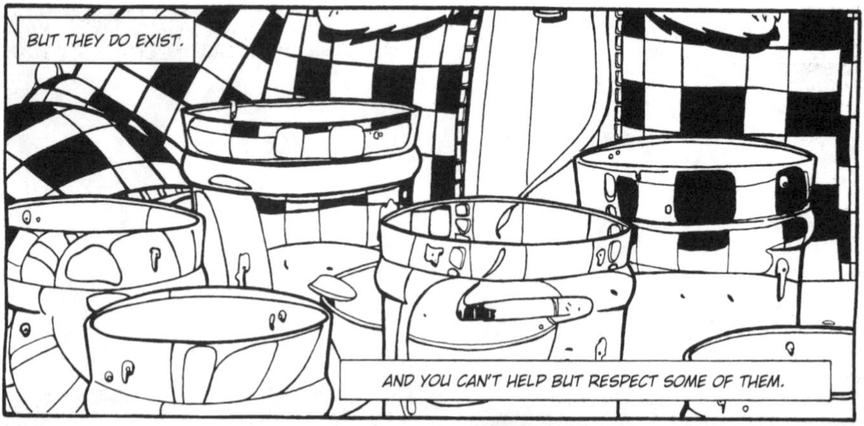
BUT THEY DO EXIST.
AND YOU CAN'T HELP BUT RESPECT SOME OF THEM.

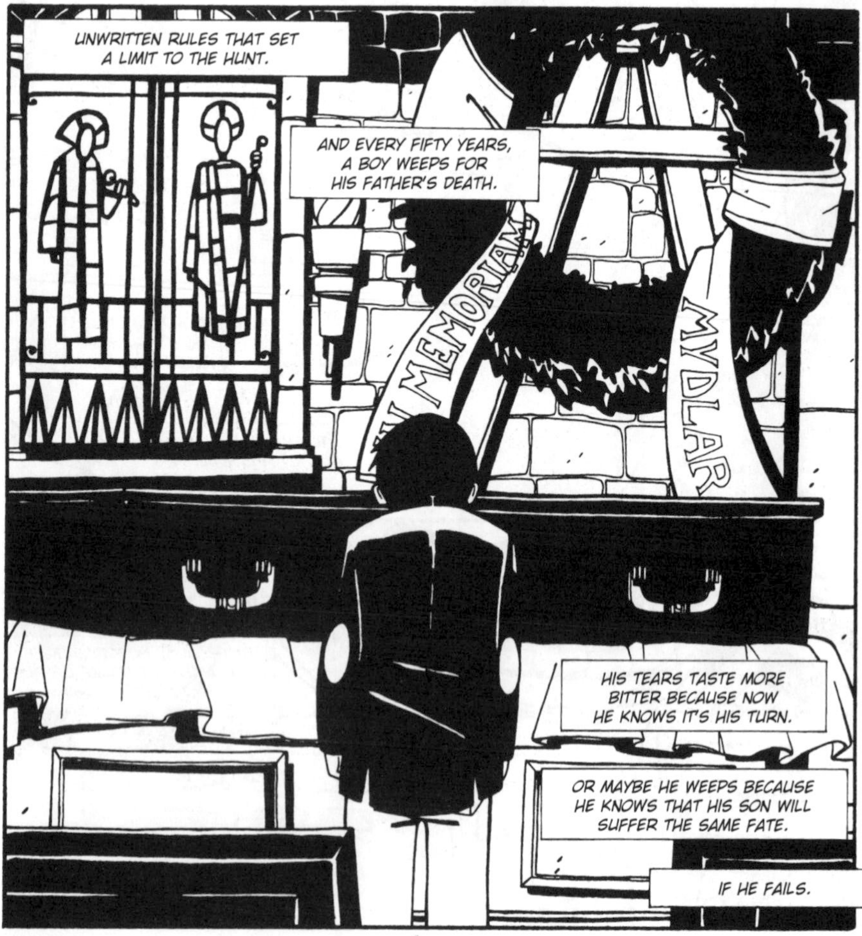
UNWRITTEN RULES THAT SET A LIMIT TO THE HUNT.
AND EVERY FIFTY YEARS, A BOY WEEPS FOR HIS FATHER'S DEATH.
IN MEMORIAM
MYDLAR
HIS TEARS TASTE MORE BITTER BECAUSE NOW HE KNOWS IT'S HIS TURN.
OR MAYBE HE WEEPS BECAUSE HE KNOWS THAT HIS SON WILL SUFFER THE SAME FATE.
IF HE FAILS.

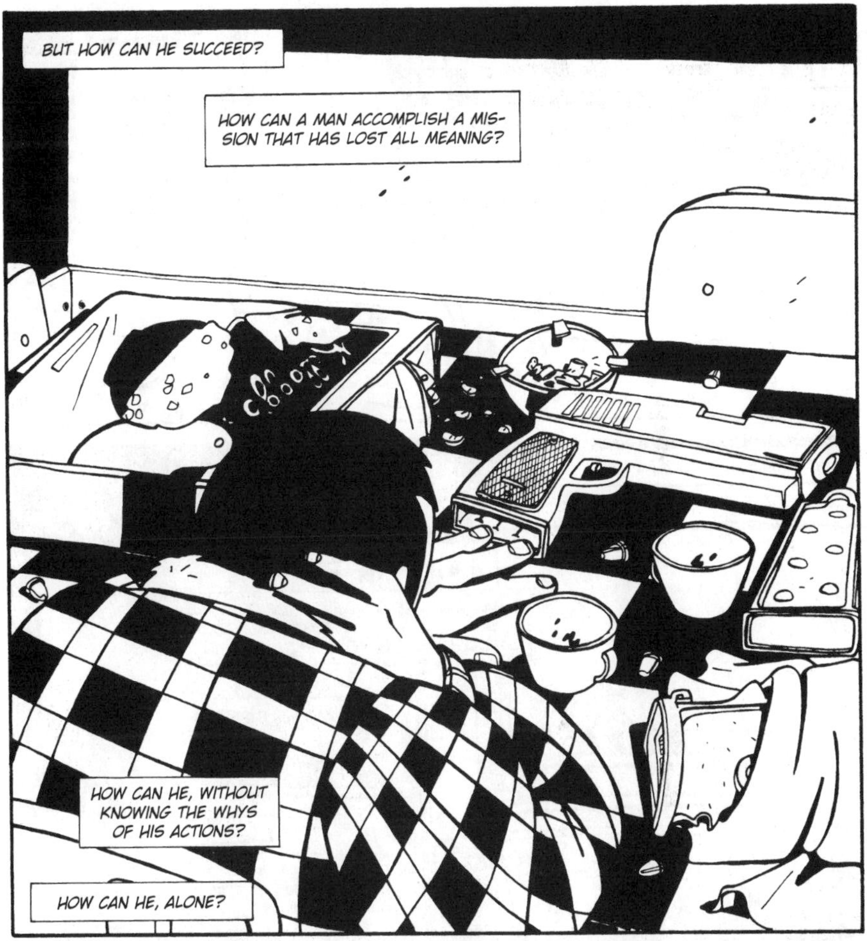
BUT HOW CAN HE SUCCEED?
HOW CAN A MAN ACCOMPLISH A MISSION THAT HAS LOST ALL MEANING?
HOW CAN HE, WITHOUT KNOWING THE WHYS OF HIS ACTIONS?
HOW CAN HE, ALONE?

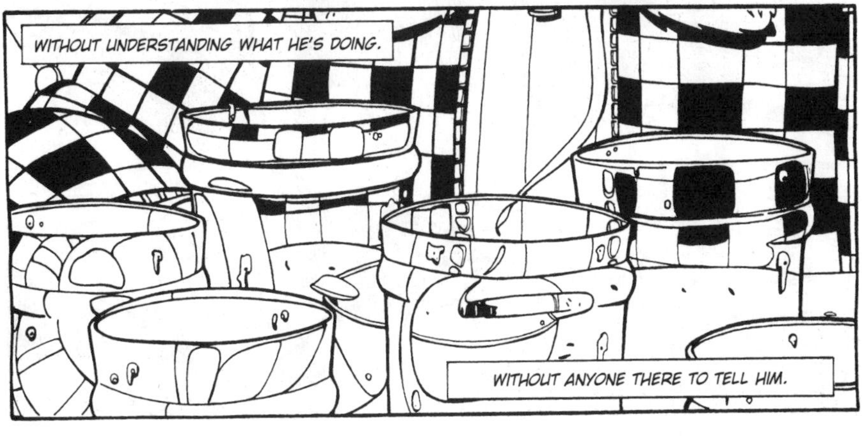
WITHOUT UNDERSTANDING WHAT HE'S DOING.
WITHOUT ANYONE THERE TO TELL HIM.

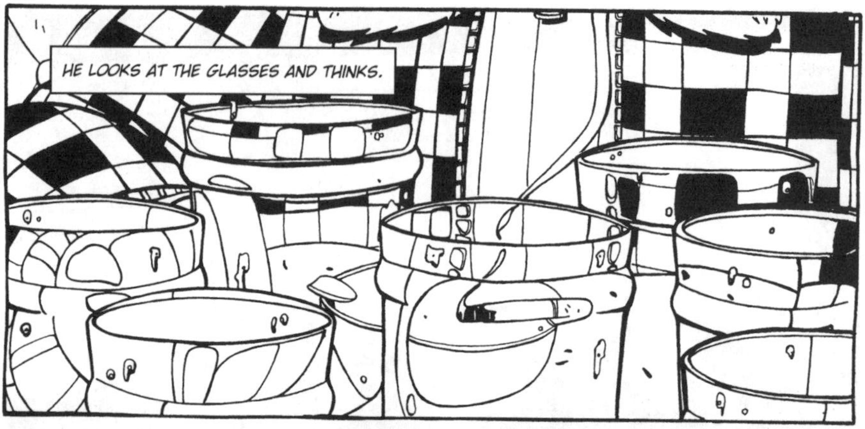
HE LOOKS AT THE GLASSES AND THINKS.

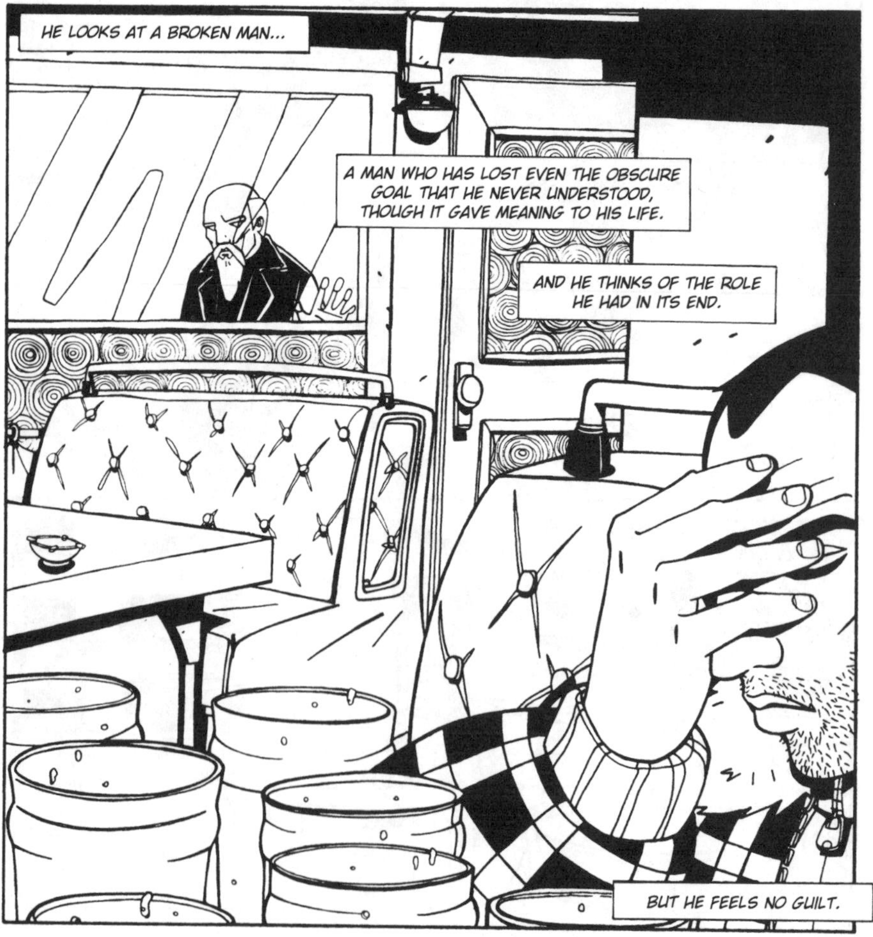
HE LOOKS AT A BROKEN MAN...
A MAN WHO HAS LOST EVEN THE OBSCURE GOAL THAT HE NEVER UNDERSTOOD, THOUGH IT GAVE MEANING TO HIS LIFE.
AND HE THINKS OF THE ROLE HE HAD IN ITS END.
BUT HE FEELS NO GUILT.

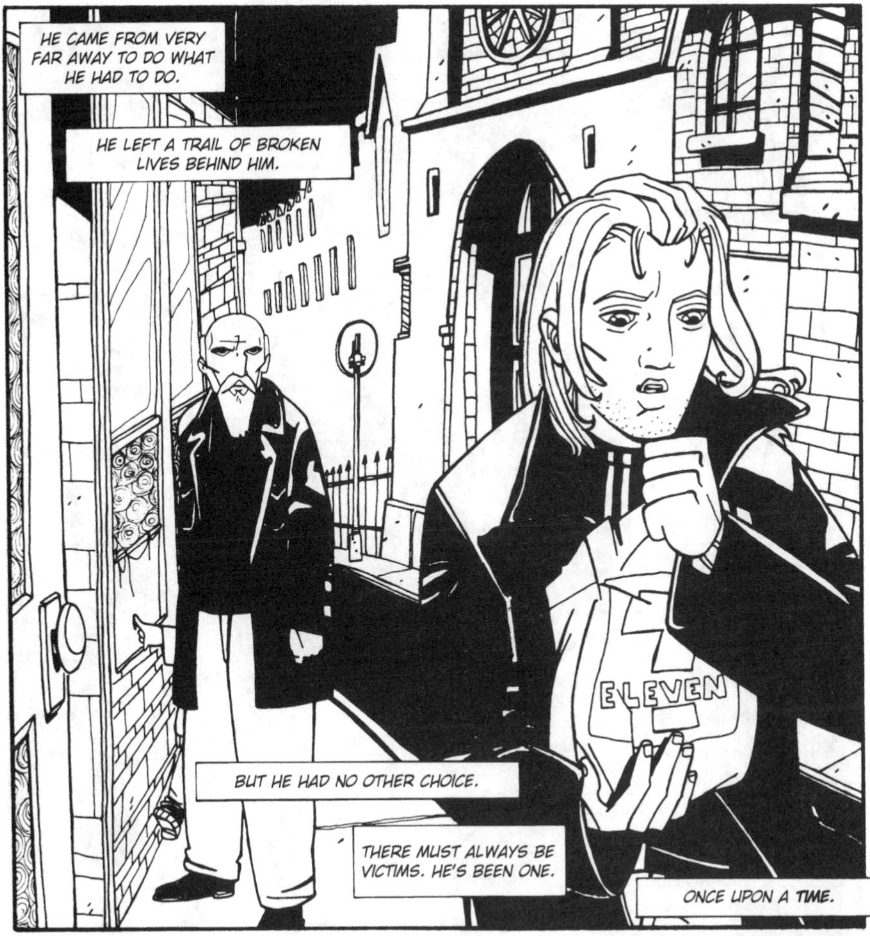
HE CAME FROM VERY FAR AWAY TO DO WHAT HE HAD TO DO.
HE LEFT A TRAIL OF BROKEN LIVES BEHIND HIM.
ELEVEN
BUT HE HAD NO OTHER CHOICE.
THERE MUST ALWAYS BE VICTIMS. HE'S BEEN ONE.
ONCE UPON A TIME.

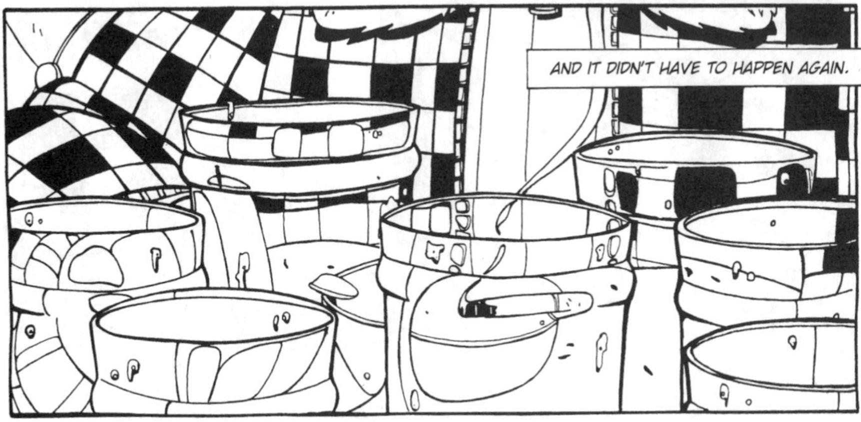
AND IT DIDN'T HAVE TO HAPPEN AGAIN.

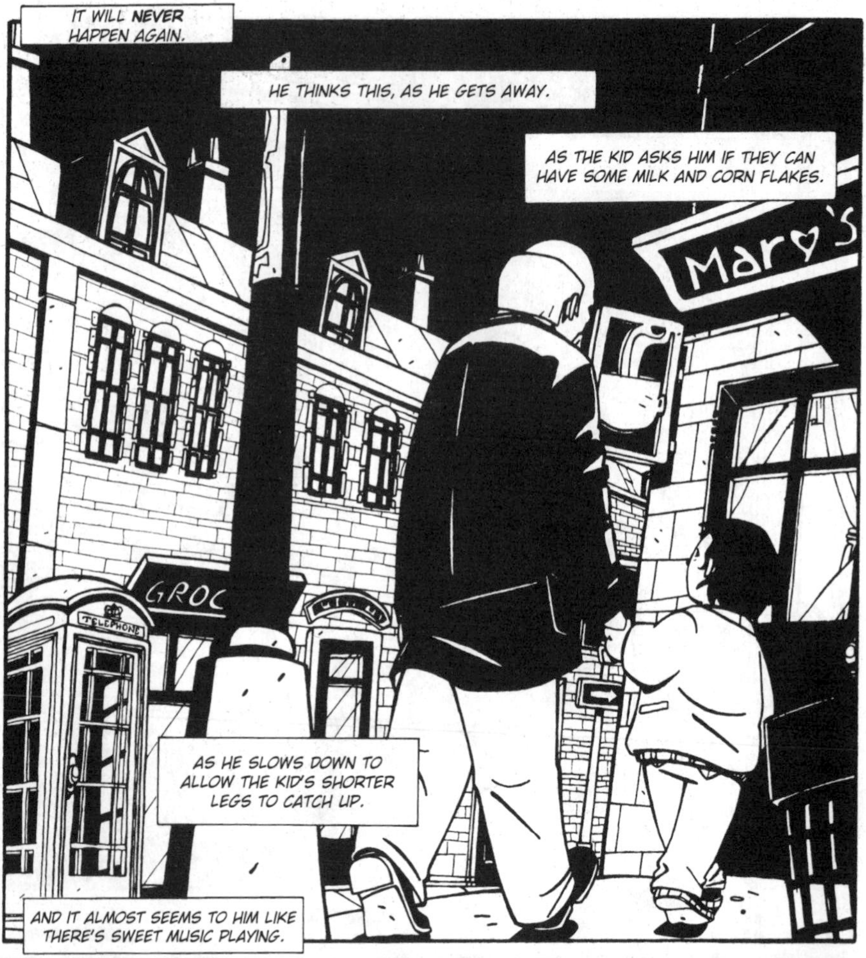
IT WILL NEVER HAPPEN AGAIN.
HE THINKS THIS, AS HE GETS AWAY.
AS THE KID ASKS HIM IF THEY CAN HAVE SOME MILK AND CORN FLAKES.
Mary's
GROC
TELEPHONE
AS HE SLOWS DOWN TO ALLOW THE KID'S SHORTER LEGS TO CATCH UP.
AND IT ALMOST SEEMS TO HIM LIKE THERE'S SWEET MUSIC PLAYING.

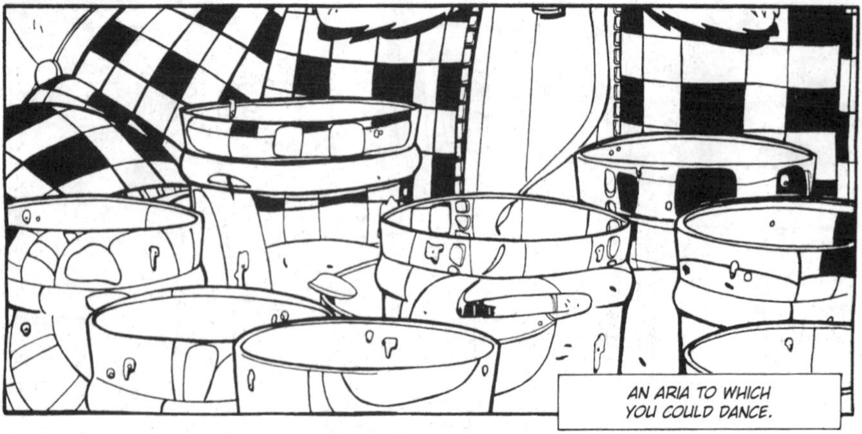
AN ARIA TO WHICH YOU COULD DANCE.

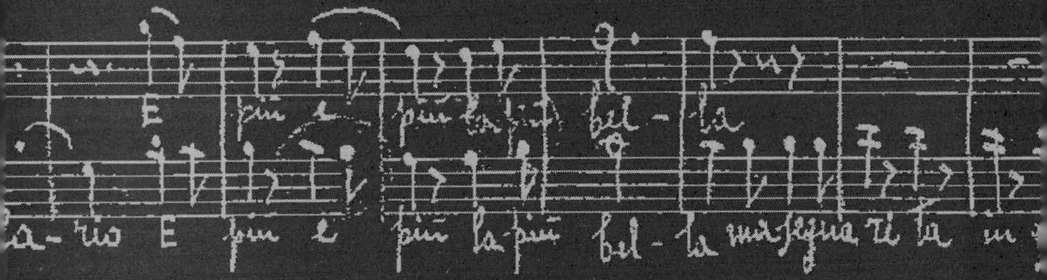

chapter one

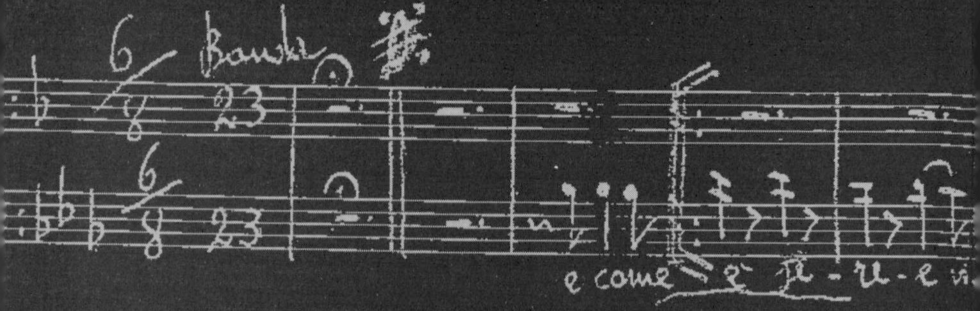
e come

Story
MATTEO CASALI

Art
ALESSANDRO DeANGELIS

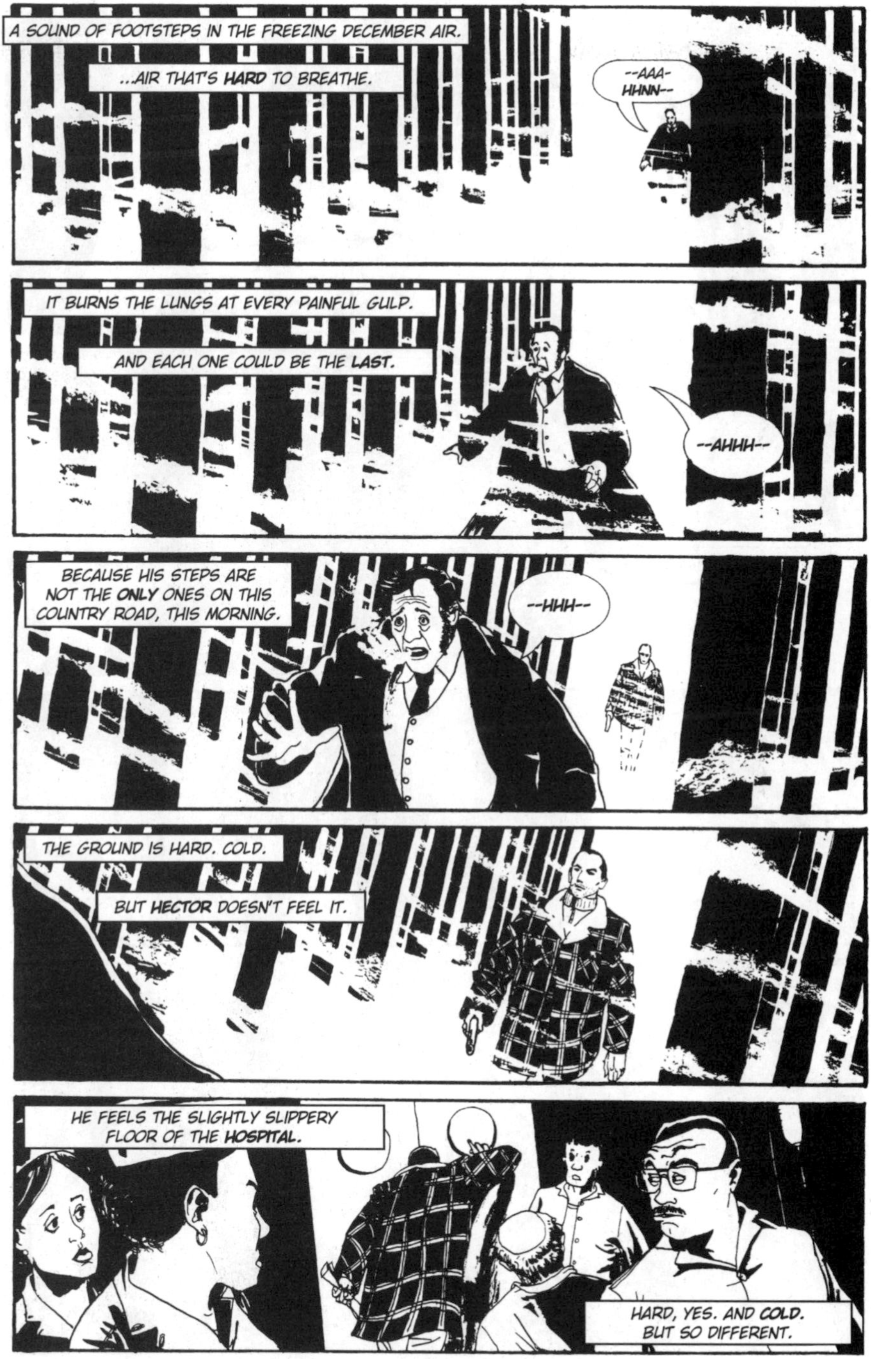
A SOUND OF FOOTSTEPS IN THE FREEZING DECEMBER AIR.
...AIR THAT'S HARD TO BREATHE.
--AAA-HHNN--
IT BURNS THE LUNGS AT EVERY PAINFUL GULP.
AND EACH ONE COULD BE THE LAST.
--AHHH--
BECAUSE HIS STEPS ARE NOT THE ONLY ONES ON THIS COUNTRY ROAD, THIS MORNING.
--HHH--
THE GROUND IS HARD. COLD.
BUT HECTOR DOESN'T FEEL IT.
HE FEELS THE SLIGHTLY SLIPPERY FLOOR OF THE HOSPITAL.
HARD, YES. AND COLD. BUT SO DIFFERENT.

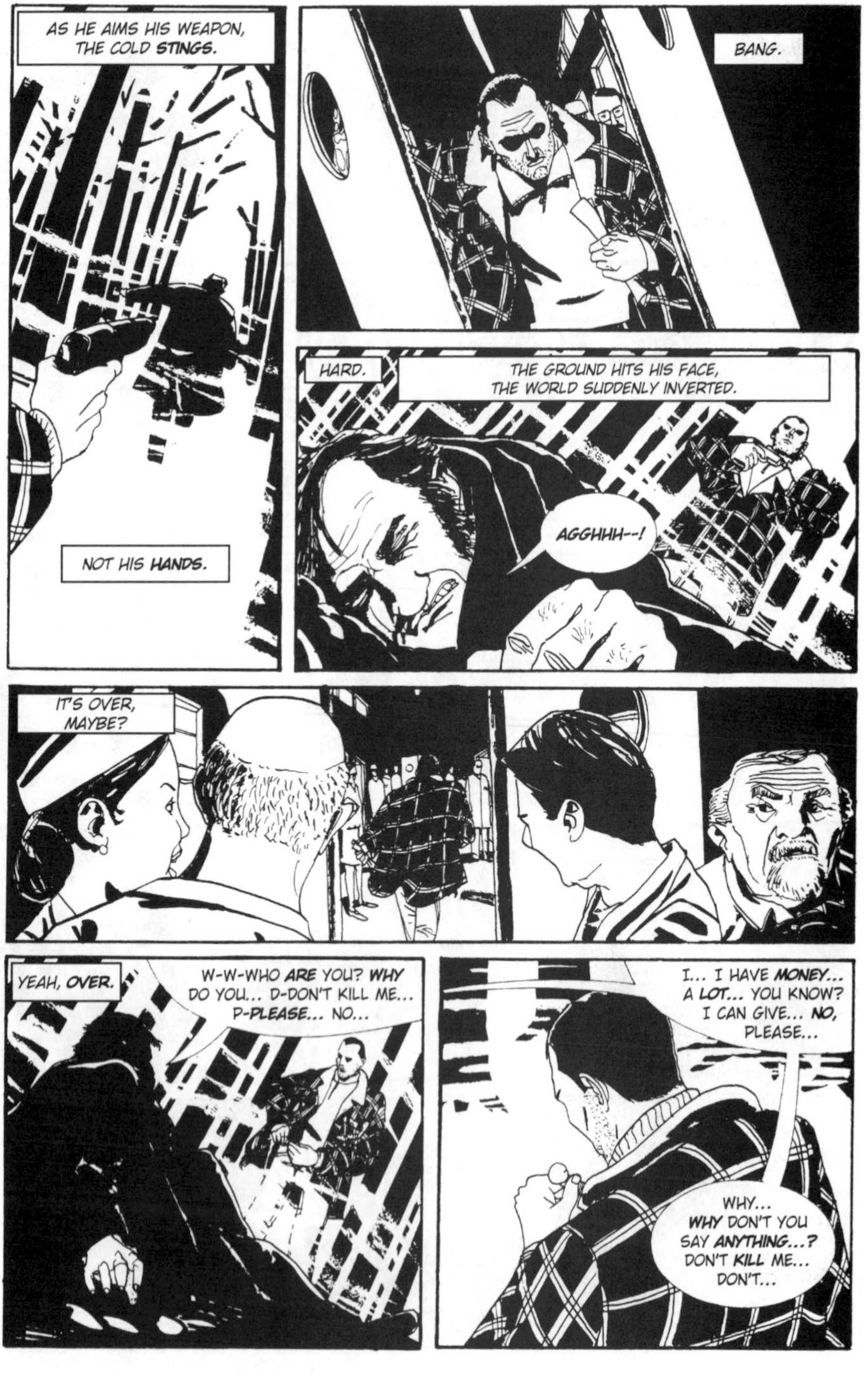
AS HE AIMS HIS WEAPON, THE COLD STINGS.
NOT HIS HANDS.
BANG.
HARD.
THE GROUND HITS HIS FACE, THE WORLD SUDDENLY INVERTED.
AGGHHH--!
IT'S OVER, MAYBE?
YEAH, OVER.
W-W-WHO ARE YOU? WHY DO YOU... D-DON'T KILL ME... P-PLEASE... NO...
I... I HAVE MONEY... A LOT... YOU KNOW? I CAN GIVE... NO, PLEASE...
WHY... WHY DON'T YOU SAY ANYTHING...? DON'T KILL ME... DON'T...

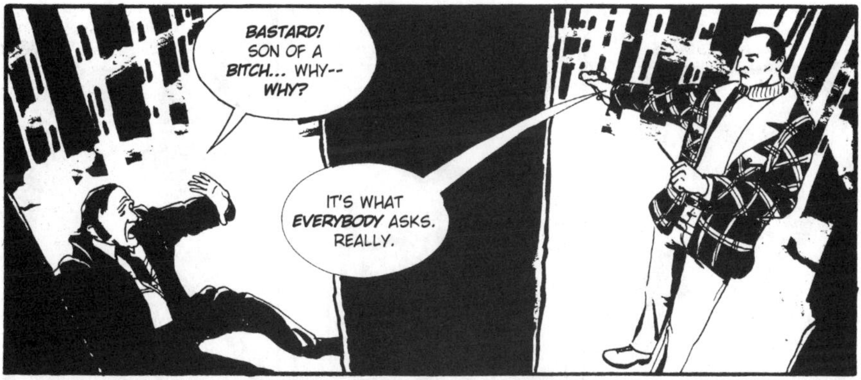
BASTARD! SON OF A BITCH... WHY-- WHY?
IT'S WHAT EVERYBODY ASKS. REALLY.

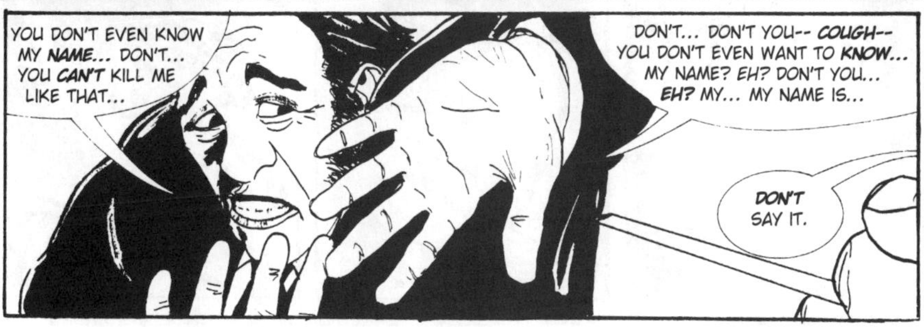
YOU DON'T EVEN KNOW MY NAME... DON'T... YOU CAN'T KILL ME LIKE THAT...
DON'T... DON'T YOU-- COUGH-- YOU DON'T EVEN WANT TO KNOW... MY NAME? EH? DON'T YOU... EH? MY... MY NAME IS...
DON'T SAY IT.

don't ask. don't tell

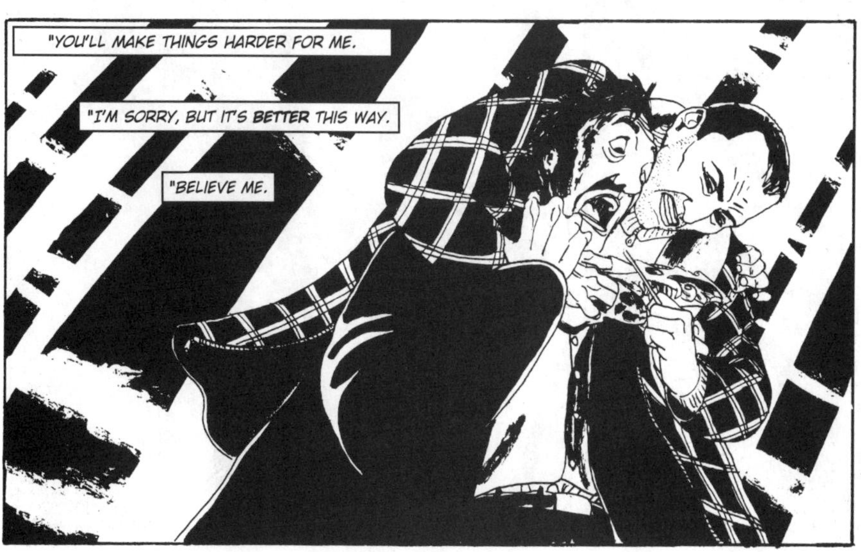
"YOU'LL MAKE THINGS HARDER FOR ME.
"I'M SORRY, BUT IT'S BETTER THIS WAY.
"BELIEVE ME.

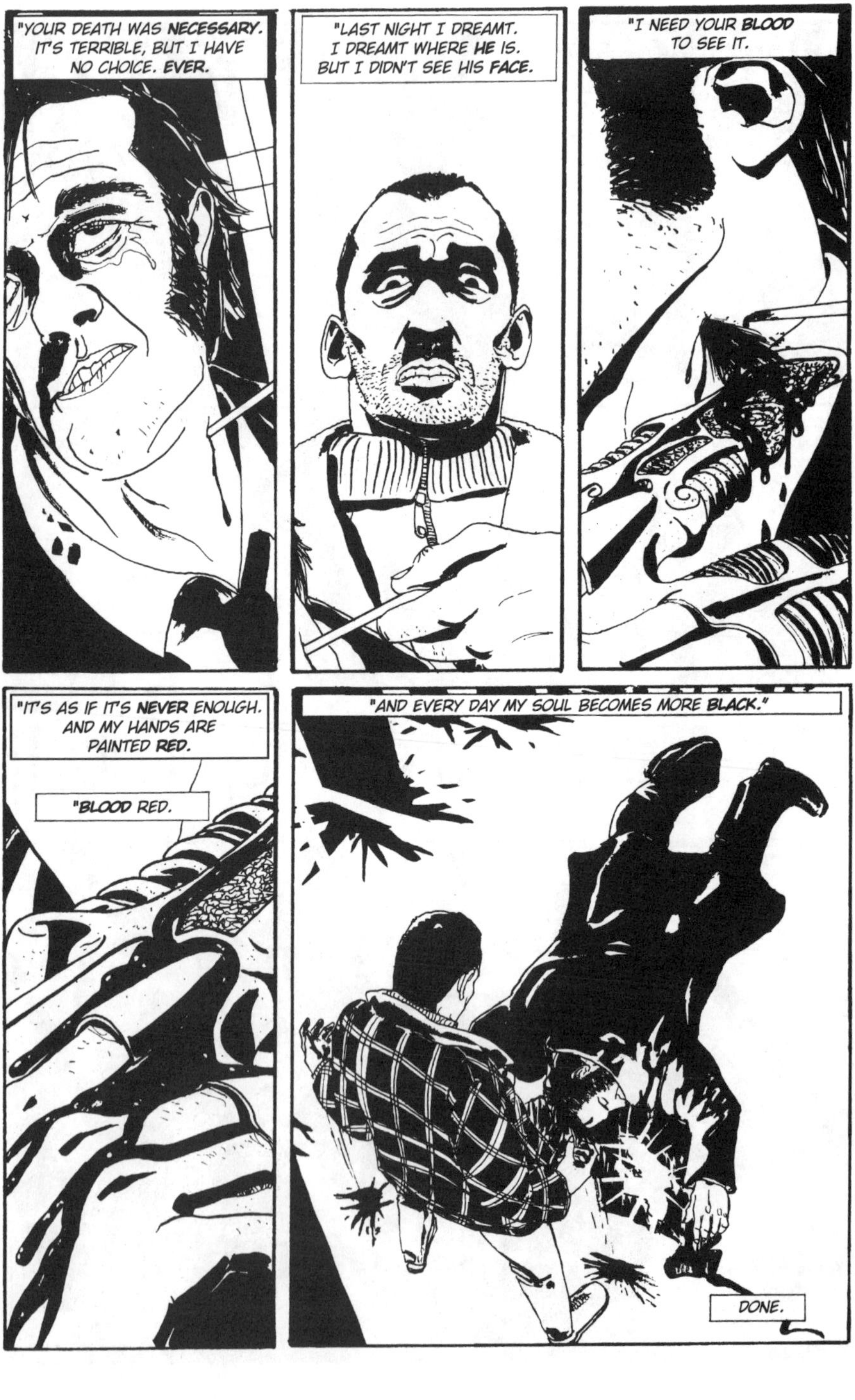
"YOUR DEATH WAS NECESSARY. IT'S TERRIBLE, BUT I HAVE NO CHOICE. EVER.
"LAST NIGHT I DREAMT. I DREAMT WHERE HE IS. BUT I DIDN'T SEE HIS FACE.
"I NEED YOUR BLOOD TO SEE IT.
"IT'S AS IF IT'S NEVER ENOUGH. AND MY HANDS ARE PAINTED RED.
"BLOOD RED.
"AND EVERY DAY MY SOUL BECOMES MORE BLACK."
DONE.

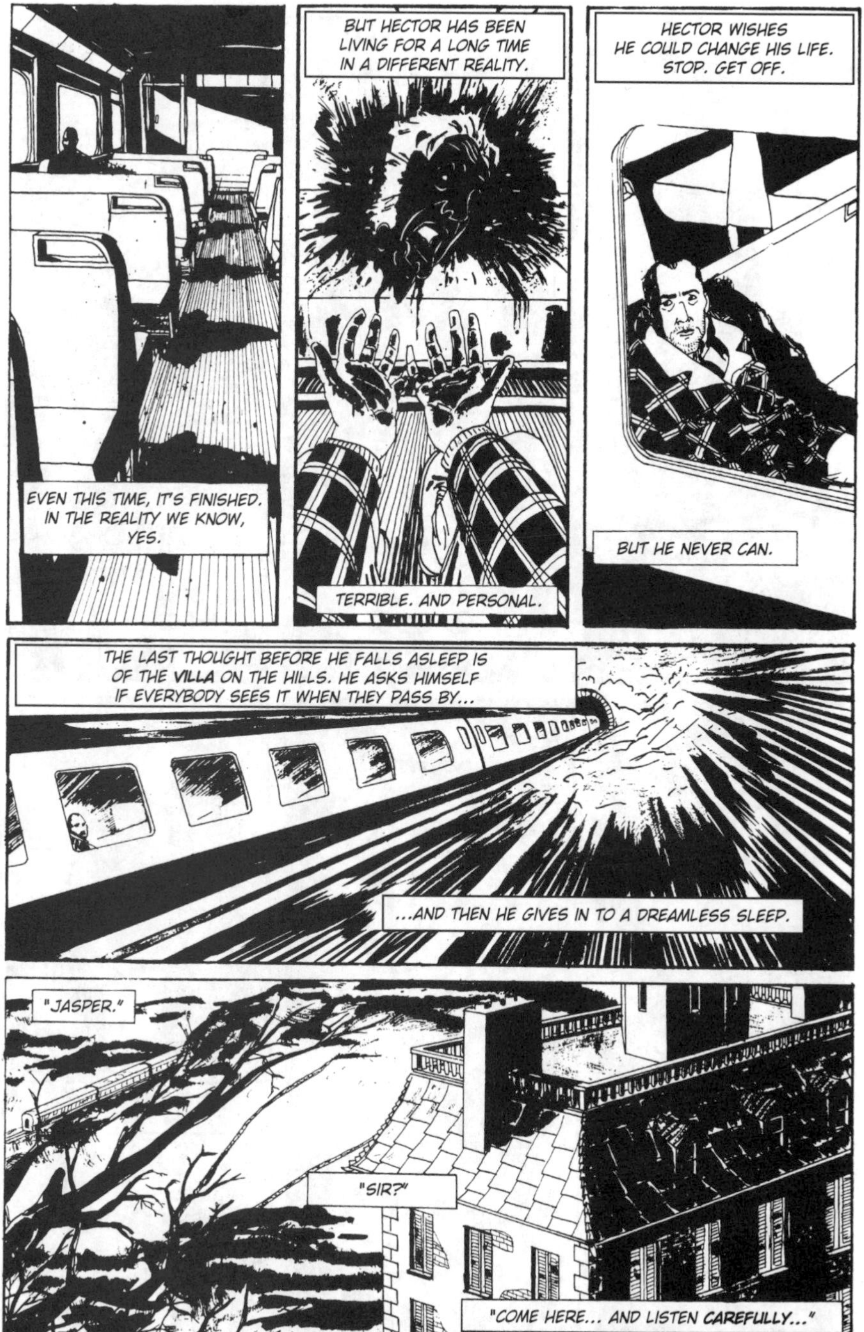
EVEN THIS TIME, IT'S FINISHED. IN THE REALITY WE KNOW, YES.
BUT HECTOR HAS BEEN LIVING FOR A LONG TIME IN A DIFFERENT REALITY.
TERRIBLE. AND PERSONAL.
HECTOR WISHES HE COULD CHANGE HIS LIFE. STOP. GET OFF.
BUT HE NEVER CAN.
THE LAST THOUGHT BEFORE HE FALLS ASLEEP IS OF THE VILLA ON THE HILLS. HE ASKS HIMSELF IF EVERYBODY SEES IT WHEN THEY PASS BY...
...AND THEN HE GIVES IN TO A DREAMLESS SLEEP.
"JASPER."
"SIR?"
"COME HERE... AND LISTEN CAREFULLY..."

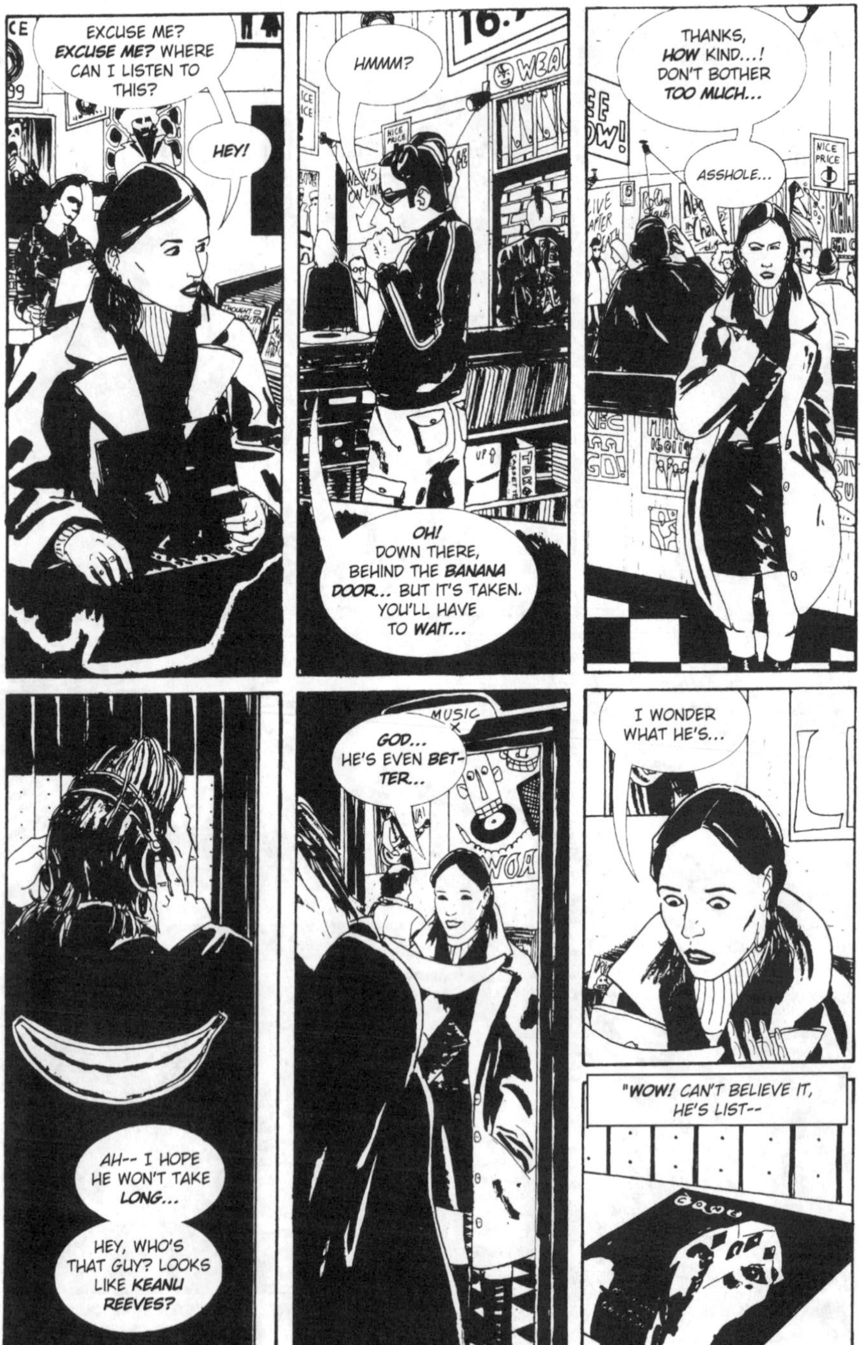

EXCUSE ME? EXCUSE ME? WHERE CAN I LISTEN TO THIS?
HEY!
HMMM?
OH! DOWN THERE, BEHIND THE BANANA DOOR... BUT IT'S TAKEN. YOU'LL HAVE TO WAIT...
THANKS, HOW KIND...! DON'T BOTHER TOO MUCH...
ASSHOLE...
AH-- I HOPE HE WON'T TAKE LONG...
HEY, WHO'S THAT GUY? LOOKS LIKE KEANU REEVES?
MUSIC
GOD... HE'S EVEN BET-TER...
I WONDER WHAT HE'S...
"WOW! CAN'T BELIEVE IT, HE'S LIST--

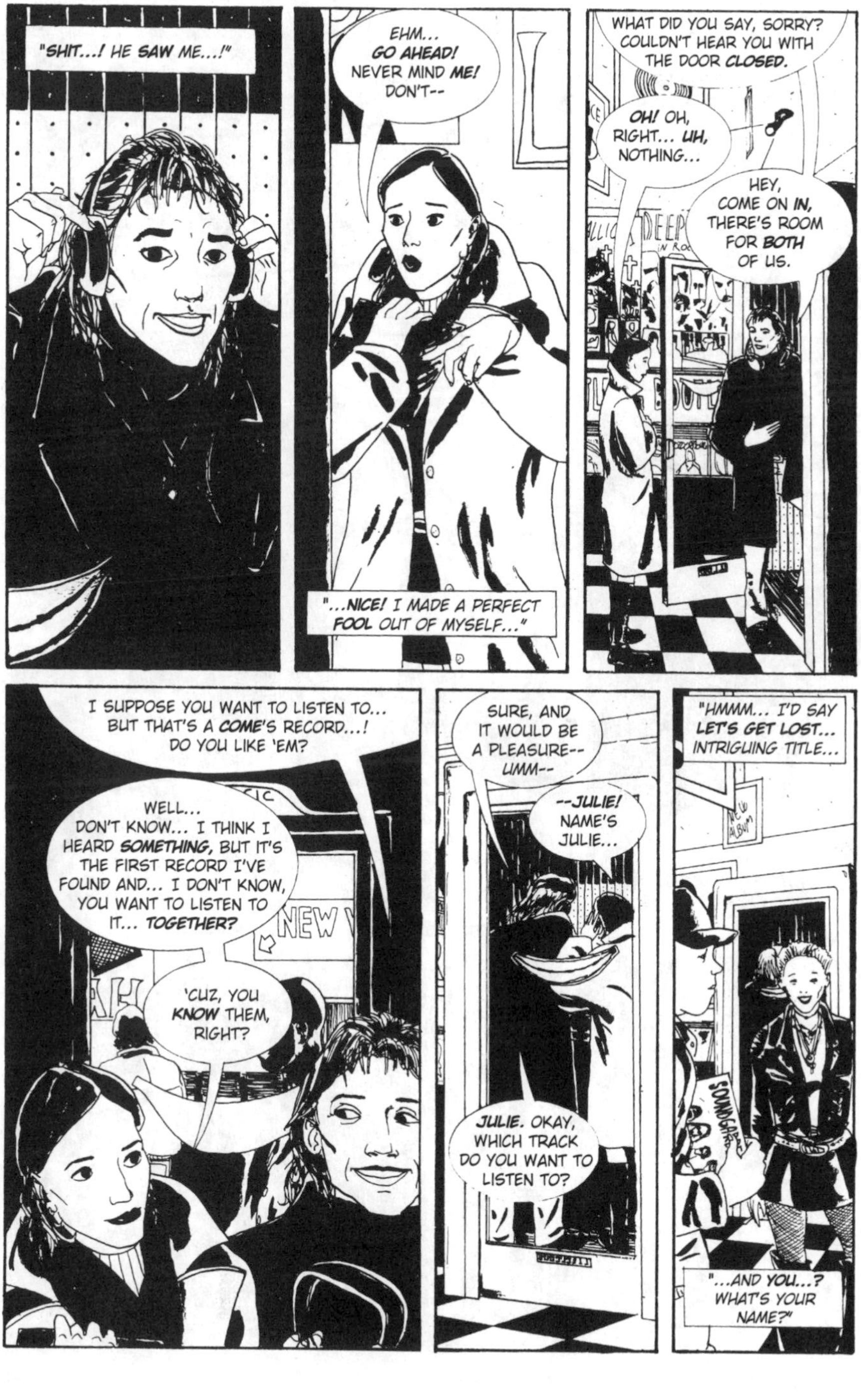
"SHIT...! HE SAW ME...!"
EHM... GO AHEAD! NEVER MIND ME! DON'T--
"...NICE! I MADE A PERFECT FOOL OUT OF MYSELF..."
WHAT DID YOU SAY, SORRY? COULDN'T HEAR YOU WITH THE DOOR CLOSED.
OH! OH, RIGHT... UH, NOTHING...
HEY, COME ON IN, THERE'S ROOM FOR BOTH OF US.
I SUPPOSE YOU WANT TO LISTEN TO... BUT THAT'S A COME'S RECORD...! DO YOU LIKE 'EM?
WELL... DON'T KNOW... I THINK I HEARD SOMETHING, BUT IT'S THE FIRST RECORD I'VE FOUND AND... I DON'T KNOW, YOU WANT TO LISTEN TO IT... TOGETHER?
'CUZ, YOU KNOW THEM, RIGHT?
NEW
SURE, AND IT WOULD BE A PLEASURE-- UMM--
--JULIE! NAME'S JULIE...
JULIE. OKAY, WHICH TRACK DO YOU WANT TO LISTEN TO?
"HMMM... I'D SAY LET'S GET LOST... INTRIGUING TITLE...
SOUNDGARDEN
"...AND YOU...? WHAT'S YOUR NAME?"

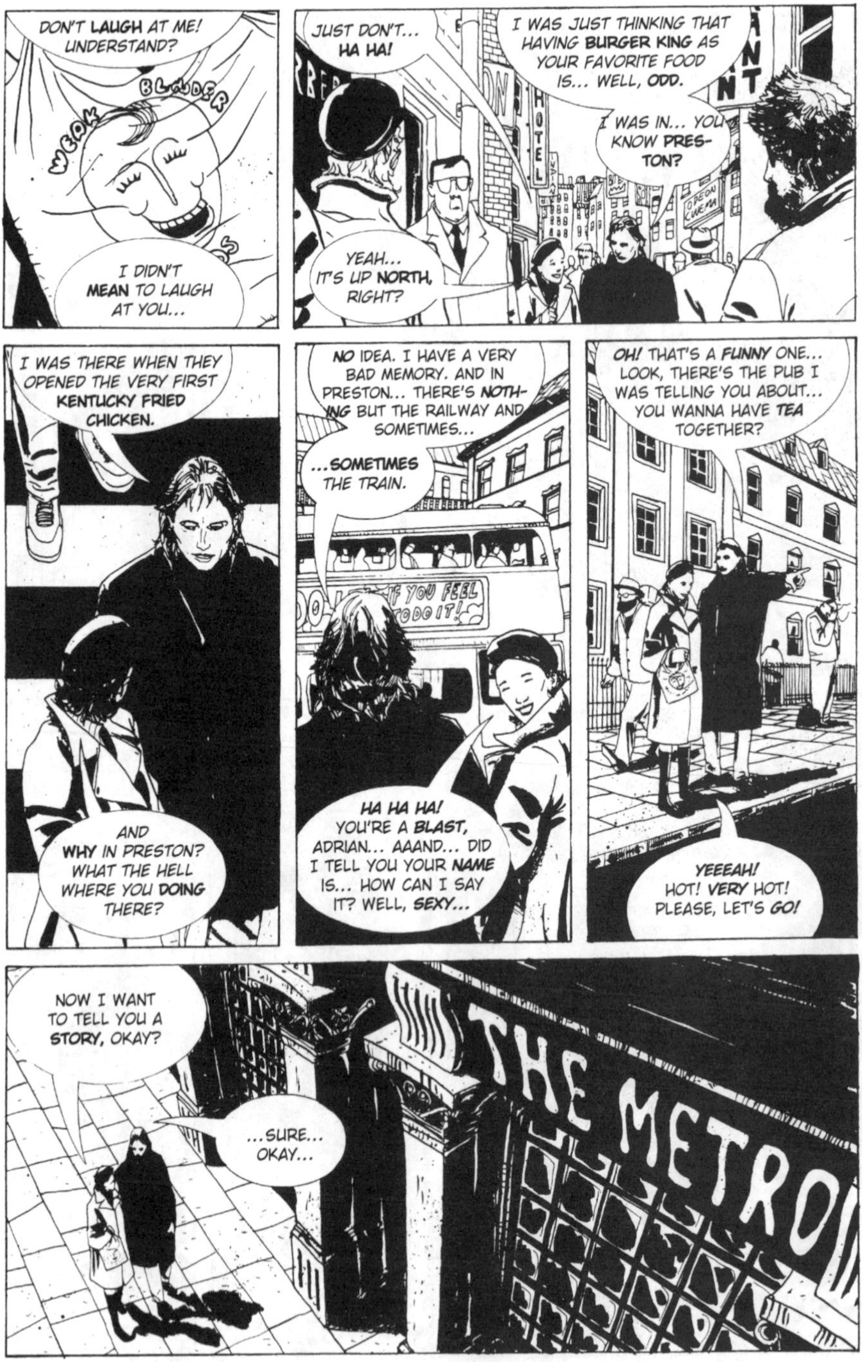
DON'T LAUGH AT ME! UNDERSTAND?
I DIDN'T MEAN TO LAUGH AT YOU...
JUST DON'T... HA HA!
I WAS JUST THINKING THAT HAVING BURGER KING AS YOUR FAVORITE FOOD IS... WELL, ODD.
I WAS IN... YOU KNOW PRESTON?
HOTEL
YEAH... IT'S UP NORTH, RIGHT?
I WAS THERE WHEN THEY OPENED THE VERY FIRST KENTUCKY FRIED CHICKEN.
AND WHY IN PRESTON? WHAT THE HELL WHERE YOU DOING THERE?
NO IDEA. I HAVE A VERY BAD MEMORY. AND IN PRESTON... THERE'S NOTHING BUT THE RAILWAY AND SOMETIMES...
...SOMETIMES THE TRAIN.
IF YOU FEEL TO DO IT!
HA HA HA! YOU'RE A BLAST, ADRIAN... AAAND... DID I TELL YOU YOUR NAME IS... HOW CAN I SAY IT? WELL, SEXY...
OH! THAT'S A FUNNY ONE... LOOK, THERE'S THE PUB I WAS TELLING YOU ABOUT... YOU WANNA HAVE TEA TOGETHER?
YEEEAH! HOT! VERY HOT! PLEASE, LET'S GO!
NOW I WANT TO TELL YOU A STORY, OKAY?
...SURE... OKAY...
THE METRO

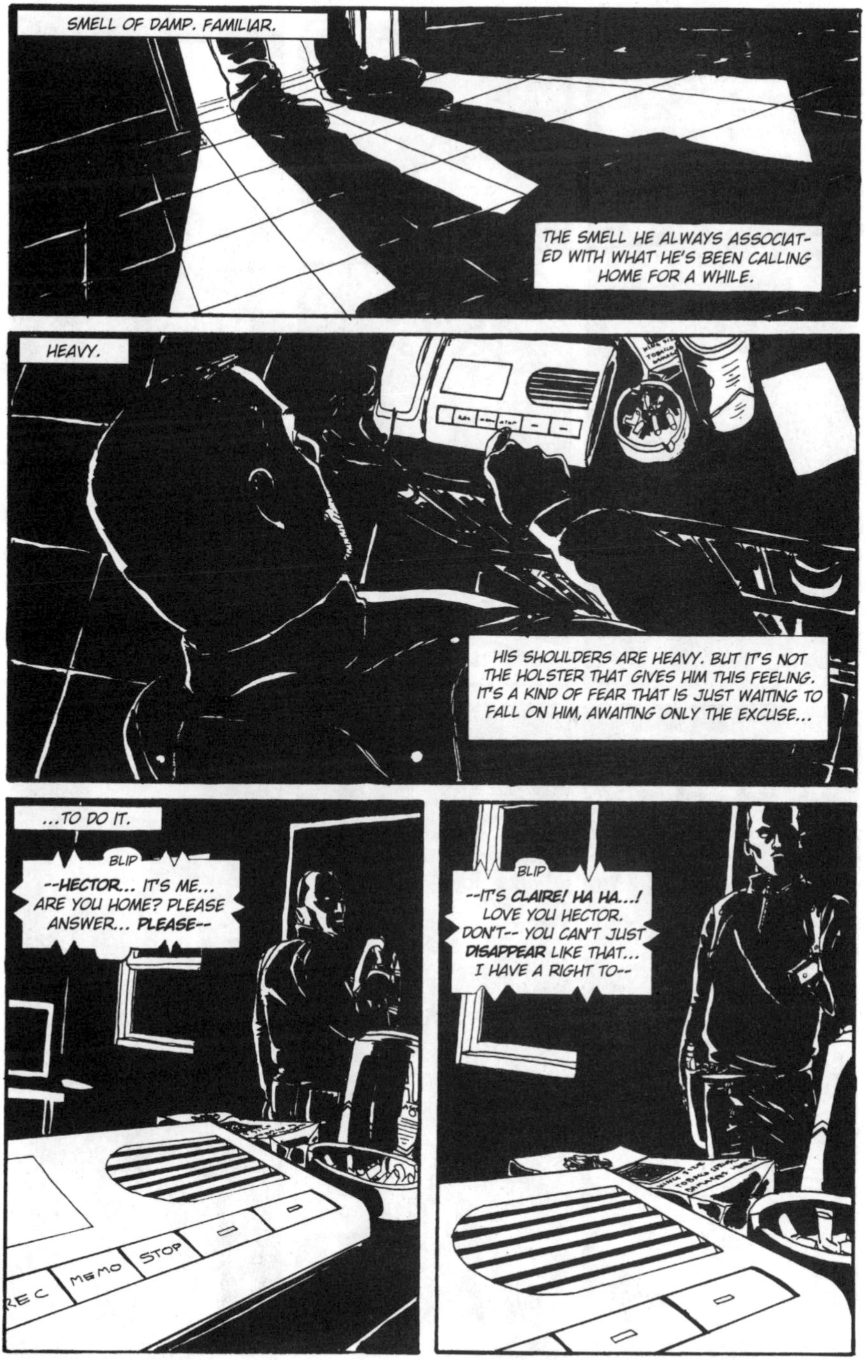
SMELL OF DAMP. FAMILIAR.
THE SMELL HE ALWAYS ASSOCIATED WITH WHAT HE'S BEEN CALLING HOME FOR A WHILE.
HEAVY.
HIS SHOULDERS ARE HEAVY. BUT IT'S NOT THE HOLSTER THAT GIVES HIM THIS FEELING. IT'S A KIND OF FEAR THAT IS JUST WAITING TO FALL ON HIM, AWAITING ONLY THE EXCUSE...
...TO DO IT.
BLIP
--HECTOR... IT'S ME... ARE YOU HOME? PLEASE ANSWER... PLEASE--
REC
MEMO
STOP
BLIP
--IT'S CLAIRE! HA HA...! LOVE YOU HECTOR. DON'T-- YOU CAN'T JUST DISAPPEAR LIKE THAT... I HAVE A RIGHT TO--

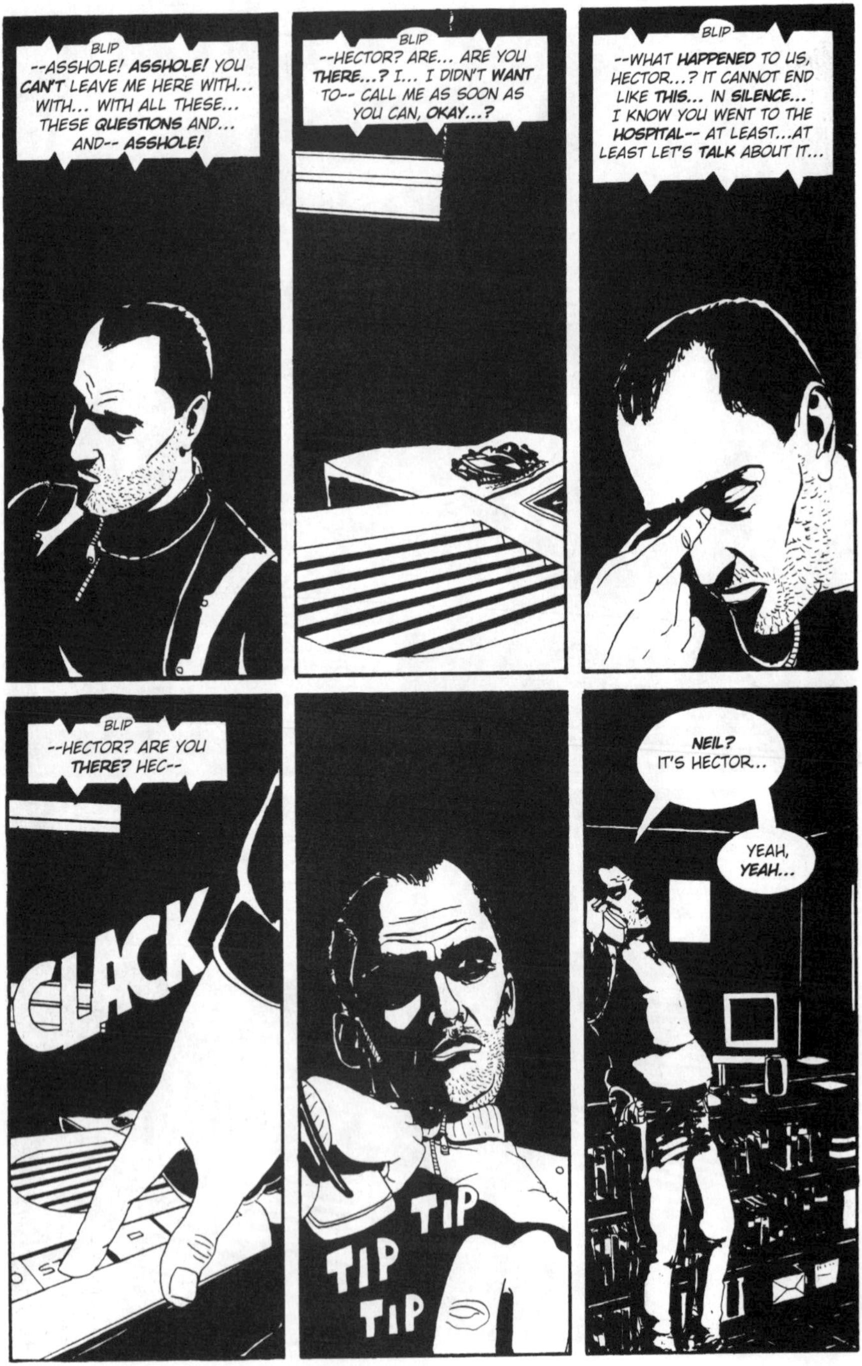
BLIP
--ASSHOLE! ASSHOLE! YOU CAN'T LEAVE ME HERE WITH... WITH... WITH ALL THESE... THESE QUESTIONS AND... AND-- ASSHOLE!
BLIP
--HECTOR? ARE... ARE YOU THERE...? I... I DIDN'T WANT TO-- CALL ME AS SOON AS YOU CAN, OKAY...?
BLIP
--WHAT HAPPENED TO US, HECTOR...? IT CANNOT END LIKE THIS... IN SILENCE... I KNOW YOU WENT TO THE HOSPITAL-- AT LEAST...AT LEAST LET'S TALK ABOUT IT...
BLIP
--HECTOR? ARE YOU THERE? HEC--
CLACK
TIP
TIP
TIP
NEIL? IT'S HECTOR...
YEAH, YEAH...

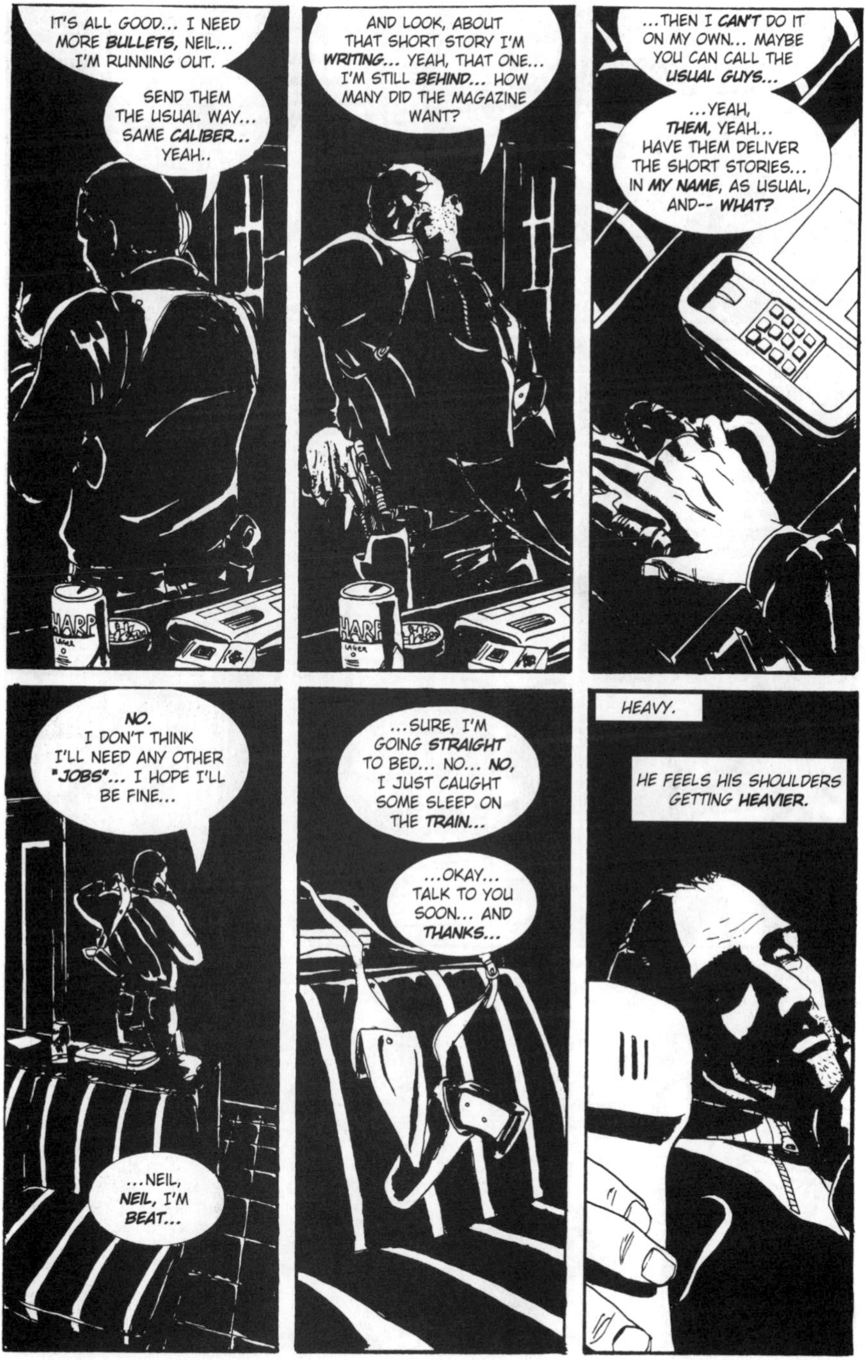

IT'S ALL GOOD... I NEED MORE BULLETS, NEIL... I'M RUNNING OUT.
SEND THEM THE USUAL WAY... SAME CALIBER... YEAH..
AND LOOK, ABOUT THAT SHORT STORY I'M WRITING... YEAH, THAT ONE... I'M STILL BEHIND... HOW MANY DID THE MAGAZINE WANT?
...THEN I CAN'T DO IT ON MY OWN... MAYBE YOU CAN CALL THE USUAL GUYS...
...YEAH, THEM, YEAH... HAVE THEM DELIVER THE SHORT STORIES... IN MY NAME, AS USUAL, AND-- WHAT?
NO. I DON'T THINK I'LL NEED ANY OTHER "JOBS"... I HOPE I'LL BE FINE...
...NEIL, NEIL, I'M BEAT...
...SURE, I'M GOING STRAIGHT TO BED... NO... NO, I JUST CAUGHT SOME SLEEP ON THE TRAIN...
...OKAY... TALK TO YOU SOON... AND THANKS...
HEAVY.
HE FEELS HIS SHOULDERS GETTING HEAVIER.

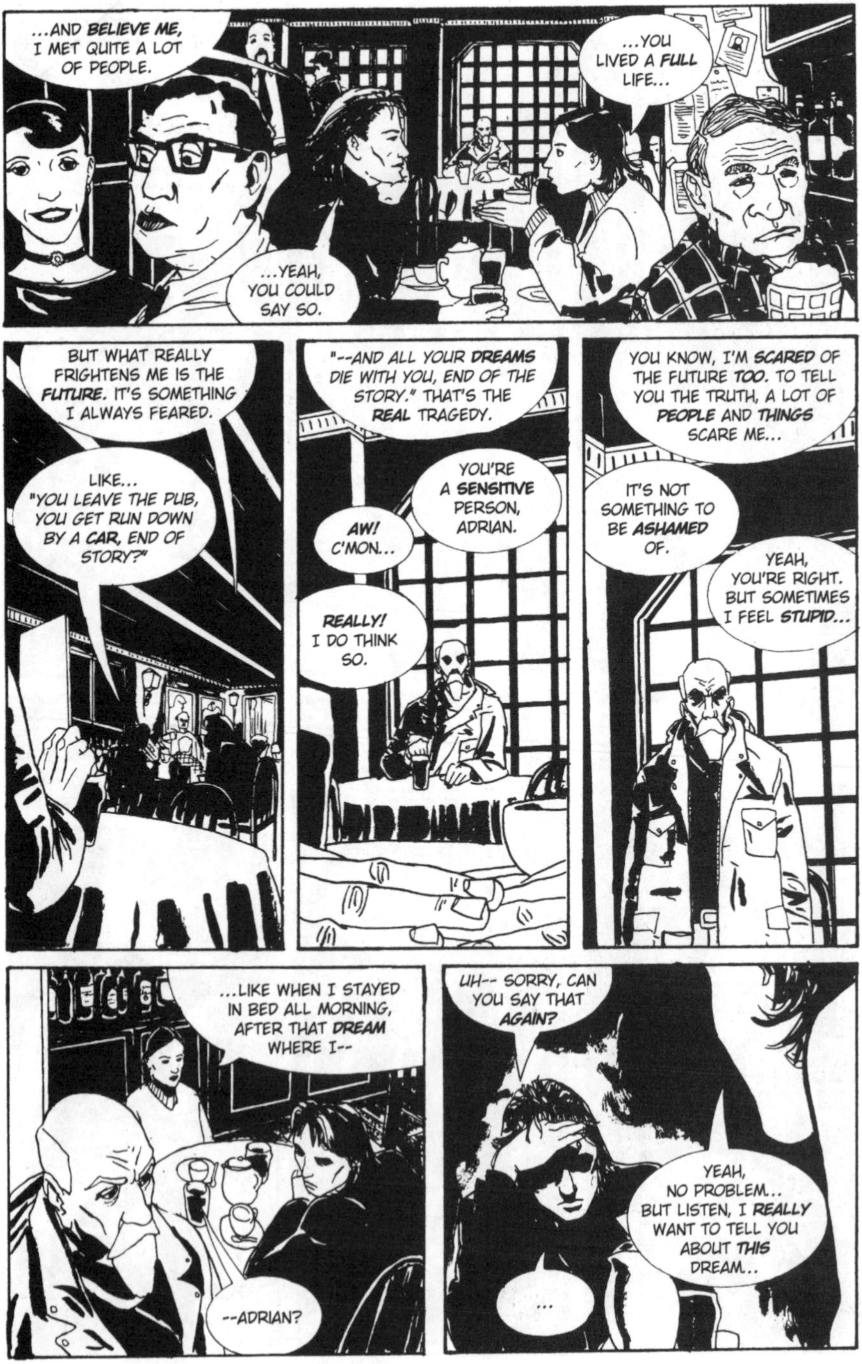
...AND BELIEVE ME, I MET QUITE A LOT OF PEOPLE.
...YOU LIVED A FULL LIFE...
...YEAH, YOU COULD SAY SO.
BUT WHAT REALLY FRIGHTENS ME IS THE FUTURE. IT'S SOMETHING I ALWAYS FEARED.
LIKE... "YOU LEAVE THE PUB, YOU GET RUN DOWN BY A CAR, END OF STORY?"
"--AND ALL YOUR DREAMS DIE WITH YOU, END OF THE STORY." THAT'S THE REAL TRAGEDY.
YOU'RE A SENSITIVE PERSON, ADRIAN.
AW! C'MON...
REALLY! I DO THINK SO.
YOU KNOW, I'M SCARED OF THE FUTURE TOO. TO TELL YOU THE TRUTH, A LOT OF PEOPLE AND THINGS SCARE ME...
IT'S NOT SOMETHING TO BE ASHAMED OF.
YEAH, YOU'RE RIGHT. BUT SOMETIMES I FEEL STUPID...
...LIKE WHEN I STAYED IN BED ALL MORNING, AFTER THAT DREAM WHERE I--
--ADRIAN?
UH-- SORRY, CAN YOU SAY THAT AGAIN?
YEAH, NO PROBLEM... BUT LISTEN, I REALLY WANT TO TELL YOU ABOUT THIS DREAM...
...

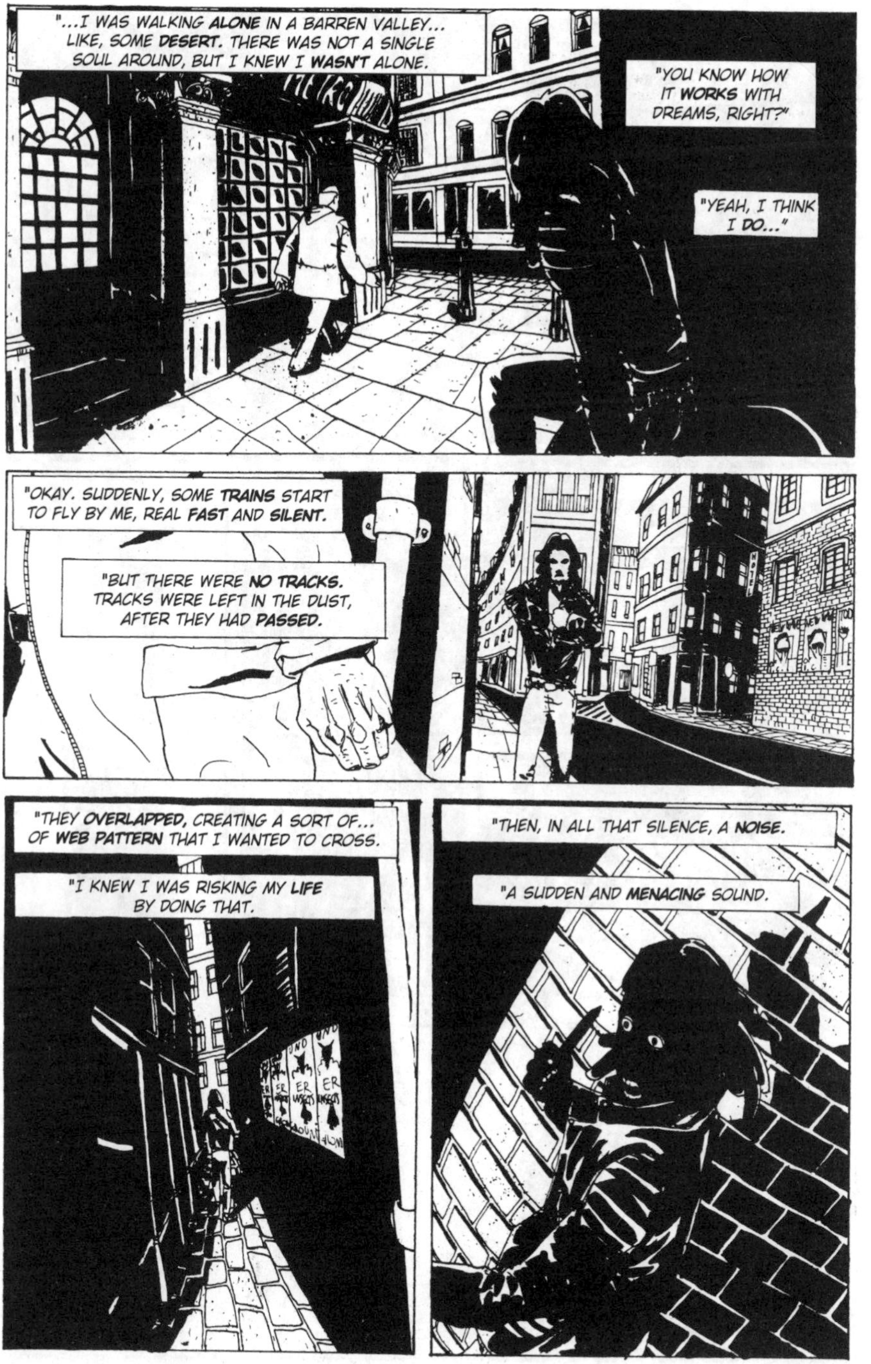
"...I WAS WALKING **ALONE** IN A BARREN VALLEY... LIKE, SOME **DESERT.** THERE WAS NOT A SINGLE SOUL AROUND, BUT I KNEW I **WASN'T** ALONE.
"YOU KNOW HOW IT **WORKS** WITH DREAMS, RIGHT?"
"YEAH, I THINK I *DO*..."
"OKAY. SUDDENLY, SOME **TRAINS** START TO FLY BY ME, REAL **FAST** AND **SILENT.**
"BUT THERE WERE **NO TRACKS.** TRACKS WERE LEFT IN THE DUST, AFTER THEY HAD **PASSED.**
"THEY **OVERLAPPED,** CREATING A SORT OF... OF **WEB PATTERN** THAT I WANTED TO CROSS.
"I KNEW I WAS RISKING MY **LIFE** BY DOING THAT.
"THEN, IN ALL THAT SILENCE, A **NOISE.**
"A SUDDEN AND **MENACING** SOUND.

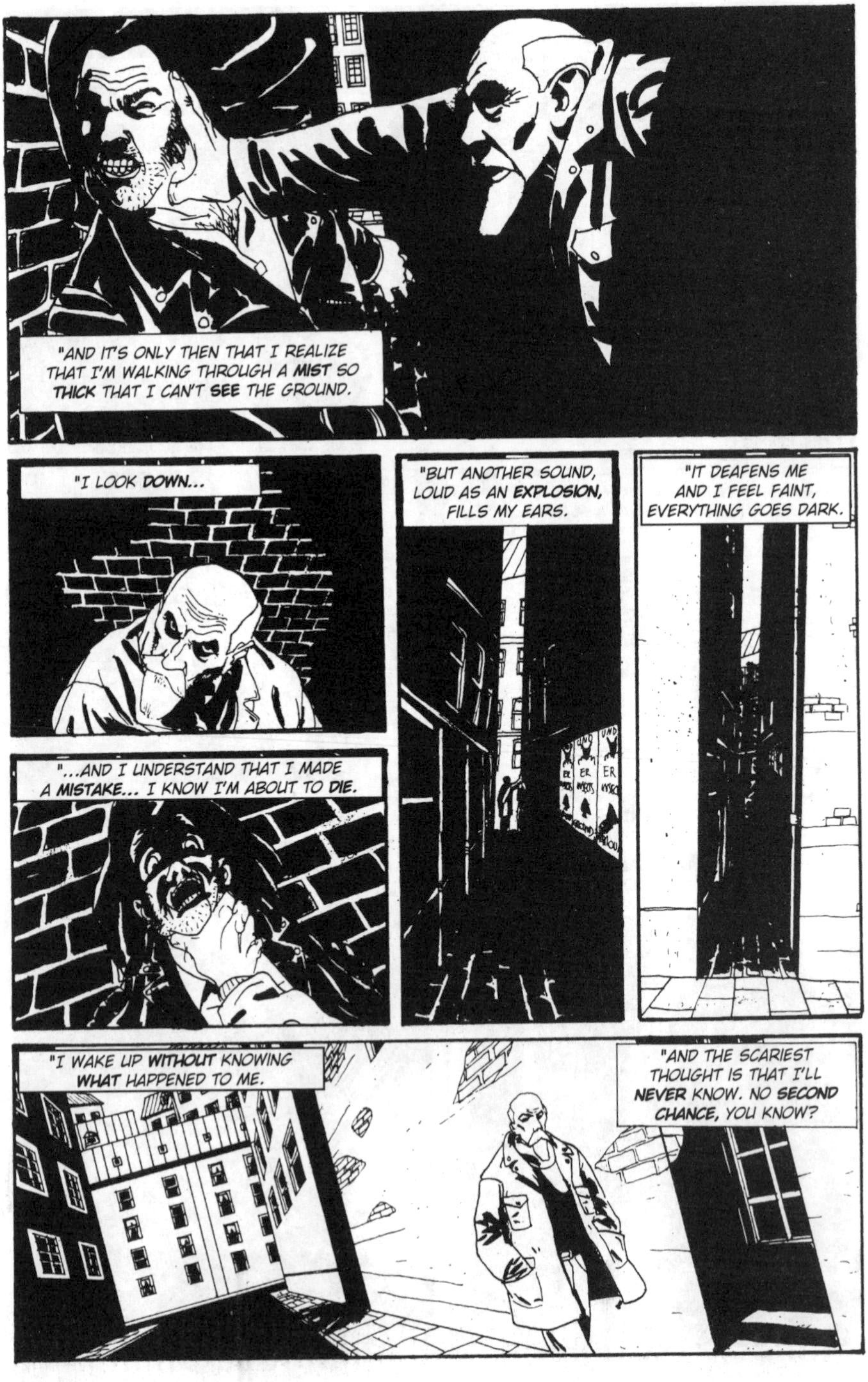
"AND IT'S ONLY THEN THAT I REALIZE THAT I'M WALKING THROUGH A MIST SO THICK THAT I CAN'T SEE THE GROUND.
"I LOOK DOWN...
"BUT ANOTHER SOUND, LOUD AS AN EXPLOSION, FILLS MY EARS.
"IT DEAFENS ME AND I FEEL FAINT, EVERYTHING GOES DARK.
"...AND I UNDERSTAND THAT I MADE A MISTAKE... I KNOW I'M ABOUT TO DIE.
"I WAKE UP WITHOUT KNOWING WHAT HAPPENED TO ME.
"AND THE SCARIEST THOUGHT IS THAT I'LL NEVER KNOW. NO SECOND CHANCE, YOU KNOW?

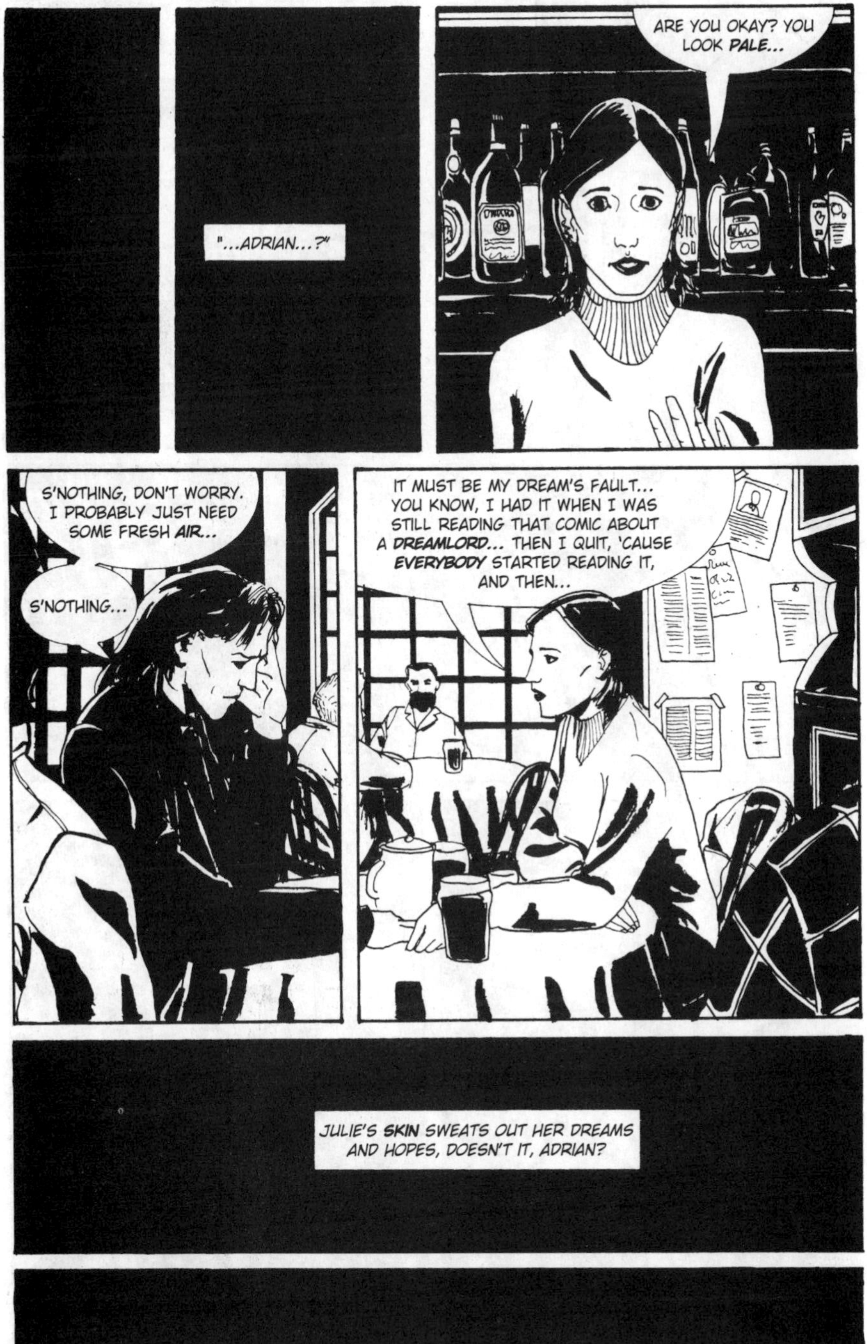
"...ADRIAN...?"
ARE YOU OKAY? YOU LOOK PALE...
S'NOTHING, DON'T WORRY. I PROBABLY JUST NEED SOME FRESH AIR...
S'NOTHING...
IT MUST BE MY DREAM'S FAULT... YOU KNOW, I HAD IT WHEN I WAS STILL READING THAT COMIC ABOUT A DREAMLORD... THEN I QUIT, 'CAUSE EVERYBODY STARTED READING IT, AND THEN...
JULIE'S SKIN SWEATS OUT HER DREAMS AND HOPES, DOESN'T IT, ADRIAN?

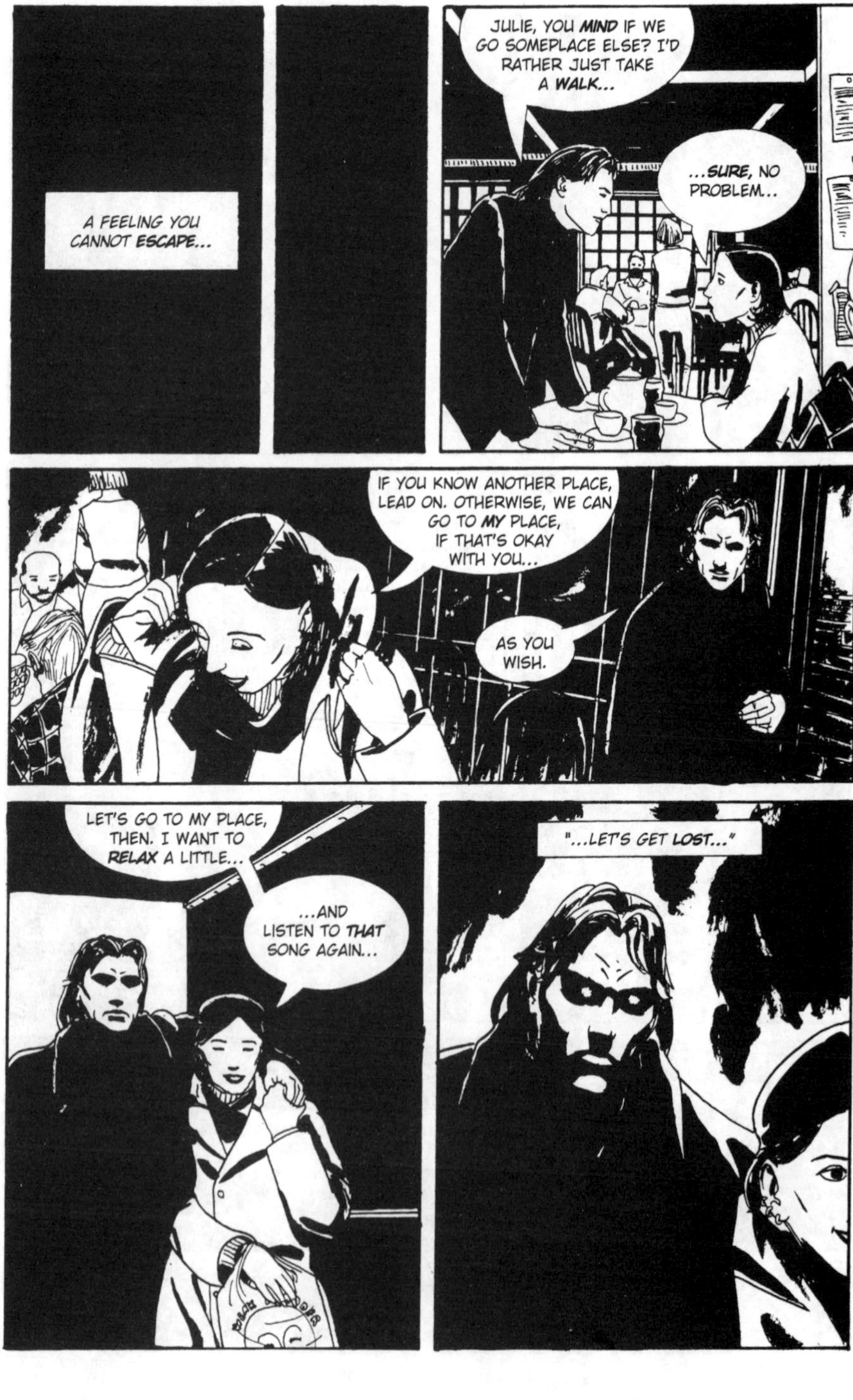
A FEELING YOU CANNOT ESCAPE...
JULIE, YOU MIND IF WE GO SOMEPLACE ELSE? I'D RATHER JUST TAKE A WALK...
...SURE, NO PROBLEM...
IF YOU KNOW ANOTHER PLACE, LEAD ON. OTHERWISE, WE CAN GO TO MY PLACE, IF THAT'S OKAY WITH YOU...
AS YOU WISH.
LET'S GO TO MY PLACE, THEN. I WANT TO RELAX A LITTLE...
...AND LISTEN TO THAT SONG AGAIN...
"...LET'S GET LOST..."

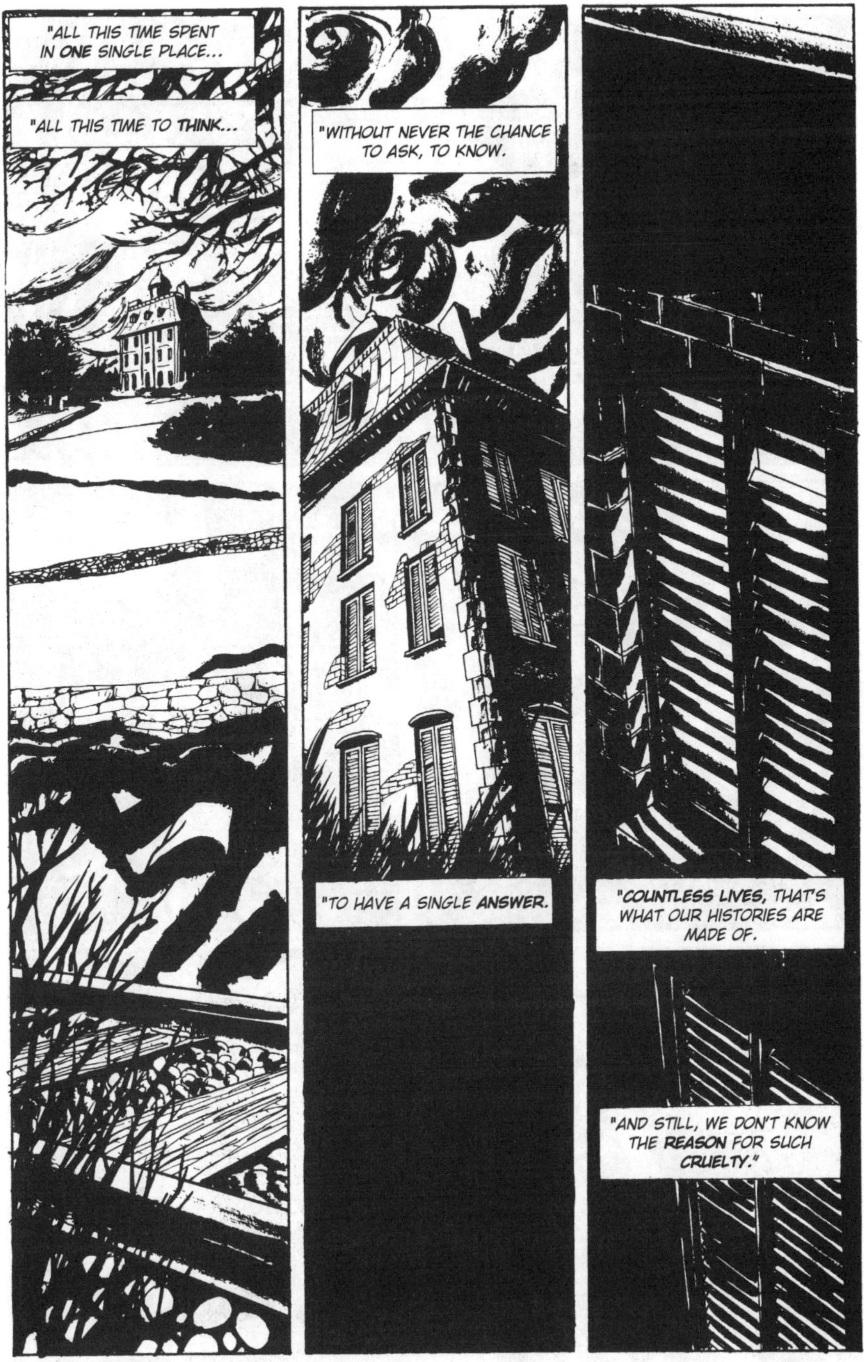
"ALL THIS TIME SPENT IN ONE SINGLE PLACE...
"ALL THIS TIME TO THINK...
"WITHOUT NEVER THE CHANCE TO ASK, TO KNOW.
"TO HAVE A SINGLE ANSWER.
"COUNTLESS LIVES, THAT'S WHAT OUR HISTORIES ARE MADE OF.
"AND STILL, WE DON'T KNOW THE REASON FOR SUCH CRUELTY."

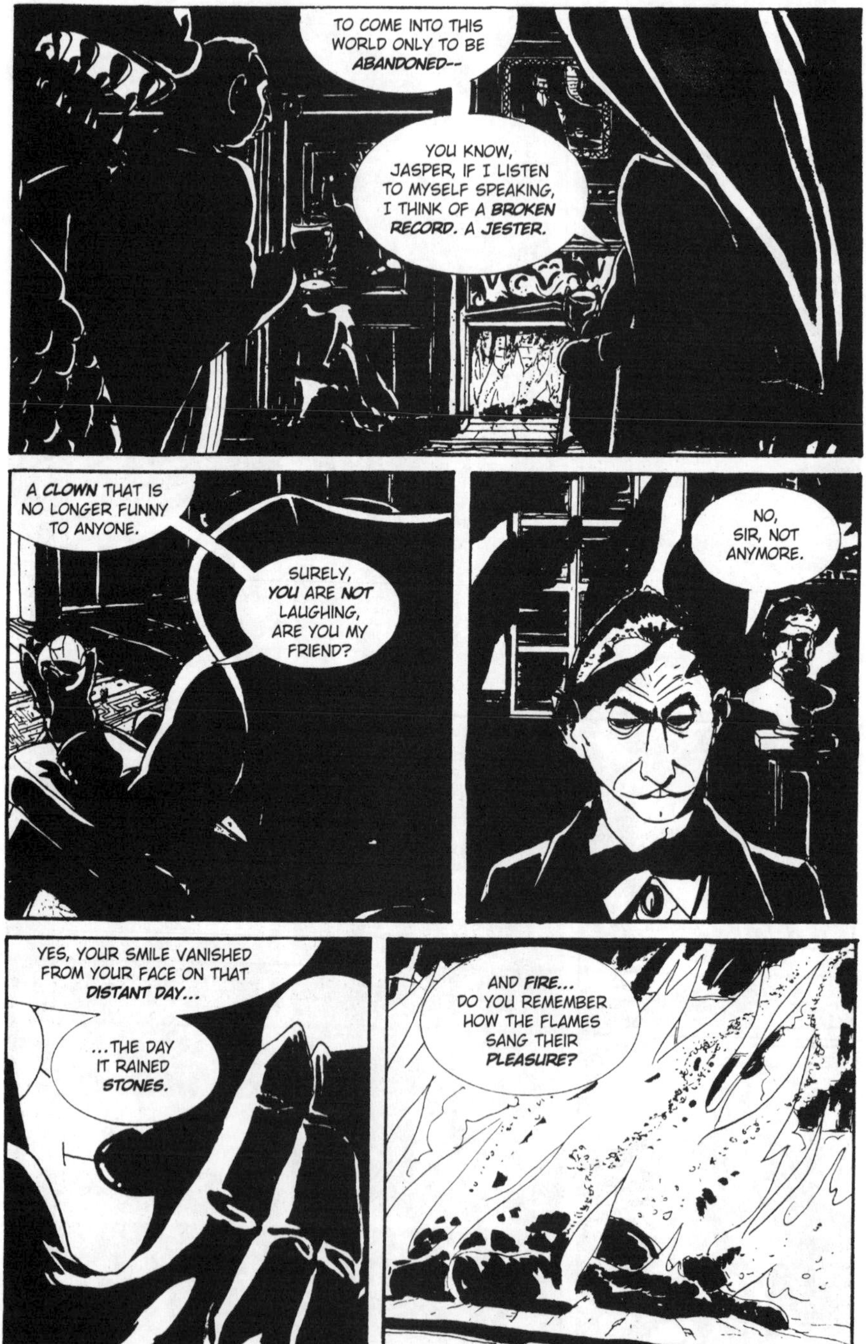
TO COME INTO THIS WORLD ONLY TO BE ABANDONED--
YOU KNOW, JASPER, IF I LISTEN TO MYSELF SPEAKING, I THINK OF A BROKEN RECORD. A JESTER.
A CLOWN THAT IS NO LONGER FUNNY TO ANYONE.
SURELY, YOU ARE NOT LAUGHING, ARE YOU MY FRIEND?
NO, SIR, NOT ANYMORE.
YES, YOUR SMILE VANISHED FROM YOUR FACE ON THAT DISTANT DAY...
...THE DAY IT RAINED STONES.
AND FIRE... DO YOU REMEMBER HOW THE FLAMES SANG THEIR PLEASURE?

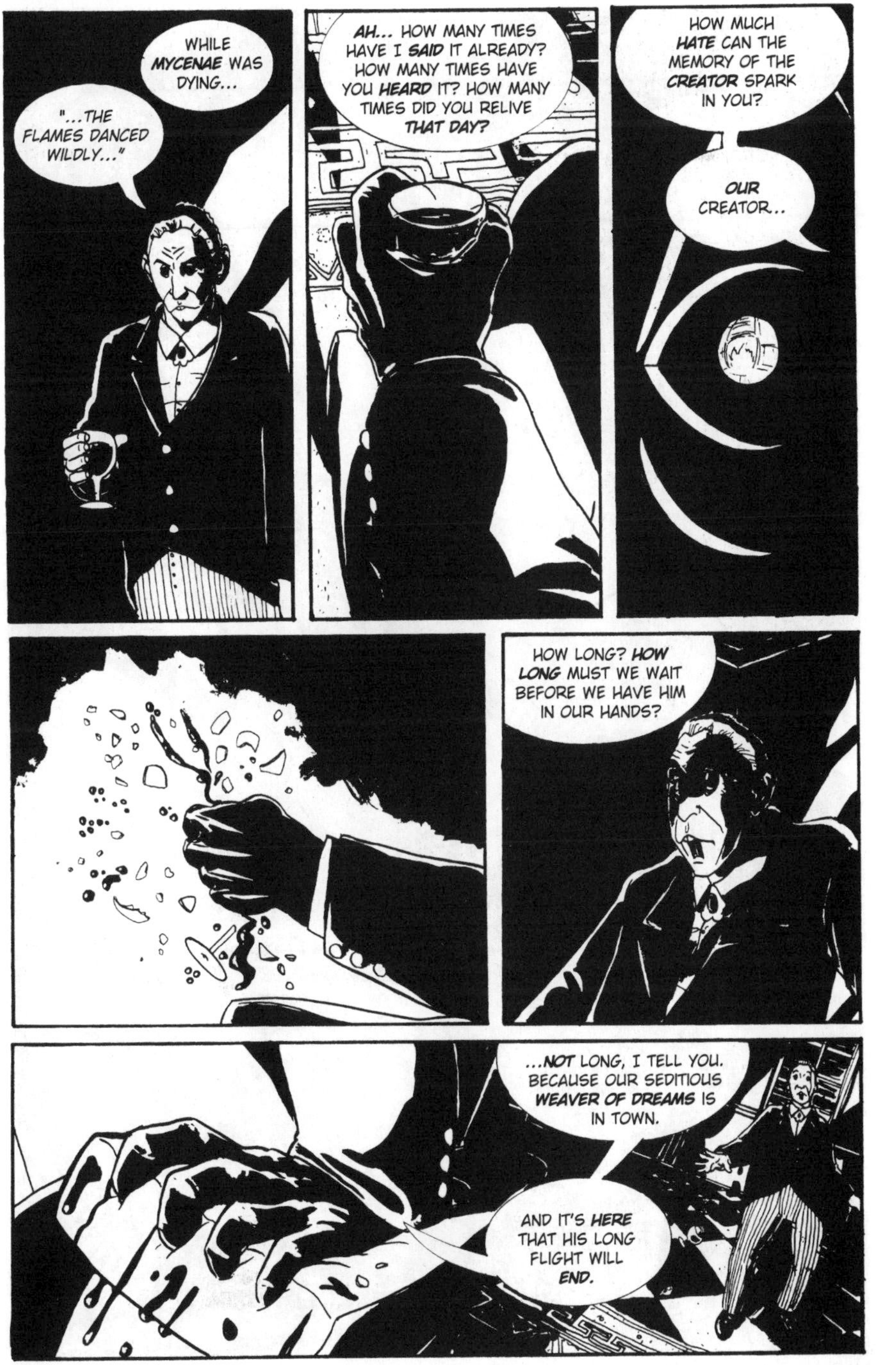
WHILE MYCENAE WAS DYING...
"...THE FLAMES DANCED WILDLY..."
AH... HOW MANY TIMES HAVE I SAID IT ALREADY? HOW MANY TIMES HAVE YOU HEARD IT? HOW MANY TIMES DID YOU RELIVE THAT DAY?
HOW MUCH HATE CAN THE MEMORY OF THE CREATOR SPARK IN YOU?
OUR CREATOR...
HOW LONG? HOW LONG MUST WE WAIT BEFORE WE HAVE HIM IN OUR HANDS?
...NOT LONG, I TELL YOU. BECAUSE OUR SEDITIOUS WEAVER OF DREAMS IS IN TOWN.
AND IT'S HERE THAT HIS LONG FLIGHT WILL END.

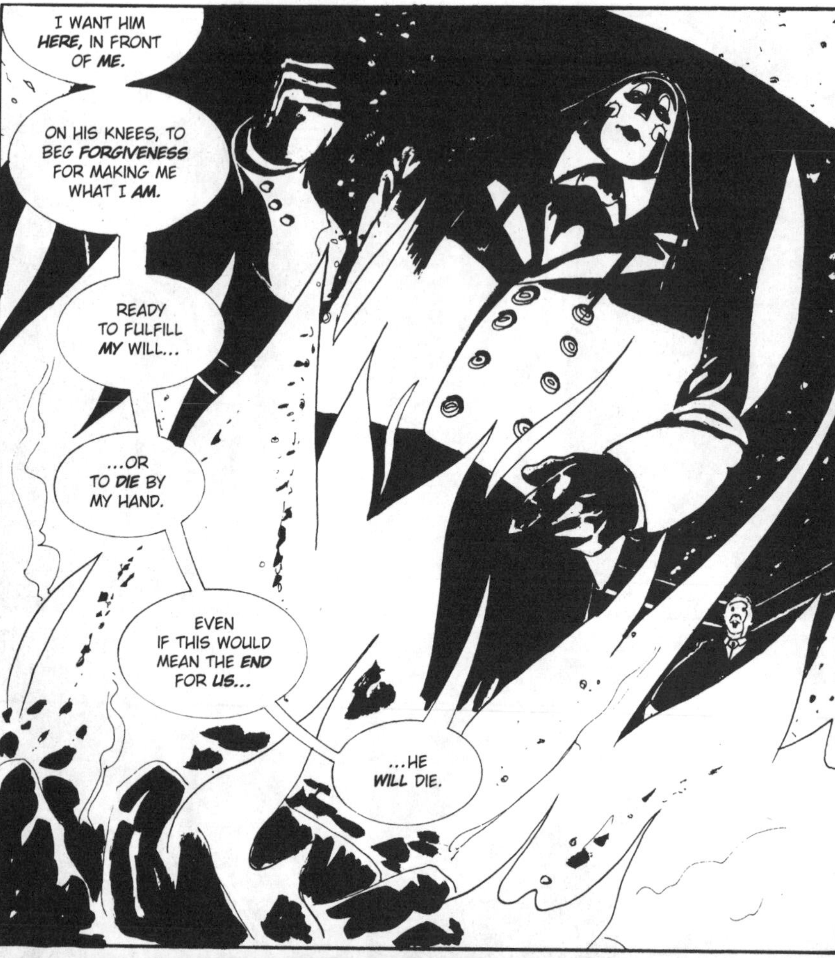
I WANT HIM *HERE,* IN FRONT OF *ME.*
ON HIS KNEES, TO BEG *FORGIVENESS* FOR MAKING ME WHAT I *AM.*
READY TO FULFILL *MY* WILL...
...OR TO *DIE* BY MY HAND.
EVEN IF THIS WOULD MEAN THE *END* FOR *US...*
...HE *WILL* DIE.

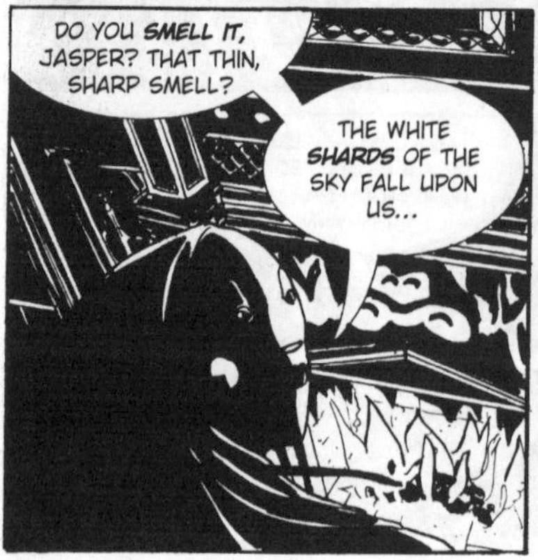
DO YOU *SMELL IT,* JASPER? THAT THIN, SHARP SMELL?
THE WHITE *SHARDS* OF THE SKY FALL UPON US...

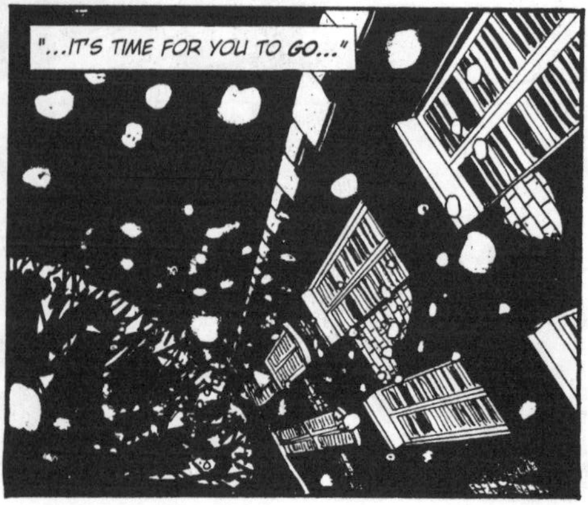
"...IT'S TIME FOR YOU TO *GO...*"

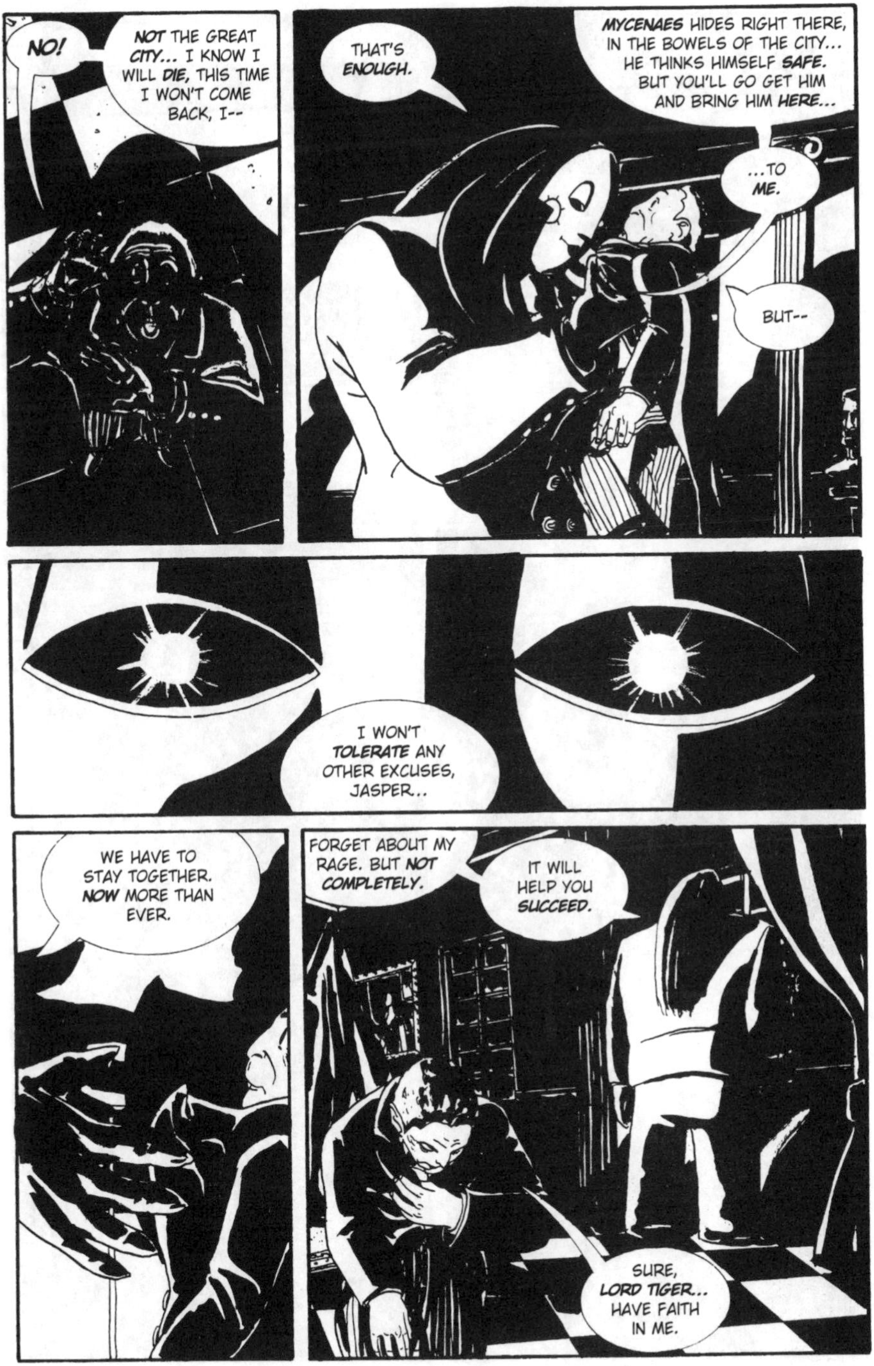
NO!
NOT THE GREAT CITY... I KNOW I WILL DIE, THIS TIME I WON'T COME BACK, I--
THAT'S ENOUGH.
MYCENAES HIDES RIGHT THERE, IN THE BOWELS OF THE CITY... HE THINKS HIMSELF SAFE. BUT YOU'LL GO GET HIM AND BRING HIM HERE...
...TO ME.
BUT--
I WON'T TOLERATE ANY OTHER EXCUSES, JASPER...
WE HAVE TO STAY TOGETHER. NOW MORE THAN EVER.
FORGET ABOUT MY RAGE. BUT NOT COMPLETELY.
IT WILL HELP YOU SUCCEED.
SURE, LORD TIGER... HAVE FAITH IN ME.

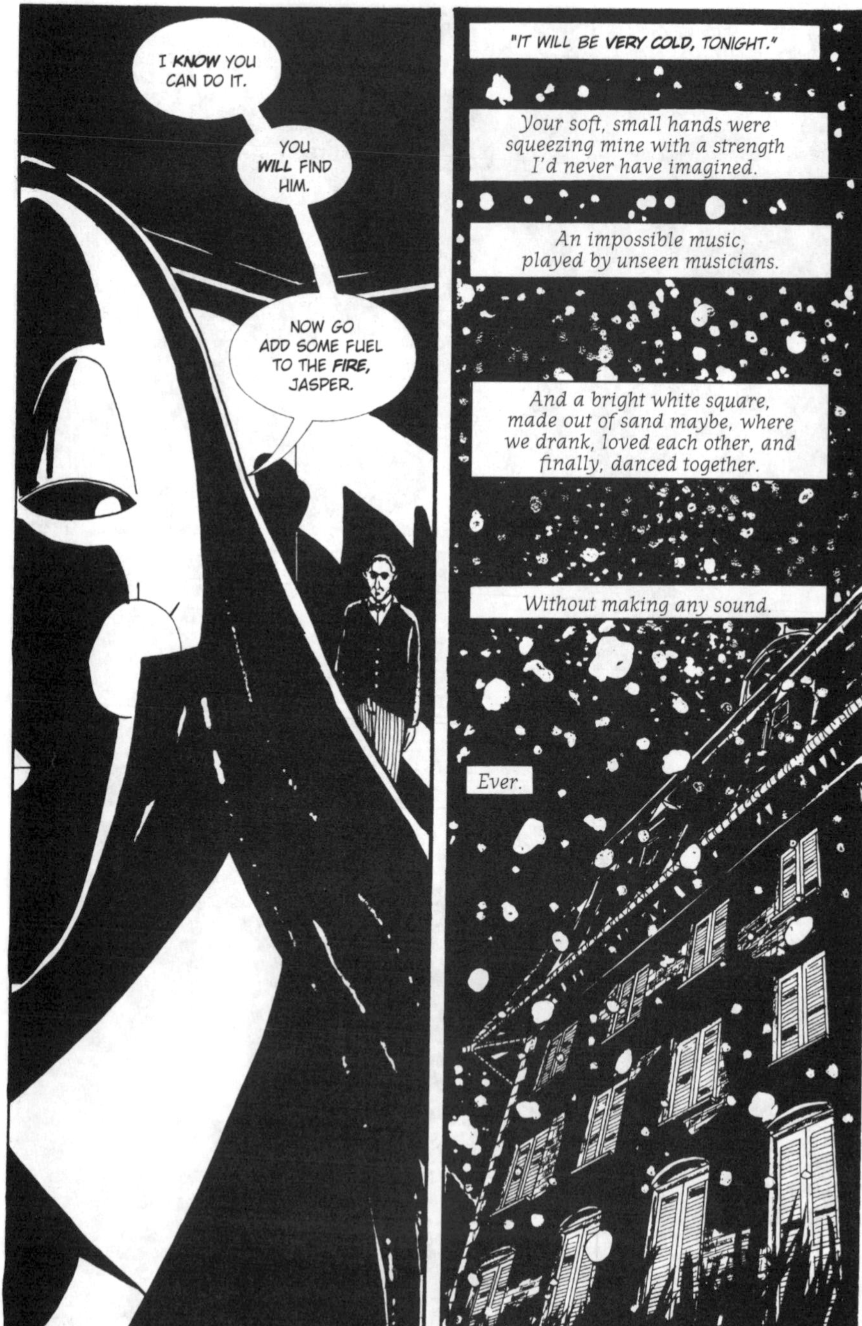
I **KNOW** YOU CAN DO IT.
YOU **WILL** FIND HIM.
NOW GO ADD SOME FUEL TO THE **FIRE**, JASPER.
"IT WILL BE **VERY COLD,** TONIGHT."
Your soft, small hands were squeezing mine with a strength I'd never have imagined.
An impossible music, played by unseen musicians.
And a bright white square, made out of sand maybe, where we drank, loved each other, and finally, danced together.
Without making any sound.
Ever.

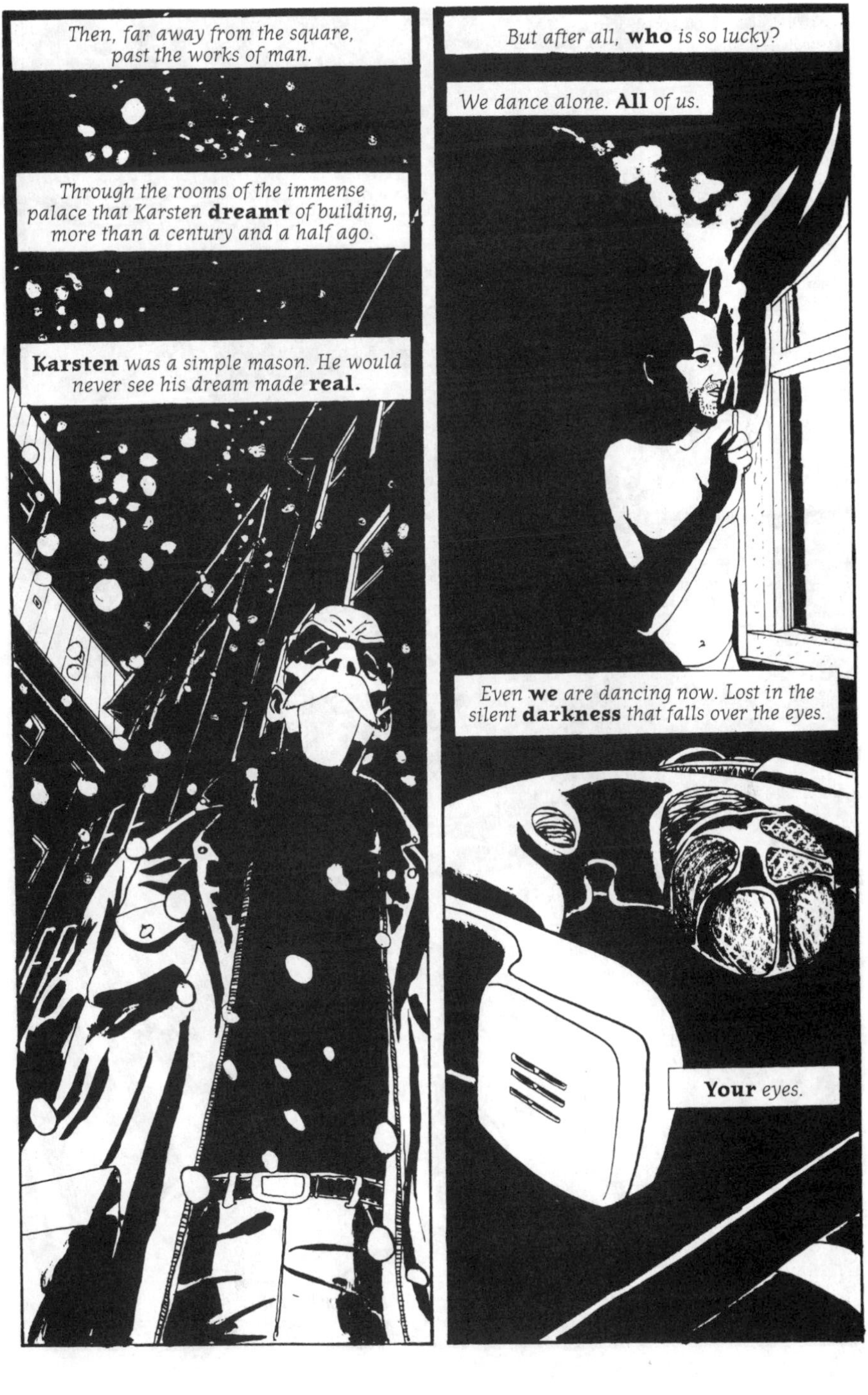
Then, far away from the square, past the works of man.
Through the rooms of the immense palace that Karsten **dreamt** of building, more than a century and a half ago.
Karsten was a simple mason. He would never see his dream made **real.**
But after all, **who** is so lucky?
We dance alone. **All** of us.
Even **we** are dancing now. Lost in the silent **darkness** that falls over the eyes.
Your eyes.

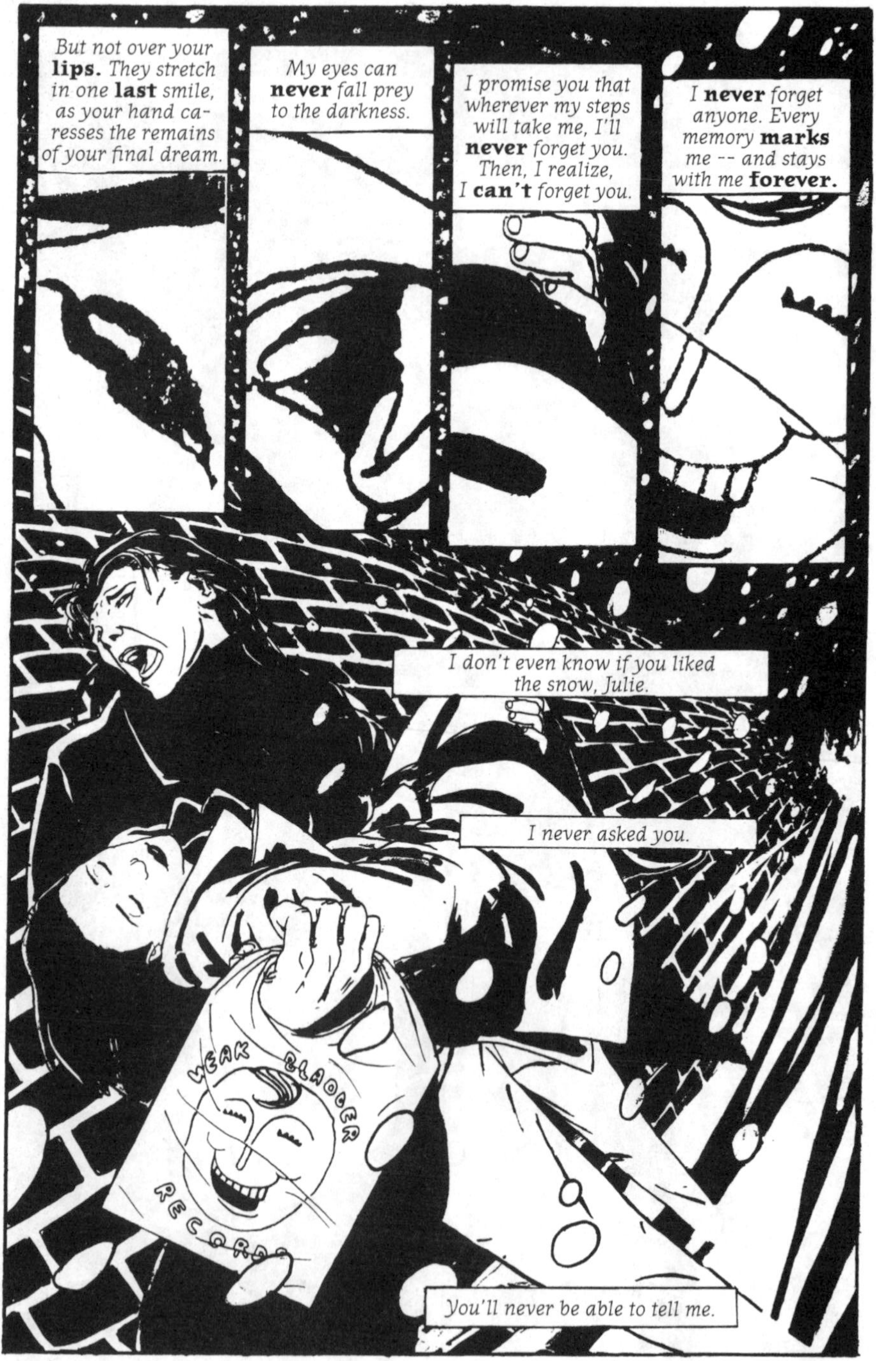
But not over your **lips.** They stretch in one **last** smile, as your hand caresses the remains of your final dream.
My eyes can **never** fall prey to the darkness.
I promise you that wherever my steps will take me, I'll **never** forget you. Then, I realize, I **can't** forget you.
I **never** forget anyone. Every memory **marks** me -- and stays with me **forever.**
I don't even know if you liked the snow, Julie.
I never asked you.
WEAK BLADDER RECORDS
You'll never be able to tell me.

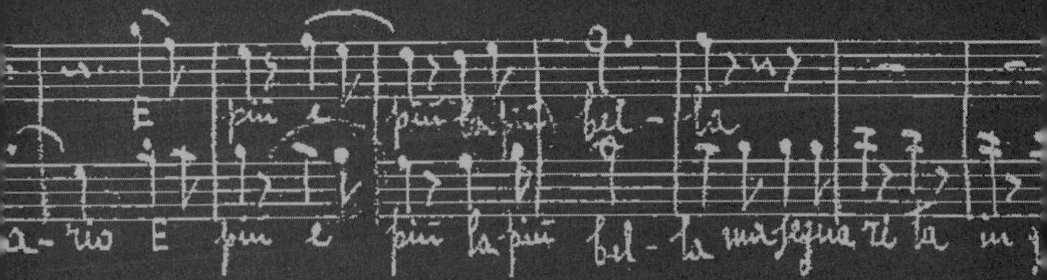

chapter two

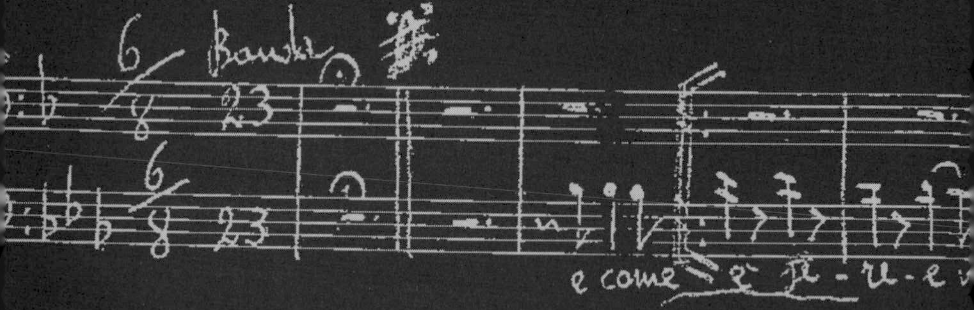
e come

Story
MATTEO CASALI

Art
GRAZIA LOBACCARO

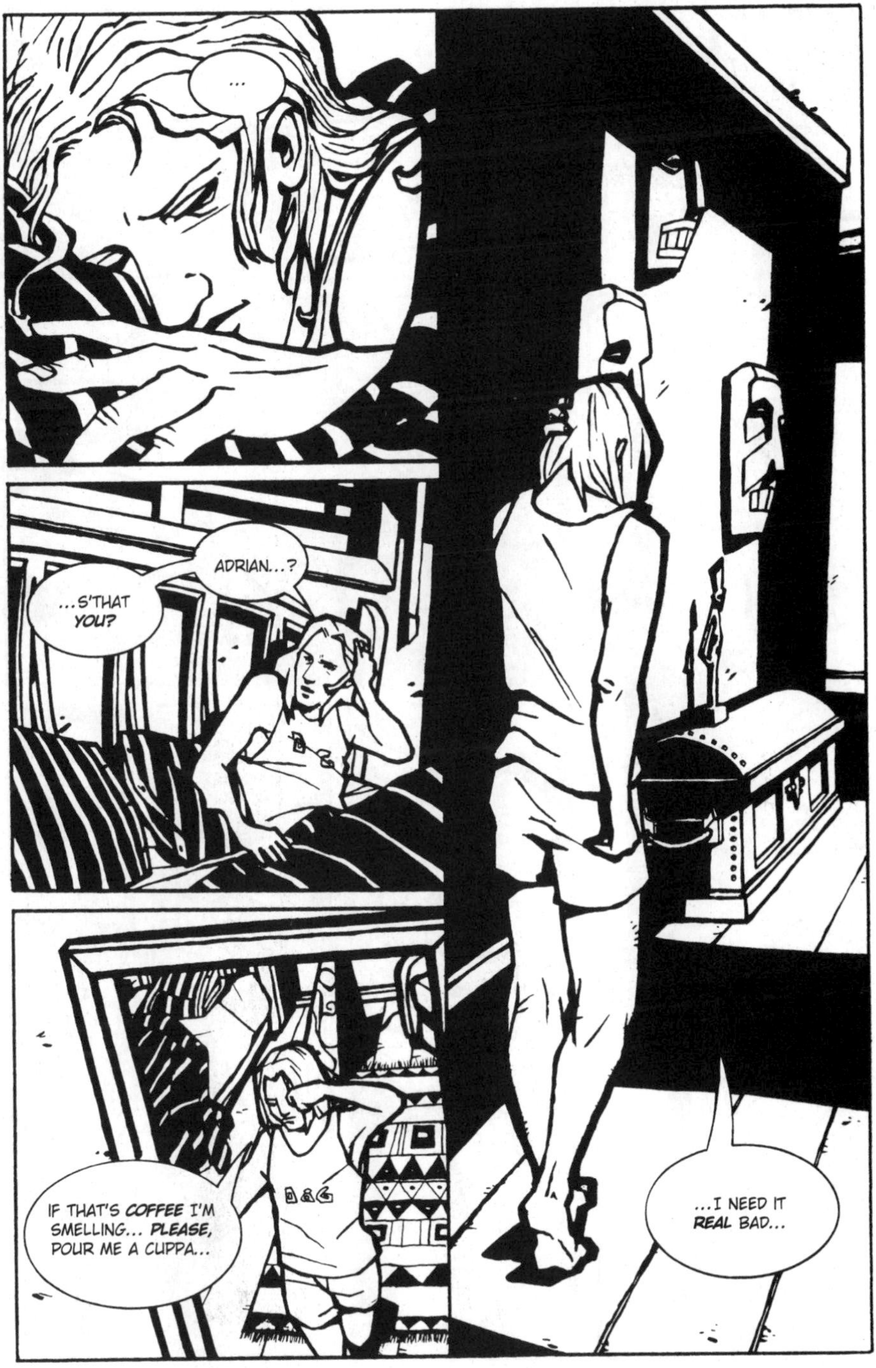
...
ADRIAN...?
...S'THAT *YOU?*
IF THAT'S *COFFEE* I'M SMELLING... *PLEASE,* POUR ME A CUPPA...
...I NEED IT *REAL* BAD...

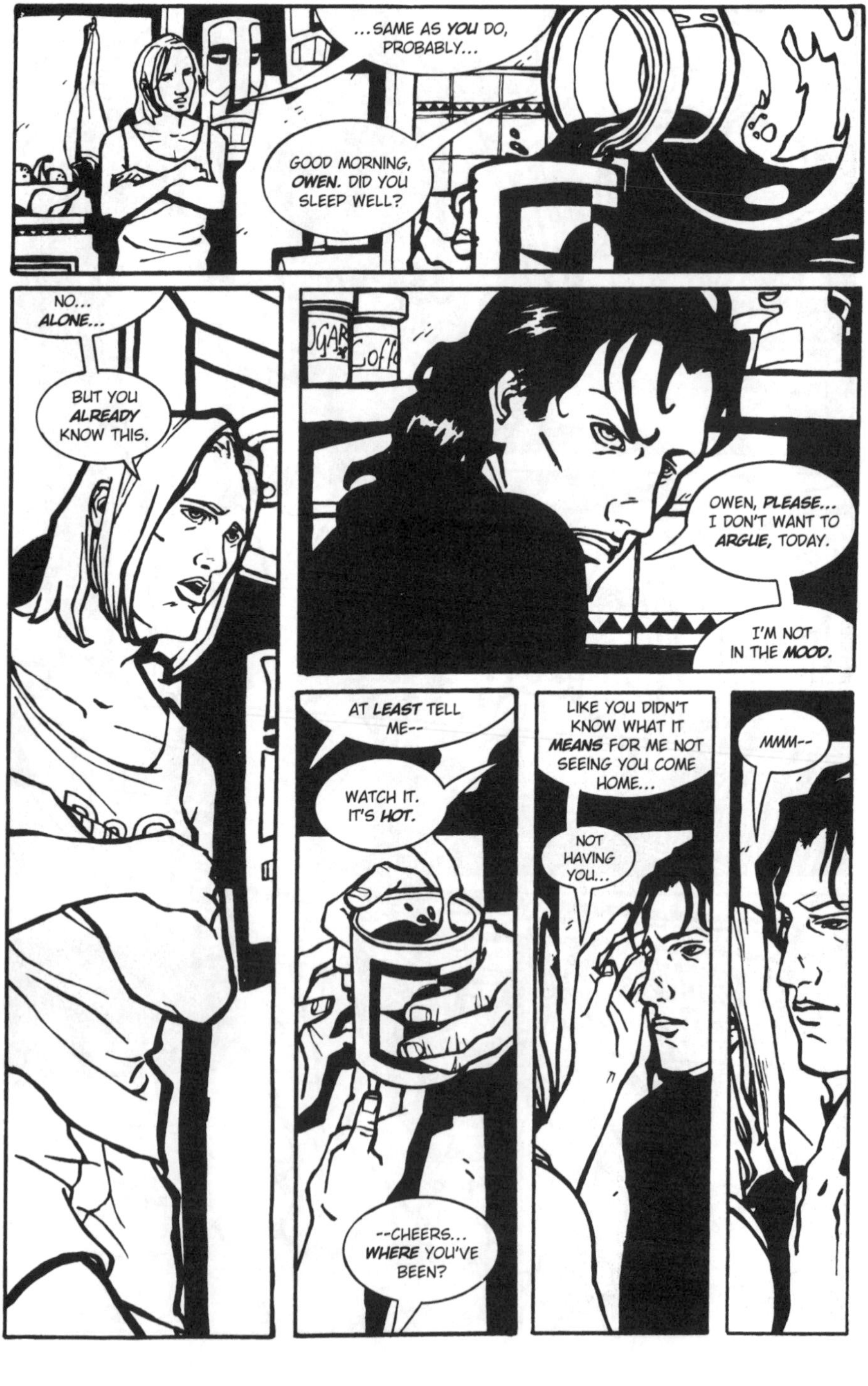

GOOD MORNING, OWEN. DID YOU SLEEP WELL?
...SAME AS YOU DO, PROBABLY...
NO... ALONE...
BUT YOU ALREADY KNOW THIS.
OWEN, PLEASE... I DON'T WANT TO ARGUE, TODAY.
I'M NOT IN THE MOOD.
AT LEAST TELL ME--
WATCH IT. IT'S HOT.
--CHEERS... WHERE YOU'VE BEEN?
LIKE YOU DIDN'T KNOW WHAT IT MEANS FOR ME NOT SEEING YOU COME HOME...
NOT HAVING YOU...
MMM--

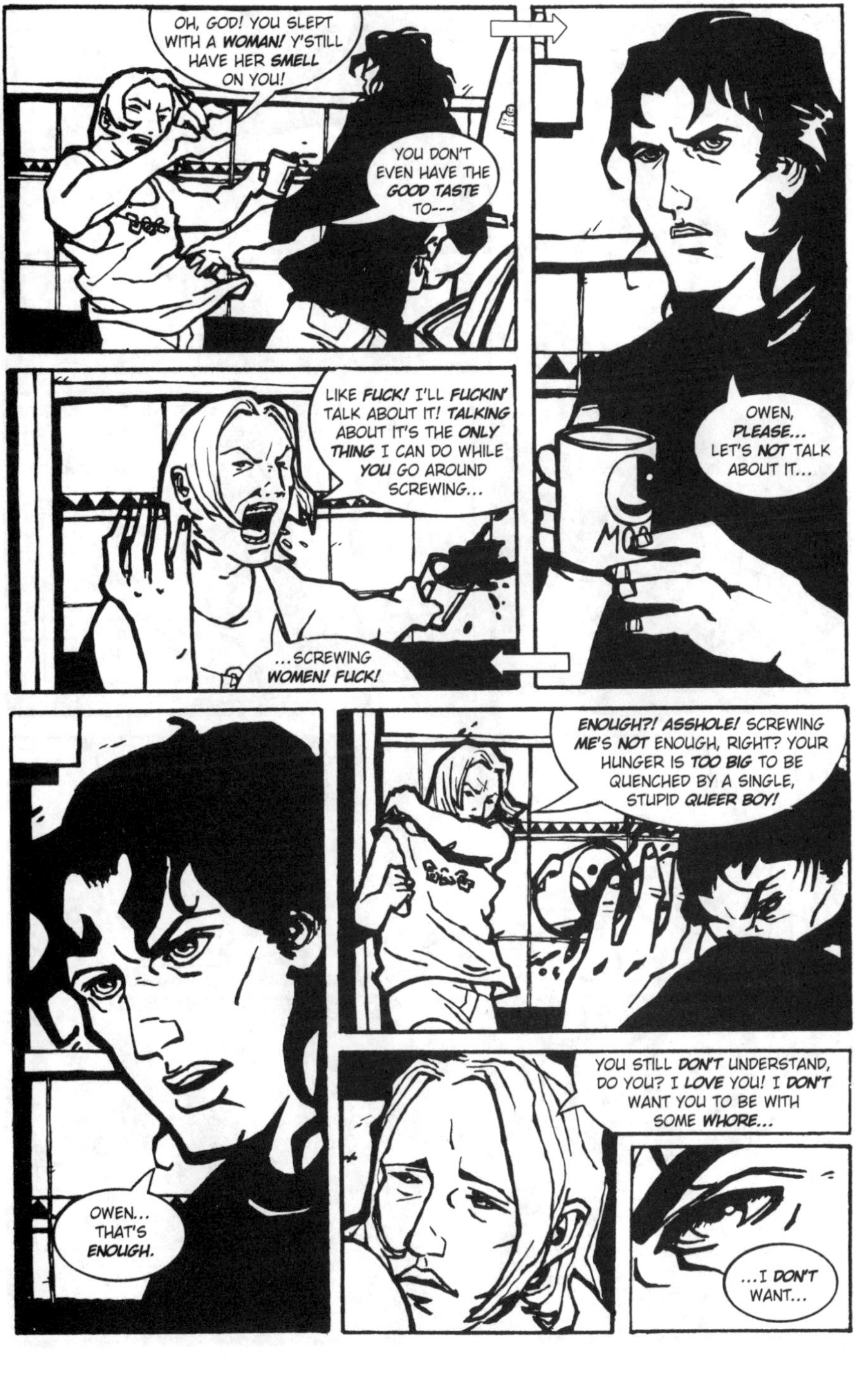
OH, GOD! YOU SLEPT WITH A WOMAN! Y'STILL HAVE HER SMELL ON YOU!
YOU DON'T EVEN HAVE THE GOOD TASTE TO---
OWEN, PLEASE... LET'S NOT TALK ABOUT IT...
LIKE FUCK! I'LL FUCKIN' TALK ABOUT IT! TALKING ABOUT IT'S THE ONLY THING I CAN DO WHILE YOU GO AROUND SCREWING...
...SCREWING WOMEN! FUCK!
OWEN... THAT'S ENOUGH.
ENOUGH?! ASSHOLE! SCREWING ME'S NOT ENOUGH, RIGHT? YOUR HUNGER IS TOO BIG TO BE QUENCHED BY A SINGLE, STUPID QUEER BOY!
YOU STILL DON'T UNDERSTAND, DO YOU? I LOVE YOU! I DON'T WANT YOU TO BE WITH SOME WHORE...
...I DON'T WANT...

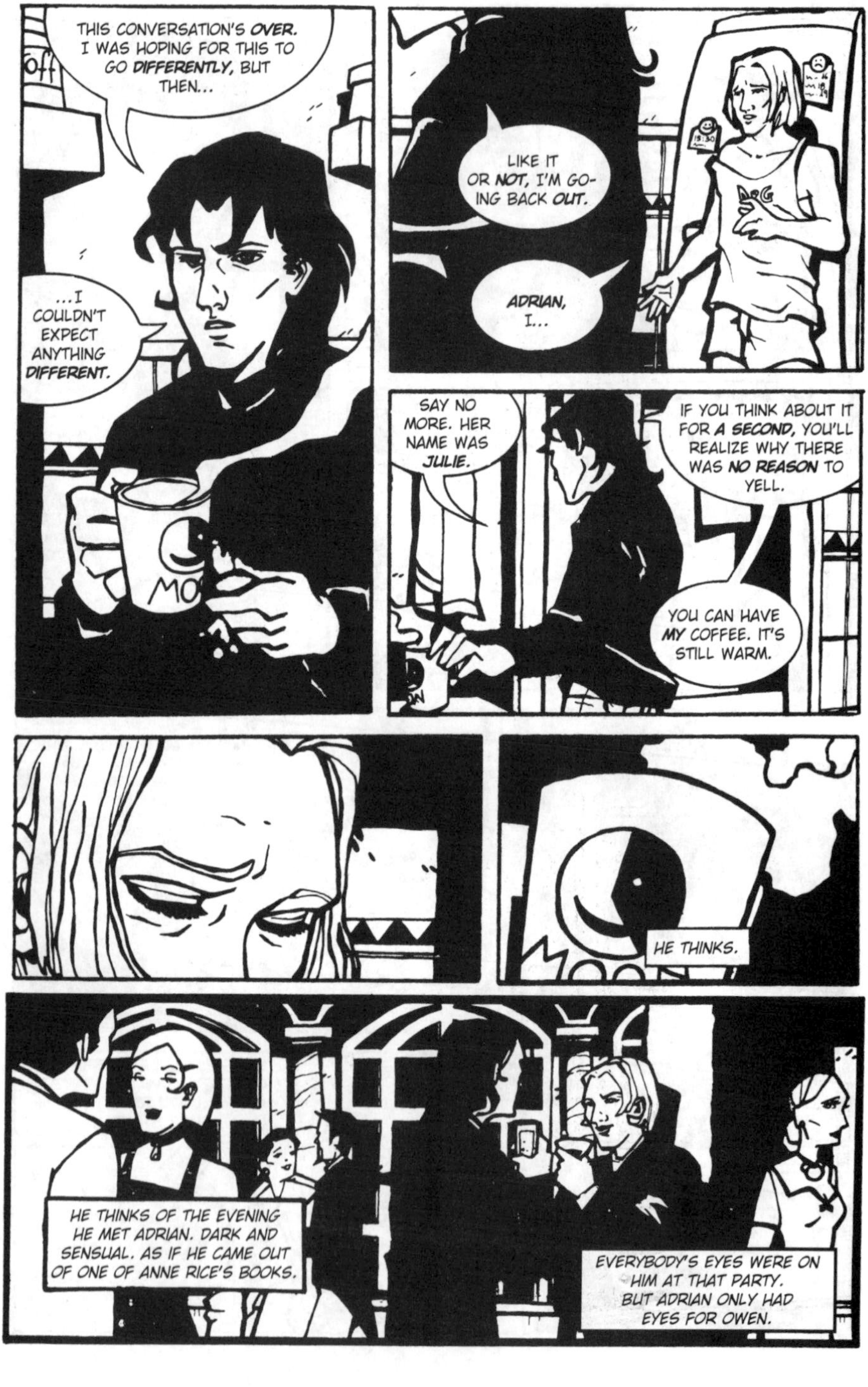
THIS CONVERSATION'S OVER. I WAS HOPING FOR THIS TO GO DIFFERENTLY, BUT THEN...
...I COULDN'T EXPECT ANYTHING DIFFERENT.
LIKE IT OR NOT, I'M GOING BACK OUT.
ADRIAN, I...
SAY NO MORE. HER NAME WAS JULIE.
IF YOU THINK ABOUT IT FOR A SECOND, YOU'LL REALIZE WHY THERE WAS NO REASON TO YELL.
YOU CAN HAVE MY COFFEE. IT'S STILL WARM.
HE THINKS.
HE THINKS OF THE EVENING HE MET ADRIAN. DARK AND SENSUAL. AS IF HE CAME OUT OF ONE OF ANNE RICE'S BOOKS.
EVERYBODY'S EYES WERE ON HIM AT THAT PARTY. BUT ADRIAN ONLY HAD EYES FOR OWEN.

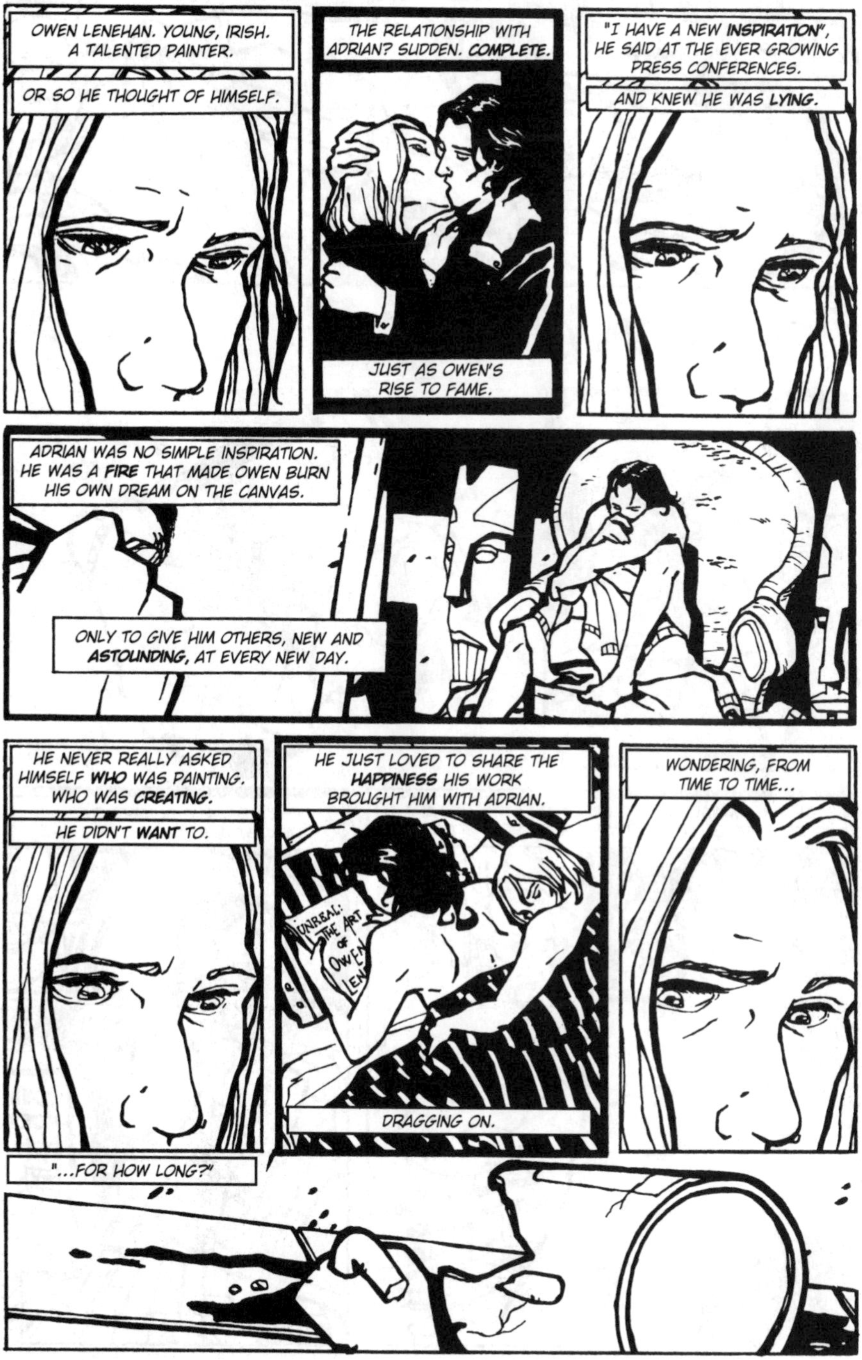
OWEN LENEHAN. YOUNG, IRISH. A TALENTED PAINTER.
OR SO HE THOUGHT OF HIMSELF.
THE RELATIONSHIP WITH ADRIAN? SUDDEN. COMPLETE.
JUST AS OWEN'S RISE TO FAME.
"I HAVE A NEW INSPIRATION", HE SAID AT THE EVER GROWING PRESS CONFERENCES.
AND KNEW HE WAS LYING.
ADRIAN WAS NO SIMPLE INSPIRATION. HE WAS A FIRE THAT MADE OWEN BURN HIS OWN DREAM ON THE CANVAS.
ONLY TO GIVE HIM OTHERS, NEW AND ASTOUNDING, AT EVERY NEW DAY.
HE NEVER REALLY ASKED HIMSELF WHO WAS PAINTING. WHO WAS CREATING.
HE DIDN'T WANT TO.
HE JUST LOVED TO SHARE THE HAPPINESS HIS WORK BROUGHT HIM WITH ADRIAN.
UNREAL: THE ART OF
DRAGGING ON.
WONDERING, FROM TIME TO TIME...
"...FOR HOW LONG?"

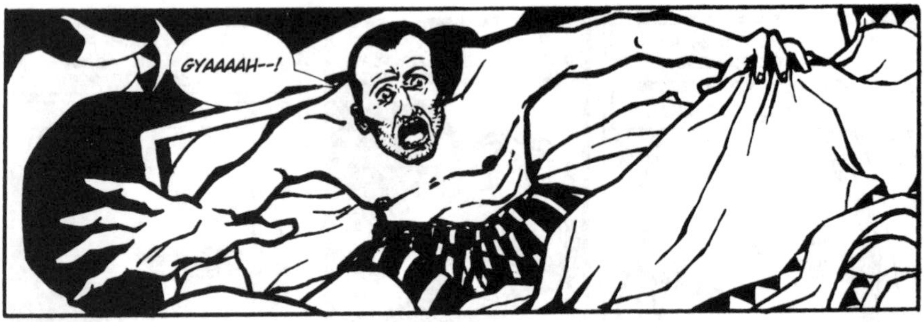
GYAAAAH--!

first round

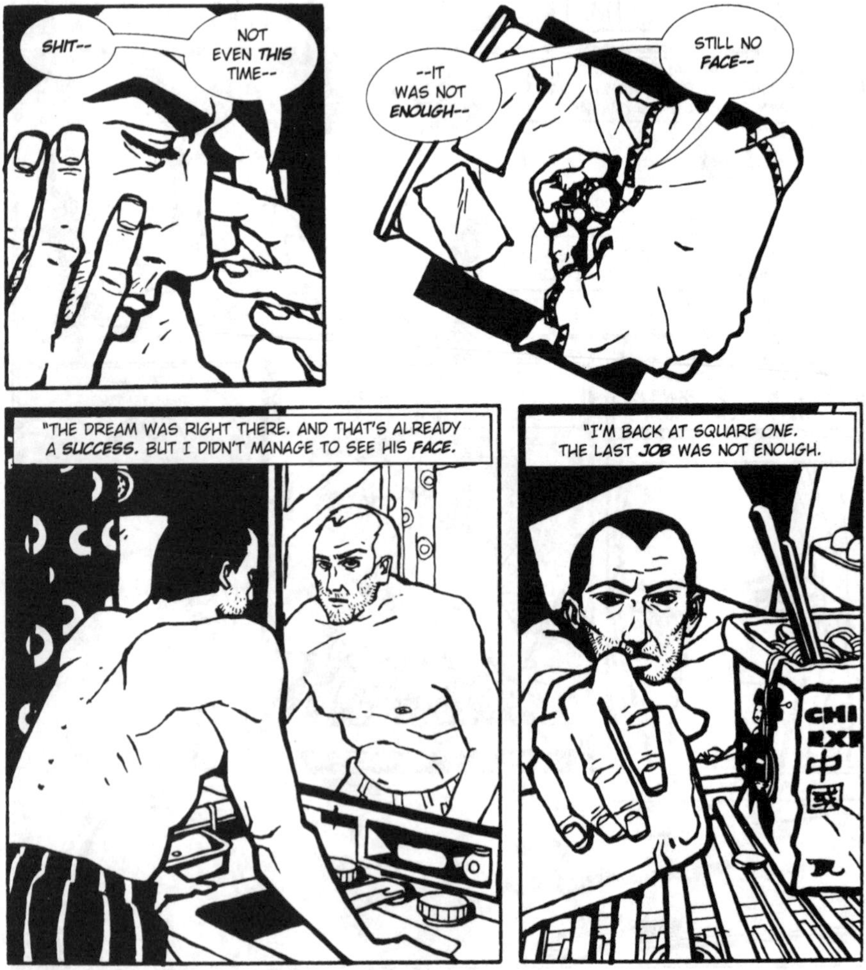
SHIT--
NOT EVEN THIS TIME--
STILL NO FACE--
--IT WAS NOT ENOUGH--
"THE DREAM WAS RIGHT THERE. AND THAT'S ALREADY A SUCCESS. BUT I DIDN'T MANAGE TO SEE HIS FACE.
"I'M BACK AT SQUARE ONE. THE LAST JOB WAS NOT ENOUGH.

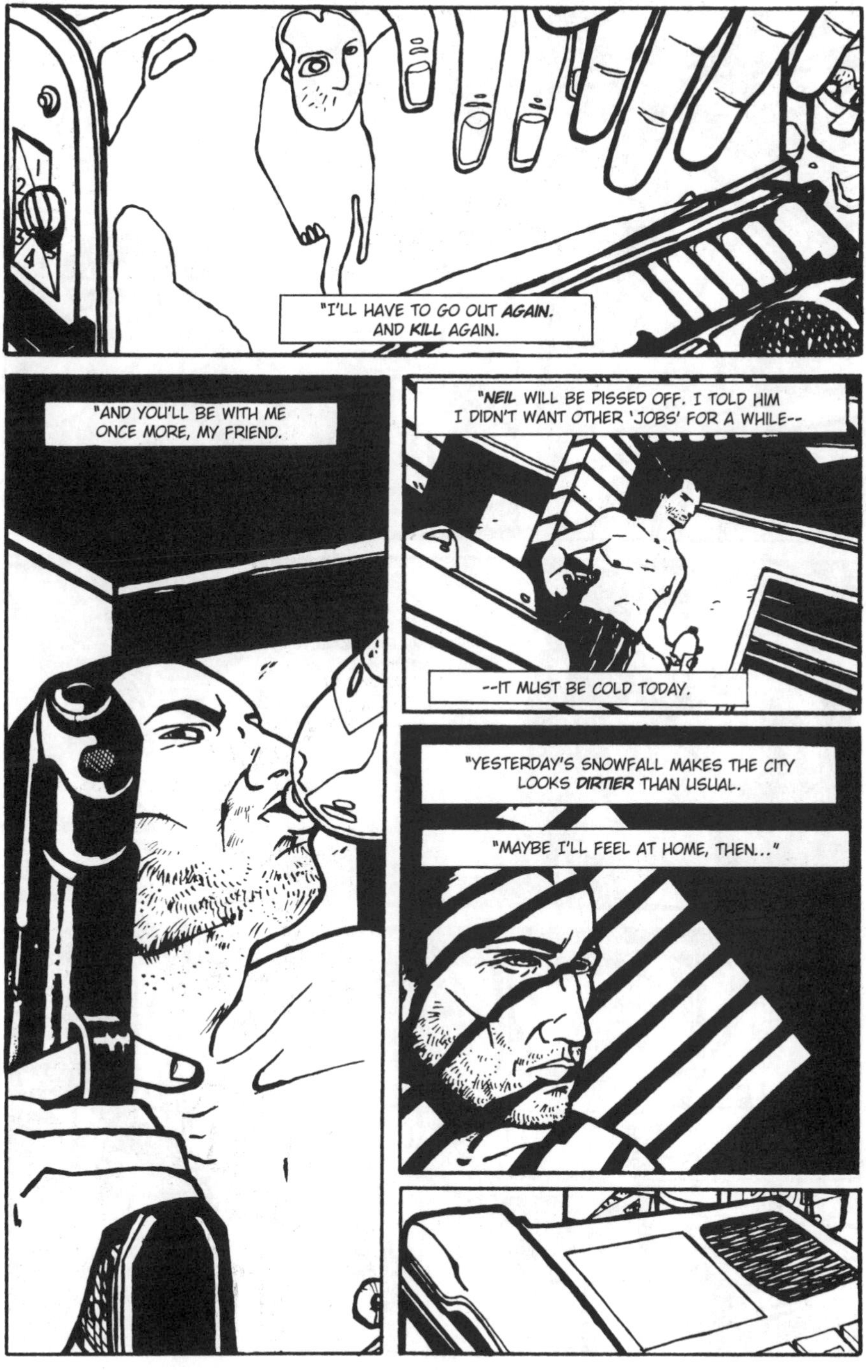
"I'LL HAVE TO GO OUT AGAIN.
AND KILL AGAIN.
"AND YOU'LL BE WITH ME ONCE MORE, MY FRIEND.
"NEIL WILL BE PISSED OFF. I TOLD HIM I DIDN'T WANT OTHER 'JOBS' FOR A WHILE--
--IT MUST BE COLD TODAY.
"YESTERDAY'S SNOWFALL MAKES THE CITY LOOKS DIRTIER THAN USUAL.
"MAYBE I'LL FEEL AT HOME, THEN..."

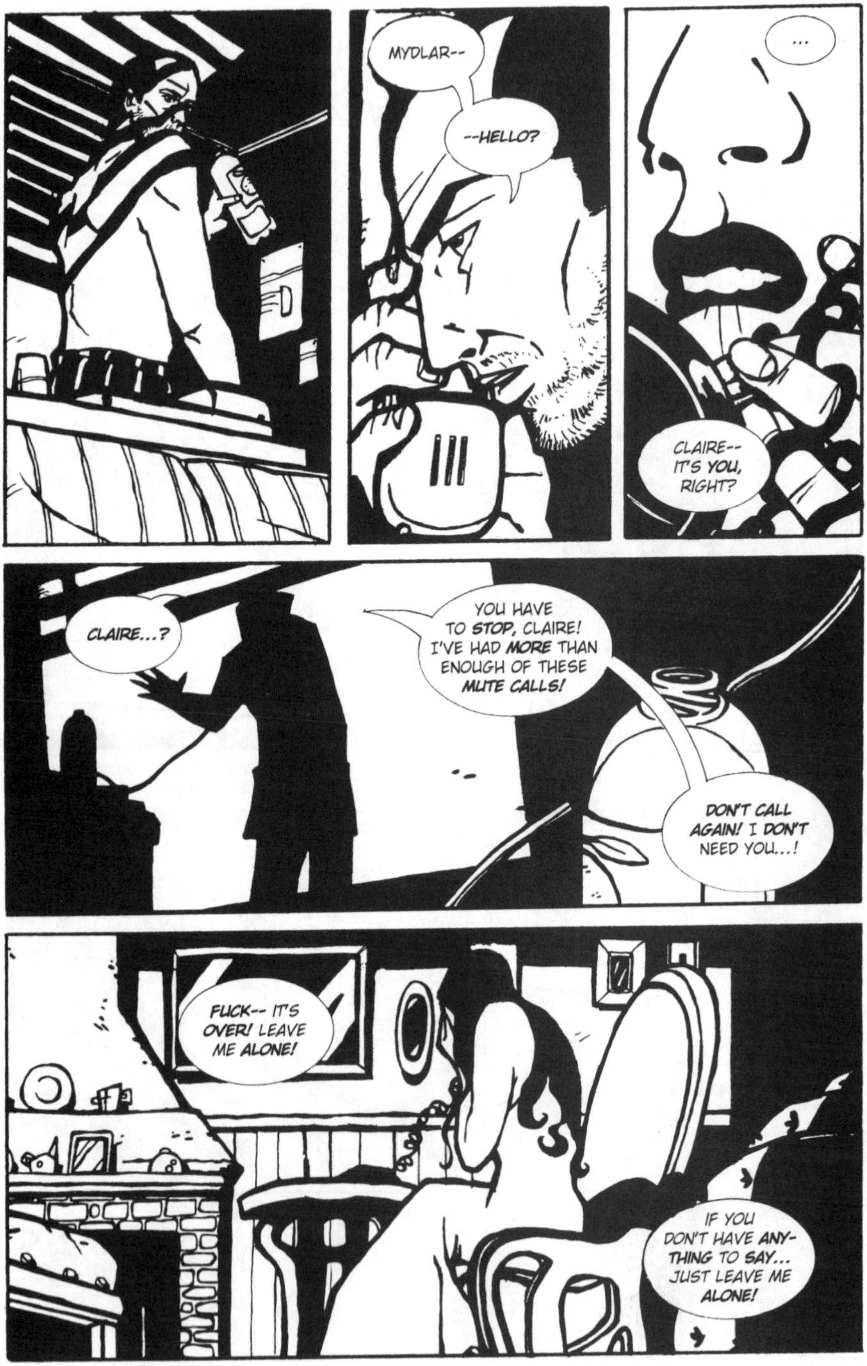
MYDLAR--
--HELLO?
...
CLAIRE-- IT'S YOU, RIGHT?
CLAIRE...?
YOU HAVE TO STOP, CLAIRE! I'VE HAD MORE THAN ENOUGH OF THESE MUTE CALLS!
DON'T CALL AGAIN! I DON'T NEED YOU...!
FUCK-- IT'S OVER! LEAVE ME ALONE!
IF YOU DON'T HAVE ANY-THING TO SAY... JUST LEAVE ME ALONE!

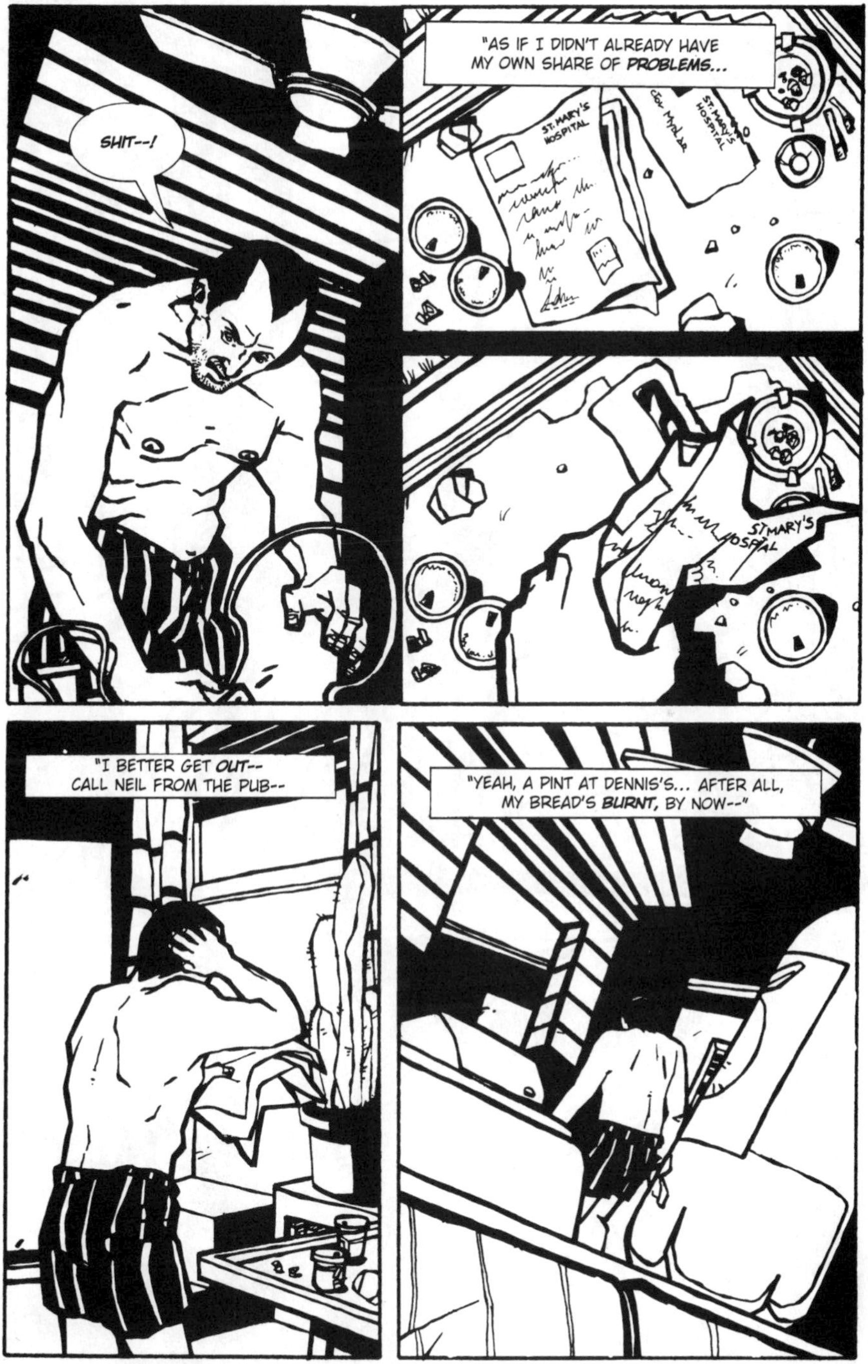
SHIT--!
"AS IF I DIDN'T ALREADY HAVE MY OWN SHARE OF PROBLEMS...
ST. MARY'S HOSPITAL
ST. MARY'S HOSPITAL
ST. MARY'S HOSPITAL
"I BETTER GET OUT-- CALL NEIL FROM THE PUB--
"YEAH, A PINT AT DENNIS'S... AFTER ALL, MY BREAD'S BURNT, BY NOW--"

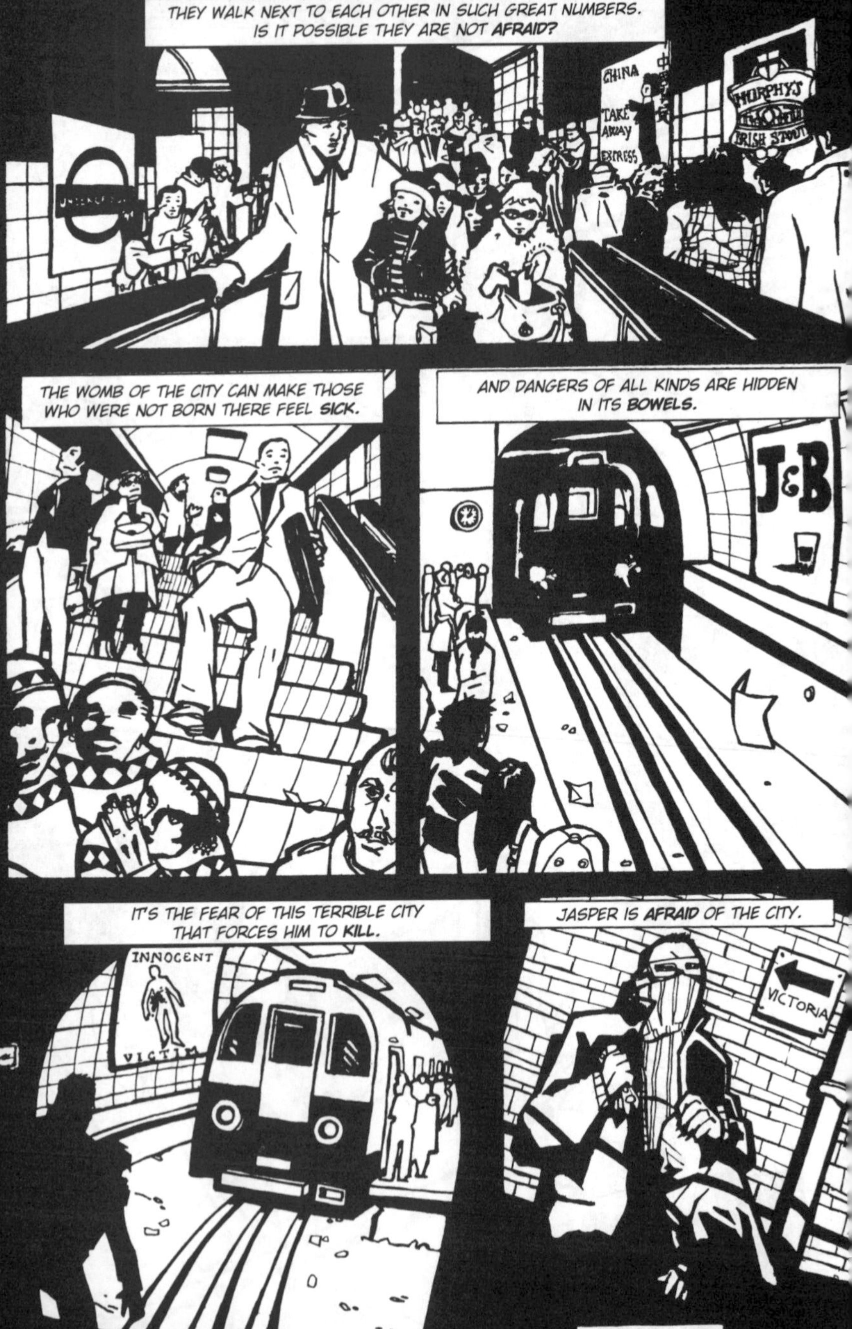
THEY WALK NEXT TO EACH OTHER IN SUCH GREAT NUMBERS. IS IT POSSIBLE THEY ARE NOT AFRAID?
CHINA
TAKE AWAY
EXPRESS
MURPHY'S
IRISH STOUT
THE WOMB OF THE CITY CAN MAKE THOSE WHO WERE NOT BORN THERE FEEL SICK.
AND DANGERS OF ALL KINDS ARE HIDDEN IN ITS BOWELS.
J&B
IT'S THE FEAR OF THIS TERRIBLE CITY THAT FORCES HIM TO KILL.
INNOCENT
VICTIM
JASPER IS AFRAID OF THE CITY.
VICTORIA
AND HE HATES IT.

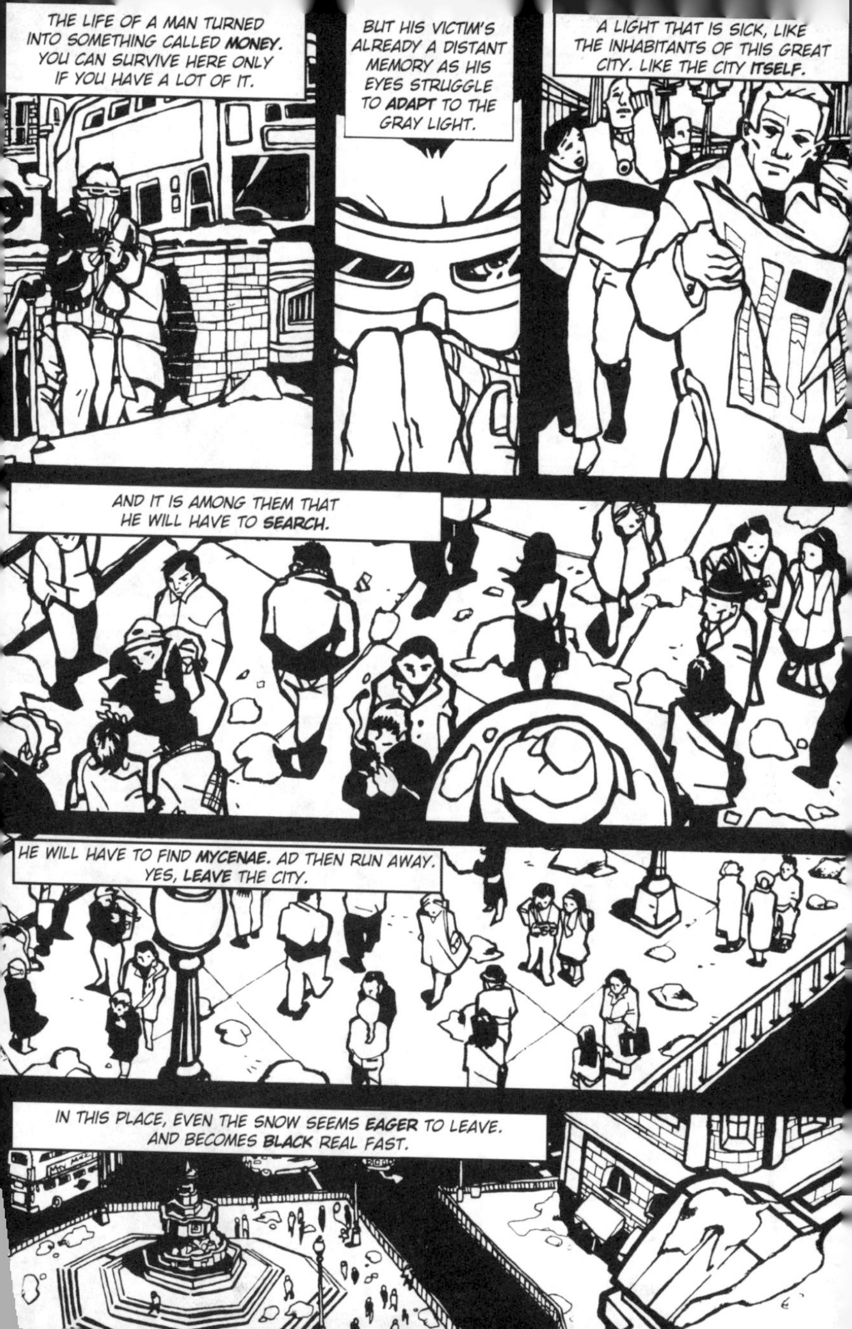
THE LIFE OF A MAN TURNED INTO SOMETHING CALLED MONEY. YOU CAN SURVIVE HERE ONLY IF YOU HAVE A LOT OF IT.
BUT HIS VICTIM'S ALREADY A DISTANT MEMORY AS HIS EYES STRUGGLE TO ADAPT TO THE GRAY LIGHT.
A LIGHT THAT IS SICK, LIKE THE INHABITANTS OF THIS GREAT CITY. LIKE THE CITY ITSELF.
AND IT IS AMONG THEM THAT HE WILL HAVE TO SEARCH.
HE WILL HAVE TO FIND MYCENAE. AD THEN RUN AWAY. YES, LEAVE THE CITY.
IN THIS PLACE, EVEN THE SNOW SEEMS EAGER TO LEAVE. AND BECOMES BLACK REAL FAST.

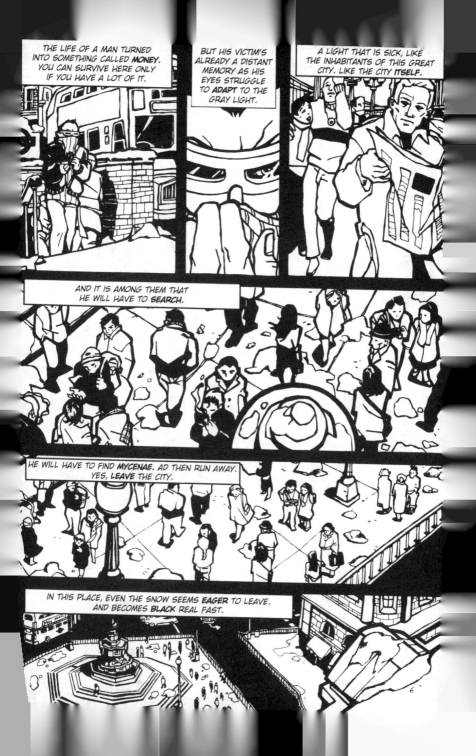

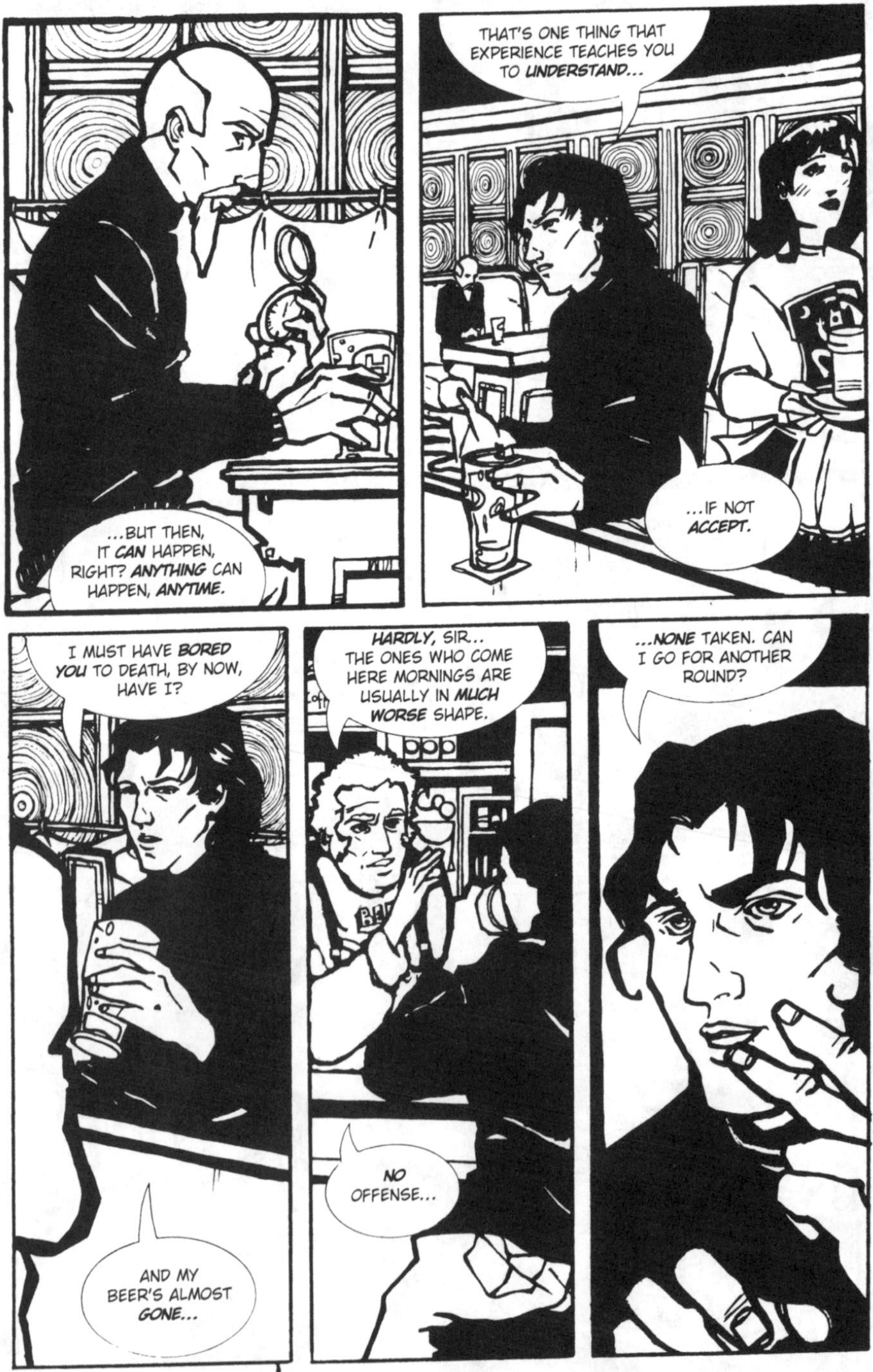
...BUT THEN, IT CAN HAPPEN, RIGHT? ANYTHING CAN HAPPEN, ANYTIME.
THAT'S ONE THING THAT EXPERIENCE TEACHES YOU TO UNDERSTAND...
...IF NOT ACCEPT.
I MUST HAVE BORED YOU TO DEATH, BY NOW, HAVE I?
AND MY BEER'S ALMOST GONE...
HARDLY, SIR... THE ONES WHO COME HERE MORNINGS ARE USUALLY IN MUCH WORSE SHAPE.
NO OFFENSE...
...NONE TAKEN. CAN I GO FOR ANOTHER ROUND?

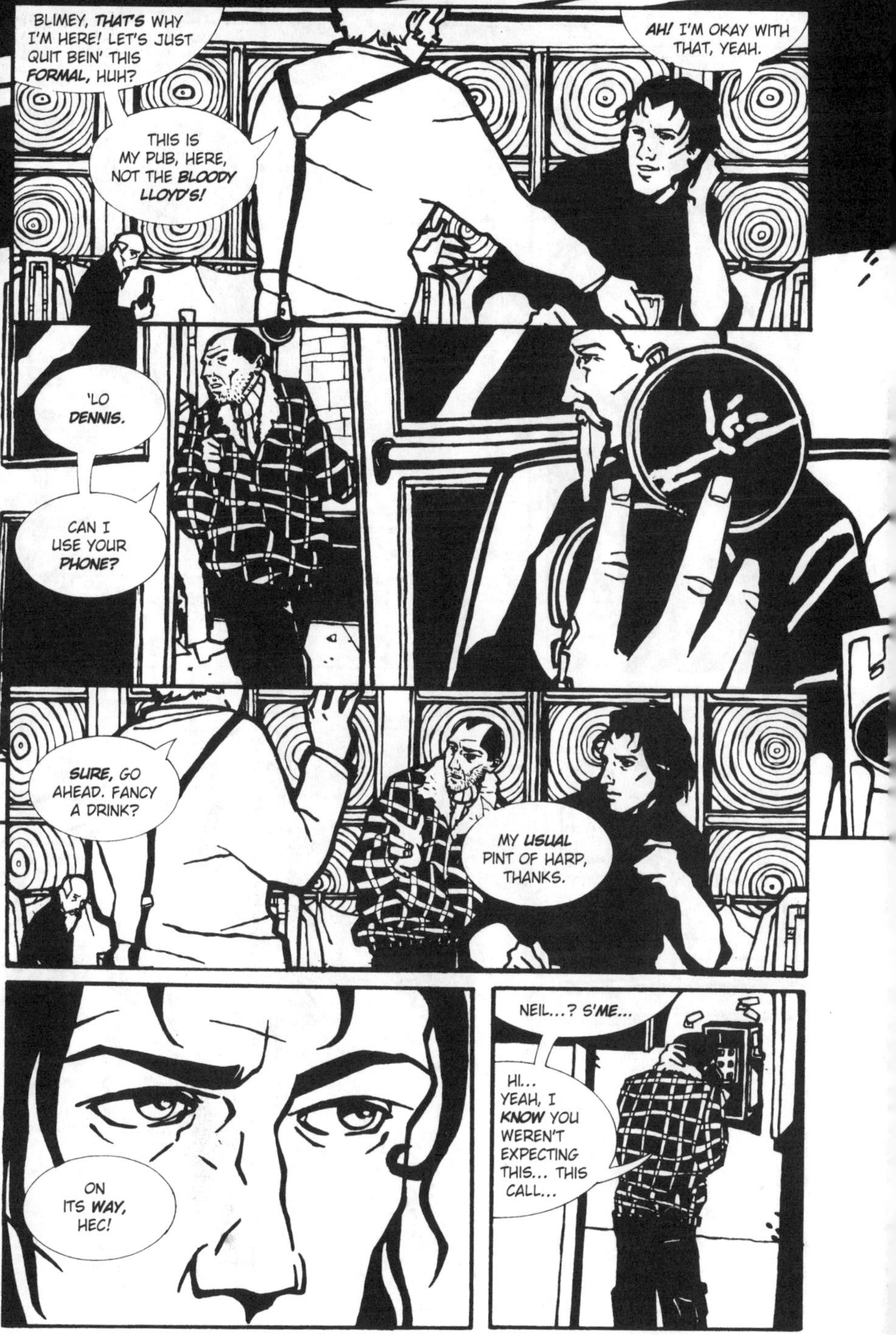
BLIMEY, THAT'S WHY I'M HERE! LET'S JUST QUIT BEIN' THIS FORMAL, HUH?
THIS IS MY PUB, HERE, NOT THE BLOODY LLOYD'S!
AH! I'M OKAY WITH THAT, YEAH.
'LO DENNIS.
CAN I USE YOUR PHONE?
SURE, GO AHEAD. FANCY A DRINK?
MY USUAL PINT OF HARP, THANKS.
ON ITS WAY, HEC!
NEIL...? S'ME...
HI... YEAH, I KNOW YOU WEREN'T EXPECTING THIS... THIS CALL...

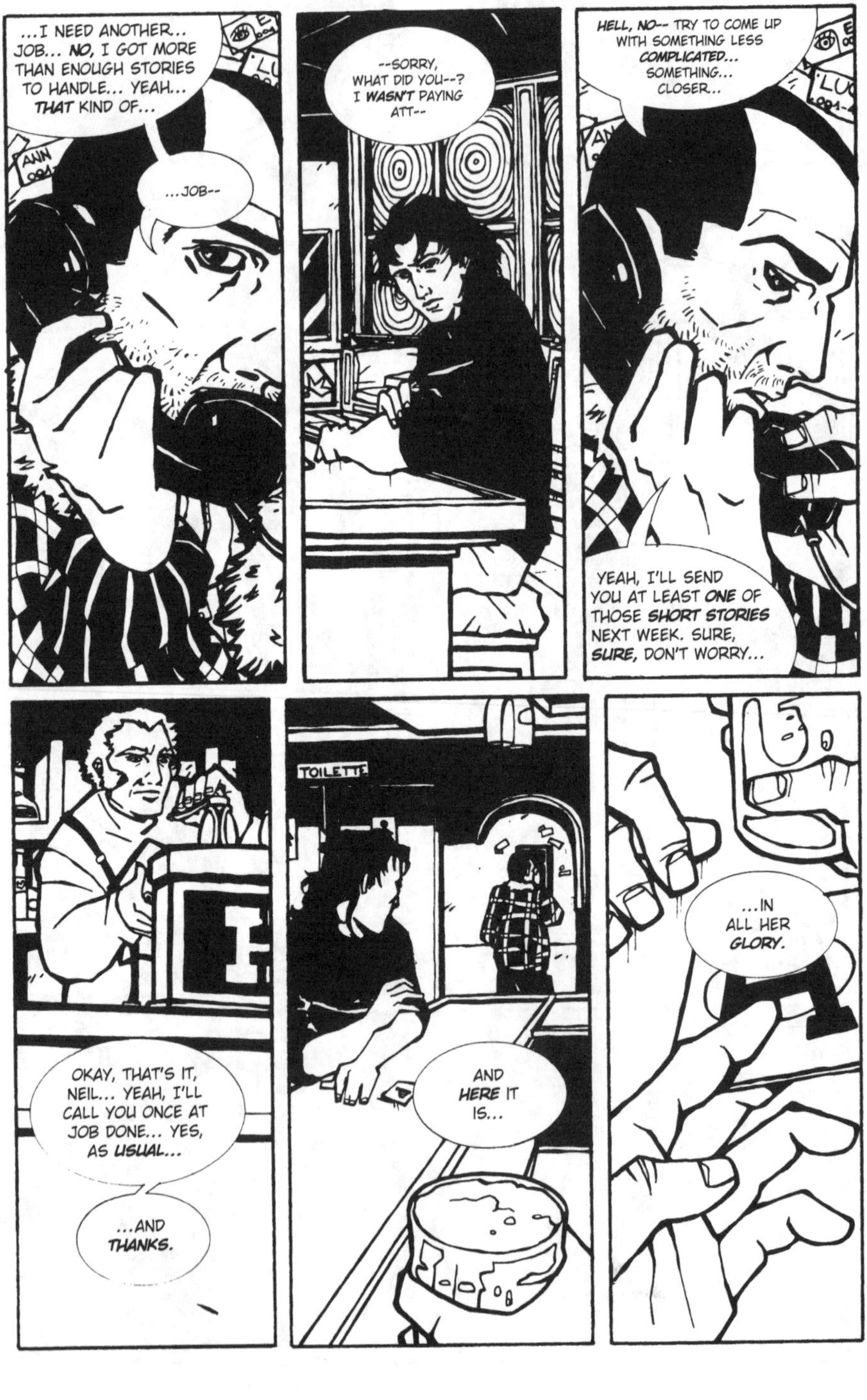
...I NEED ANOTHER... JOB... NO, I GOT MORE THAN ENOUGH STORIES TO HANDLE... YEAH... THAT KIND OF...
...JOB--
--SORRY, WHAT DID YOU--? I WASN'T PAYING ATT--
HELL, NO-- TRY TO COME UP WITH SOMETHING LESS COMPLICATED... SOMETHING... CLOSER...
YEAH, I'LL SEND YOU AT LEAST ONE OF THOSE SHORT STORIES NEXT WEEK. SURE, SURE, DON'T WORRY...
OKAY, THAT'S IT, NEIL... YEAH, I'LL CALL YOU ONCE AT JOB DONE... YES, AS USUAL...
...AND THANKS.
TOILETTE
AND HERE IT IS...
...IN ALL HER GLORY.

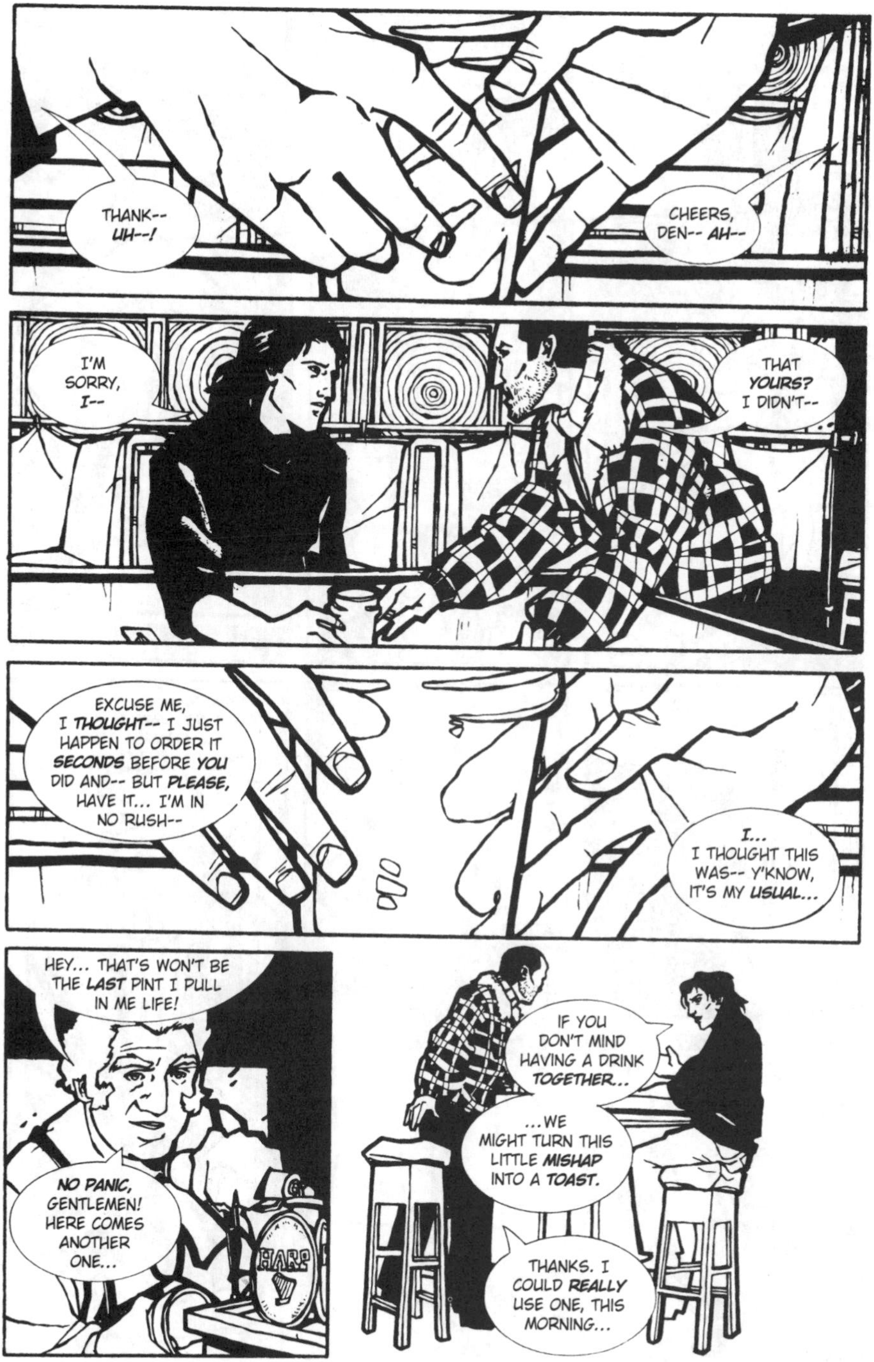
THANK-- UH--!
CHEERS, DEN-- AH--
I'M SORRY, I--
THAT YOURS? I DIDN'T--
EXCUSE ME, I THOUGHT-- I JUST HAPPEN TO ORDER IT SECONDS BEFORE YOU DID AND-- BUT PLEASE, HAVE IT... I'M IN NO RUSH--
I... I THOUGHT THIS WAS-- Y'KNOW, IT'S MY USUAL...
HEY... THAT'S WON'T BE THE LAST PINT I PULL IN ME LIFE!
NO PANIC, GENTLEMEN! HERE COMES ANOTHER ONE...
IF YOU DON'T MIND HAVING A DRINK TOGETHER...
...WE MIGHT TURN THIS LITTLE MISHAP INTO A TOAST.
THANKS. I COULD REALLY USE ONE, THIS MORNING...

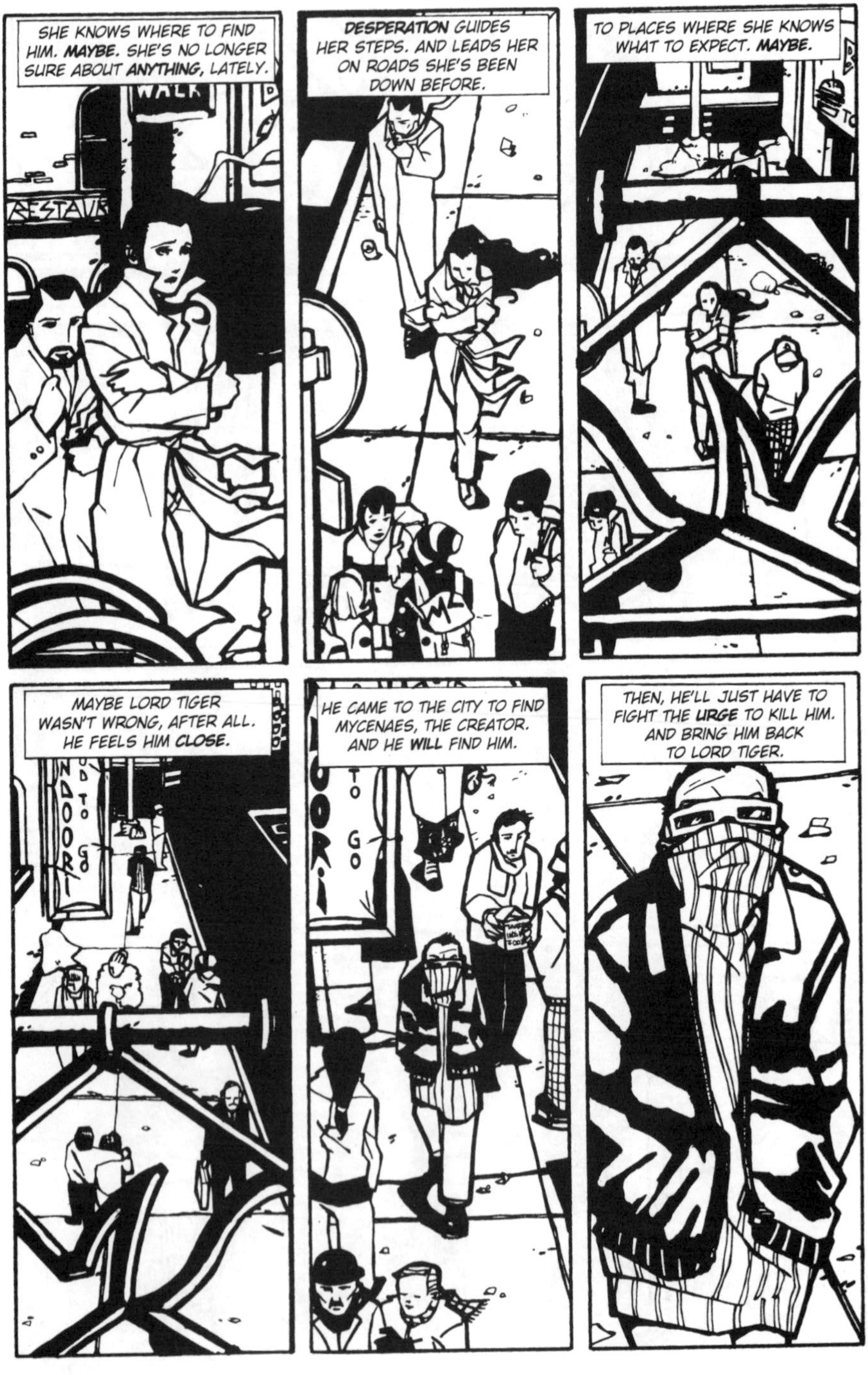

SHE KNOWS WHERE TO FIND HIM. **MAYBE.** SHE'S NO LONGER SURE ABOUT **ANYTHING,** LATELY.
WALK
RESTAU
DESPERATION GUIDES HER STEPS. AND LEADS HER ON ROADS SHE'S BEEN DOWN BEFORE.
TO PLACES WHERE SHE KNOWS WHAT TO EXPECT. **MAYBE.**
MAYBE LORD TIGER WASN'T WRONG, AFTER ALL. HE FEELS HIM **CLOSE.**
HE CAME TO THE CITY TO FIND MYCENAES, THE CREATOR. AND HE **WILL** FIND HIM.
TO GO
THEN, HE'LL JUST HAVE TO FIGHT THE **URGE** TO KILL HIM. AND BRING HIM BACK TO LORD TIGER.

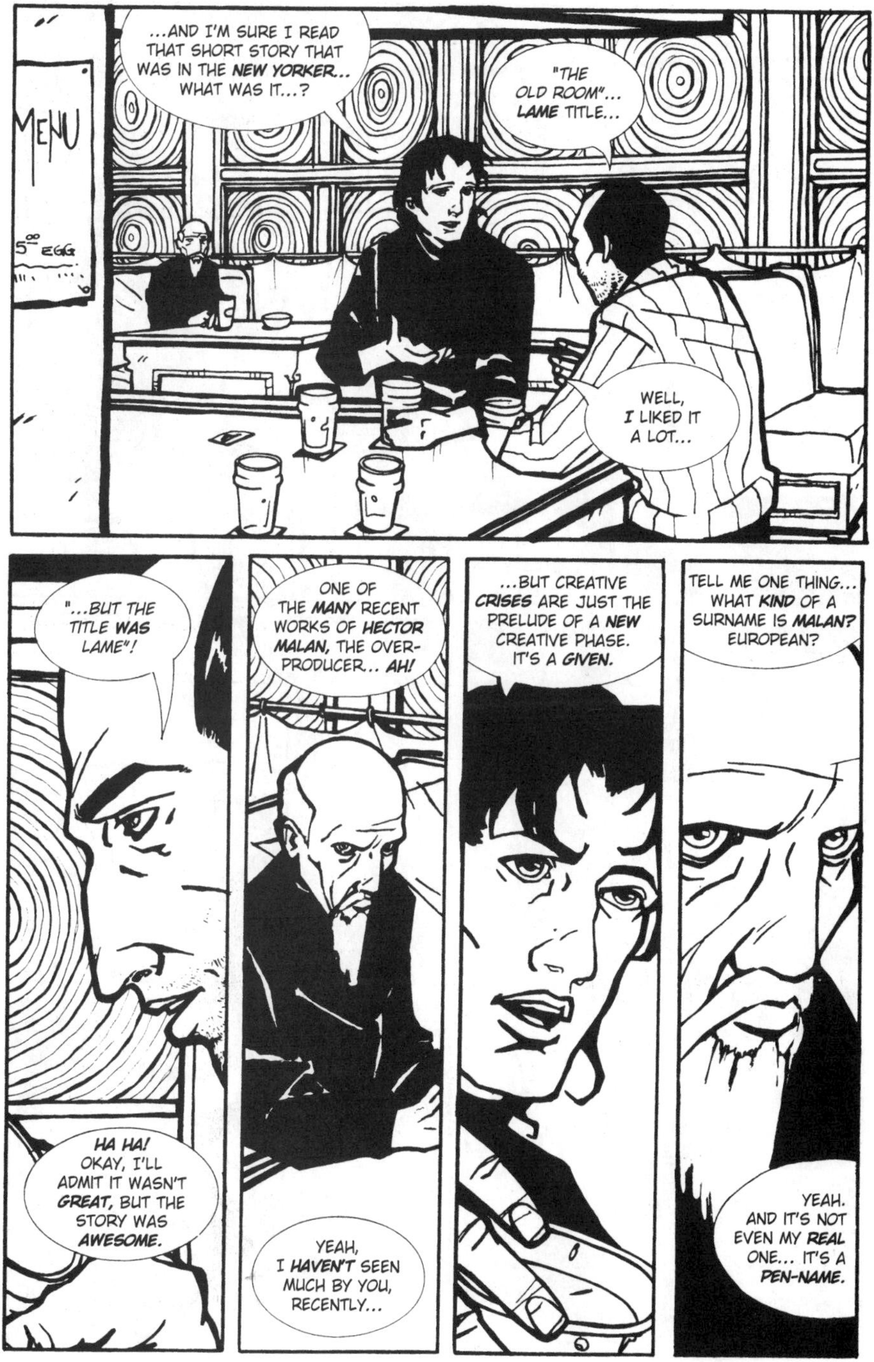
...AND I'M SURE I READ THAT SHORT STORY THAT WAS IN THE NEW YORKER... WHAT WAS IT...?
"THE OLD ROOM"... LAME TITLE...
MENU
5.00 EGG
WELL, I LIKED IT A LOT...
"...BUT THE TITLE WAS LAME"!
HA HA! OKAY, I'LL ADMIT IT WASN'T GREAT, BUT THE STORY WAS AWESOME.
ONE OF THE MANY RECENT WORKS OF HECTOR MALAN, THE OVER-PRODUCER... AH!
YEAH, I HAVEN'T SEEN MUCH BY YOU, RECENTLY...
...BUT CREATIVE CRISES ARE JUST THE PRELUDE OF A NEW CREATIVE PHASE. IT'S A GIVEN.
TELL ME ONE THING... WHAT KIND OF A SURNAME IS MALAN? EUROPEAN?
YEAH. AND IT'S NOT EVEN MY REAL ONE... IT'S A PEN-NAME.

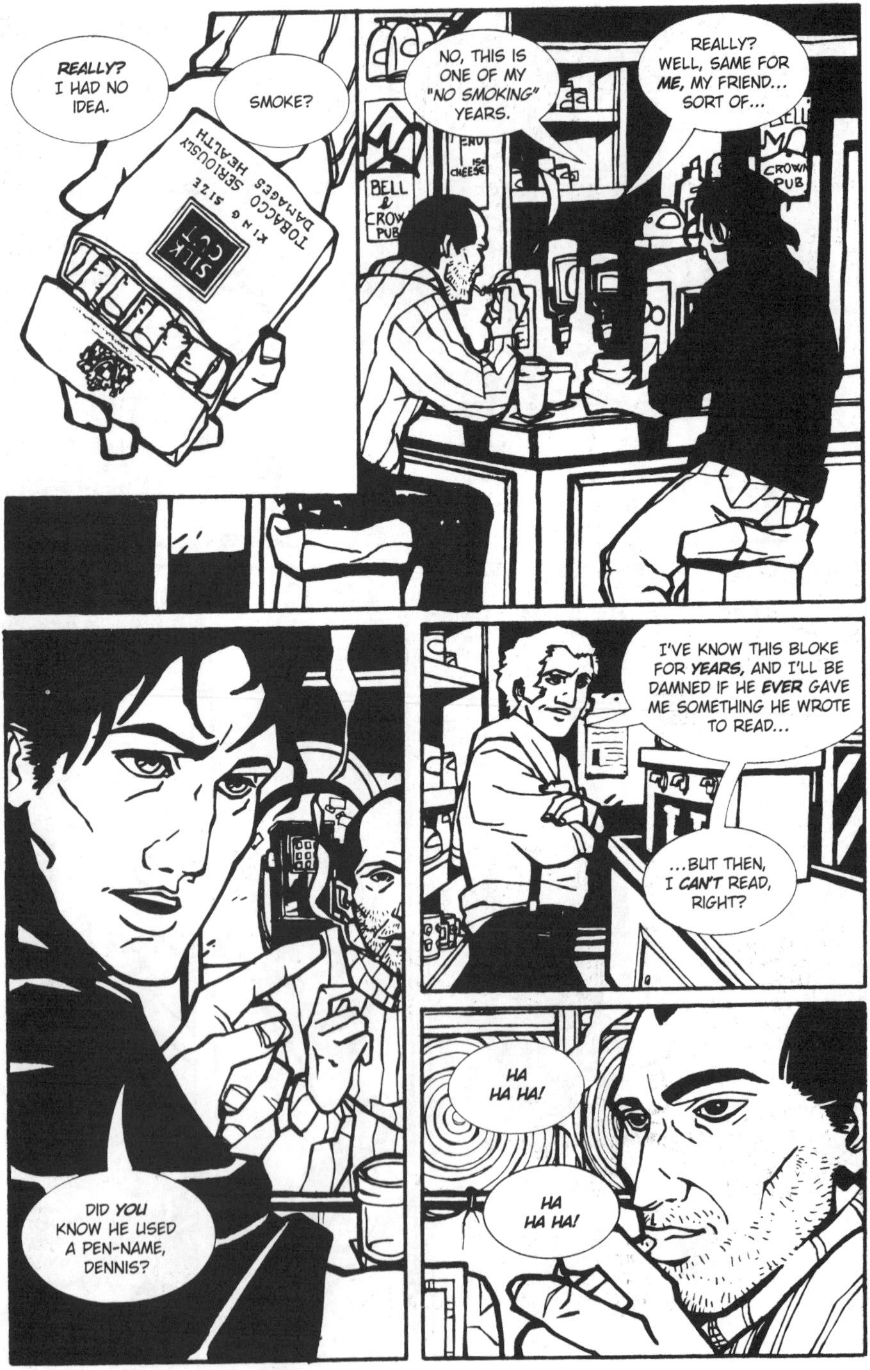
REALLY? I HAD NO IDEA.
SMOKE?
SILK CUT
KING SIZE
TOBACCO SERIOUSLY DAMAGES HEALTH
NO, THIS IS ONE OF MY "NO SMOKING" YEARS.
REALLY? WELL, SAME FOR ME, MY FRIEND... SORT OF...
BELL & CROWN PUB
CHEESE
DID YOU KNOW HE USED A PEN-NAME, DENNIS?
I'VE KNOW THIS BLOKE FOR YEARS, AND I'LL BE DAMNED IF HE EVER GAVE ME SOMETHING HE WROTE TO READ...
...BUT THEN, I CAN'T READ, RIGHT?
HA HA HA!
HA HA HA!

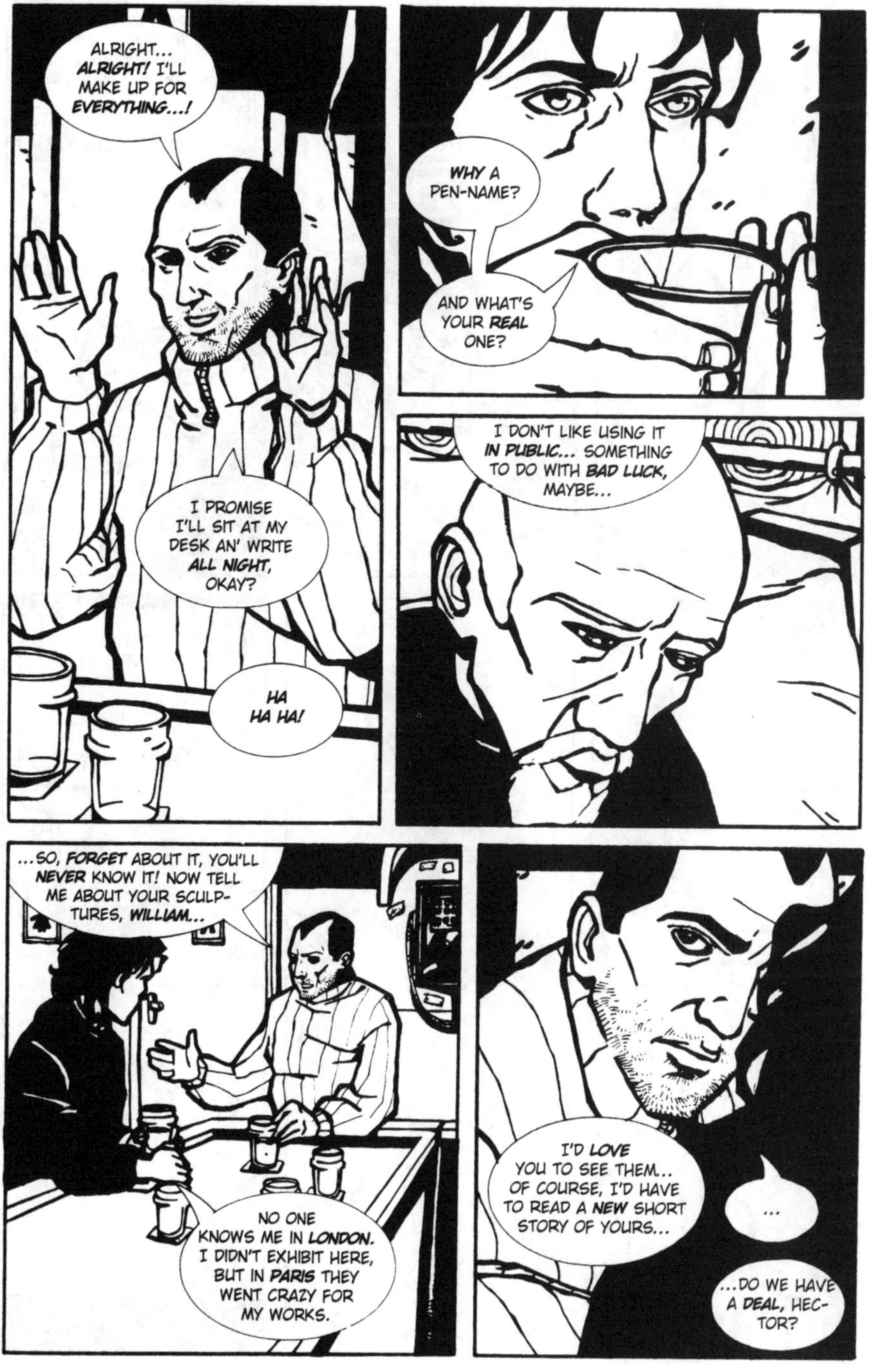
ALRIGHT... ALRIGHT! I'LL MAKE UP FOR EVERYTHING...!
I PROMISE I'LL SIT AT MY DESK AN' WRITE ALL NIGHT, OKAY?
HA HA HA!
WHY A PEN-NAME?
AND WHAT'S YOUR REAL ONE?
I DON'T LIKE USING IT IN PUBLIC... SOMETHING TO DO WITH BAD LUCK, MAYBE...
...SO, FORGET ABOUT IT, YOU'LL NEVER KNOW IT! NOW TELL ME ABOUT YOUR SCULP-TURES, WILLIAM...
NO ONE KNOWS ME IN LONDON. I DIDN'T EXHIBIT HERE, BUT IN PARIS THEY WENT CRAZY FOR MY WORKS.
I'D LOVE YOU TO SEE THEM... OF COURSE, I'D HAVE TO READ A NEW SHORT STORY OF YOURS...
...
...DO WE HAVE A DEAL, HEC-TOR?

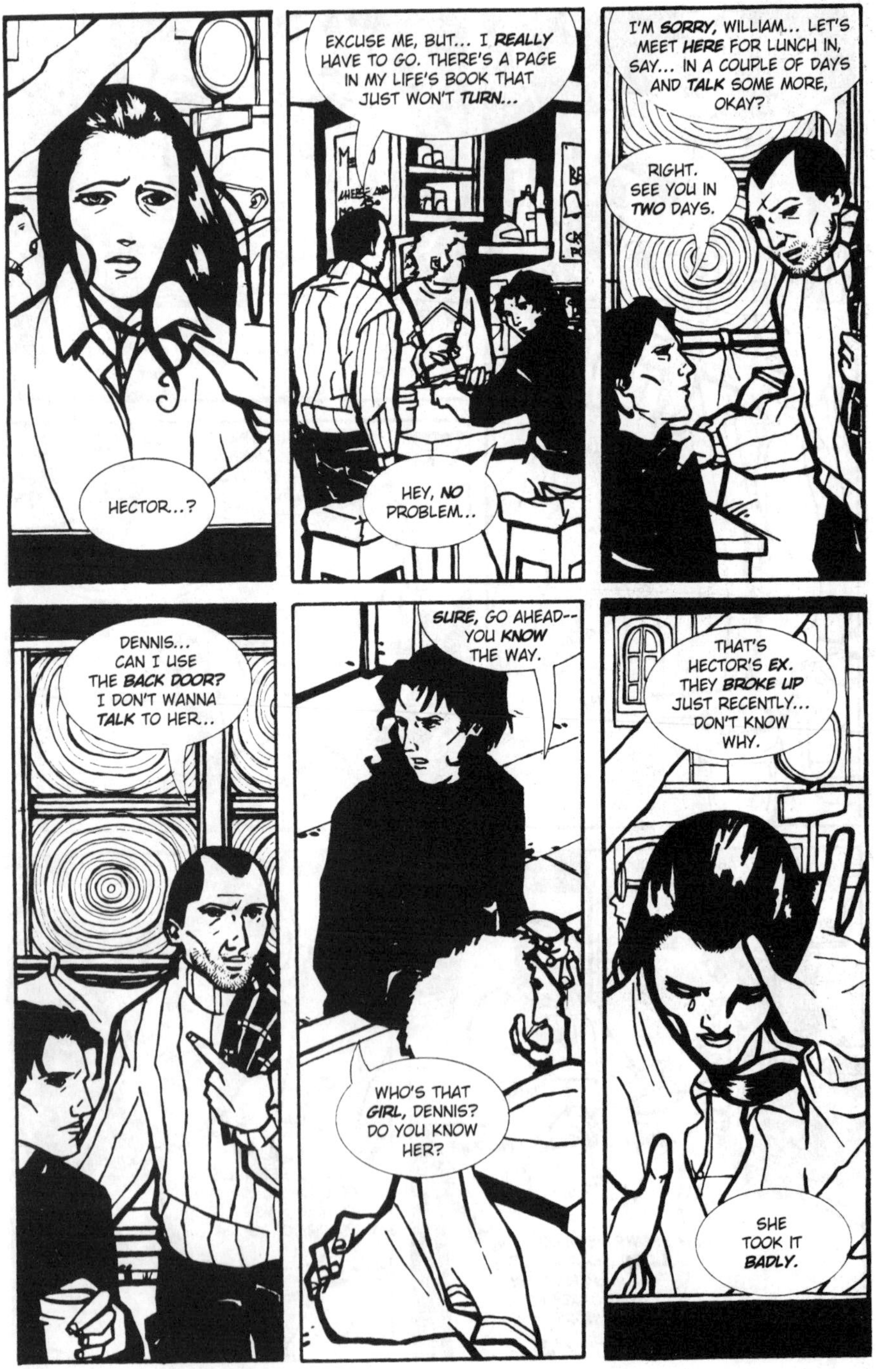
HECTOR...?
EXCUSE ME, BUT... I REALLY HAVE TO GO. THERE'S A PAGE IN MY LIFE'S BOOK THAT JUST WON'T TURN...
HEY, NO PROBLEM...
I'M SORRY, WILLIAM... LET'S MEET HERE FOR LUNCH IN, SAY... IN A COUPLE OF DAYS AND TALK SOME MORE, OKAY?
RIGHT. SEE YOU IN TWO DAYS.
DENNIS... CAN I USE THE BACK DOOR? I DON'T WANNA TALK TO HER...
SURE, GO AHEAD-- YOU KNOW THE WAY.
WHO'S THAT GIRL, DENNIS? DO YOU KNOW HER?
THAT'S HECTOR'S EX. THEY BROKE UP JUST RECENTLY... DON'T KNOW WHY.
SHE TOOK IT BADLY.

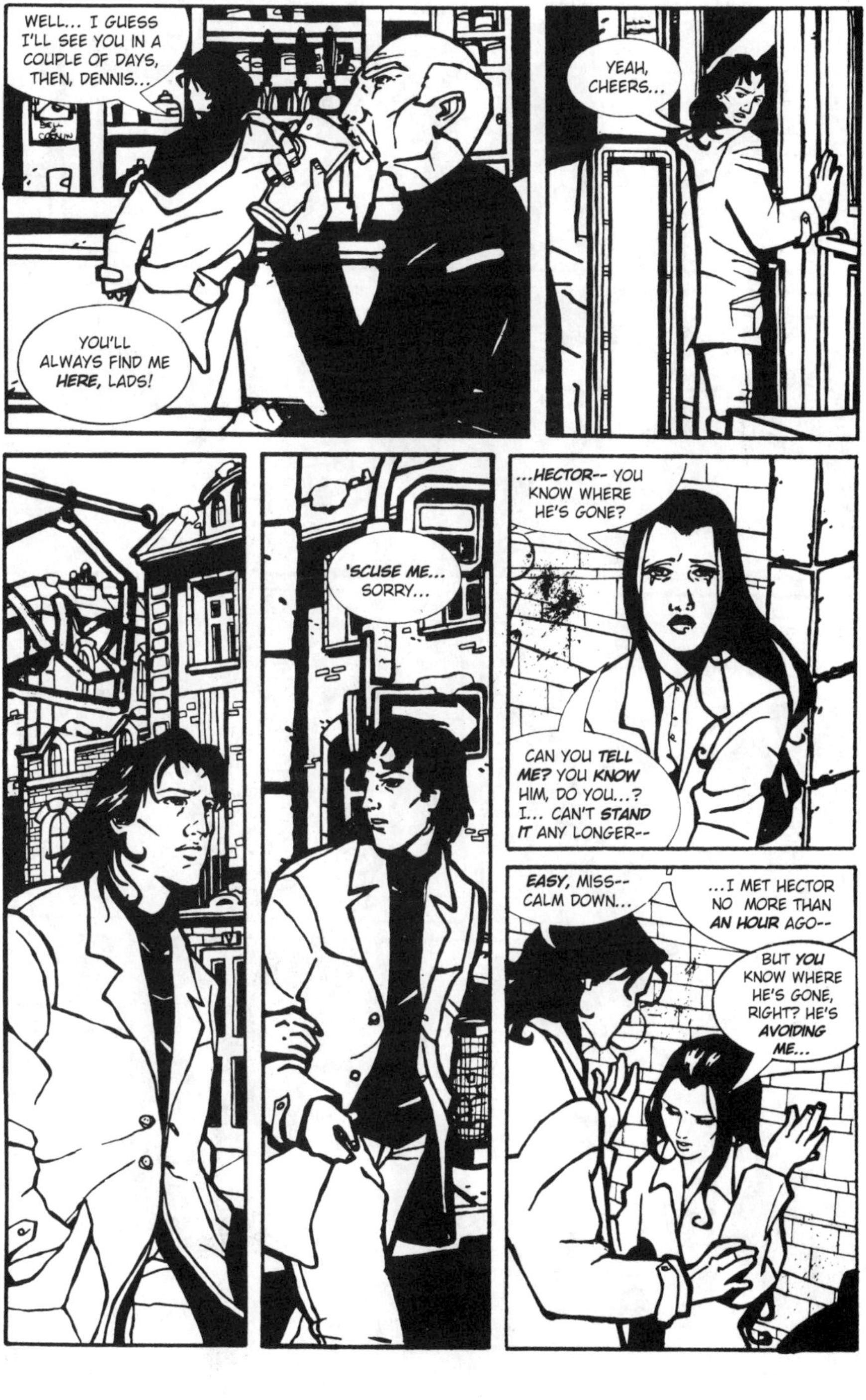
WELL... I GUESS I'LL SEE YOU IN A COUPLE OF DAYS, THEN, DENNIS...
YOU'LL ALWAYS FIND ME **HERE,** LADS!
YEAH, CHEERS...
'SCUSE ME... SORRY...
...HECTOR-- YOU KNOW WHERE HE'S GONE?
CAN YOU **TELL ME?** YOU **KNOW** HIM, DO YOU...? I... CAN'T **STAND IT** ANY LONGER--
EASY, MISS-- CALM DOWN...
...I MET HECTOR NO MORE THAN **AN HOUR** AGO--
BUT **YOU** KNOW WHERE HE'S GONE, RIGHT? HE'S **AVOIDING ME...**

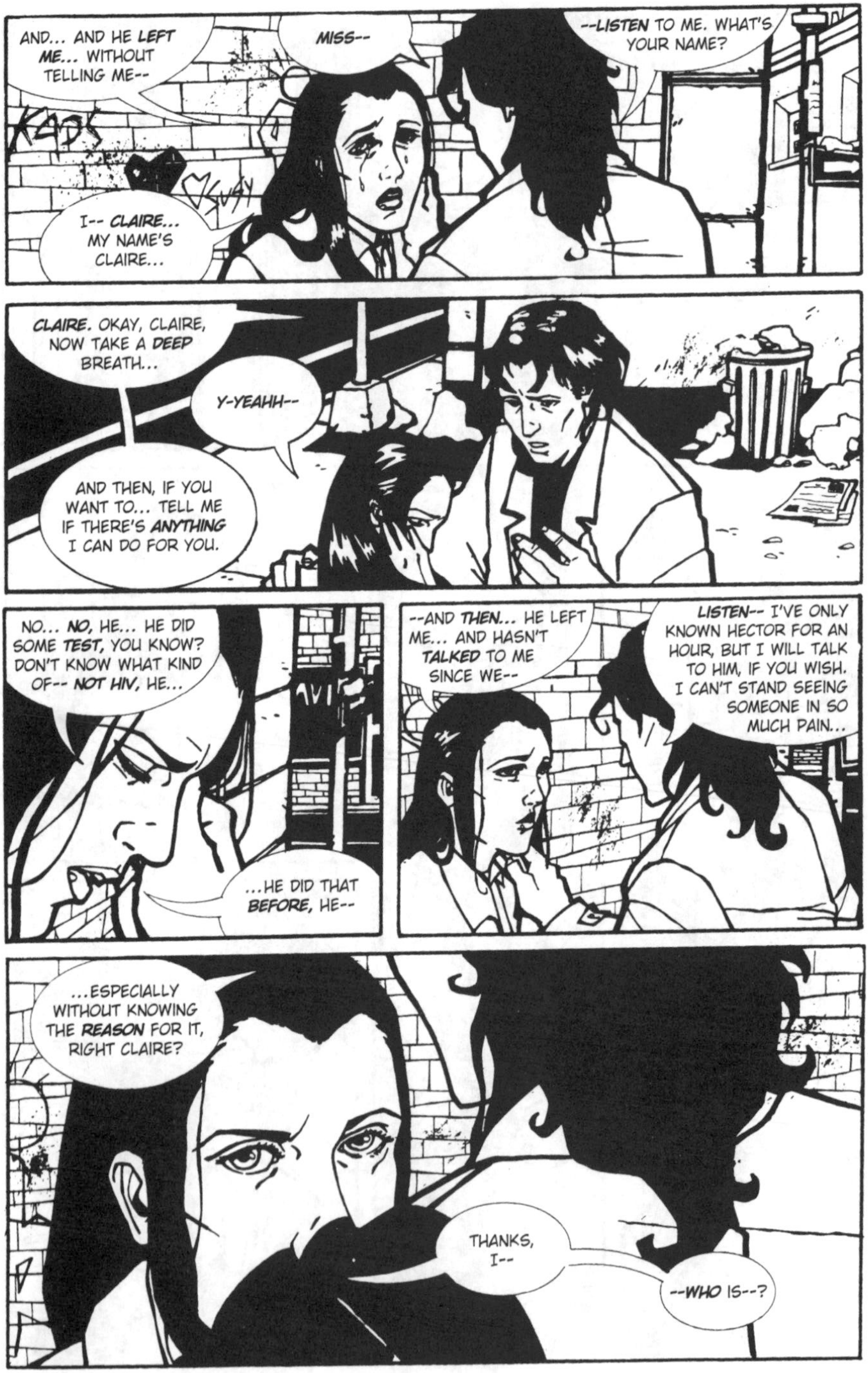

AND... AND HE LEFT ME... WITHOUT TELLING ME--
MISS--
--LISTEN TO ME. WHAT'S YOUR NAME?
I-- CLAIRE... MY NAME'S CLAIRE...
CLAIRE. OKAY, CLAIRE, NOW TAKE A DEEP BREATH...
Y-YEAHH--
AND THEN, IF YOU WANT TO... TELL ME IF THERE'S ANYTHING I CAN DO FOR YOU.
NO... NO, HE... HE DID SOME TEST, YOU KNOW? DON'T KNOW WHAT KIND OF-- NOT HIV, HE...
...HE DID THAT BEFORE, HE--
--AND THEN... HE LEFT ME... AND HASN'T TALKED TO ME SINCE WE--
LISTEN-- I'VE ONLY KNOWN HECTOR FOR AN HOUR, BUT I WILL TALK TO HIM, IF YOU WISH. I CAN'T STAND SEEING SOMEONE IN SO MUCH PAIN...
...ESPECIALLY WITHOUT KNOWING THE REASON FOR IT, RIGHT CLAIRE?
THANKS, I--
--WHO IS--?

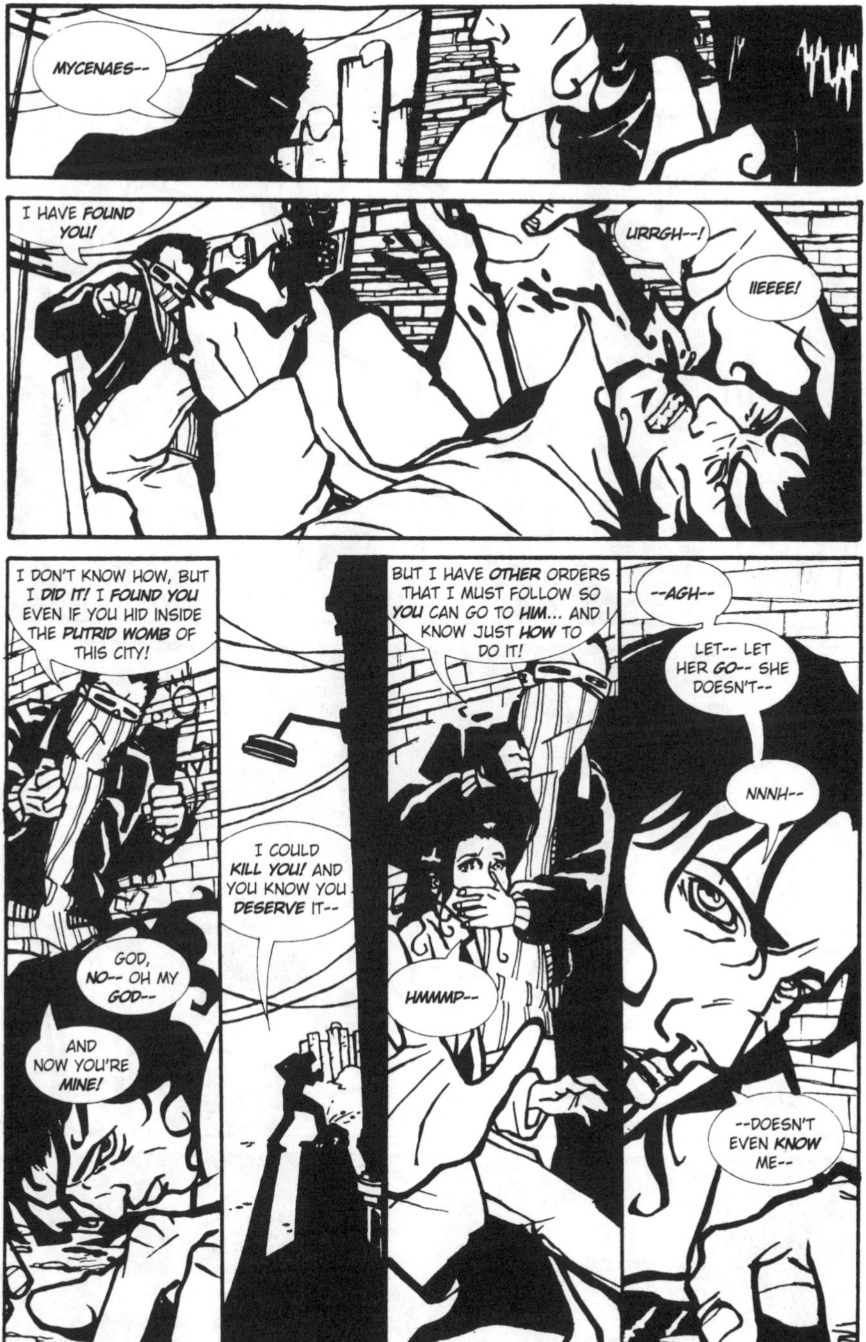
MYCENAES--
I HAVE FOUND YOU!
URRGH--!
IIEEEE!
I DON'T KNOW HOW, BUT I DID IT! I FOUND YOU EVEN IF YOU HID INSIDE THE PUTRID WOMB OF THIS CITY!
GOD, NO-- OH MY GOD--
AND NOW YOU'RE MINE!
I COULD KILL YOU! AND YOU KNOW YOU DESERVE IT--
BUT I HAVE OTHER ORDERS THAT I MUST FOLLOW SO YOU CAN GO TO HIM... AND I KNOW JUST HOW TO DO IT!
HMMMP--
--AGH--
LET-- LET HER GO-- SHE DOESN'T--
NNNH--
--DOESN'T EVEN KNOW ME--

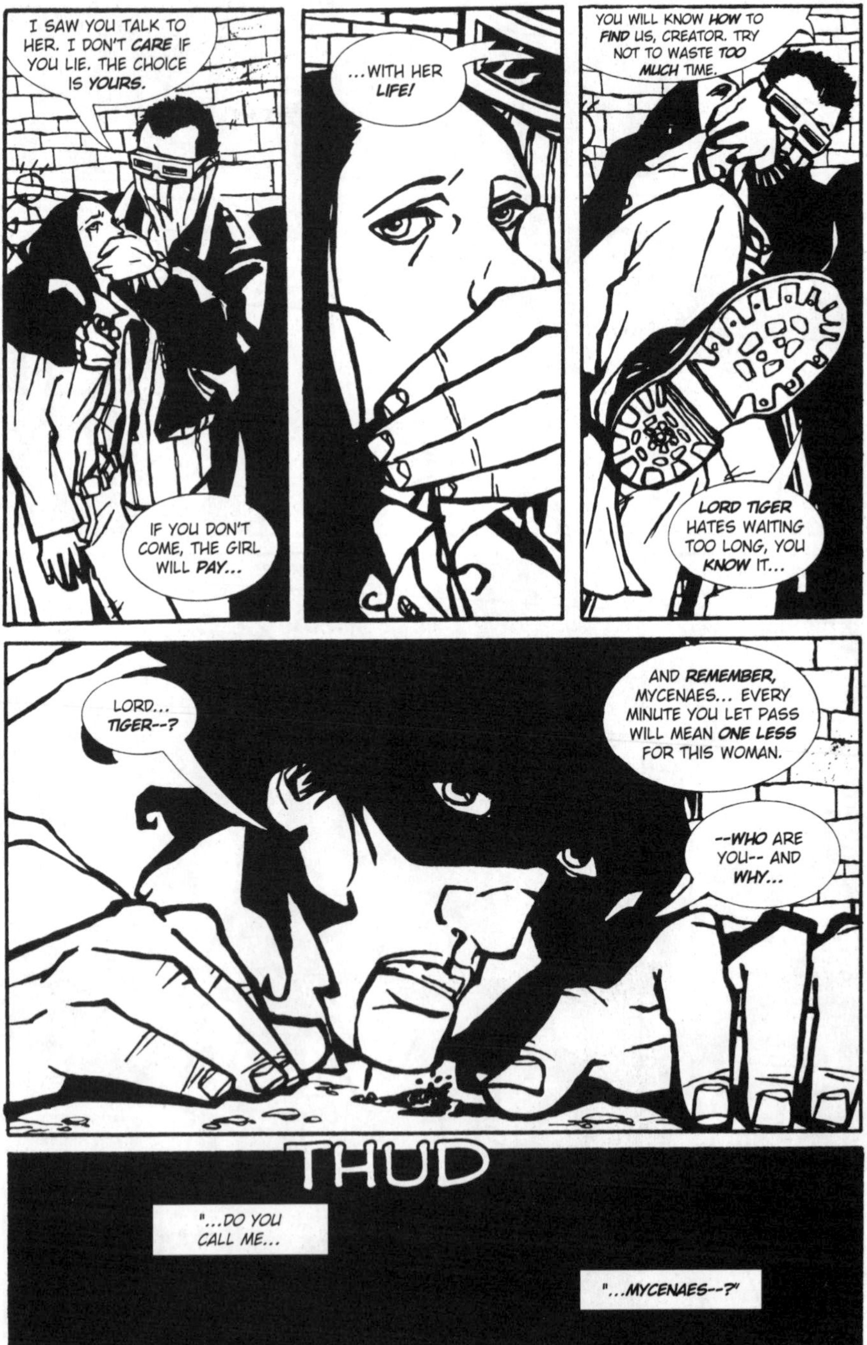
I SAW YOU TALK TO HER. I DON'T CARE IF YOU LIE. THE CHOICE IS YOURS.
IF YOU DON'T COME, THE GIRL WILL PAY...
...WITH HER LIFE!
YOU WILL KNOW HOW TO FIND US, CREATOR. TRY NOT TO WASTE TOO MUCH TIME.
LORD TIGER HATES WAITING TOO LONG, YOU KNOW IT...
LORD... TIGER--?
AND REMEMBER, MYCENAES... EVERY MINUTE YOU LET PASS WILL MEAN ONE LESS FOR THIS WOMAN.
--WHO ARE YOU-- AND WHY...
THUD
"...DO YOU CALL ME...
"...MYCENAES--?"

chapter three

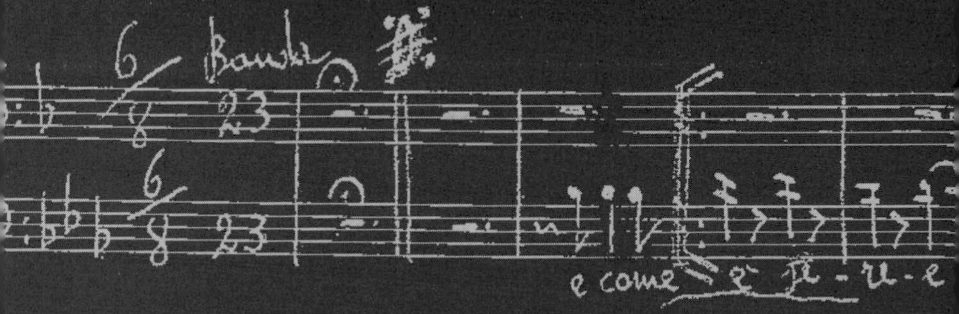
e come

Story
MATTEO CASALI

Art
GRAZIA LOBACCARO

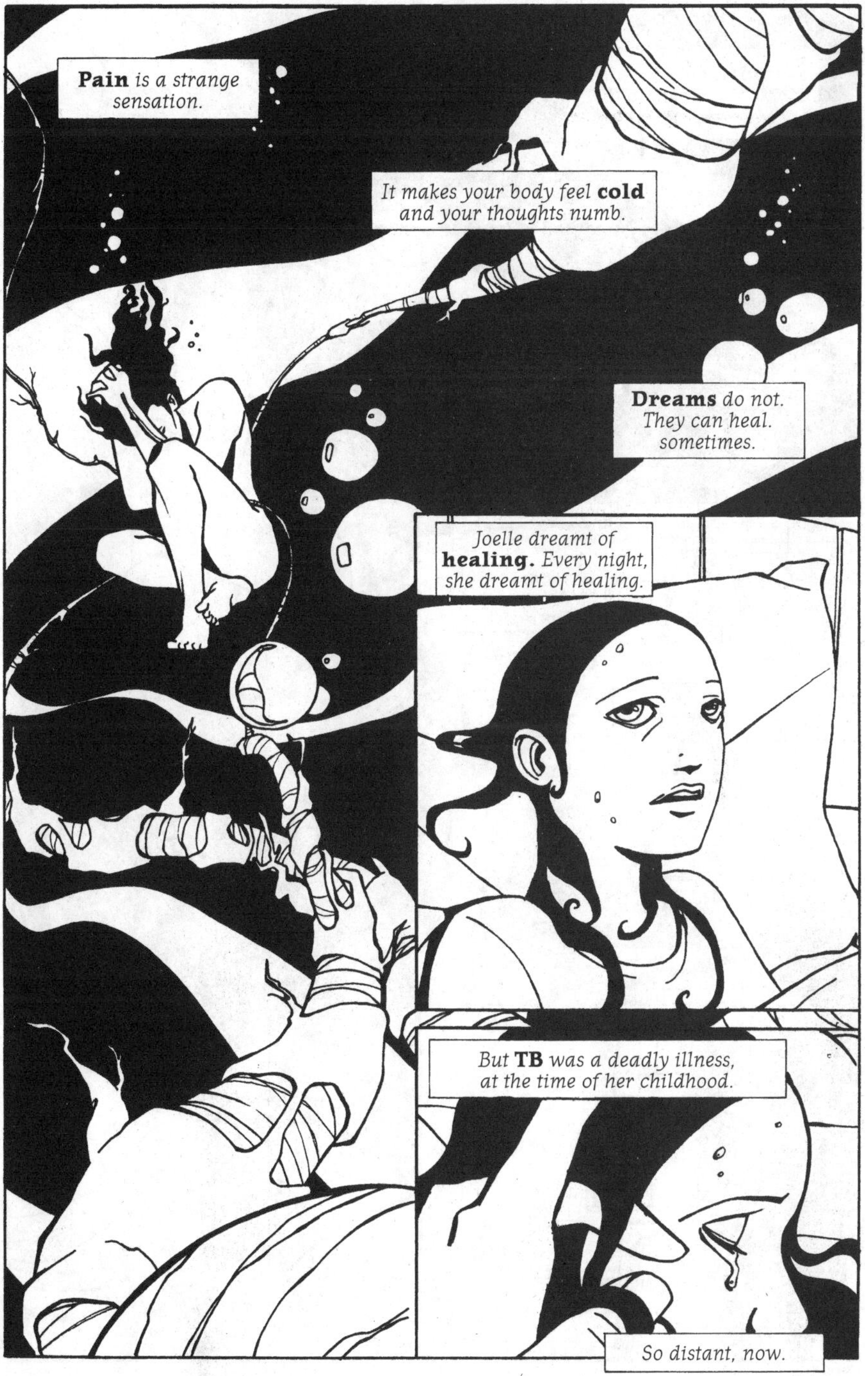
Pain *is a strange sensation.*
It makes your body feel **cold** *and your thoughts numb.*
Dreams *do not. They can heal. sometimes.*
Joelle dreamt of **healing.** *Every night, she dreamt of healing.*
But **TB** *was a deadly illness, at the time of her childhood.*
So distant, now.

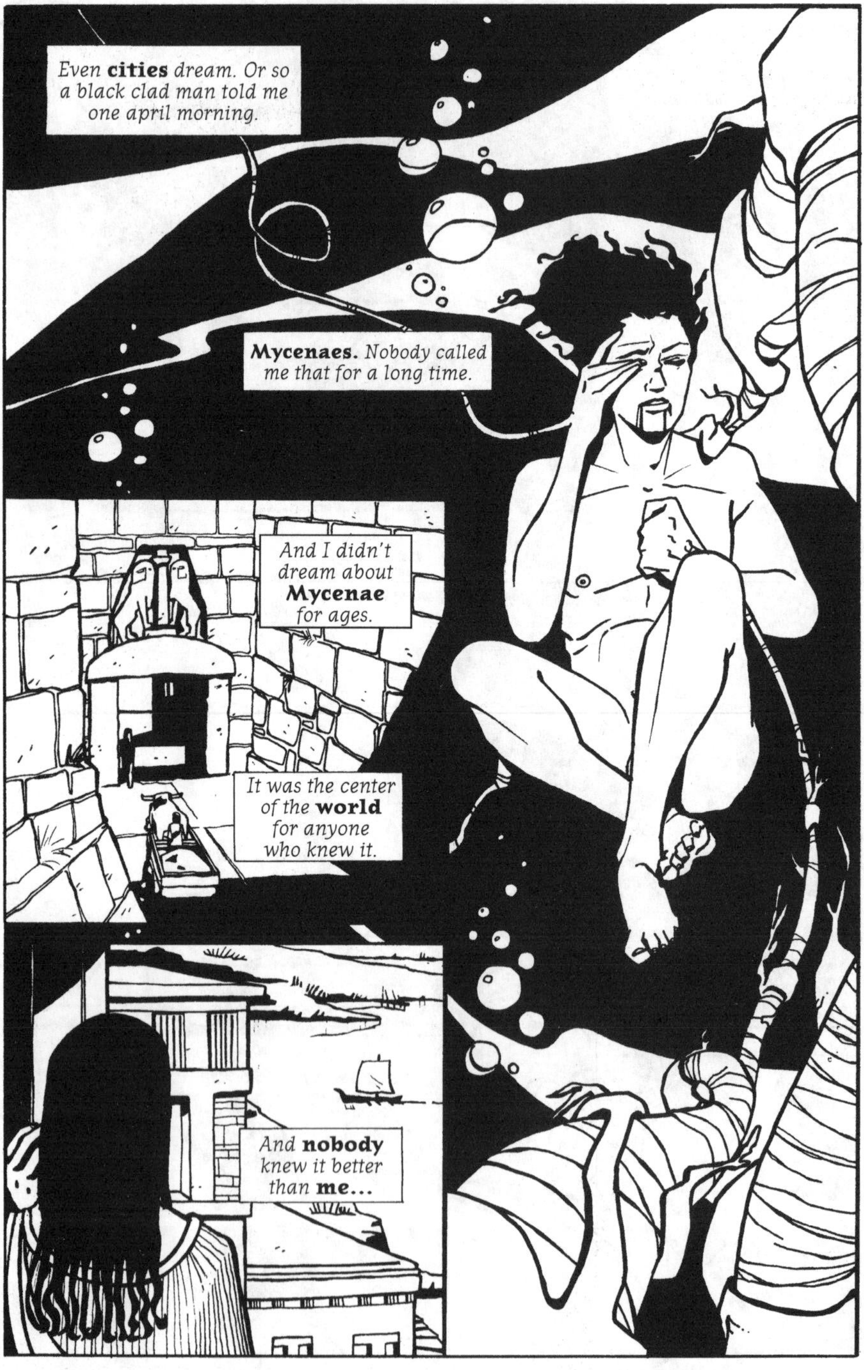
Even **cities** dream. Or so a black clad man told me one april morning.
Mycenaes. Nobody called me that for a long time.
And I didn't dream about **Mycenae** for ages.
It was the center of the **world** for anyone who knew it.
And **nobody** knew it better than **me...**

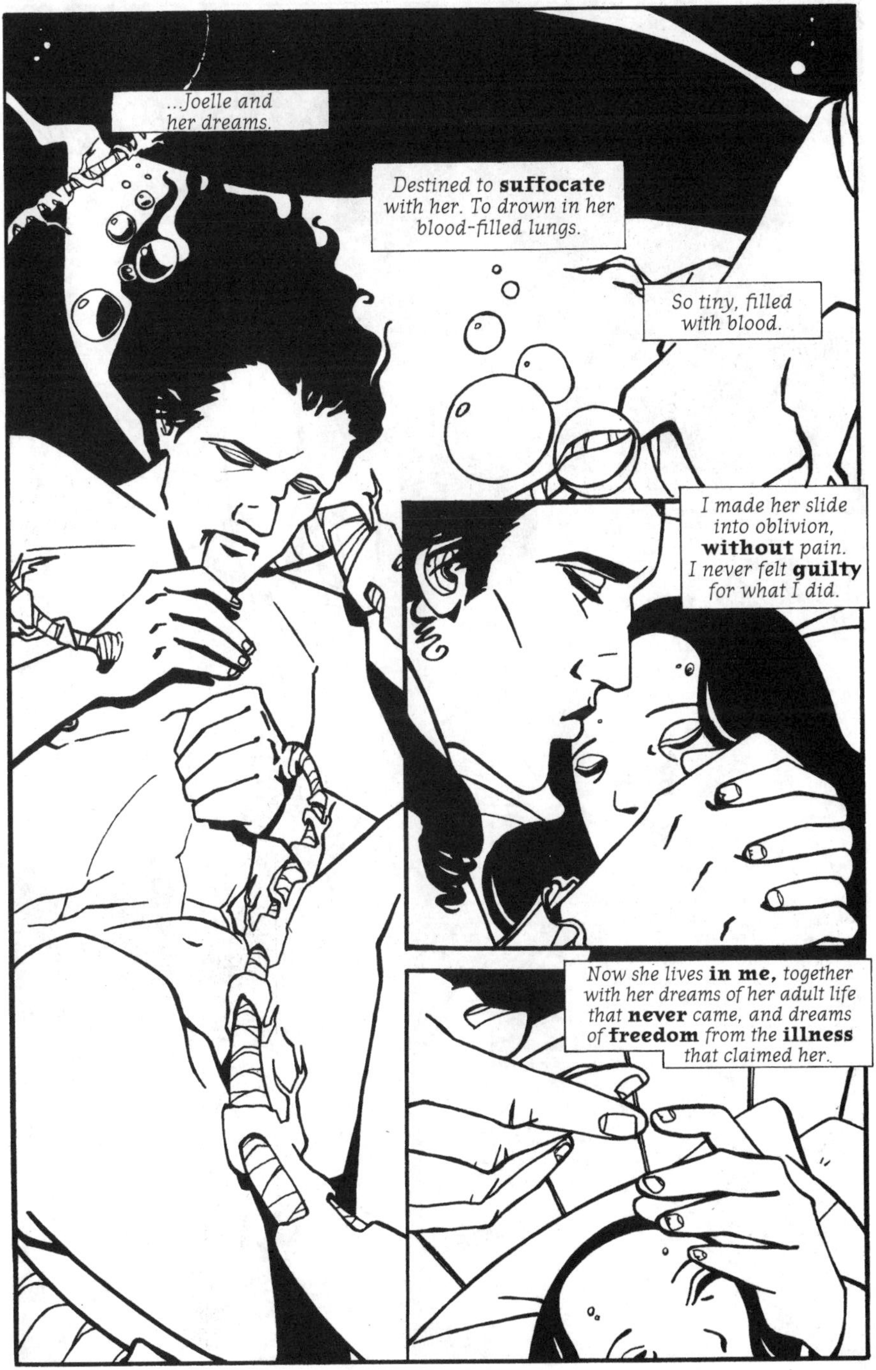

...Joelle and her dreams.
Destined to **suffocate** with her. To drown in her blood-filled lungs.
So tiny, filled with blood.
I made her slide into oblivion, **without** pain. I never felt **guilty** for what I did.
Now she lives **in me,** together with her dreams of her adult life that **never** came, and dreams of **freedom** from the **illness** that claimed her..

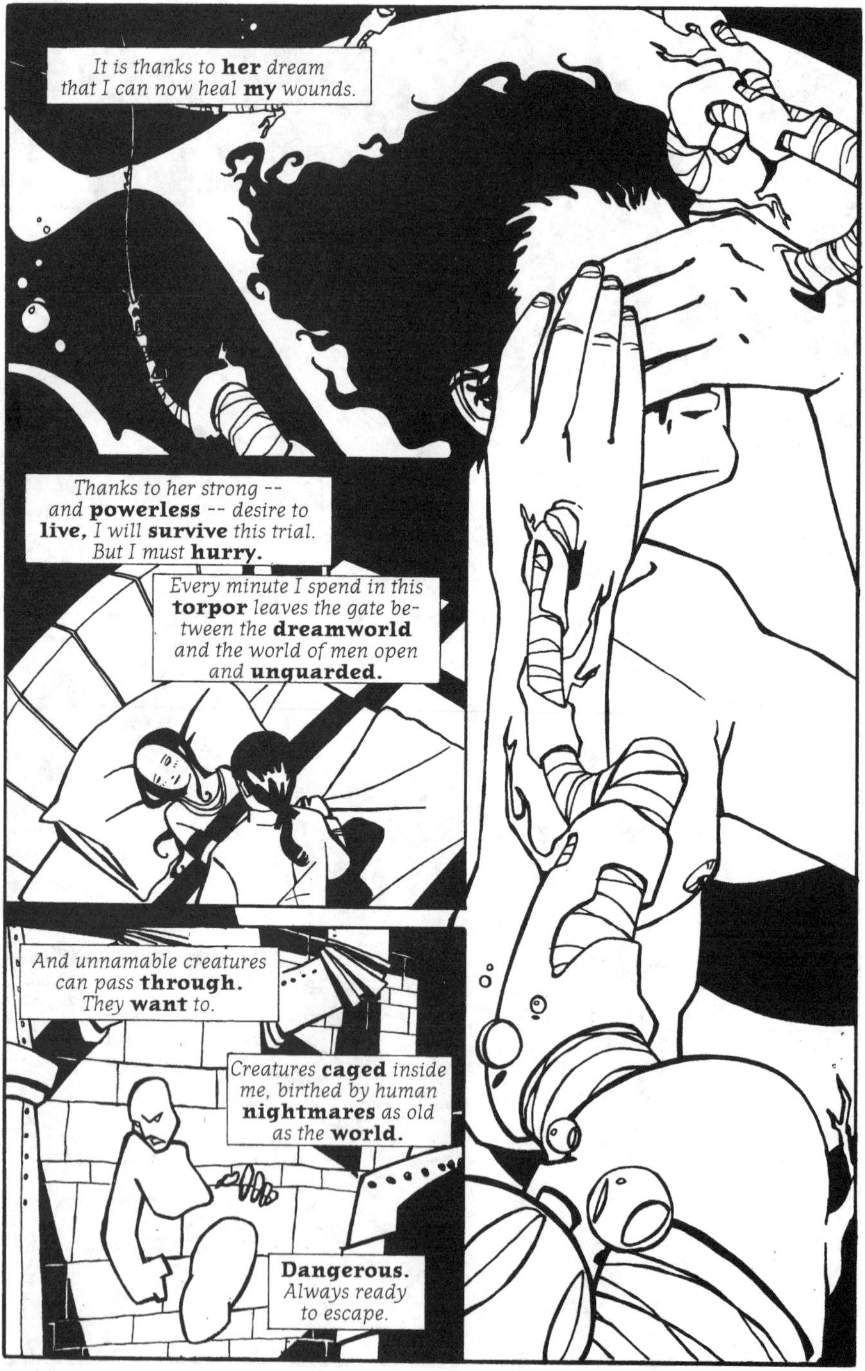
It is thanks to **her** dream that I can now heal **my** wounds.
Thanks to her strong -- and **powerless** -- desire to **live,** I will **survive** this trial. But I must **hurry.**
Every minute I spend in this **torpor** leaves the gate between the **dreamworld** and the world of men open and **unguarded.**
And unnamable creatures can pass **through.** They **want** to.
Creatures **caged** inside me, birthed by human **nightmares** as old as the **world.**
Dangerous. Always ready to escape.

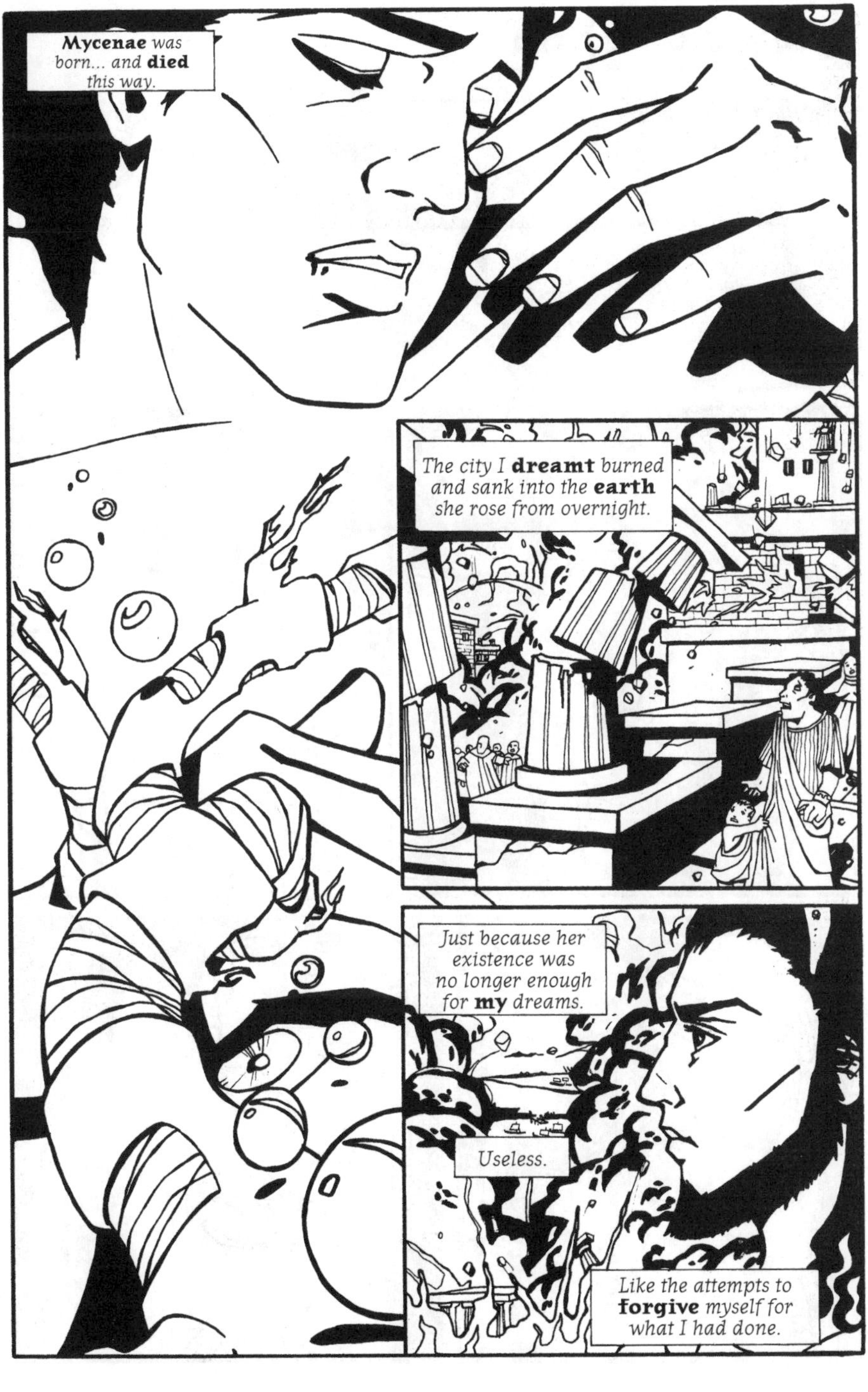
Mycenae was born... and **died** this way.
The city I **dreamt** burned and sank into the **earth** she rose from overnight.
Just because her existence was no longer enough for **my** dreams.
Useless.
Like the attempts to **forgive** myself for what I had done.

cold as steel

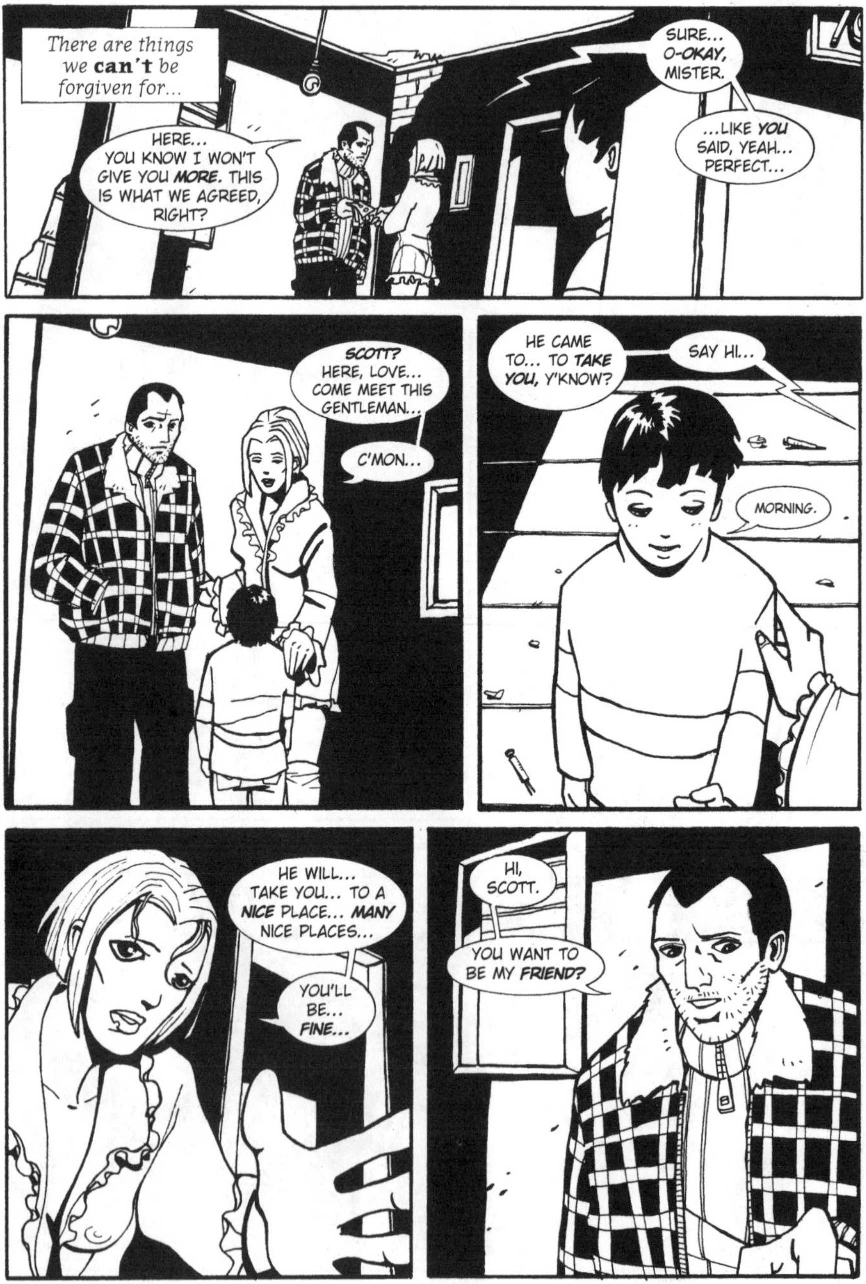

There are things we **can't** be forgiven for...
HERE... YOU KNOW I WON'T GIVE YOU *MORE.* THIS IS WHAT WE AGREED, RIGHT?
SURE... *O-OKAY,* MISTER.
...LIKE *YOU* SAID, YEAH... PERFECT...
SCOTT? HERE, LOVE... COME MEET THIS GENTLEMAN...
C'MON...
HE CAME TO... TO *TAKE YOU,* Y'KNOW?
SAY HI...
MORNING.
HE WILL... TAKE YOU... TO A *NICE* PLACE... *MANY* NICE PLACES...
YOU'LL BE... *FINE...*
HI, SCOTT.
YOU WANT TO BE MY *FRIEND?*

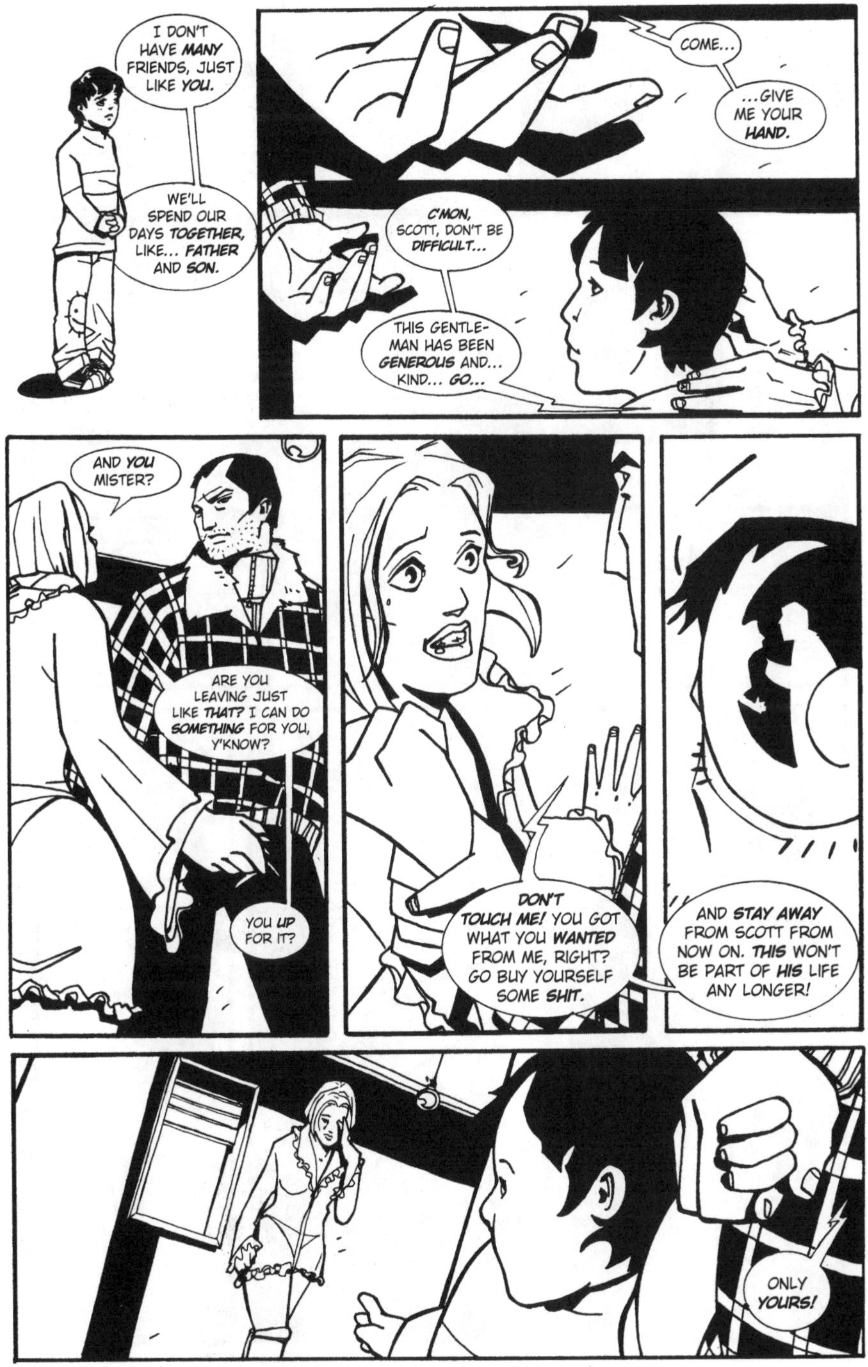

I DON'T HAVE MANY FRIENDS, JUST LIKE YOU.
WE'LL SPEND OUR DAYS TOGETHER, LIKE... FATHER AND SON.
COME...
...GIVE ME YOUR HAND.
C'MON, SCOTT, DON'T BE DIFFICULT...
THIS GENTLE-MAN HAS BEEN GENEROUS AND... KIND... GO...
AND YOU MISTER?
ARE YOU LEAVING JUST LIKE THAT? I CAN DO SOMETHING FOR YOU, Y'KNOW?
YOU UP FOR IT?
DON'T TOUCH ME! YOU GOT WHAT YOU WANTED FROM ME, RIGHT? GO BUY YOURSELF SOME SHIT.
AND STAY AWAY FROM SCOTT FROM NOW ON. THIS WON'T BE PART OF HIS LIFE ANY LONGER!
ONLY YOURS!

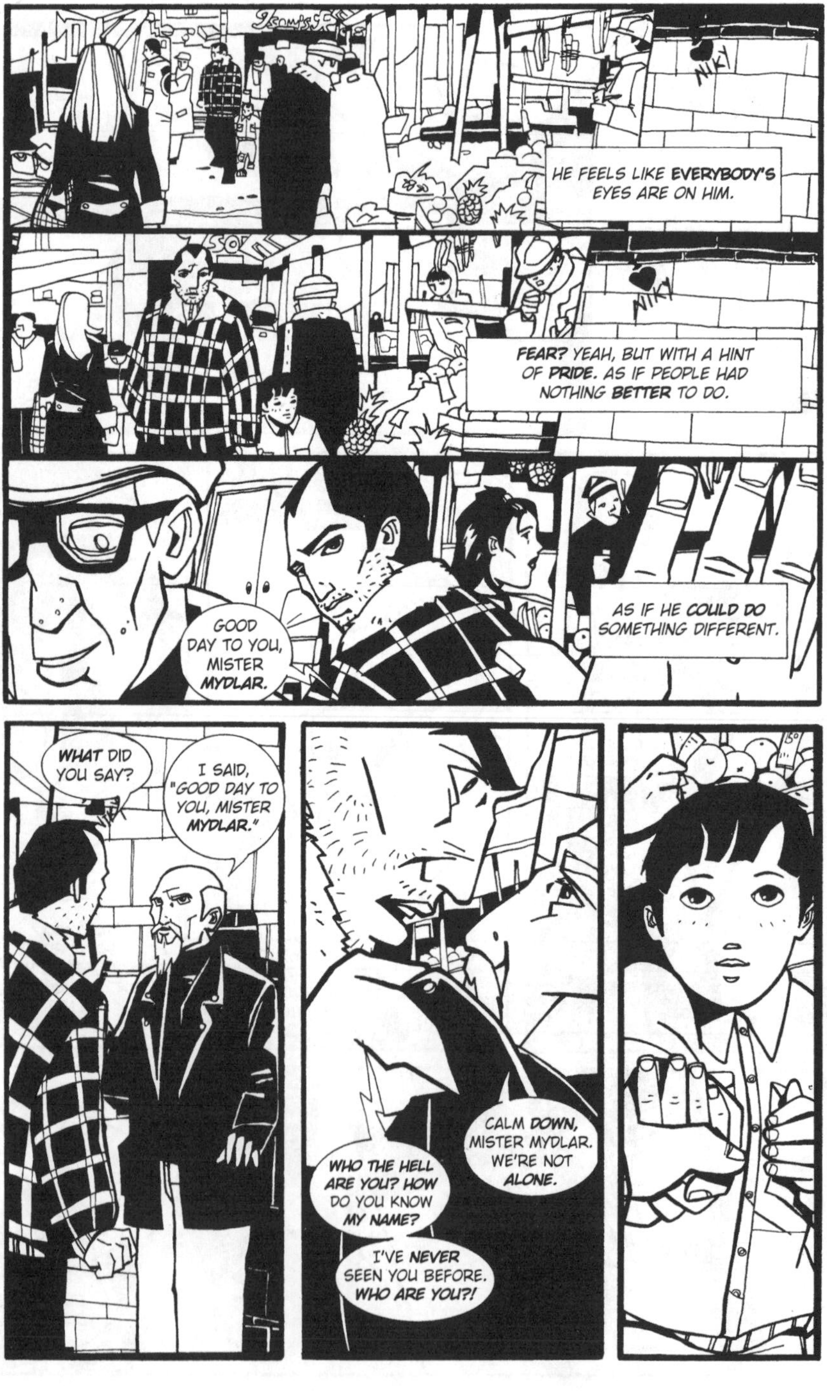
NIKY
HE FEELS LIKE EVERYBODY'S EYES ARE ON HIM.
NIKY
FEAR? YEAH, BUT WITH A HINT OF PRIDE. AS IF PEOPLE HAD NOTHING BETTER TO DO.
GOOD DAY TO YOU, MISTER MYDLAR.
AS IF HE COULD DO SOMETHING DIFFERENT.
WHAT DID YOU SAY?
I SAID, "GOOD DAY TO YOU, MISTER MYDLAR."
CALM DOWN, MISTER MYDLAR. WE'RE NOT ALONE.
WHO THE HELL ARE YOU? HOW DO YOU KNOW MY NAME?
I'VE NEVER SEEN YOU BEFORE. WHO ARE YOU?!

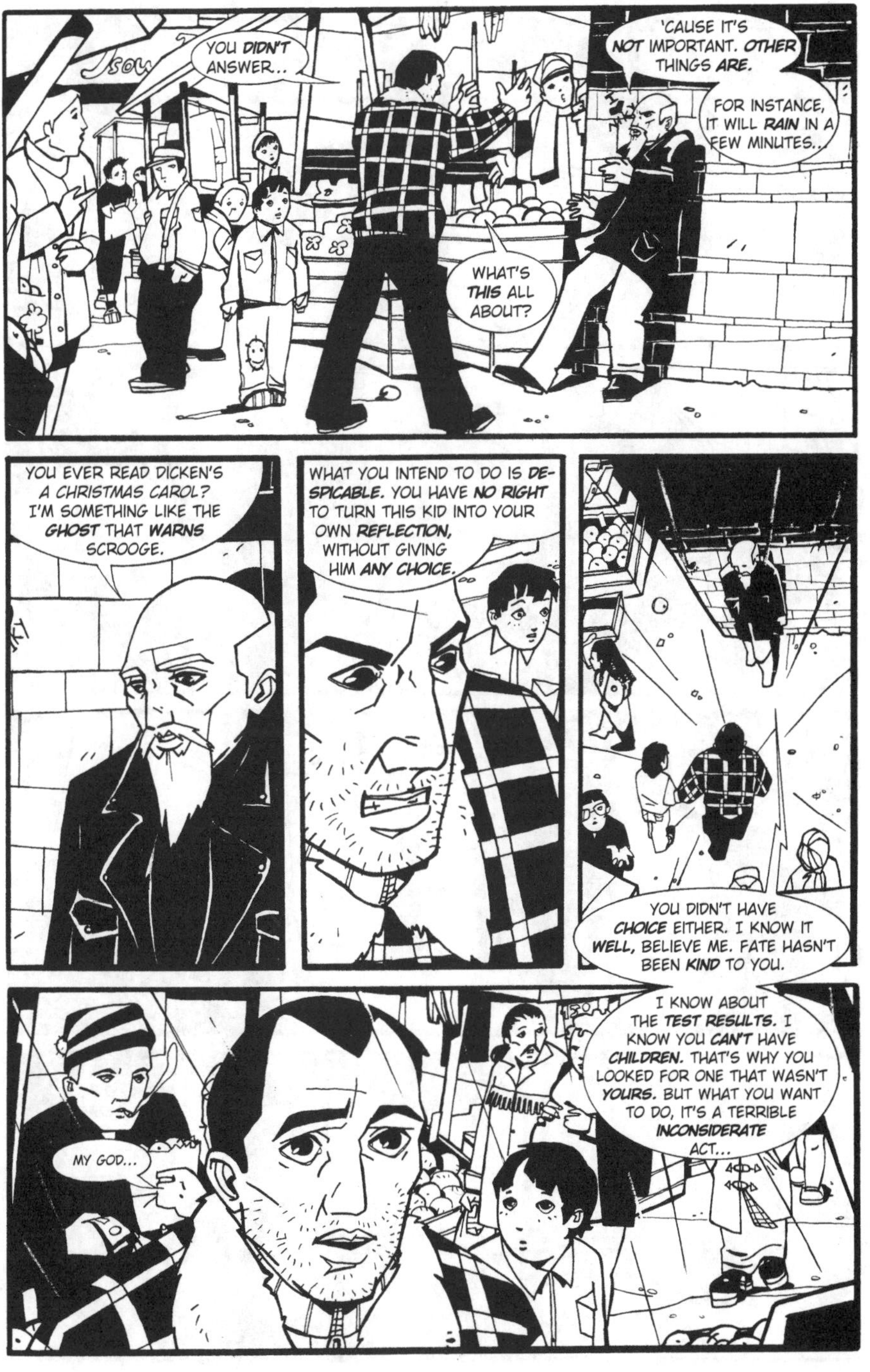
YOU DIDN'T ANSWER...
'CAUSE IT'S NOT IMPORTANT. OTHER THINGS ARE.
FOR INSTANCE, IT WILL RAIN IN A FEW MINUTES...
WHAT'S THIS ALL ABOUT?
YOU EVER READ DICKEN'S A CHRISTMAS CAROL? I'M SOMETHING LIKE THE GHOST THAT WARNS SCROOGE.
WHAT YOU INTEND TO DO IS DESPICABLE. YOU HAVE NO RIGHT TO TURN THIS KID INTO YOUR OWN REFLECTION, WITHOUT GIVING HIM ANY CHOICE.
YOU DIDN'T HAVE CHOICE EITHER. I KNOW IT WELL, BELIEVE ME. FATE HASN'T BEEN KIND TO YOU.
I KNOW ABOUT THE TEST RESULTS. I KNOW YOU CAN'T HAVE CHILDREN. THAT'S WHY YOU LOOKED FOR ONE THAT WASN'T YOURS. BUT WHAT YOU WANT TO DO, IT'S A TERRIBLE INCONSIDERATE ACT...
MY GOD...

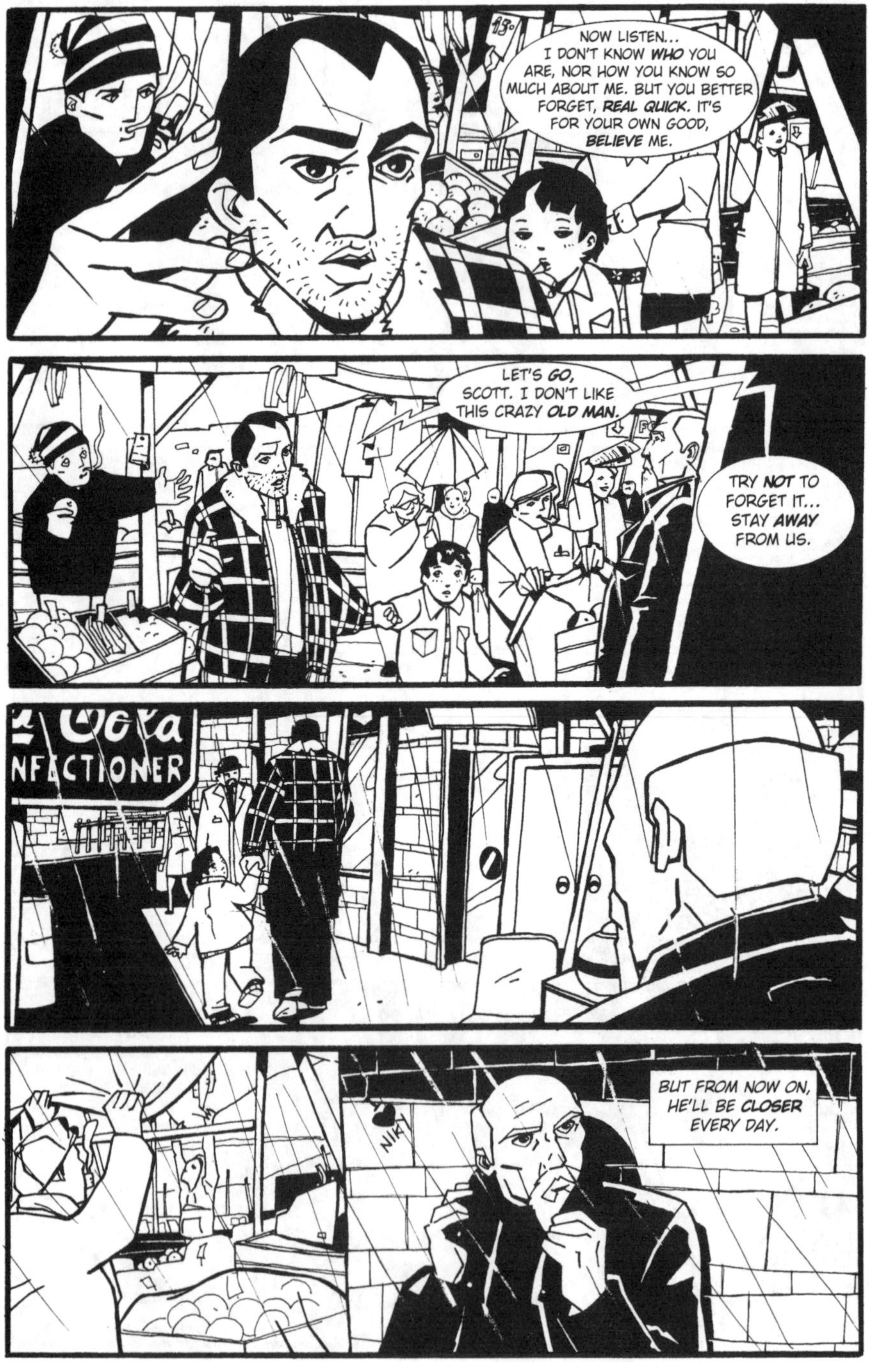
NOW LISTEN... I DON'T KNOW **WHO** YOU ARE, NOR HOW YOU KNOW SO MUCH ABOUT ME. BUT YOU BETTER FORGET, **REAL QUICK**. IT'S FOR YOUR OWN GOOD, **BELIEVE** ME.
LET'S **GO**, SCOTT. I DON'T LIKE THIS CRAZY **OLD MAN**.
TRY **NOT** TO FORGET IT... STAY **AWAY** FROM US.
NFECTIONER
BUT FROM NOW ON, HE'LL BE **CLOSER** EVERY DAY.

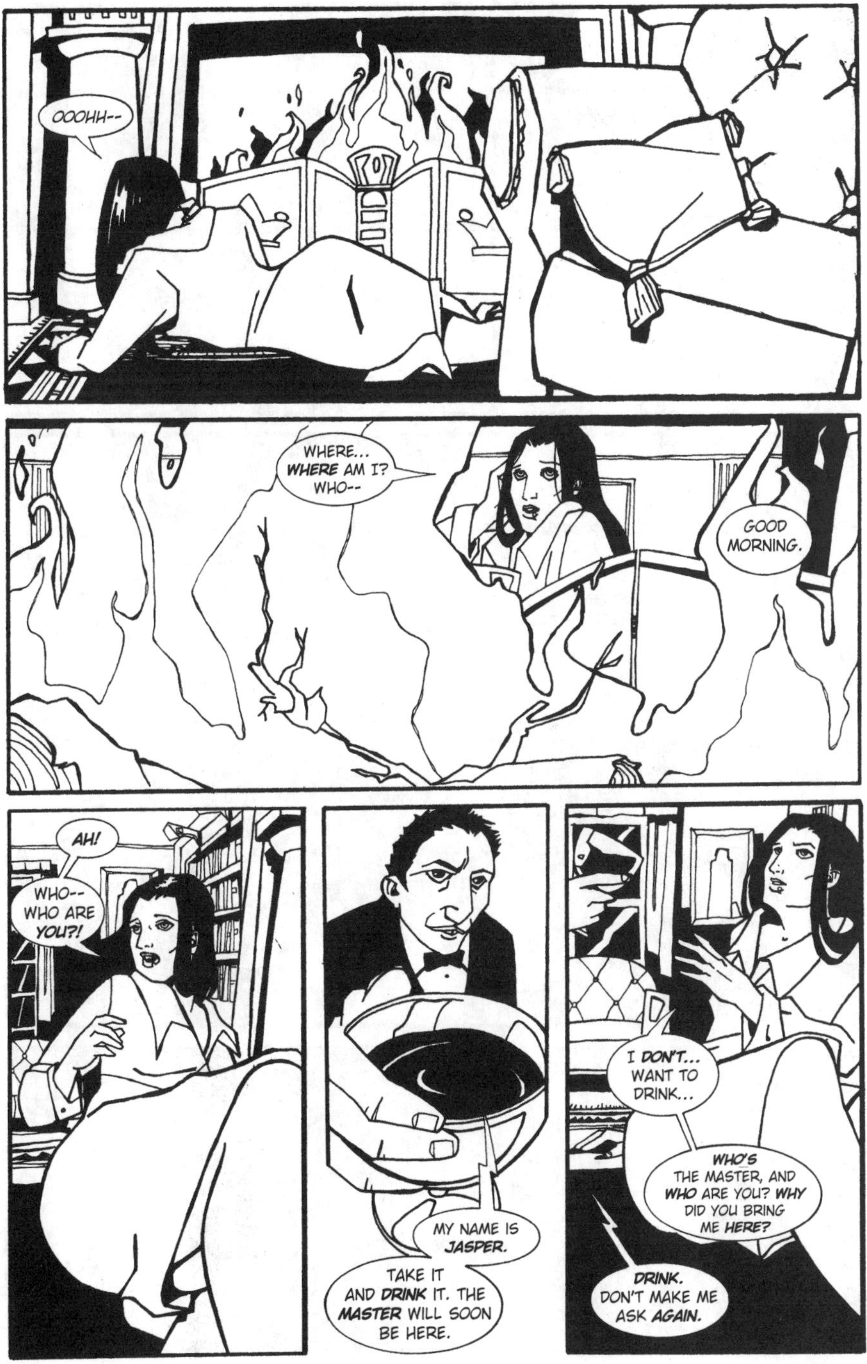
OOOHH--
WHERE... WHERE AM I? WHO--
GOOD MORNING.
AH!
WHO-- WHO ARE YOU?!
MY NAME IS JASPER.
TAKE IT AND DRINK IT. THE MASTER WILL SOON BE HERE.
I DON'T... WANT TO DRINK...
WHO'S THE MASTER, AND WHO ARE YOU? WHY DID YOU BRING ME HERE?
DRINK. DON'T MAKE ME ASK AGAIN.

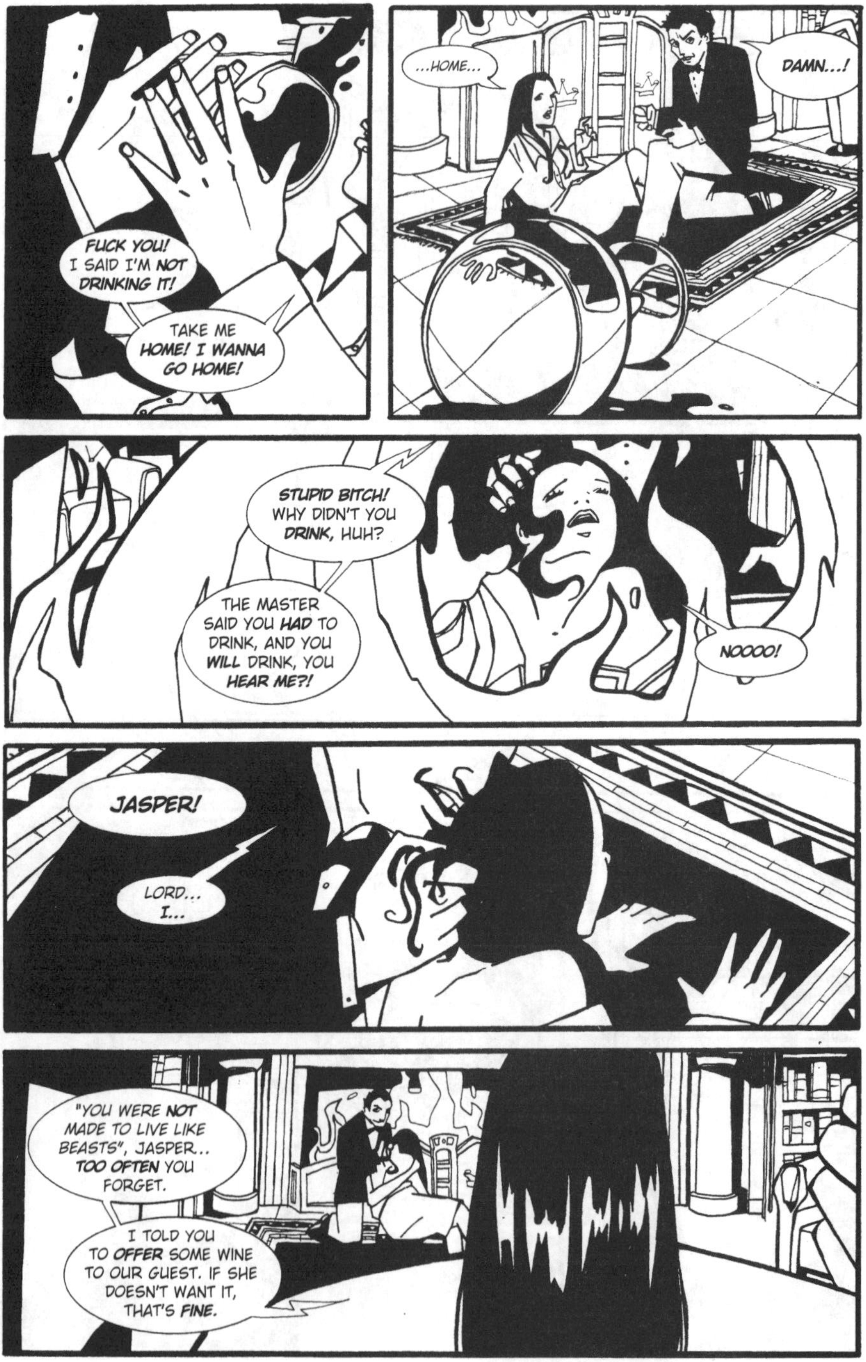
FUCK YOU! I SAID I'M NOT DRINKING IT!
TAKE ME HOME! I WANNA GO HOME!
...HOME...
DAMN...!
STUPID BITCH! WHY DIDN'T YOU DRINK, HUH?
THE MASTER SAID YOU HAD TO DRINK, AND YOU WILL DRINK, YOU HEAR ME?!
NOOOO!
JASPER!
LORD... I...
"YOU WERE NOT MADE TO LIVE LIKE BEASTS", JASPER... TOO OFTEN YOU FORGET.
I TOLD YOU TO OFFER SOME WINE TO OUR GUEST. IF SHE DOESN'T WANT IT, THAT'S FINE.

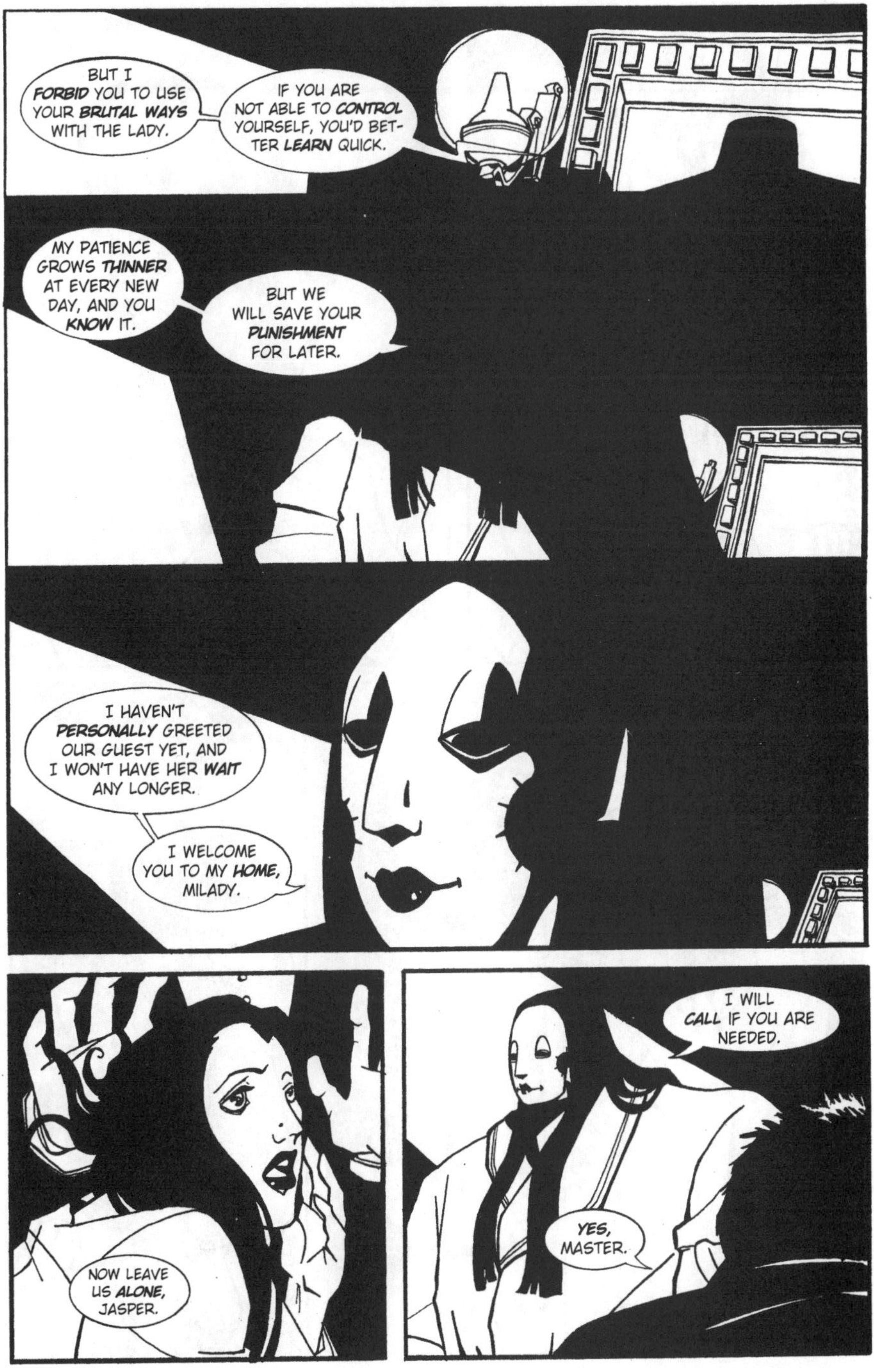
BUT I FORBID YOU TO USE YOUR BRUTAL WAYS WITH THE LADY.
IF YOU ARE NOT ABLE TO CONTROL YOURSELF, YOU'D BETTER LEARN QUICK.
MY PATIENCE GROWS THINNER AT EVERY NEW DAY, AND YOU KNOW IT.
BUT WE WILL SAVE YOUR PUNISHMENT FOR LATER.
I HAVEN'T PERSONALLY GREETED OUR GUEST YET, AND I WON'T HAVE HER WAIT ANY LONGER.
I WELCOME YOU TO MY HOME, MILADY.
NOW LEAVE US ALONE, JASPER.
I WILL CALL IF YOU ARE NEEDED.
YES, MASTER.

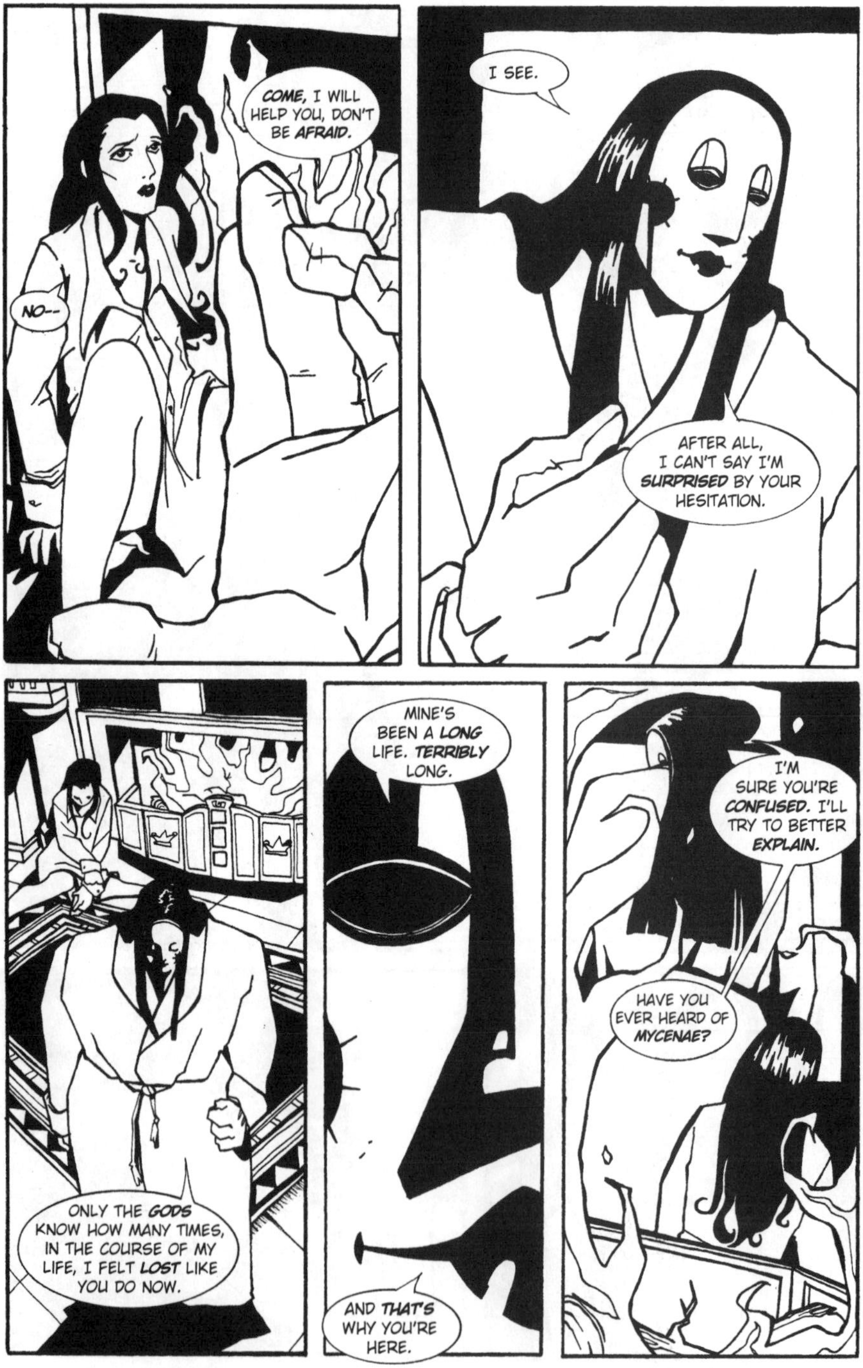
COME, I WILL HELP YOU, DON'T BE AFRAID.
NO--
I SEE.
AFTER ALL, I CAN'T SAY I'M SURPRISED BY YOUR HESITATION.
ONLY THE GODS KNOW HOW MANY TIMES, IN THE COURSE OF MY LIFE, I FELT LOST LIKE YOU DO NOW.
MINE'S BEEN A LONG LIFE. TERRIBLY LONG.
AND THAT'S WHY YOU'RE HERE.
I'M SURE YOU'RE CONFUSED. I'LL TRY TO BETTER EXPLAIN.
HAVE YOU EVER HEARD OF MYCENAE?

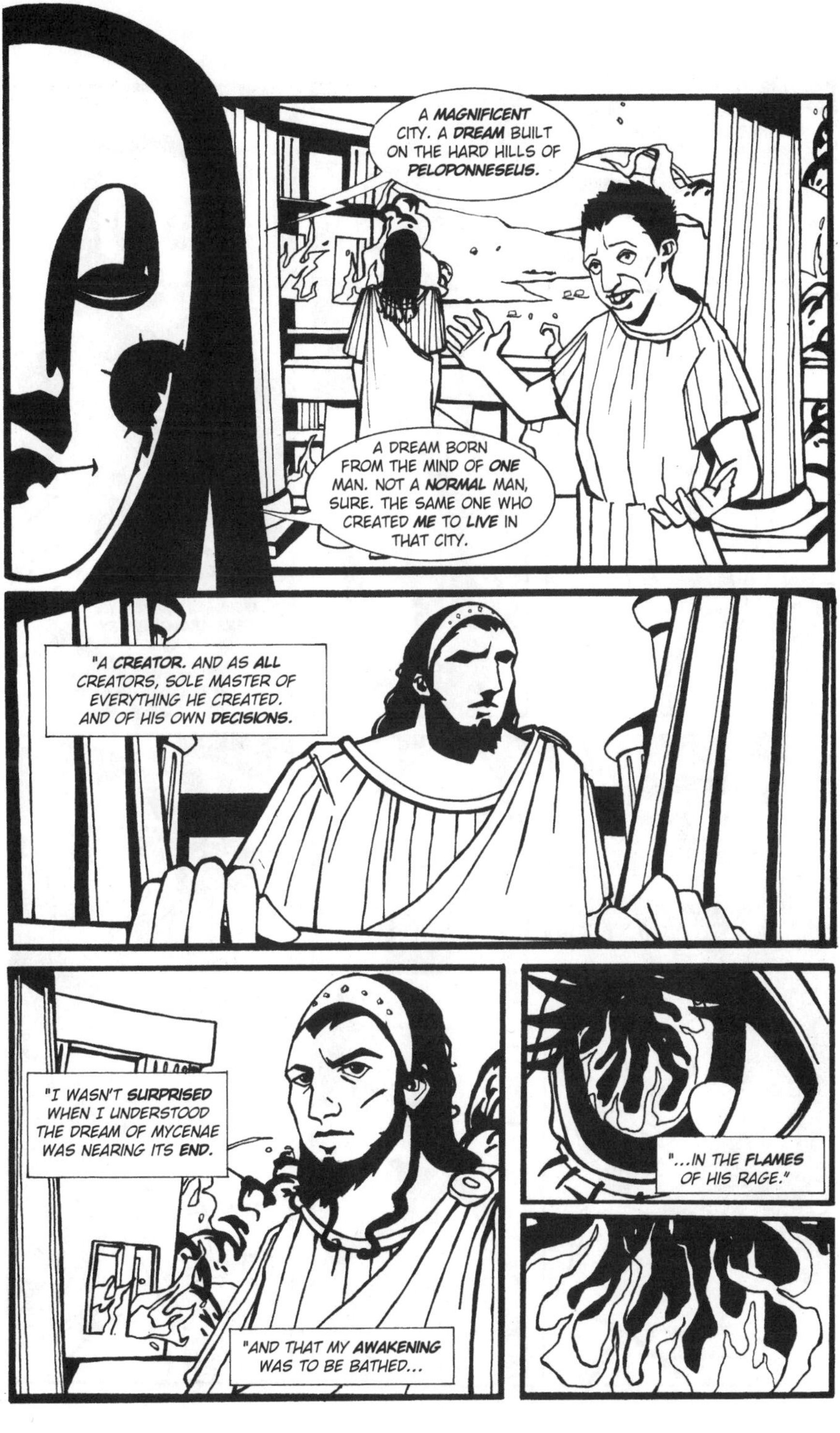
A MAGNIFICENT CITY. A DREAM BUILT ON THE HARD HILLS OF PELOPONNESEUS.
A DREAM BORN FROM THE MIND OF ONE MAN. NOT A NORMAL MAN, SURE. THE SAME ONE WHO CREATED ME TO LIVE IN THAT CITY.
"A CREATOR. AND AS ALL CREATORS, SOLE MASTER OF EVERYTHING HE CREATED. AND OF HIS OWN DECISIONS.
"I WASN'T SURPRISED WHEN I UNDERSTOOD THE DREAM OF MYCENAE WAS NEARING ITS END.
"AND THAT MY AWAKENING WAS TO BE BATHED...
"...IN THE FLAMES OF HIS RAGE."

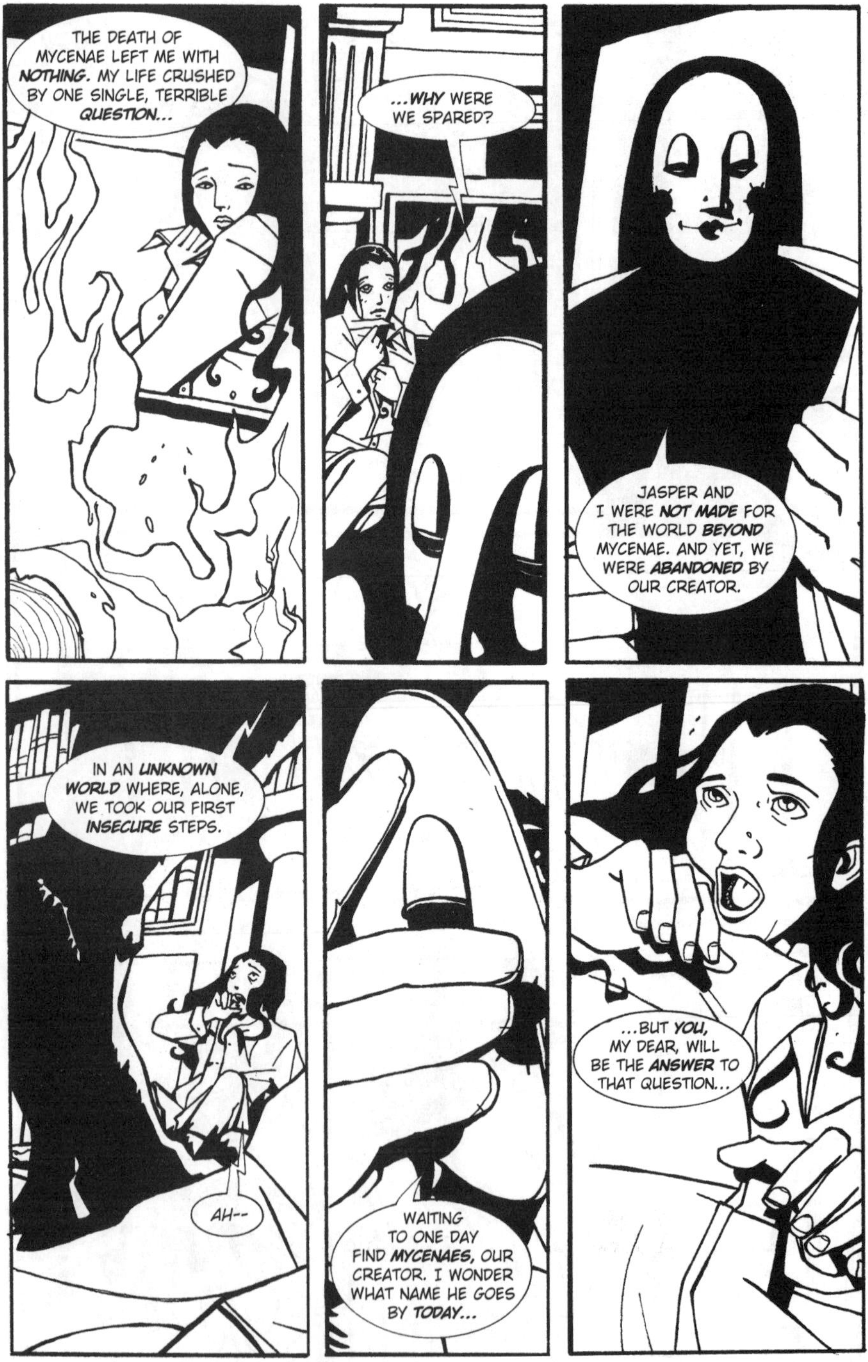
THE DEATH OF MYCENAE LEFT ME WITH NOTHING. MY LIFE CRUSHED BY ONE SINGLE, TERRIBLE QUESTION...
...WHY WERE WE SPARED?
JASPER AND I WERE NOT MADE FOR THE WORLD BEYOND MYCENAE. AND YET, WE WERE ABANDONED BY OUR CREATOR.
IN AN UNKNOWN WORLD WHERE, ALONE, WE TOOK OUR FIRST INSECURE STEPS.
AH--
WAITING TO ONE DAY FIND MYCENAES, OUR CREATOR. I WONDER WHAT NAME HE GOES BY TODAY...
...BUT YOU, MY DEAR, WILL BE THE ANSWER TO THAT QUESTION...

I'm coming **back.** Joelle **leaves,** and I come **back** to the world.

The smells are **telling.** Strong, unpleasant.

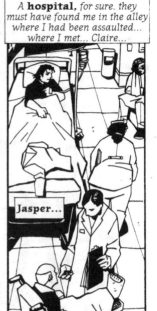

A **hospital,** for sure. they must have found me in the alley where I had been assaulted... where I met... Claire...

Jasper...

I must go, it's happening something I **never** thought could happen.

And then, I have no **ID** on me...

...it would be **annoying** to answer the doctors' questions.

I don't even **need** medical care any-more...

...Joelle did for me what she couldn't do for **herself.**

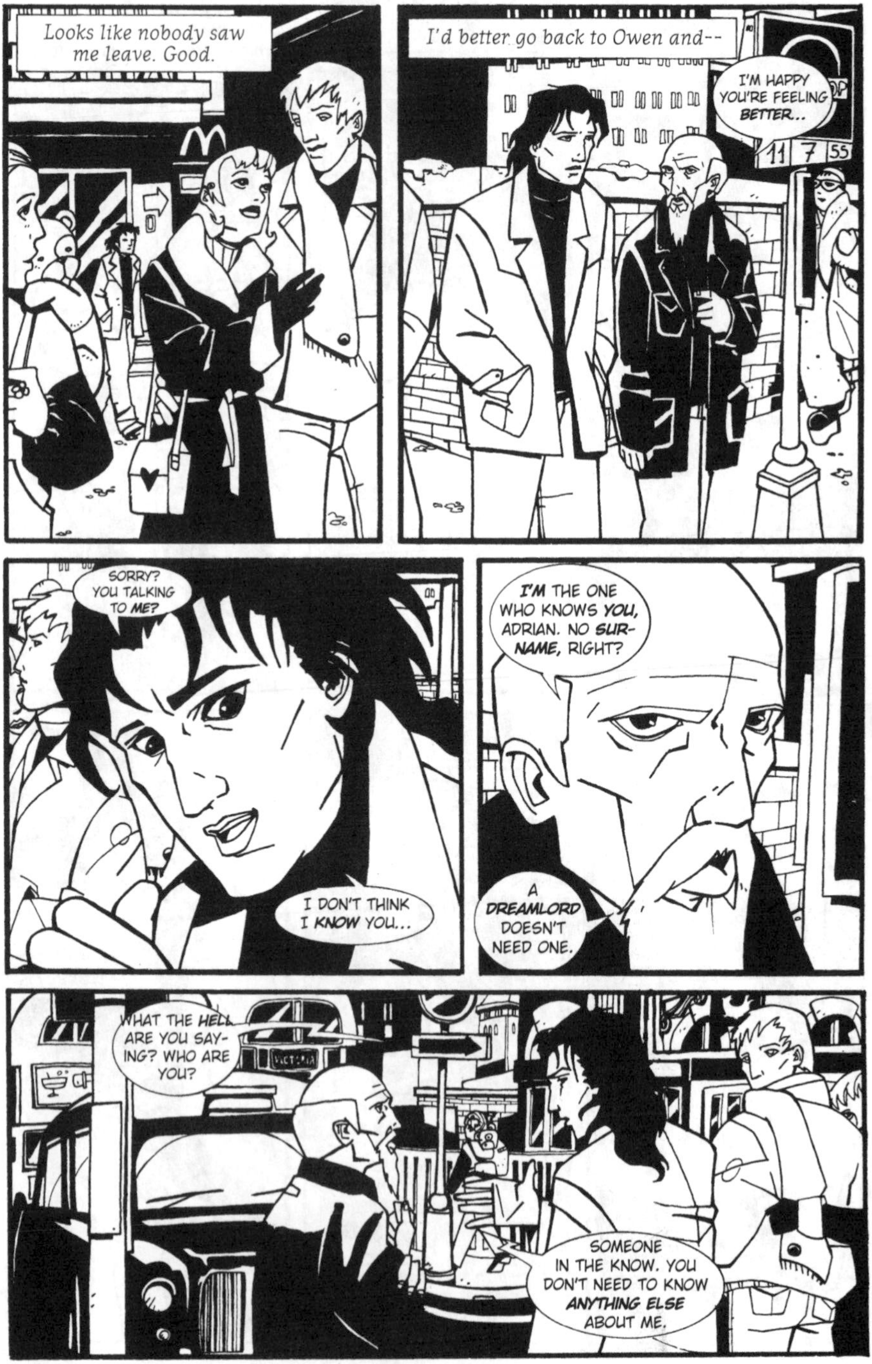
Looks like nobody saw me leave. Good.
I'd better go back to Owen and--
I'M HAPPY YOU'RE FEELING BETTER...
SORRY? YOU TALKING TO ME?
I DON'T THINK I KNOW YOU...
I'M THE ONE WHO KNOWS YOU, ADRIAN. NO SURNAME, RIGHT?
A DREAMLORD DOESN'T NEED ONE.
WHAT THE HELL ARE YOU SAYING? WHO ARE YOU?
SOMEONE IN THE KNOW. YOU DON'T NEED TO KNOW ANYTHING ELSE ABOUT ME.

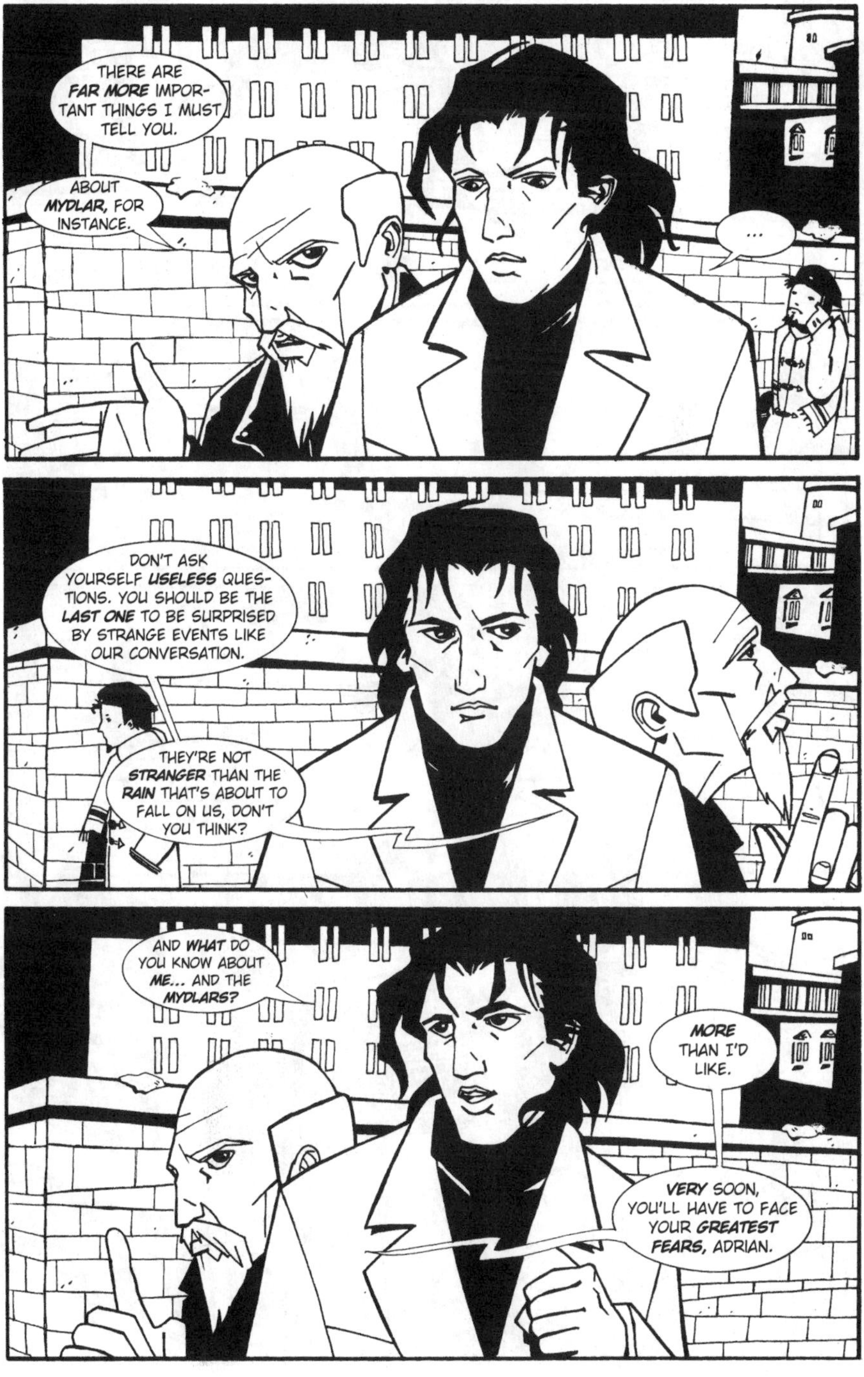
THERE ARE **FAR MORE** IMPORTANT THINGS I MUST TELL YOU.
ABOUT **MYDLAR,** FOR INSTANCE.
...
DON'T ASK YOURSELF **USELESS** QUESTIONS. YOU SHOULD BE THE **LAST ONE** TO BE SURPRISED BY STRANGE EVENTS LIKE OUR CONVERSATION.
THEY'RE NOT **STRANGER** THAN THE **RAIN** THAT'S ABOUT TO FALL ON US, DON'T YOU THINK?
AND **WHAT** DO YOU KNOW ABOUT **ME...** AND THE **MYDLARS?**
MORE THAN I'D LIKE.
VERY SOON, YOU'LL HAVE TO FACE YOUR **GREATEST FEARS,** ADRIAN.

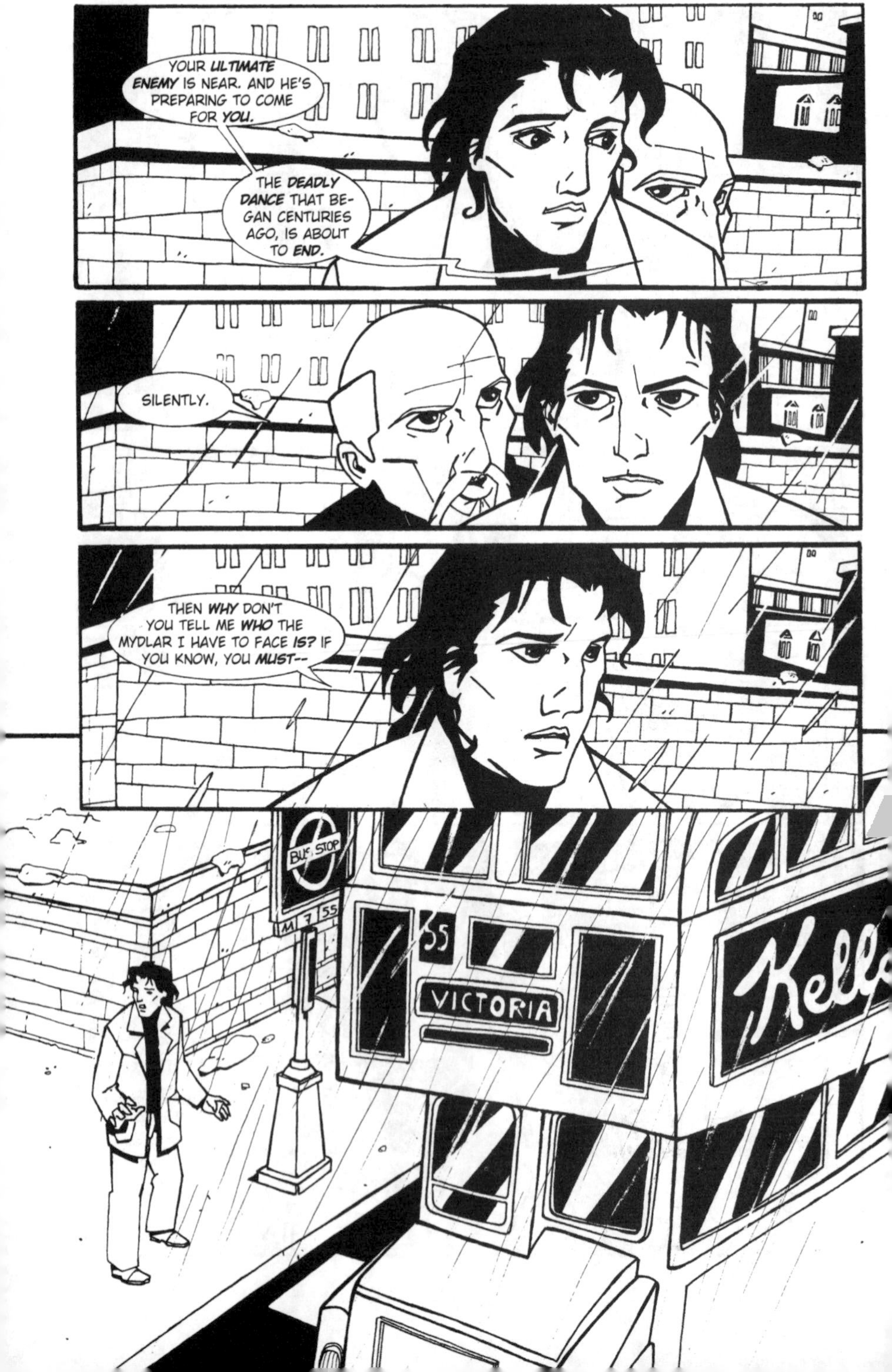
YOUR ULTIMATE ENEMY IS NEAR. AND HE'S PREPARING TO COME FOR YOU.
THE DEADLY DANCE THAT BEGAN CENTURIES AGO, IS ABOUT TO END.
SILENTLY.
THEN WHY DON'T YOU TELL ME WHO THE MYDLAR I HAVE TO FACE IS? IF YOU KNOW, YOU MUST--
BUS STOP
55
VICTORIA

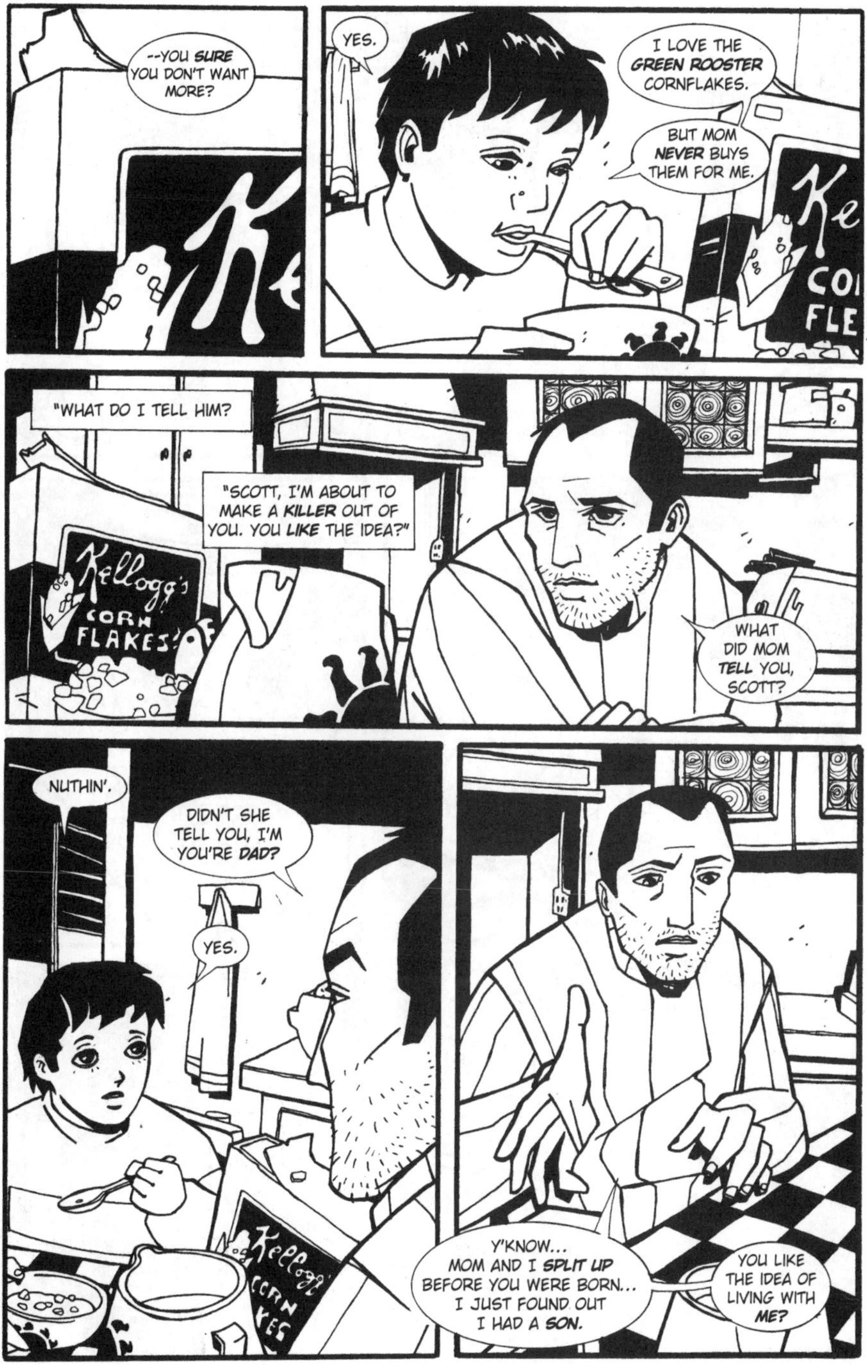
--YOU SURE YOU DON'T WANT MORE?
YES.
I LOVE THE GREEN ROOSTER CORNFLAKES.
BUT MOM NEVER BUYS THEM FOR ME.
"WHAT DO I TELL HIM?
"SCOTT, I'M ABOUT TO MAKE A KILLER OUT OF YOU. YOU LIKE THE IDEA?"
WHAT DID MOM TELL YOU, SCOTT?
NUTHIN'.
DIDN'T SHE TELL YOU, I'M YOU'RE DAD?
YES.
Y'KNOW... MOM AND I SPLIT UP BEFORE YOU WERE BORN... I JUST FOUND OUT I HAD A SON.
YOU LIKE THE IDEA OF LIVING WITH ME?

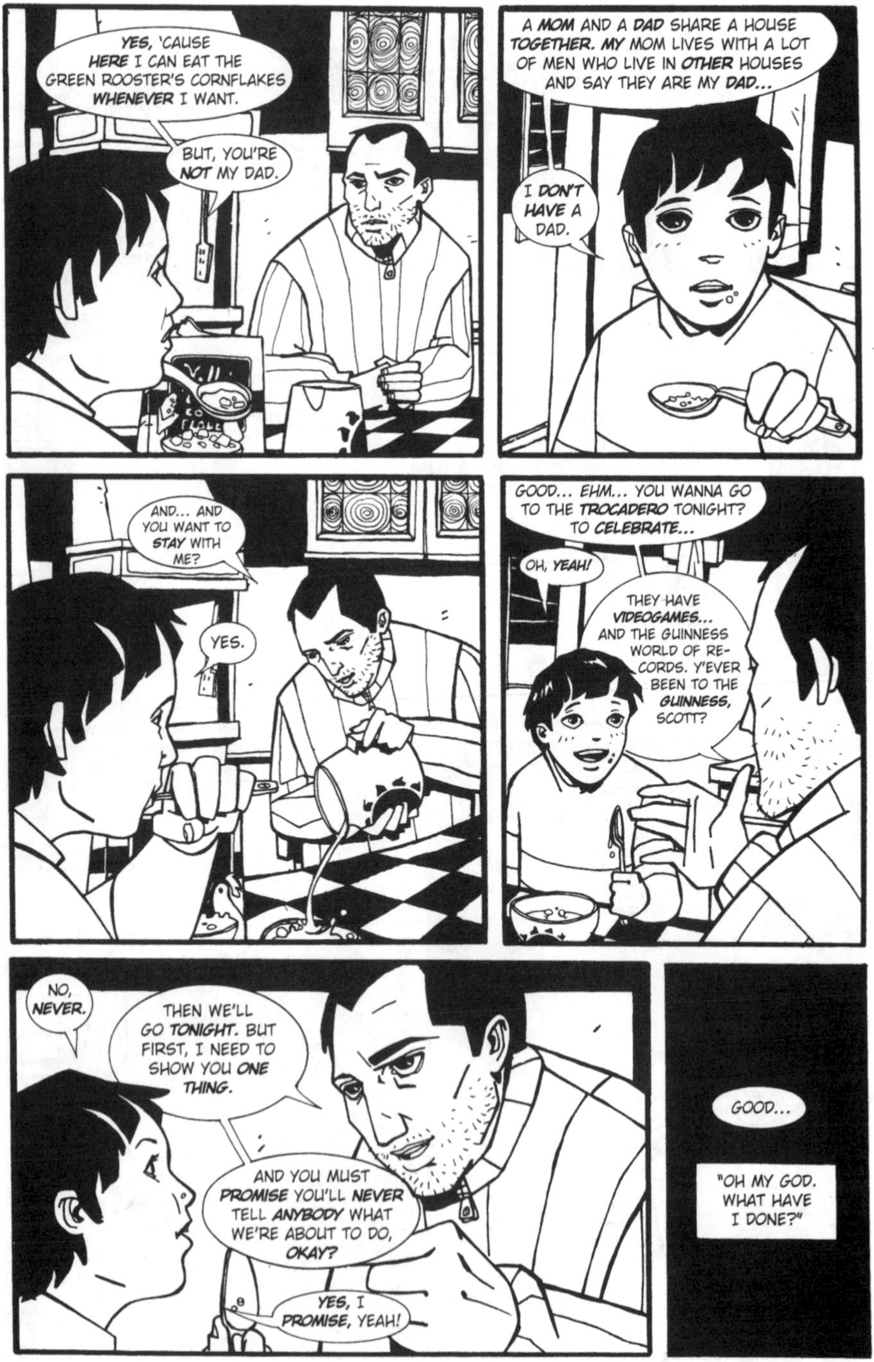
YES, 'CAUSE HERE I CAN EAT THE GREEN ROOSTER'S CORNFLAKES WHENEVER I WANT.
BUT, YOU'RE NOT MY DAD.
A MOM AND A DAD SHARE A HOUSE TOGETHER. MY MOM LIVES WITH A LOT OF MEN WHO LIVE IN OTHER HOUSES AND SAY THEY ARE MY DAD...
I DON'T HAVE A DAD.
AND... AND YOU WANT TO STAY WITH ME?
YES.
GOOD... EHM... YOU WANNA GO TO THE TROCADERO TONIGHT? TO CELEBRATE...
OH, YEAH!
THEY HAVE VIDEOGAMES... AND THE GUINNESS WORLD OF RE-CORDS. Y'EVER BEEN TO THE GUINNESS, SCOTT?
NO, NEVER.
THEN WE'LL GO TONIGHT. BUT FIRST, I NEED TO SHOW YOU ONE THING.
AND YOU MUST PROMISE YOU'LL NEVER TELL ANYBODY WHAT WE'RE ABOUT TO DO, OKAY?
YES, I PROMISE, YEAH!
GOOD...
"OH MY GOD. WHAT HAVE I DONE?"

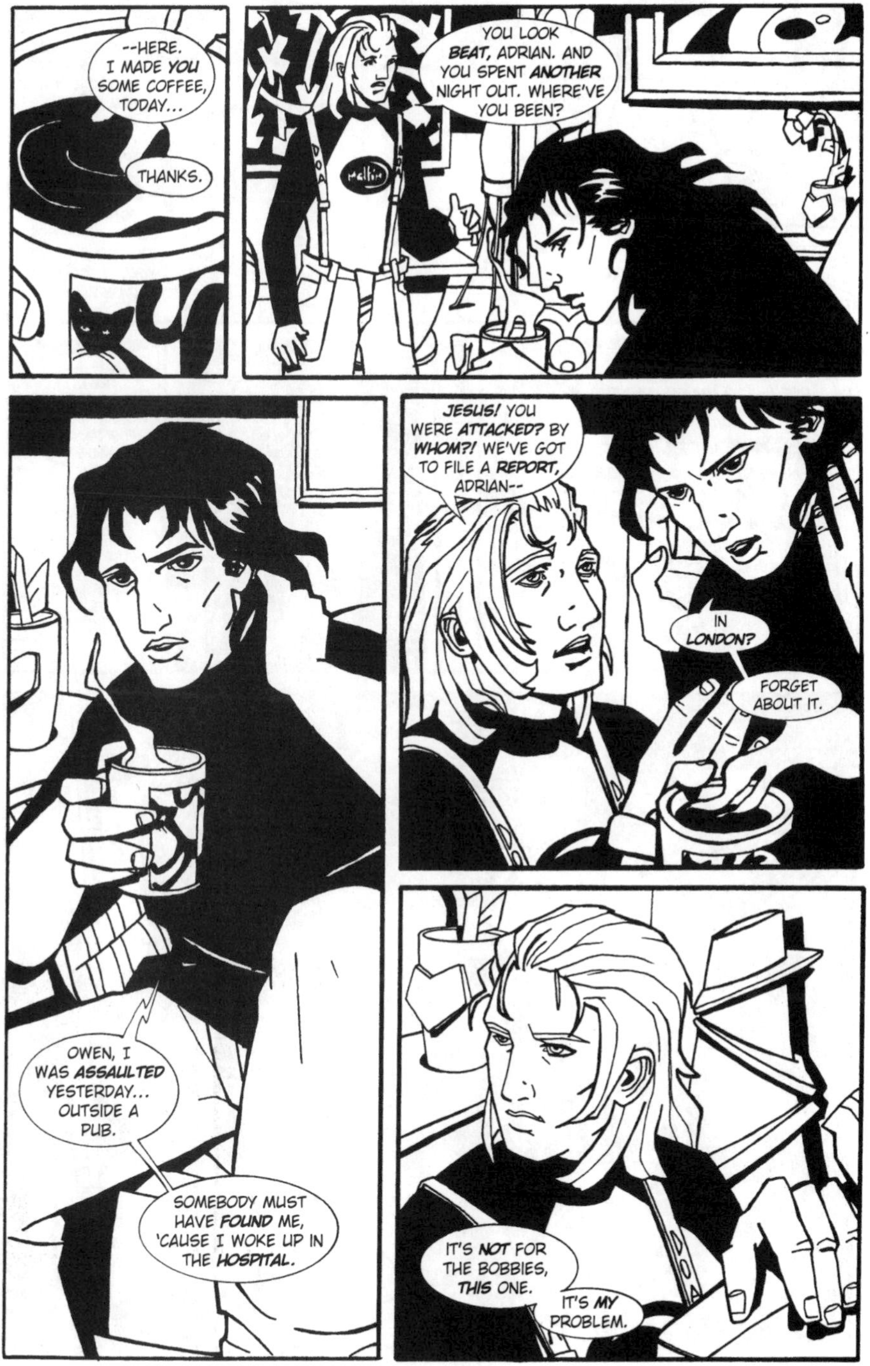
--HERE. I MADE YOU SOME COFFEE, TODAY...
THANKS.
YOU LOOK BEAT, ADRIAN. AND YOU SPENT ANOTHER NIGHT OUT. WHERE'VE YOU BEEN?
OWEN, I WAS ASSAULTED YESTERDAY... OUTSIDE A PUB.
SOMEBODY MUST HAVE FOUND ME, 'CAUSE I WOKE UP IN THE HOSPITAL.
JESUS! YOU WERE ATTACKED? BY WHOM?! WE'VE GOT TO FILE A REPORT, ADRIAN--
IN LONDON?
FORGET ABOUT IT.
IT'S NOT FOR THE BOBBIES, THIS ONE.
IT'S MY PROBLEM.

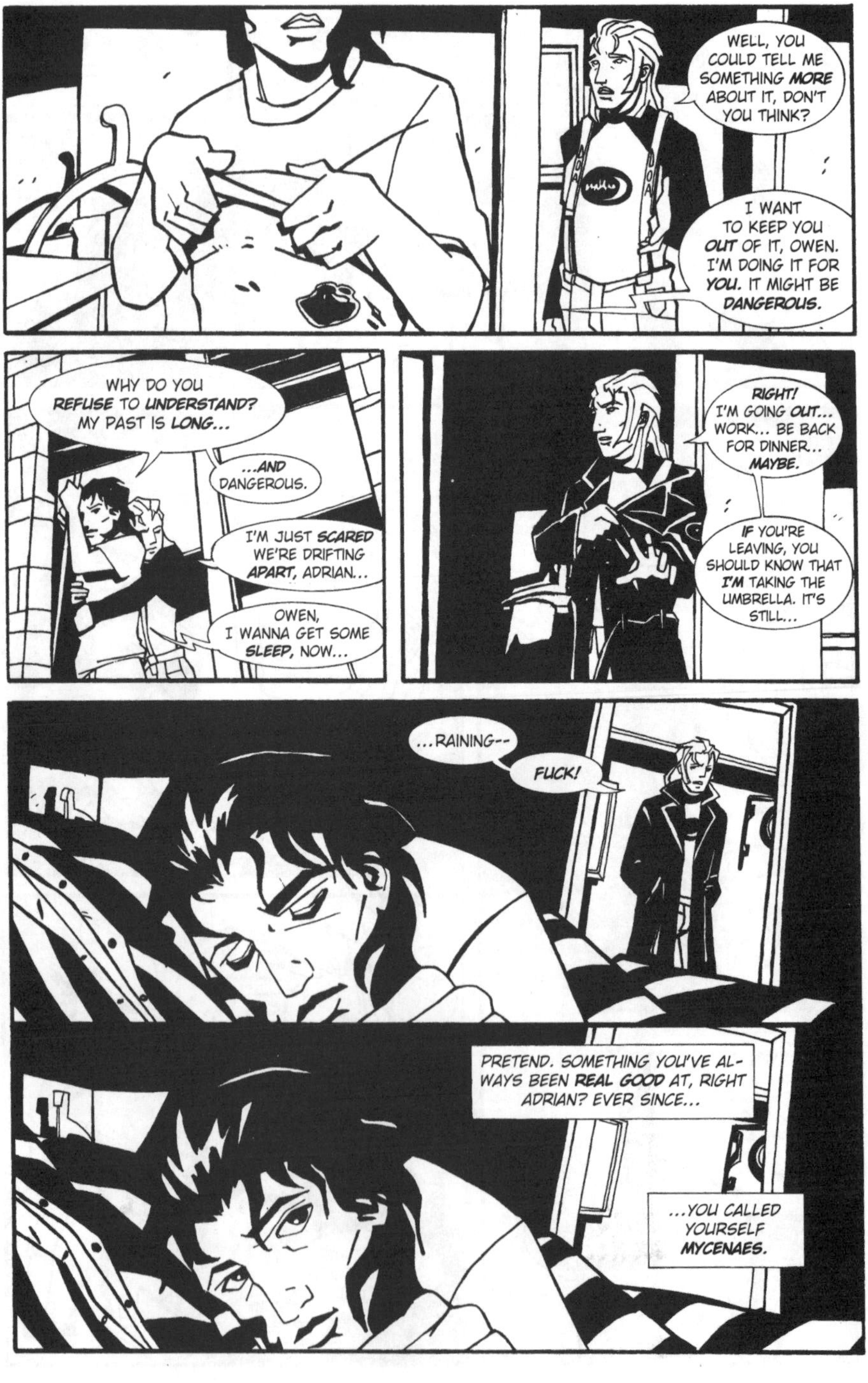
WELL, YOU COULD TELL ME SOMETHING MORE ABOUT IT, DON'T YOU THINK?
I WANT TO KEEP YOU OUT OF IT, OWEN. I'M DOING IT FOR YOU. IT MIGHT BE DANGEROUS.
WHY DO YOU REFUSE TO UNDERSTAND? MY PAST IS LONG...
...AND DANGEROUS.
I'M JUST SCARED WE'RE DRIFTING APART, ADRIAN...
OWEN, I WANNA GET SOME SLEEP, NOW...
RIGHT! I'M GOING OUT... WORK... BE BACK FOR DINNER... MAYBE.
IF YOU'RE LEAVING, YOU SHOULD KNOW THAT I'M TAKING THE UMBRELLA. IT'S STILL...
...RAINING--
FUCK!
PRETEND. SOMETHING YOU'VE ALWAYS BEEN REAL GOOD AT, RIGHT ADRIAN? EVER SINCE...
...YOU CALLED YOURSELF MYCENAES.

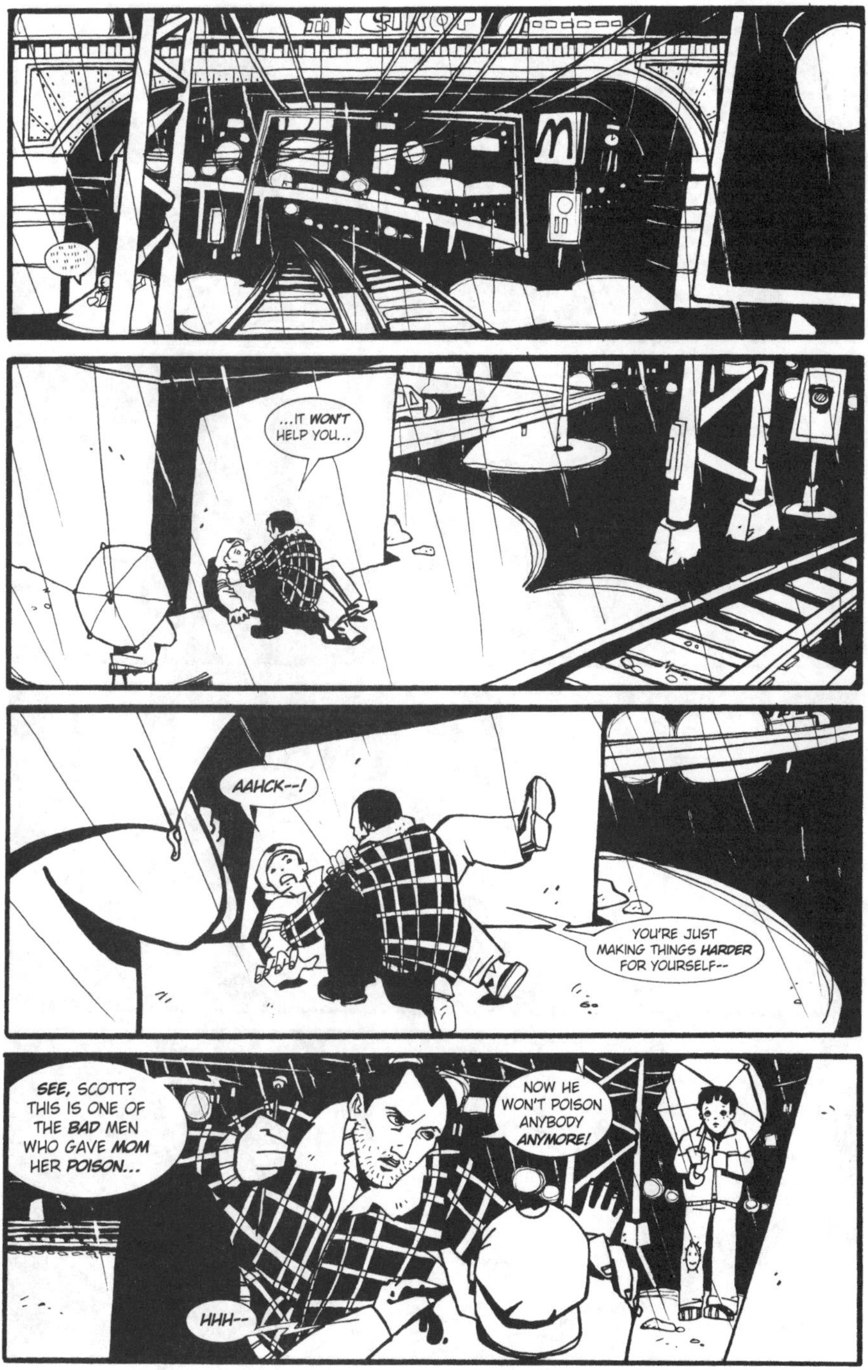
...IT WON'T HELP YOU...
AAHCK--!
YOU'RE JUST MAKING THINGS HARDER FOR YOURSELF--
SEE, SCOTT? THIS IS ONE OF THE BAD MEN WHO GAVE MOM HER POISON...
NOW HE WON'T POISON ANYBODY ANYMORE!
HHH--

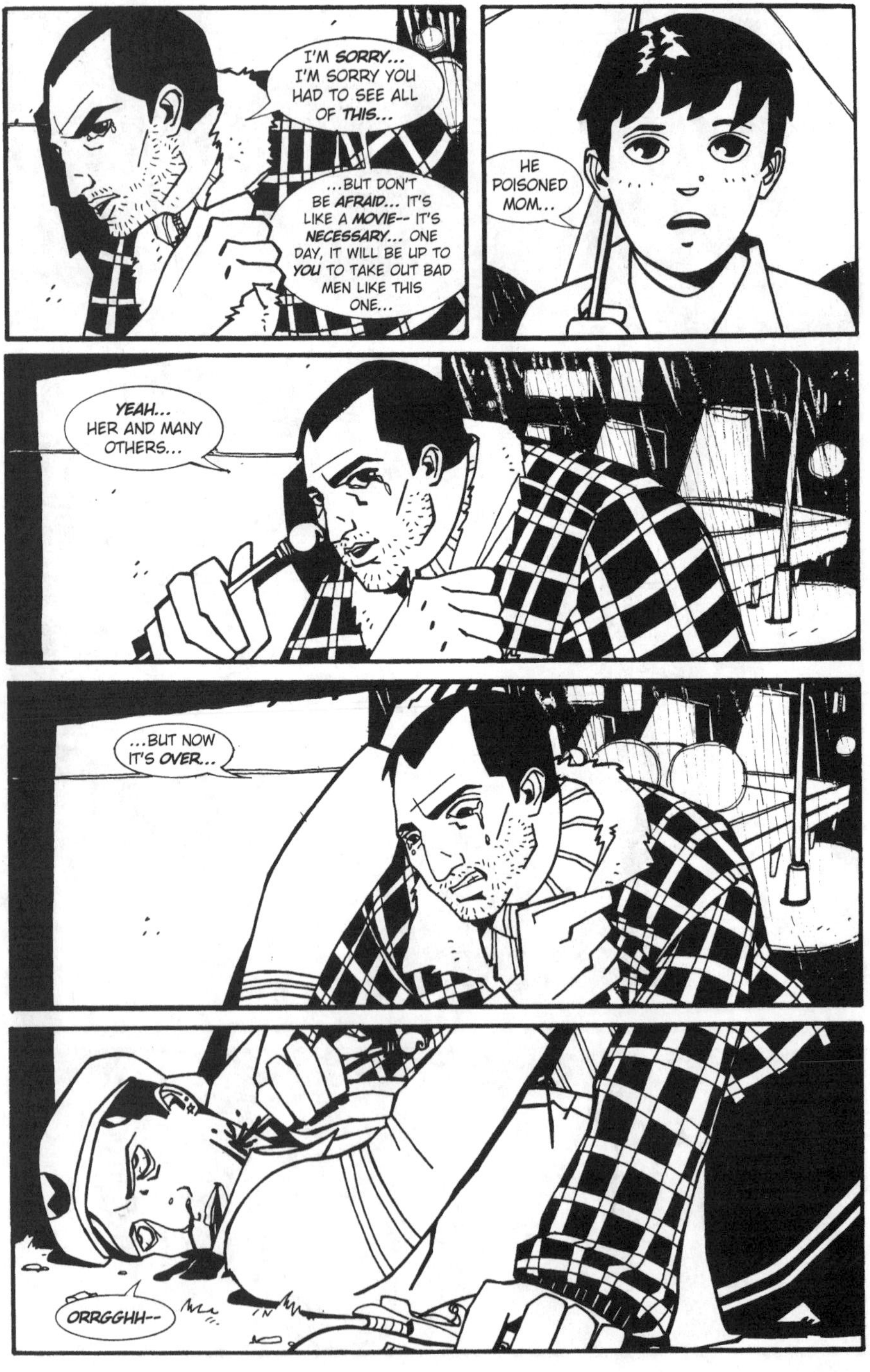
I'M SORRY... I'M SORRY YOU HAD TO SEE ALL OF THIS...
...BUT DON'T BE AFRAID... IT'S LIKE A MOVIE-- IT'S NECESSARY... ONE DAY, IT WILL BE UP TO YOU TO TAKE OUT BAD MEN LIKE THIS ONE...
HE POISONED MOM...
YEAH... HER AND MANY OTHERS...
...BUT NOW IT'S OVER...
ORRGGHH--

RESHU-IZAD DRINKS. DAMNED BE HER *THIRST*. AND LET ME BE *DAMNED* AS WELL...

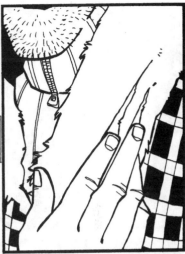

THERE, SCOTT, IT'S OVER. NOW... IT'S *OVER*...

GIVE ME A MINUTE... *ONE* MINUTE, AND WE'LL *GO*, OKAY?

AND NOW? *TROCADERO*?

YEAH, *SURE*... I *ALWAYS* KEEP A PROMISE I MAKE TO... ANOTHER *MAN*...

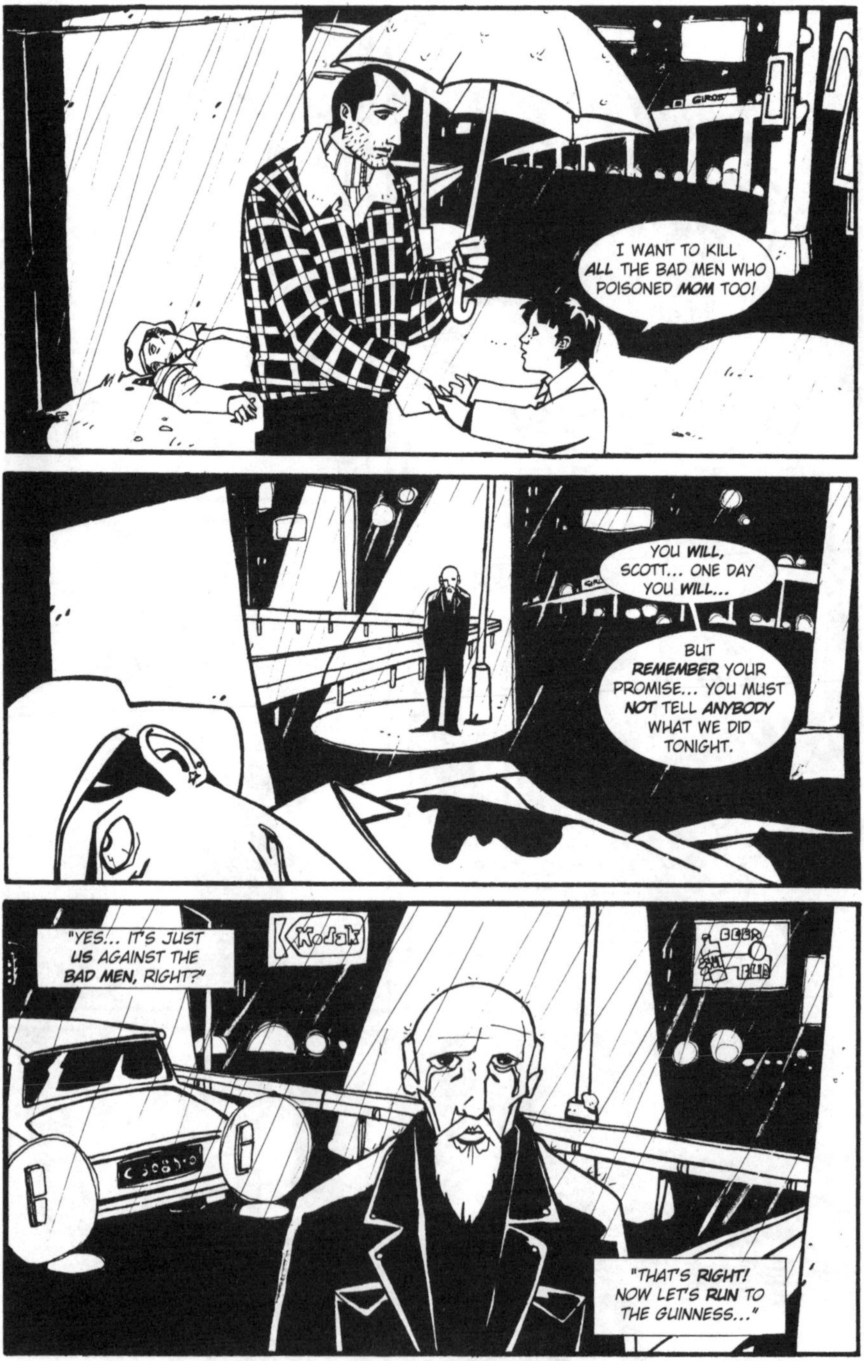
I WANT TO KILL ALL THE BAD MEN WHO POISONED MOM TOO!
YOU WILL, SCOTT... ONE DAY YOU WILL...
BUT REMEMBER YOUR PROMISE... YOU MUST NOT TELL ANYBODY WHAT WE DID TONIGHT.
"YES... IT'S JUST US AGAINST THE BAD MEN, RIGHT?"
Kodak
"THAT'S RIGHT! NOW LET'S RUN TO THE GUINNESS..."

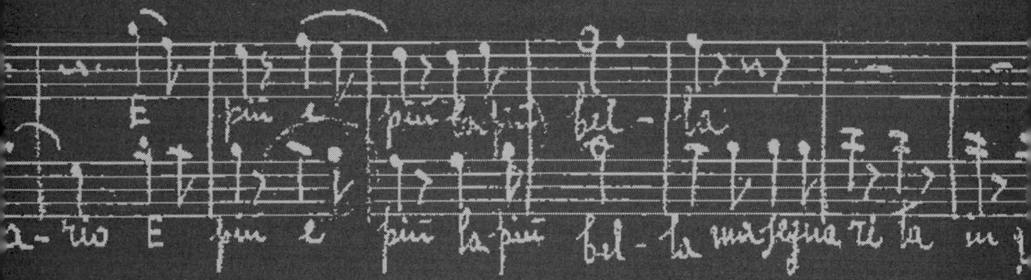

chapter four

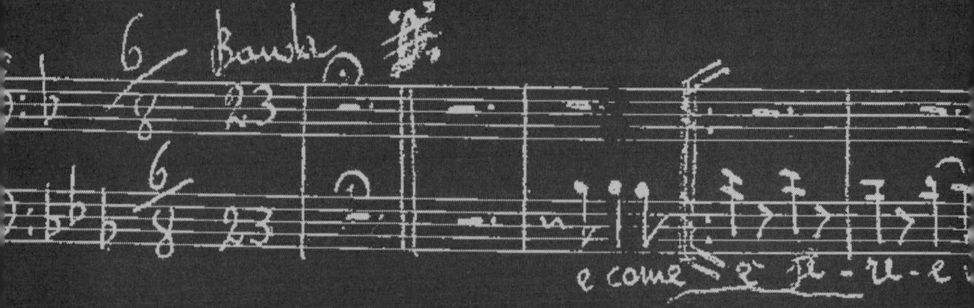
e come

Story
MATTEO CASALI

Art
GRAZIA LOBACCARO

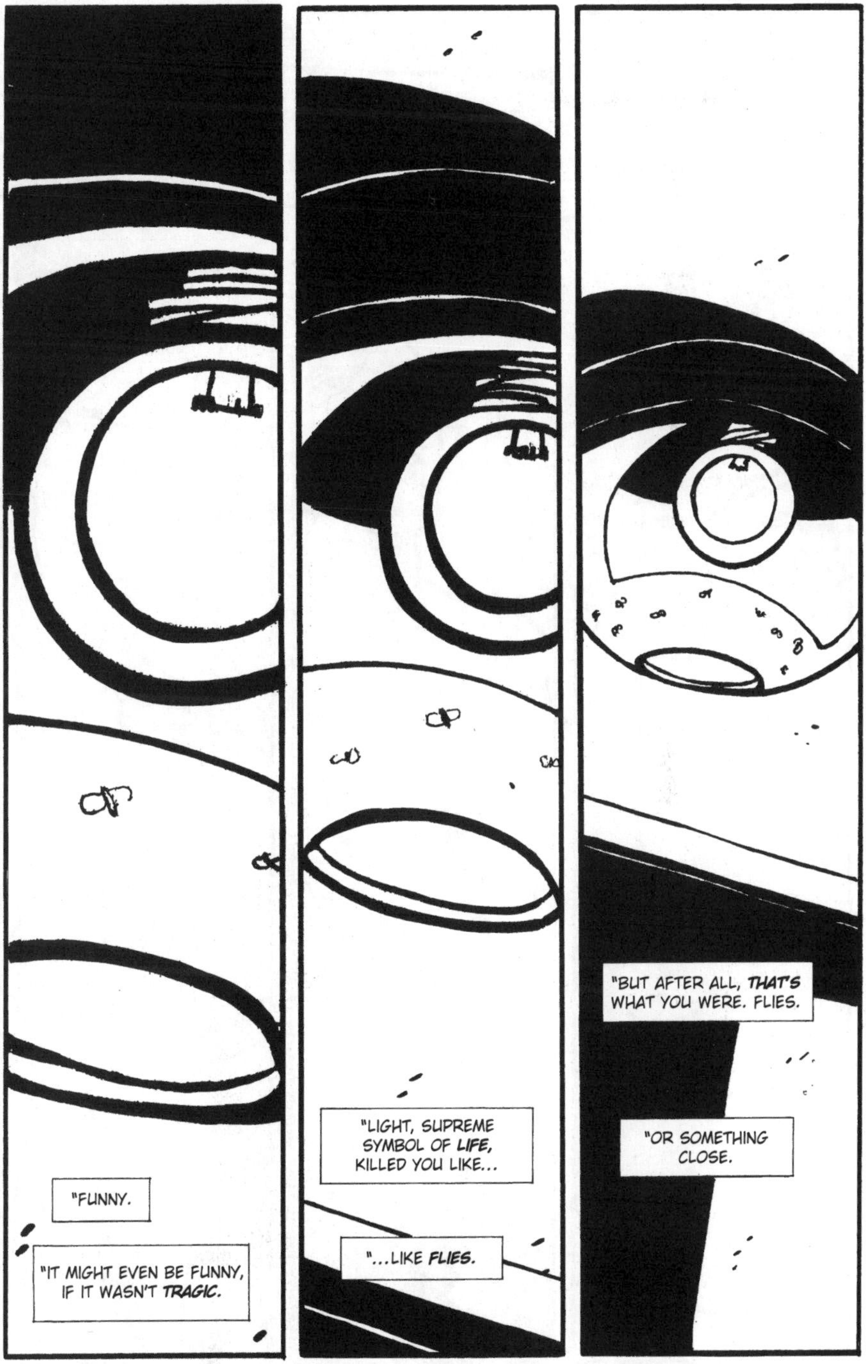
"FUNNY.
"IT MIGHT EVEN BE FUNNY, IF IT WASN'T TRAGIC.
"LIGHT, SUPREME SYMBOL OF LIFE, KILLED YOU LIKE...
"...LIKE FLIES.
"BUT AFTER ALL, THAT'S WHAT YOU WERE. FLIES.
"OR SOMETHING CLOSE.

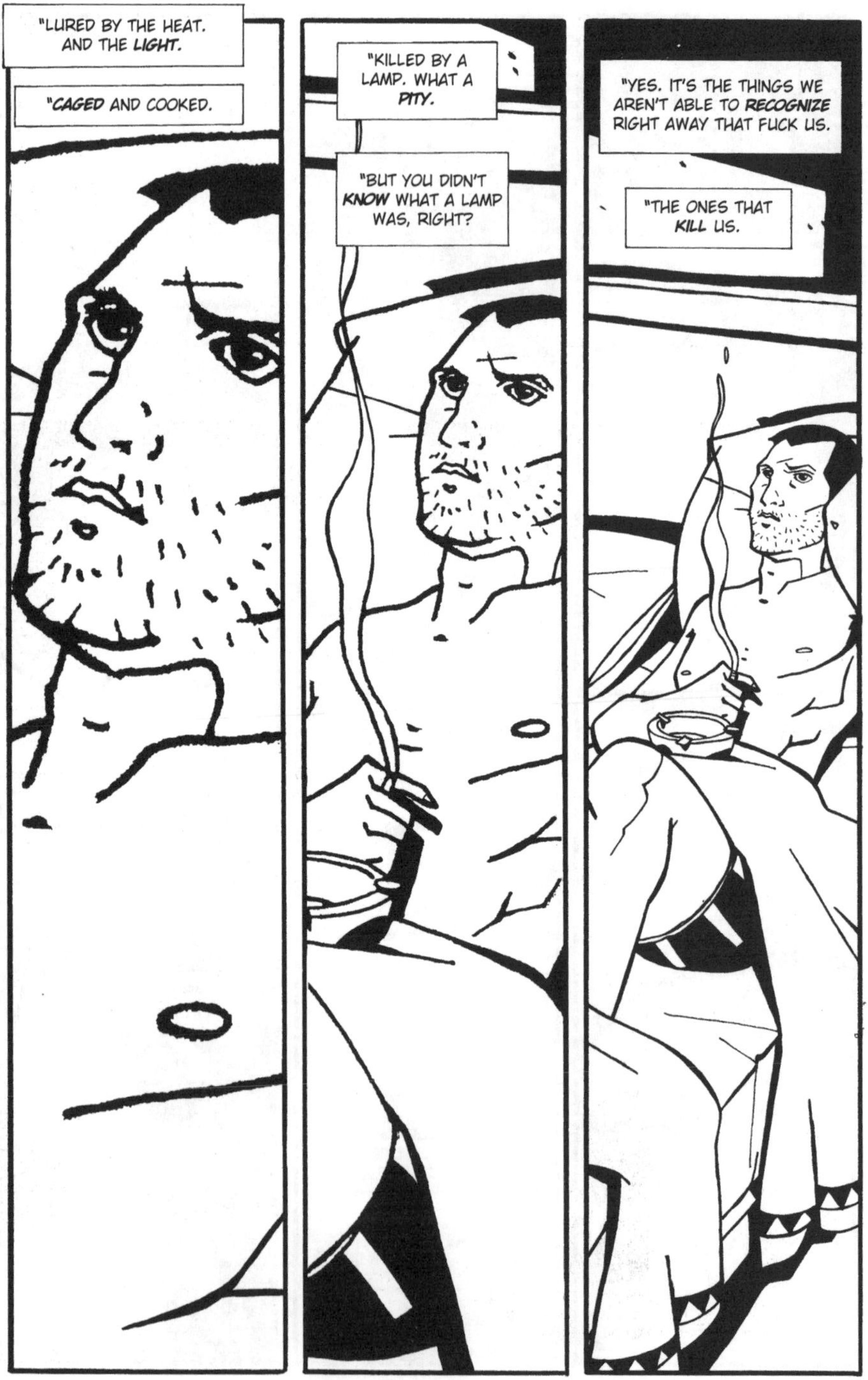
"LURED BY THE HEAT. AND THE LIGHT.
"CAGED AND COOKED.
"KILLED BY A LAMP. WHAT A PITY.
"BUT YOU DIDN'T KNOW WHAT A LAMP WAS, RIGHT?
"YES. IT'S THE THINGS WE AREN'T ABLE TO RECOGNIZE RIGHT AWAY THAT FUCK US.
"THE ONES THAT KILL US.

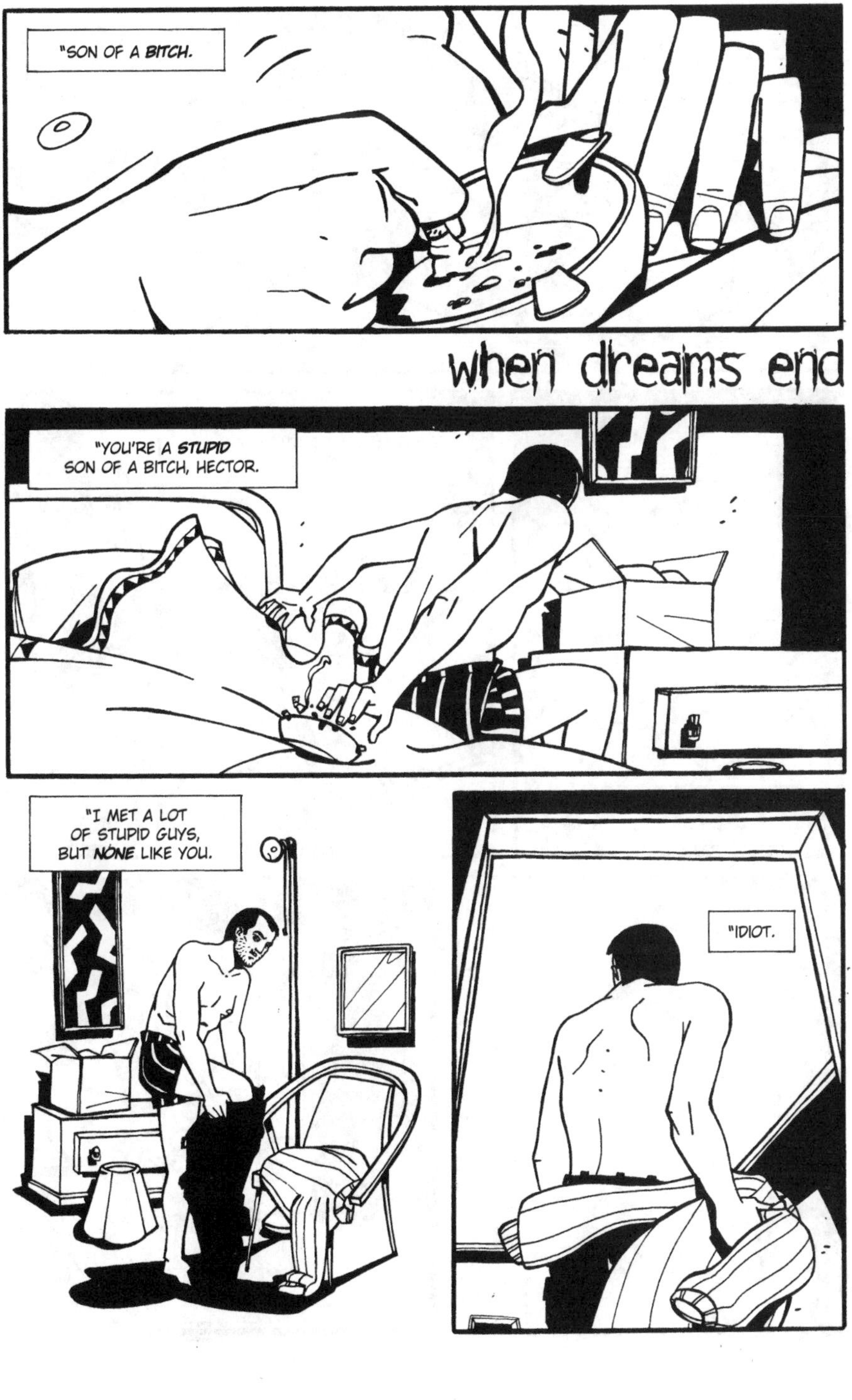
"SON OF A **BITCH**.
when dreams end
"YOU'RE A **STUPID** SON OF A BITCH, HECTOR.
"I MET A LOT OF STUPID GUYS, BUT **NONE** LIKE YOU.
"IDIOT.

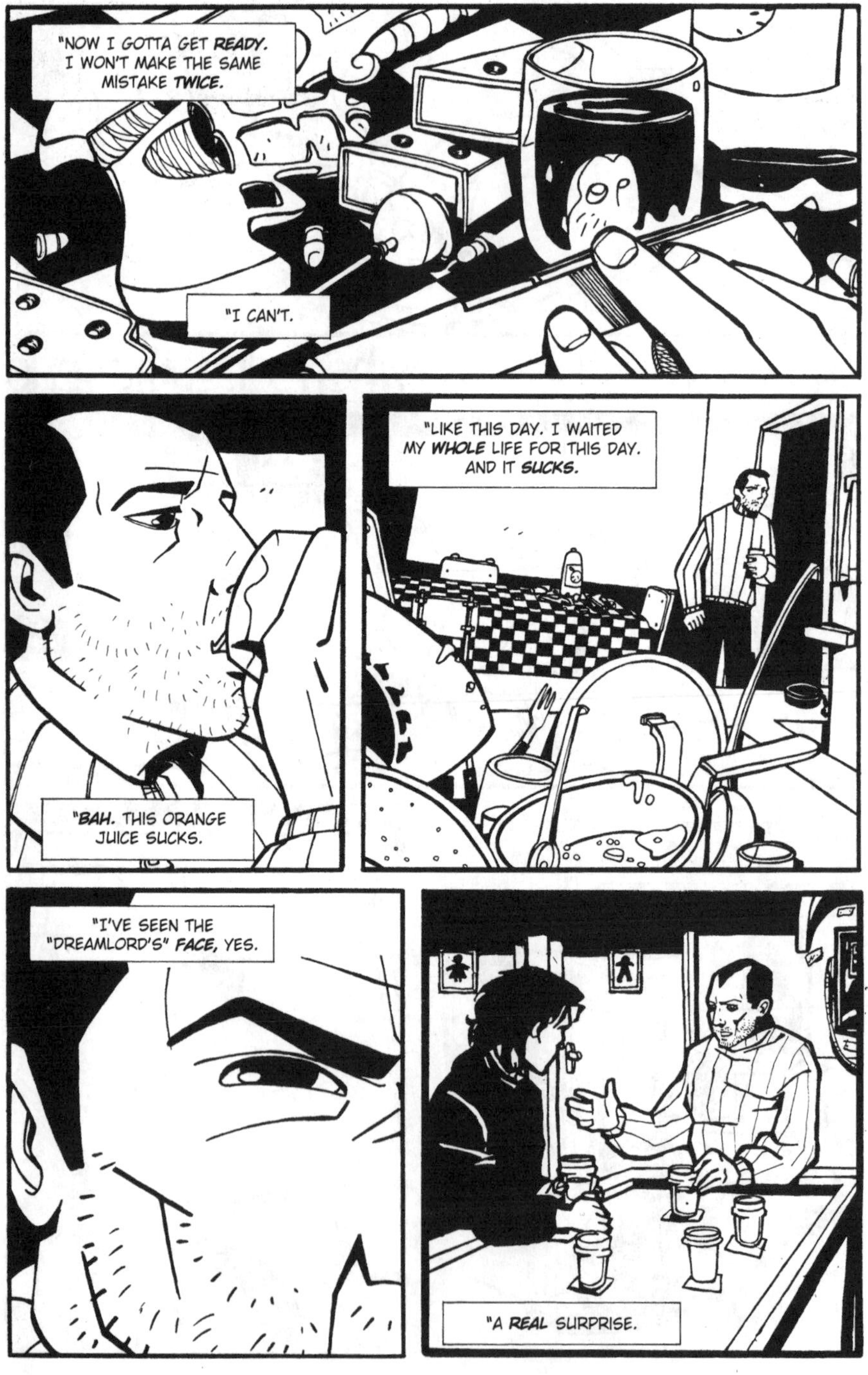
"NOW I GOTTA GET READY. I WON'T MAKE THE SAME MISTAKE TWICE.
"I CAN'T.
"BAH. THIS ORANGE JUICE SUCKS.
"LIKE THIS DAY. I WAITED MY WHOLE LIFE FOR THIS DAY. AND IT SUCKS.
"I'VE SEEN THE "DREAMLORD'S" FACE, YES.
"A REAL SURPRISE.

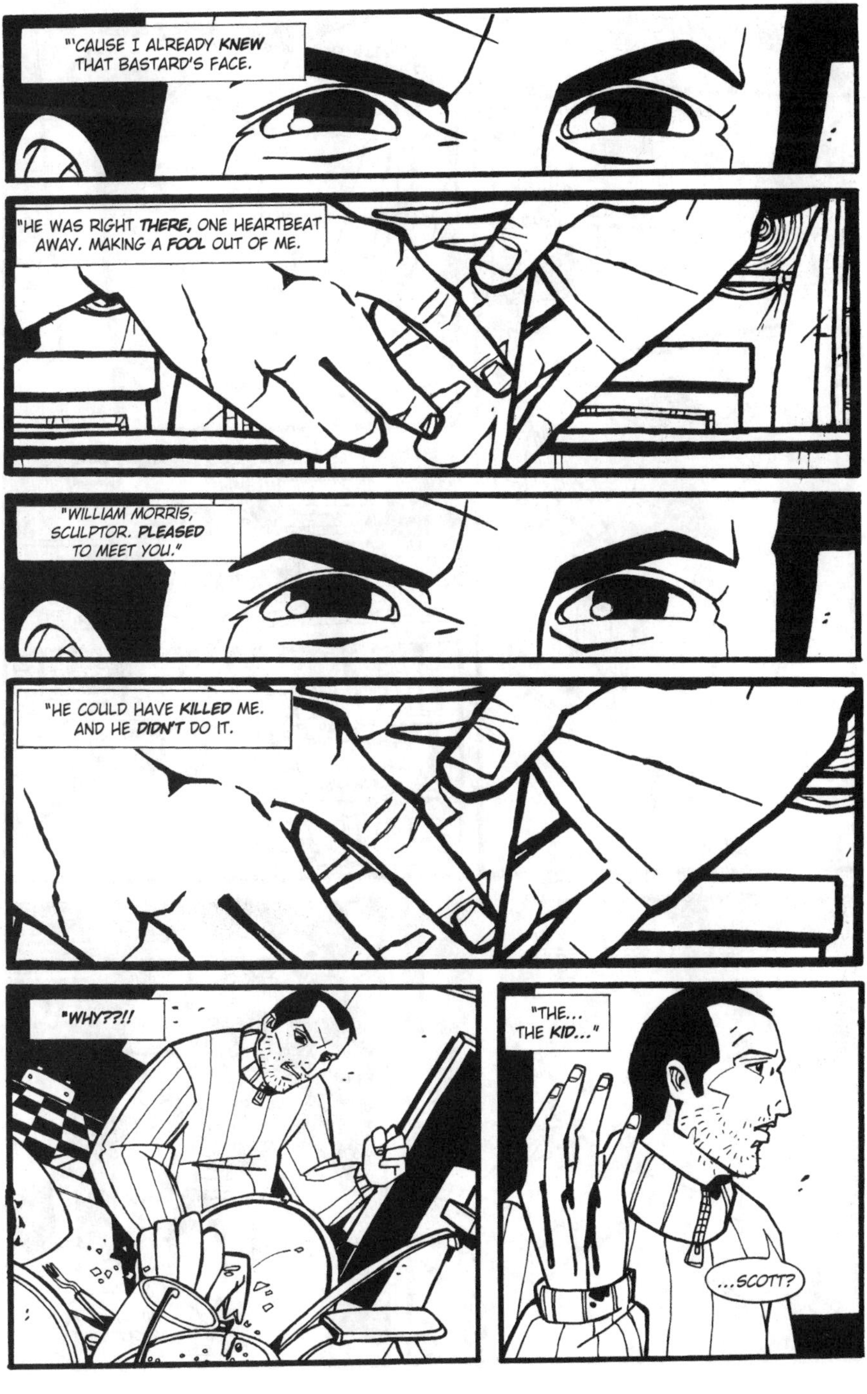
"'CAUSE I ALREADY KNEW THAT BASTARD'S FACE.
"HE WAS RIGHT THERE, ONE HEARTBEAT AWAY. MAKING A FOOL OUT OF ME.
"WILLIAM MORRIS, SCULPTOR. PLEASED TO MEET YOU."
"HE COULD HAVE KILLED ME. AND HE DIDN'T DO IT.
"WHY??!!
"THE... THE KID..."
...SCOTT?

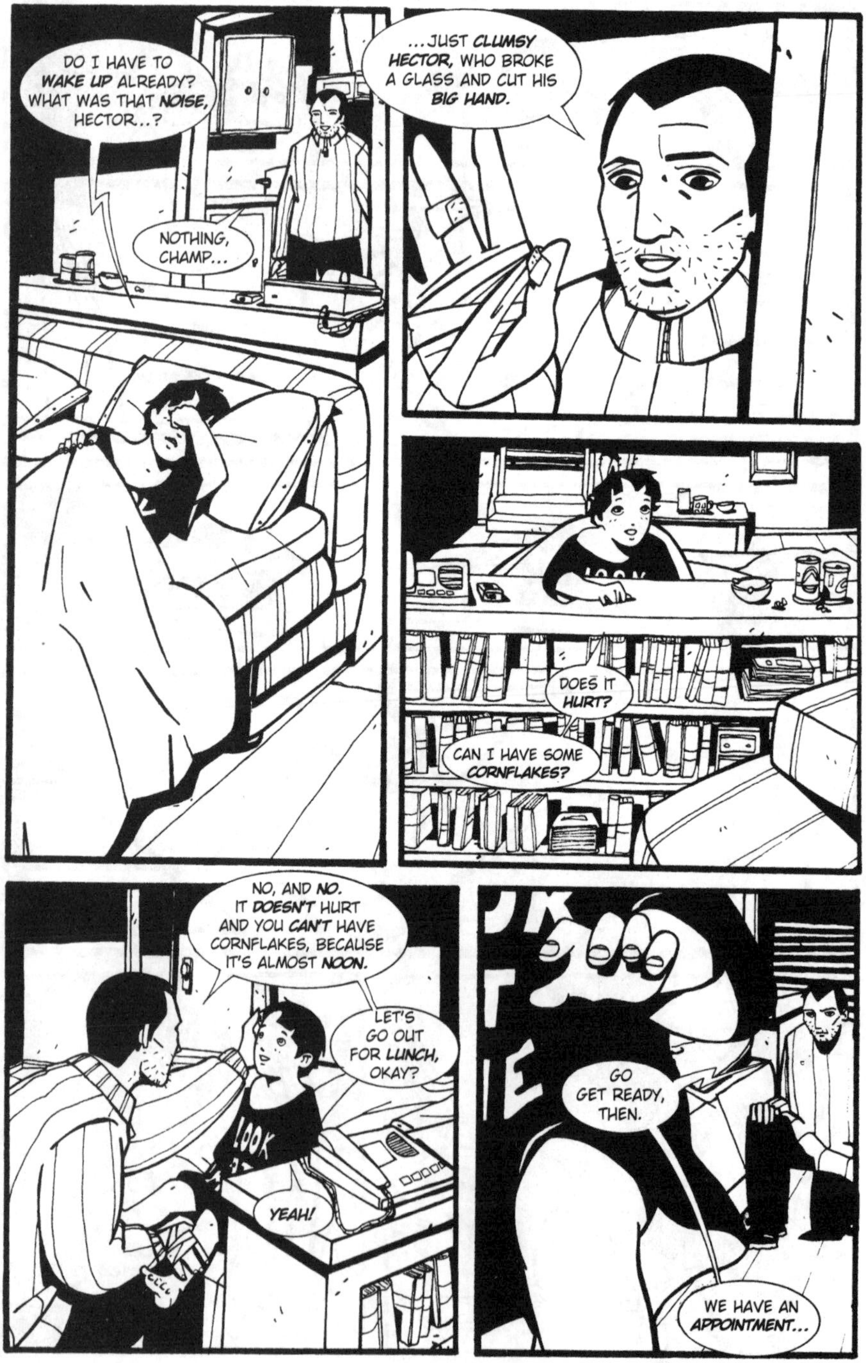
DO I HAVE TO WAKE UP ALREADY? WHAT WAS THAT NOISE, HECTOR..?
NOTHING, CHAMP...
...JUST CLUMSY HECTOR, WHO BROKE A GLASS AND CUT HIS BIG HAND.
DOES IT HURT?
CAN I HAVE SOME CORNFLAKES?
NO, AND NO. IT DOESN'T HURT AND YOU CAN'T HAVE CORNFLAKES, BECAUSE IT'S ALMOST NOON.
LET'S GO OUT FOR LUNCH, OKAY?
YEAH!
GO GET READY, THEN.
WE HAVE AN APPOINTMENT...

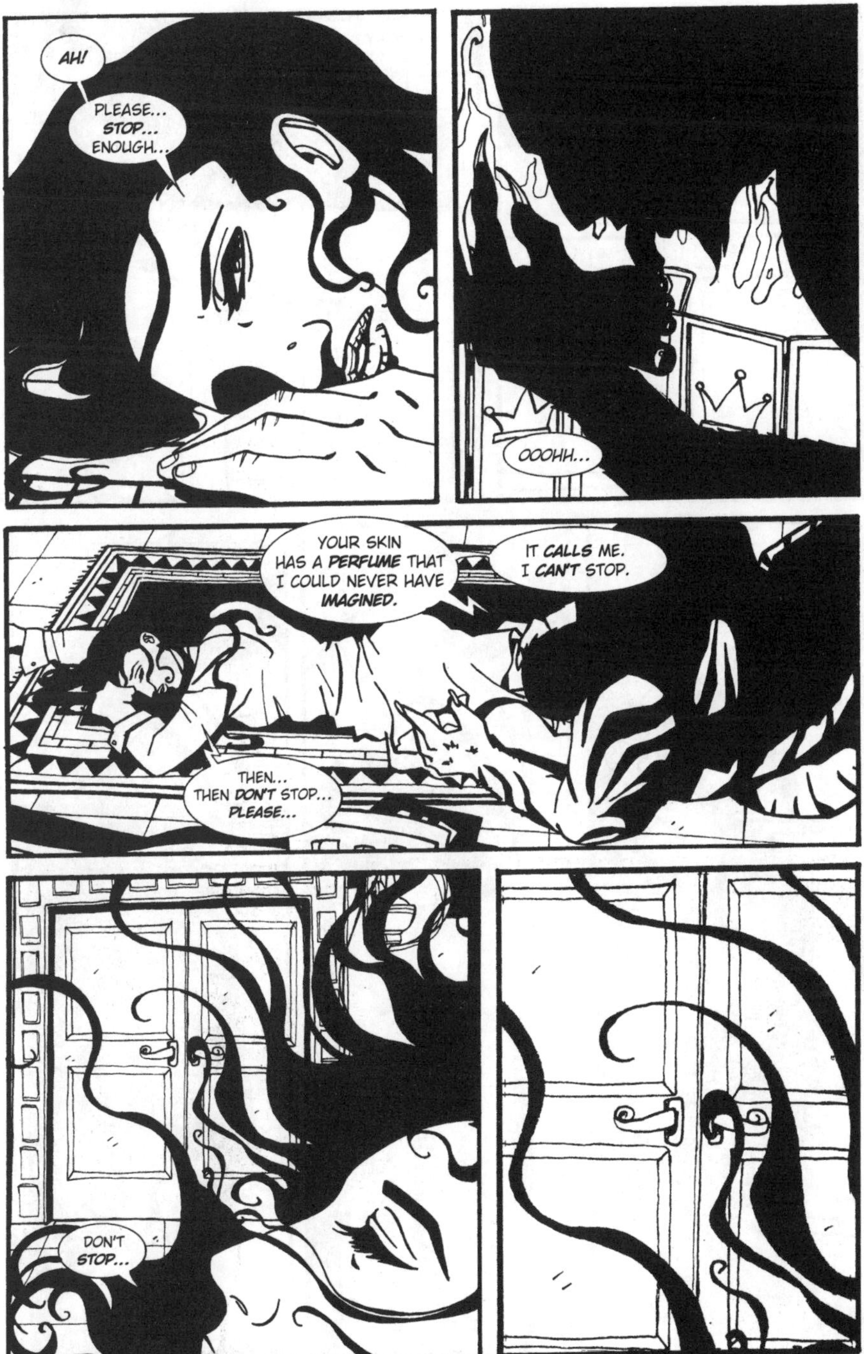

AH!
PLEASE... STOP... ENOUGH...
OOOHH...
YOUR SKIN HAS A PERFUME THAT I COULD NEVER HAVE IMAGINED.
IT CALLS ME. I CAN'T STOP.
THEN... THEN DON'T STOP... PLEASE...
DON'T STOP...

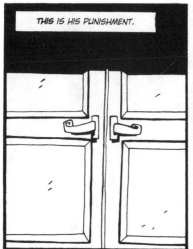

THIS IS HIS PUNISHMENT.

THE **WORST** HE COULD INFLICT ON HIM.

BUT HE **WON'T** STAY HERE AND LISTEN TO THEIR MOANS OF PLEASURE. **NO.**

THE DARKNESS AND SOLITUDE ARE BETTER THAN **THIS.**

SOLITUDE... **ALWAYS** HIS COMPANION.

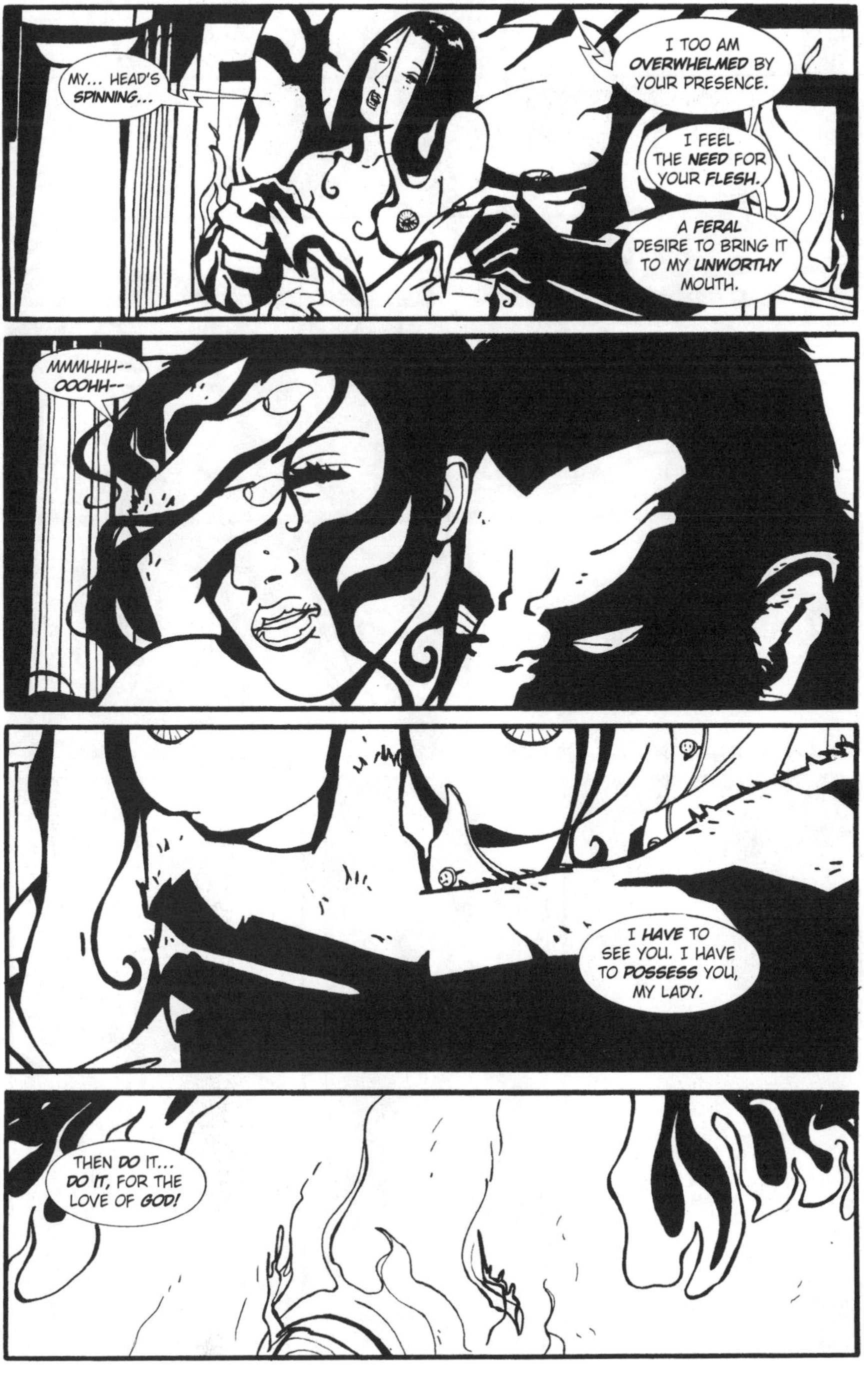
MY... HEAD'S SPINNING...
I TOO AM OVERWHELMED BY YOUR PRESENCE.
I FEEL THE NEED FOR YOUR FLESH.
A FERAL DESIRE TO BRING IT TO MY UNWORTHY MOUTH.
MMMHHH-- OOOHH--
I HAVE TO SEE YOU. I HAVE TO POSSESS YOU, MY LADY.
THEN DO IT... DO IT, FOR THE LOVE OF GOD!

I WILL GIVE MYSELF TO YOU...
...ENTIRELY. AND I WILL ASK NOTHING LESS IN RETURN.
DON'T-- YOUR WORDS DON'T SCARE ME... TOUCH ME AGAIN...
PLEASE...
MY EYES SLIDE OVER YOUR BODY AND SEE NOTHING BUT PERFECTION...
...MY CHEST IS INFLAMED AS I SAVOR YOUR CARESSES...
YESSS...
...AS I PREPARE TO ENFOLD YOU IN THE FLAMES OF MY ANCIENT PASSION.
OH! YES!
BE MY BRIDE, AND YOU WILL LIVE WITH ME FOR ALL ETERNITY.
...YES... TAKE ME... I WANT TO BE YOURS...

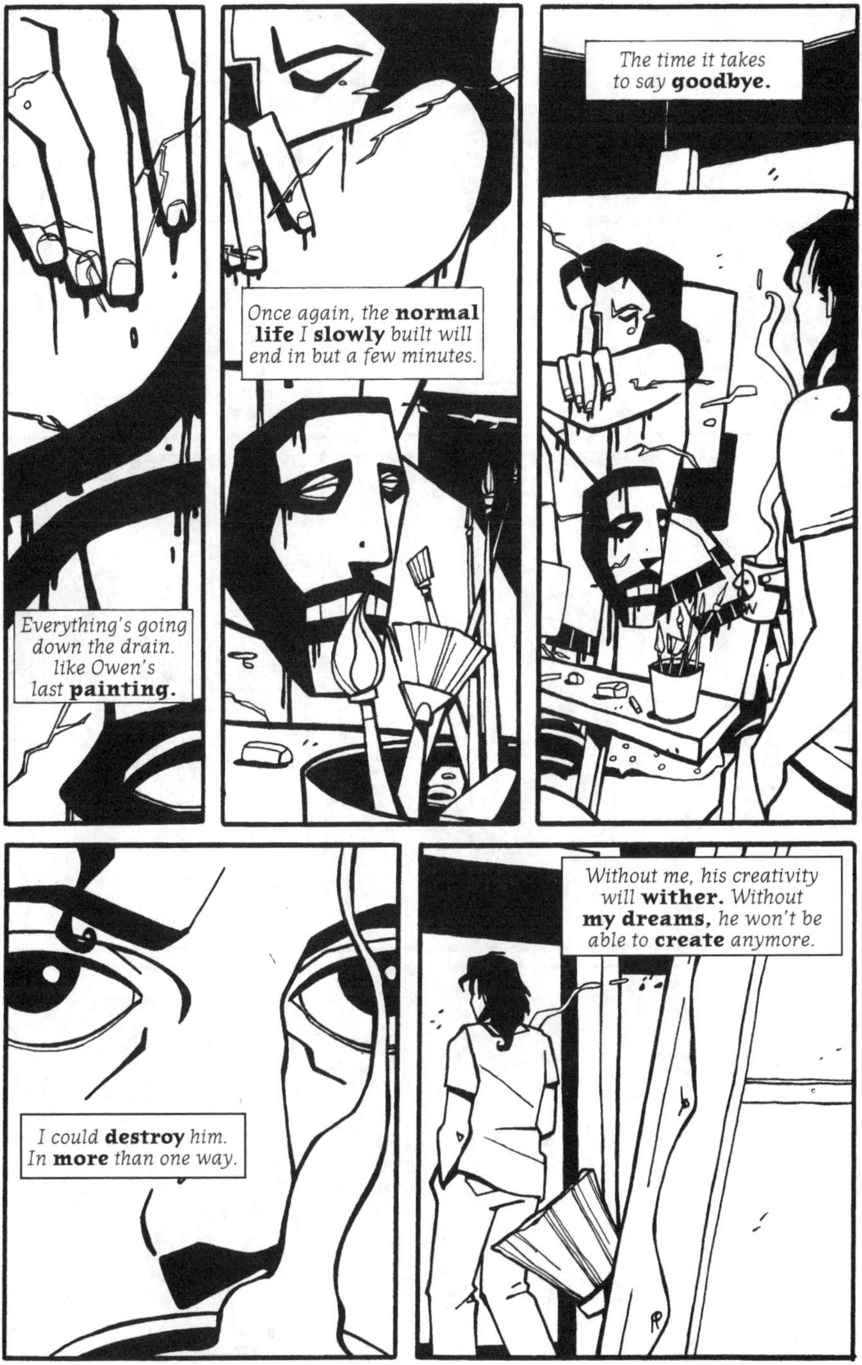
Everything's going down the drain. like Owen's last **painting.**
Once again, the **normal life** I **slowly** built will end in but a few minutes.
The time it takes to say **goodbye.**
I could **destroy** him. In **more** than one way.
Without me, his creativity will **wither.** Without **my dreams,** he won't be able to **create** anymore.

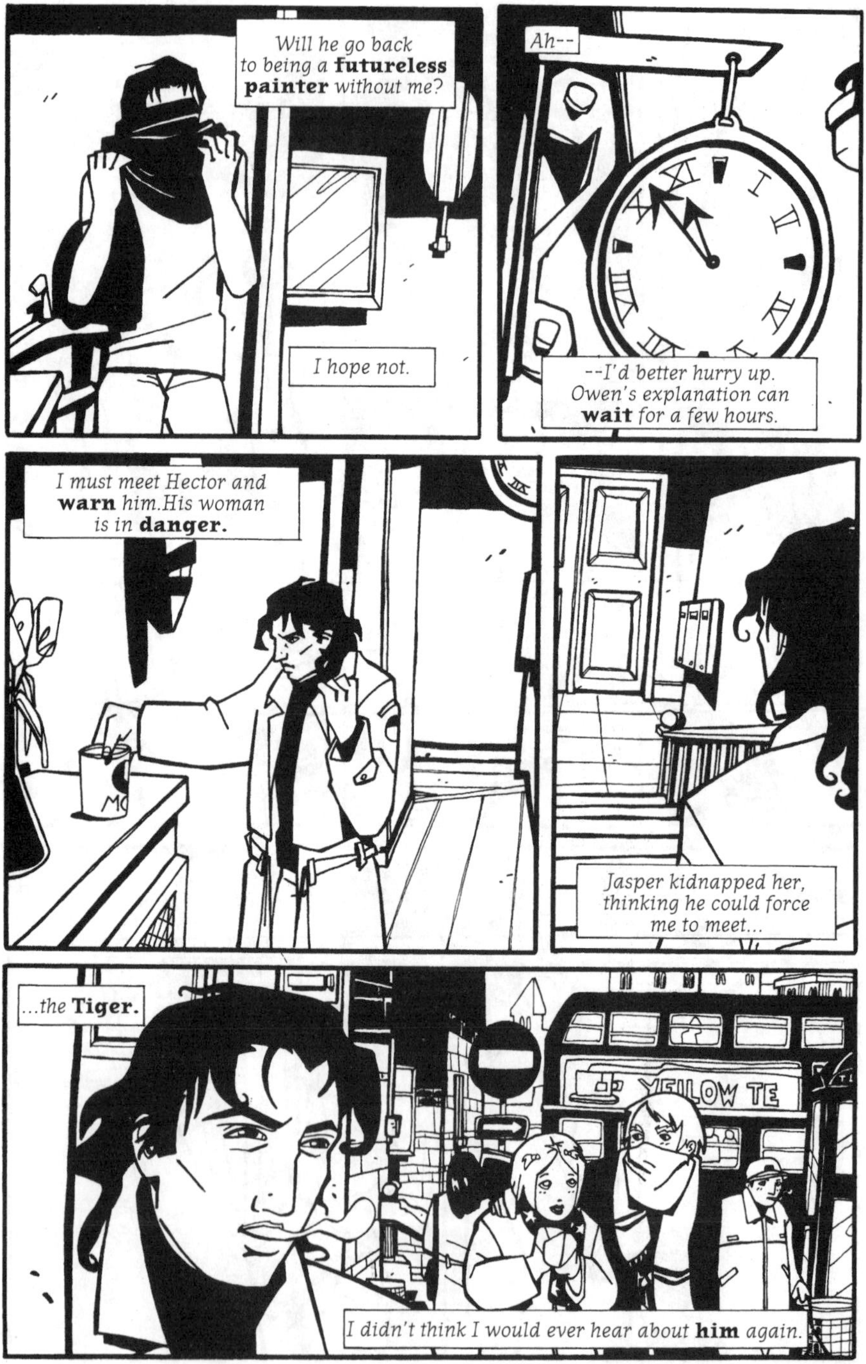
Will he go back to being a **futureless painter** without me?
I hope not.
Ah--
--I'd better hurry up. Owen's explanation can **wait** for a few hours.
I must meet Hector and **warn** him.His woman is in **danger.**
Jasper kidnapped her, thinking he could force me to meet...
...the **Tiger.**
YELLOW TE
I didn't think I would ever hear about **him** again.

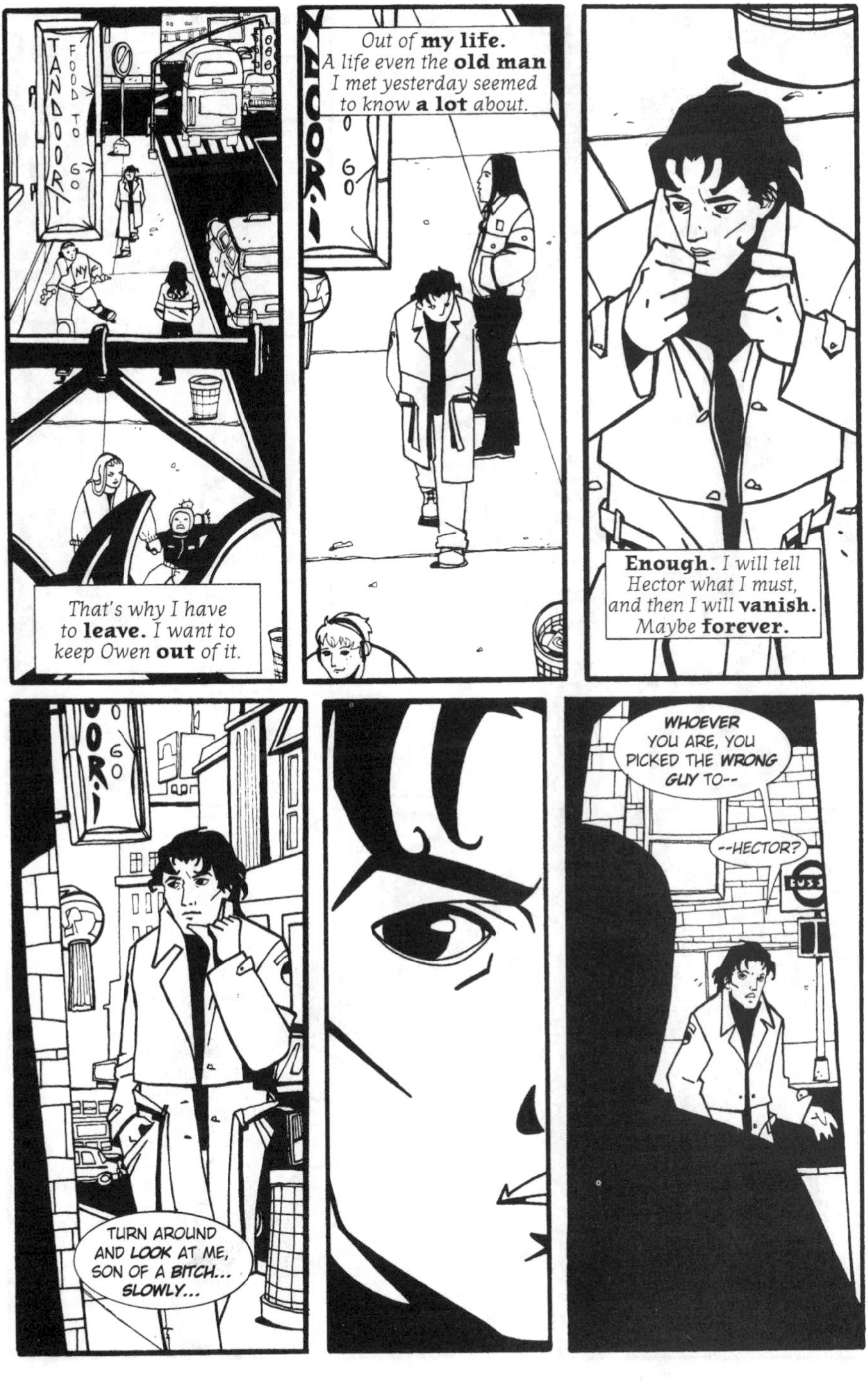
TANDOORI
FOOD TO GO
That's why I have to **leave.** I want to keep Owen **out** of it.
Out of **my life.** A life even the **old man** I met yesterday seemed to know **a lot** about.
Enough. I will tell Hector what I must, and then I will **vanish.** Maybe **forever.**
TURN AROUND AND ***LOOK*** AT ME, SON OF A ***BITCH...*** ***SLOWLY...***
WHOEVER YOU ARE, YOU PICKED THE ***WRONG GUY*** TO--
--HECTOR?

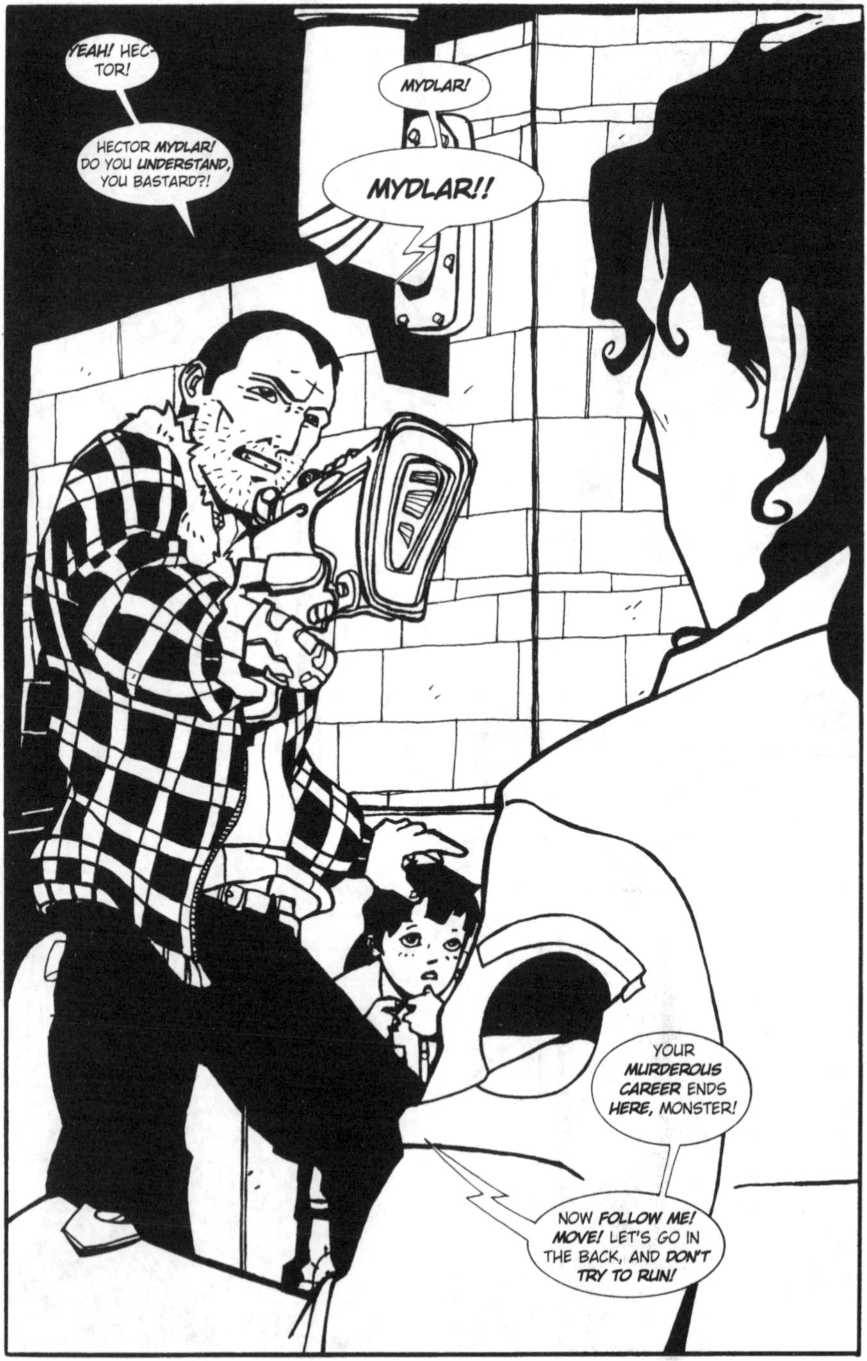
YEAH! HEC-
TOR!
HECTOR MYDLAR! DO YOU UNDERSTAND, YOU BASTARD?!
MYDLAR!
MYDLAR!!
YOUR MURDEROUS CAREER ENDS HERE, MONSTER!
NOW FOLLOW ME! MOVE! LET'S GO IN THE BACK, AND DON'T TRY TO RUN!

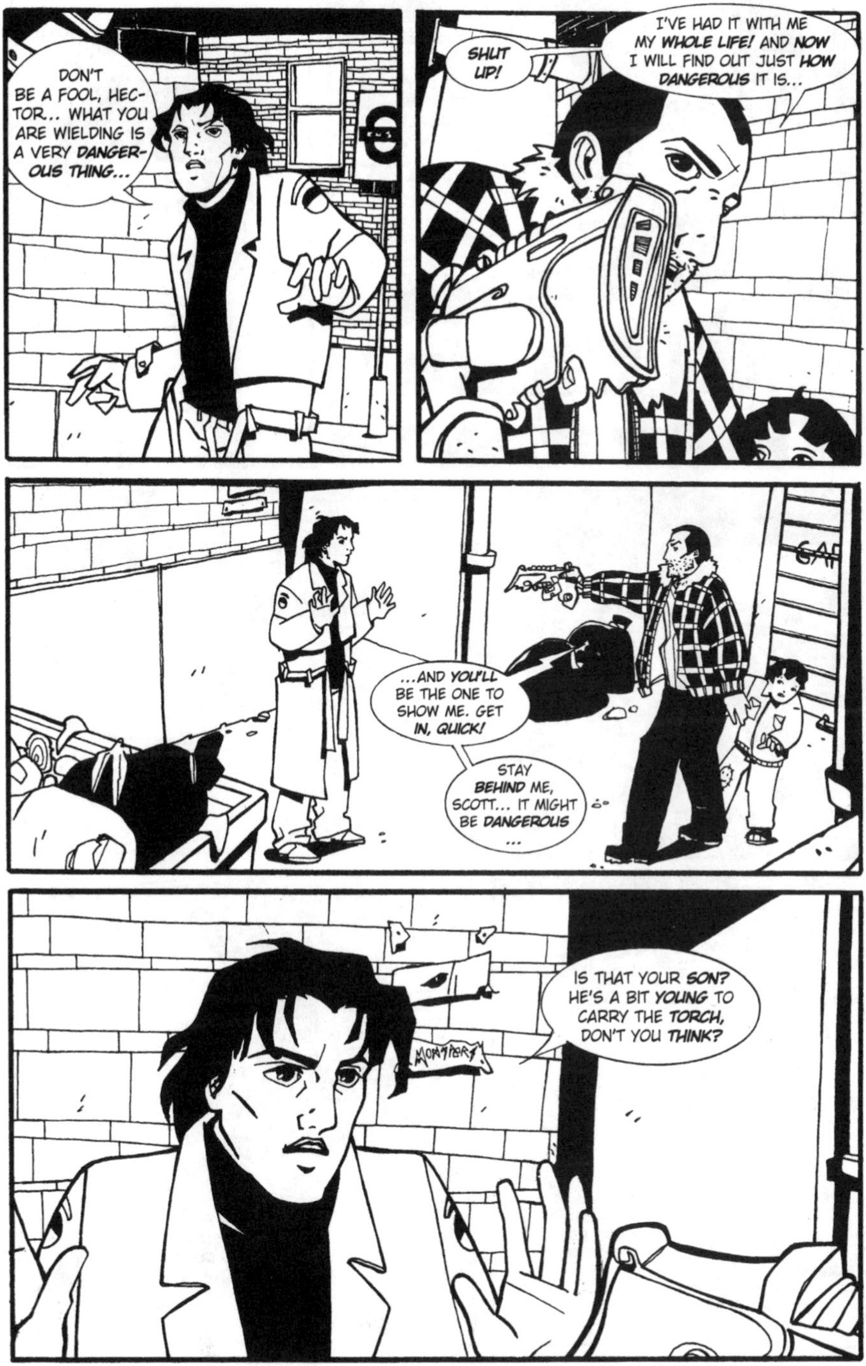
DON'T BE A FOOL, HECTOR... WHAT YOU ARE WIELDING IS A VERY DANGEROUS THING...
SHUT UP!
I'VE HAD IT WITH ME MY WHOLE LIFE! AND NOW I WILL FIND OUT JUST HOW DANGEROUS IT IS...
...AND YOU'LL BE THE ONE TO SHOW ME. GET IN, QUICK!
STAY BEHIND ME, SCOTT... IT MIGHT BE DANGEROUS ...
IS THAT YOUR SON? HE'S A BIT YOUNG TO CARRY THE TORCH, DON'T YOU THINK?

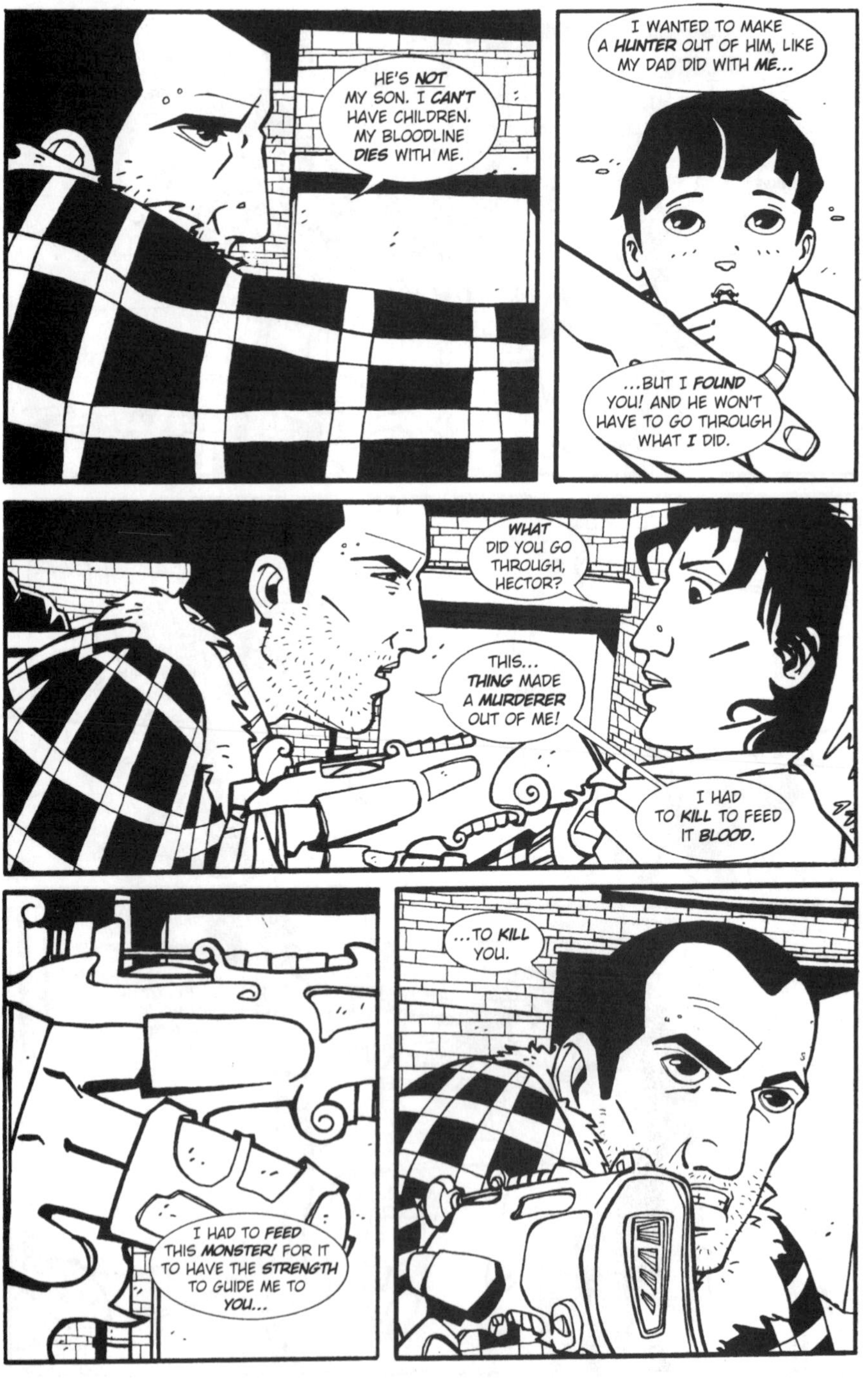
HE'S NOT MY SON. I CAN'T HAVE CHILDREN. MY BLOODLINE DIES WITH ME.
I WANTED TO MAKE A HUNTER OUT OF HIM, LIKE MY DAD DID WITH ME...
...BUT I FOUND YOU! AND HE WON'T HAVE TO GO THROUGH WHAT I DID.
WHAT DID YOU GO THROUGH, HECTOR?
THIS... THING MADE A MURDERER OUT OF ME!
I HAD TO KILL TO FEED IT BLOOD.
I HAD TO FEED THIS MONSTER! FOR IT TO HAVE THE STRENGTH TO GUIDE ME TO YOU...
...TO KILL YOU.

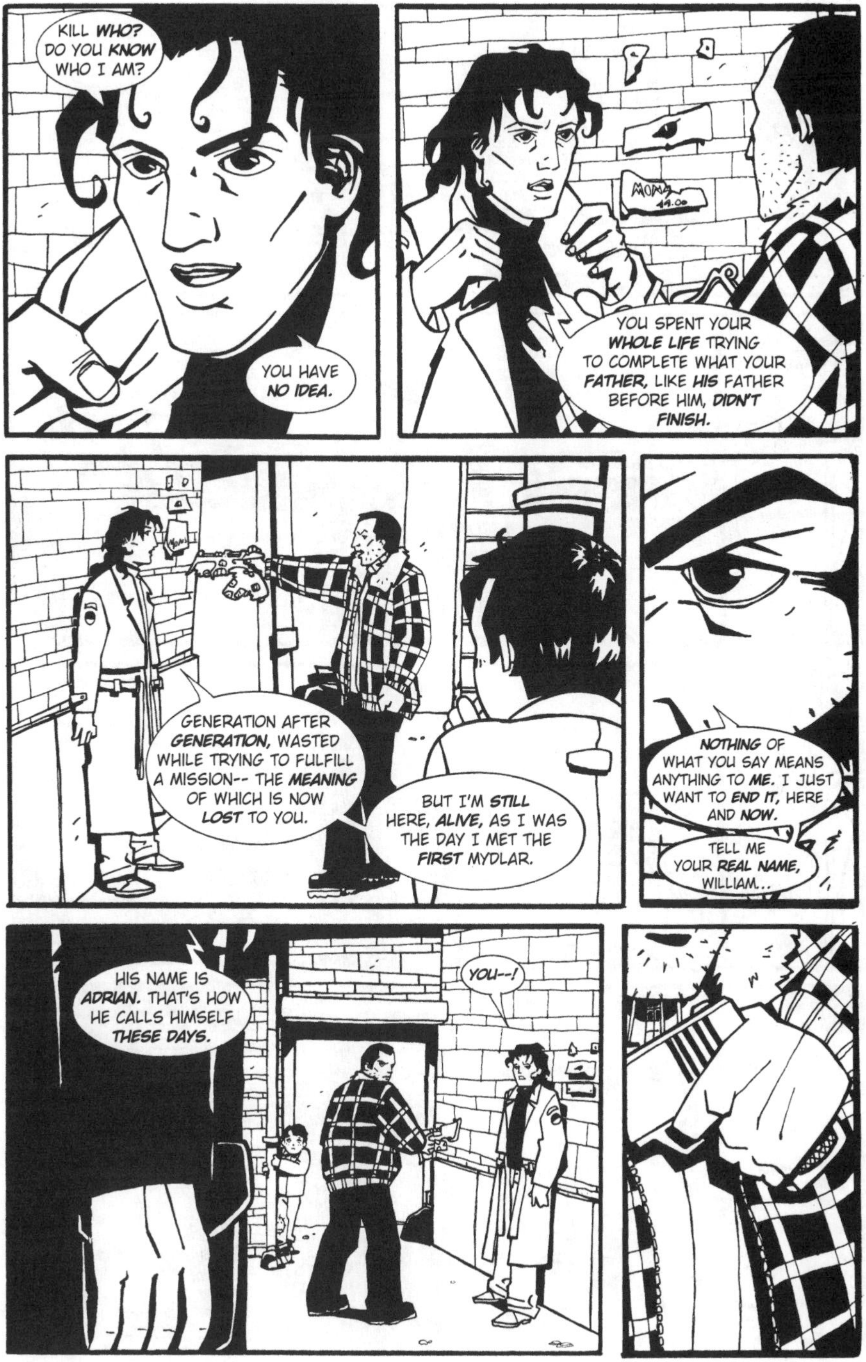
KILL WHO? DO YOU KNOW WHO I AM?
YOU HAVE NO IDEA.
YOU SPENT YOUR WHOLE LIFE TRYING TO COMPLETE WHAT YOUR FATHER, LIKE HIS FATHER BEFORE HIM, DIDN'T FINISH.
GENERATION AFTER GENERATION, WASTED WHILE TRYING TO FULFILL A MISSION-- THE MEANING OF WHICH IS NOW LOST TO YOU.
BUT I'M STILL HERE, ALIVE, AS I WAS THE DAY I MET THE FIRST MYDLAR.
NOTHING OF WHAT YOU SAY MEANS ANYTHING TO ME. I JUST WANT TO END IT, HERE AND NOW.
TELL ME YOUR REAL NAME, WILLIAM...
HIS NAME IS ADRIAN. THAT'S HOW HE CALLS HIMSELF THESE DAYS.
YOU--!

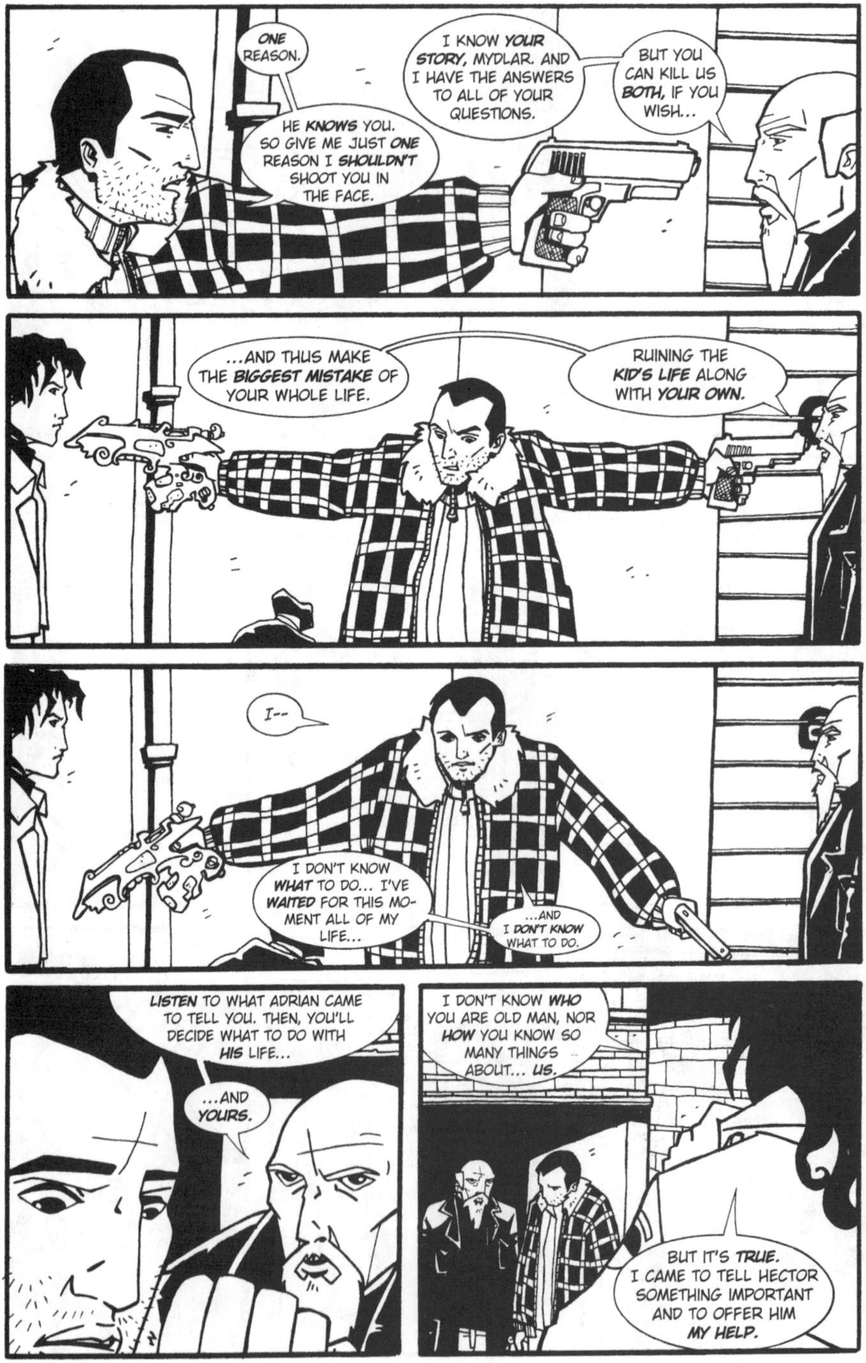
ONE REASON.
HE KNOWS YOU. SO GIVE ME JUST ONE REASON I SHOULDN'T SHOOT YOU IN THE FACE.
I KNOW YOUR STORY, MYDLAR. AND I HAVE THE ANSWERS TO ALL OF YOUR QUESTIONS.
BUT YOU CAN KILL US BOTH, IF YOU WISH...
...AND THUS MAKE THE BIGGEST MISTAKE OF YOUR WHOLE LIFE.
RUINING THE KID'S LIFE ALONG WITH YOUR OWN.
I--
I DON'T KNOW WHAT TO DO... I'VE WAITED FOR THIS MOMENT ALL OF MY LIFE...
...AND I DON'T KNOW WHAT TO DO.
LISTEN TO WHAT ADRIAN CAME TO TELL YOU. THEN, YOU'LL DECIDE WHAT TO DO WITH HIS LIFE...
...AND YOURS.
I DON'T KNOW WHO YOU ARE OLD MAN, NOR HOW YOU KNOW SO MANY THINGS ABOUT... US.
BUT IT'S TRUE. I CAME TO TELL HECTOR SOMETHING IMPORTANT AND TO OFFER HIM MY HELP.

YOUR WOMAN... *CLAIRE*... IS IN DANGER. SHE'S BEEN *KIDNAPPED* BY PEOPLE WHO WANT TO GET *TO ME* AND THOUGHT THEY COULD DO IT THROUGH HER...

...AND THROUGH *YOU.*

WHERE?! WHERE DID THEY *TAKE HER?!*

IF THIS IS *OUR* FAULT TOO, YOU WILL *PAY,* ASSHOLE!

CALM *DOWN!*

THE *CREATURES* WHO TOOK YOUR WOMAN ARE *DANGEROUS.* YOU WILL *NEED* HIM. YOU WILL NEED HIS *POWER.*

TELL ME ABOUT THEM AND HELP ME GET HER *BACK.*

THEN, I'LL DECIDE IF I'M GO- ING TO *KILL YOU.*

LET'S GET YOUR WOMAN *BACK...*

...THEN *TRY* TO KILL ME.

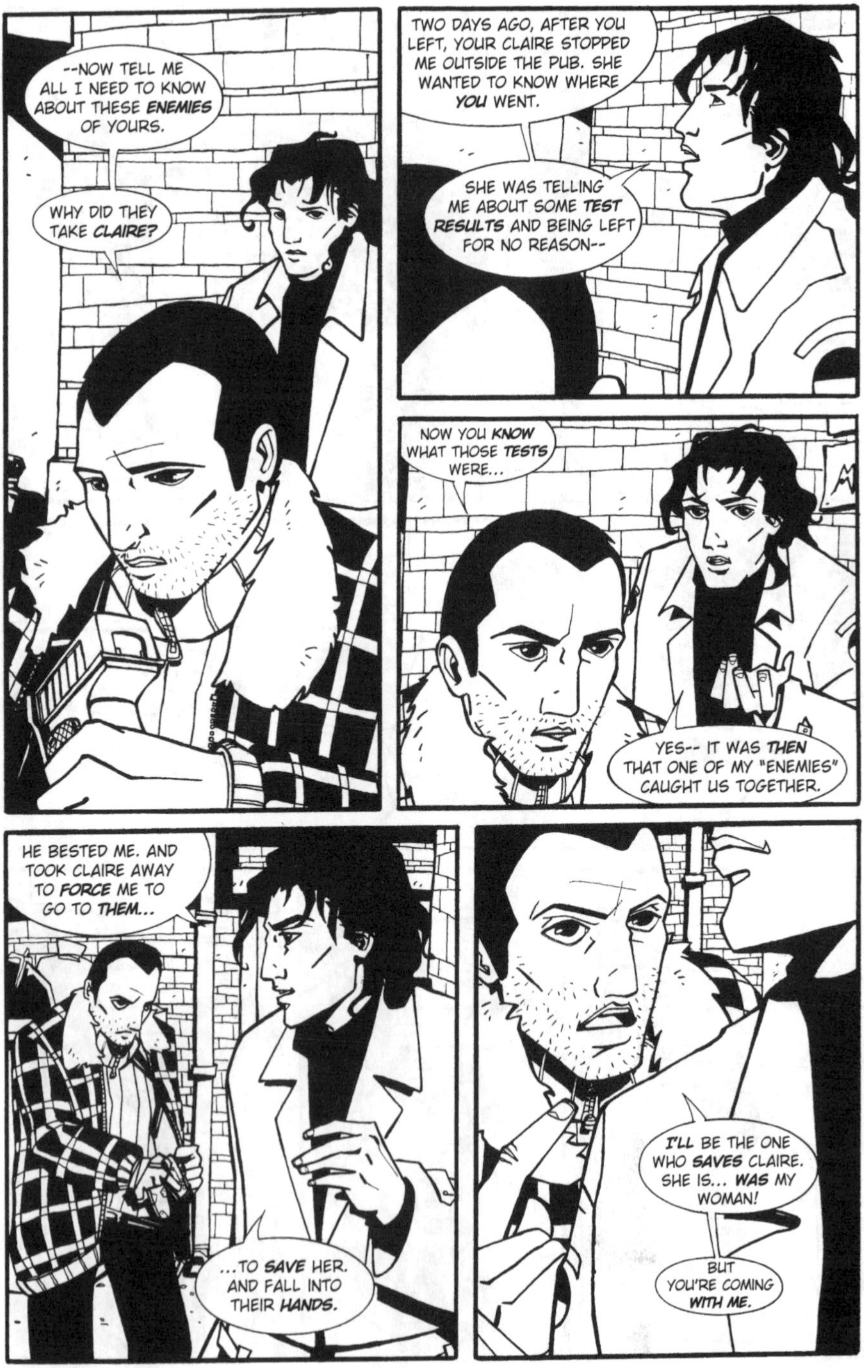
--NOW TELL ME ALL I NEED TO KNOW ABOUT THESE ENEMIES OF YOURS.
WHY DID THEY TAKE CLAIRE?
TWO DAYS AGO, AFTER YOU LEFT, YOUR CLAIRE STOPPED ME OUTSIDE THE PUB. SHE WANTED TO KNOW WHERE YOU WENT.
SHE WAS TELLING ME ABOUT SOME TEST RESULTS AND BEING LEFT FOR NO REASON--
NOW YOU KNOW WHAT THOSE TESTS WERE...
YES-- IT WAS THEN THAT ONE OF MY "ENEMIES" CAUGHT US TOGETHER.
HE BESTED ME. AND TOOK CLAIRE AWAY TO FORCE ME TO GO TO THEM...
...TO SAVE HER. AND FALL INTO THEIR HANDS.
I'LL BE THE ONE WHO SAVES CLAIRE. SHE IS... WAS MY WOMAN!
BUT YOU'RE COMING WITH ME.

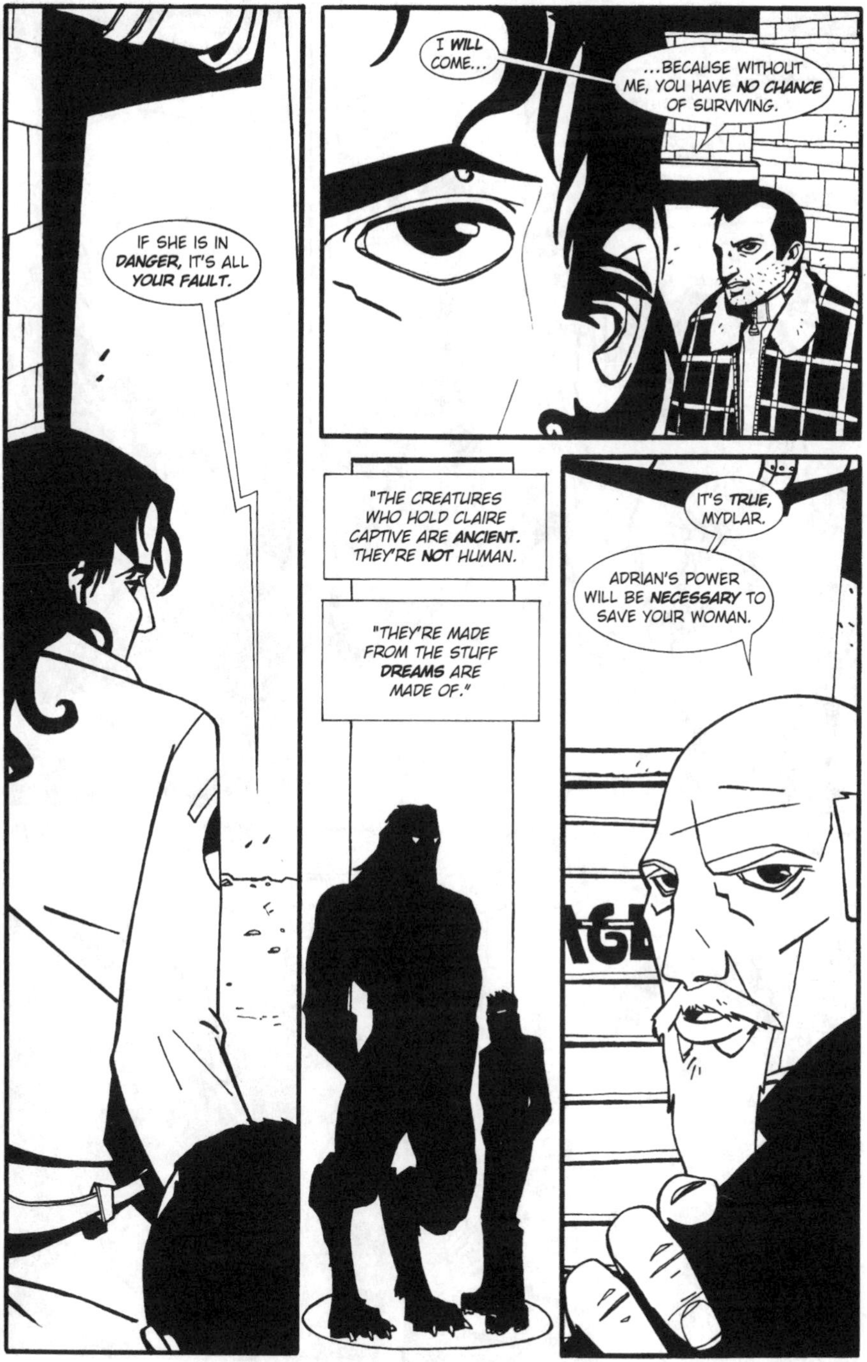

IF SHE IS IN DANGER, IT'S ALL YOUR FAULT.
I WILL COME...
...BECAUSE WITHOUT ME, YOU HAVE NO CHANCE OF SURVIVING.
"THE CREATURES WHO HOLD CLAIRE CAPTIVE ARE ANCIENT. THEY'RE NOT HUMAN.
"THEY'RE MADE FROM THE STUFF DREAMS ARE MADE OF."
IT'S TRUE, MYDLAR.
ADRIAN'S POWER WILL BE NECESSARY TO SAVE YOUR WOMAN.

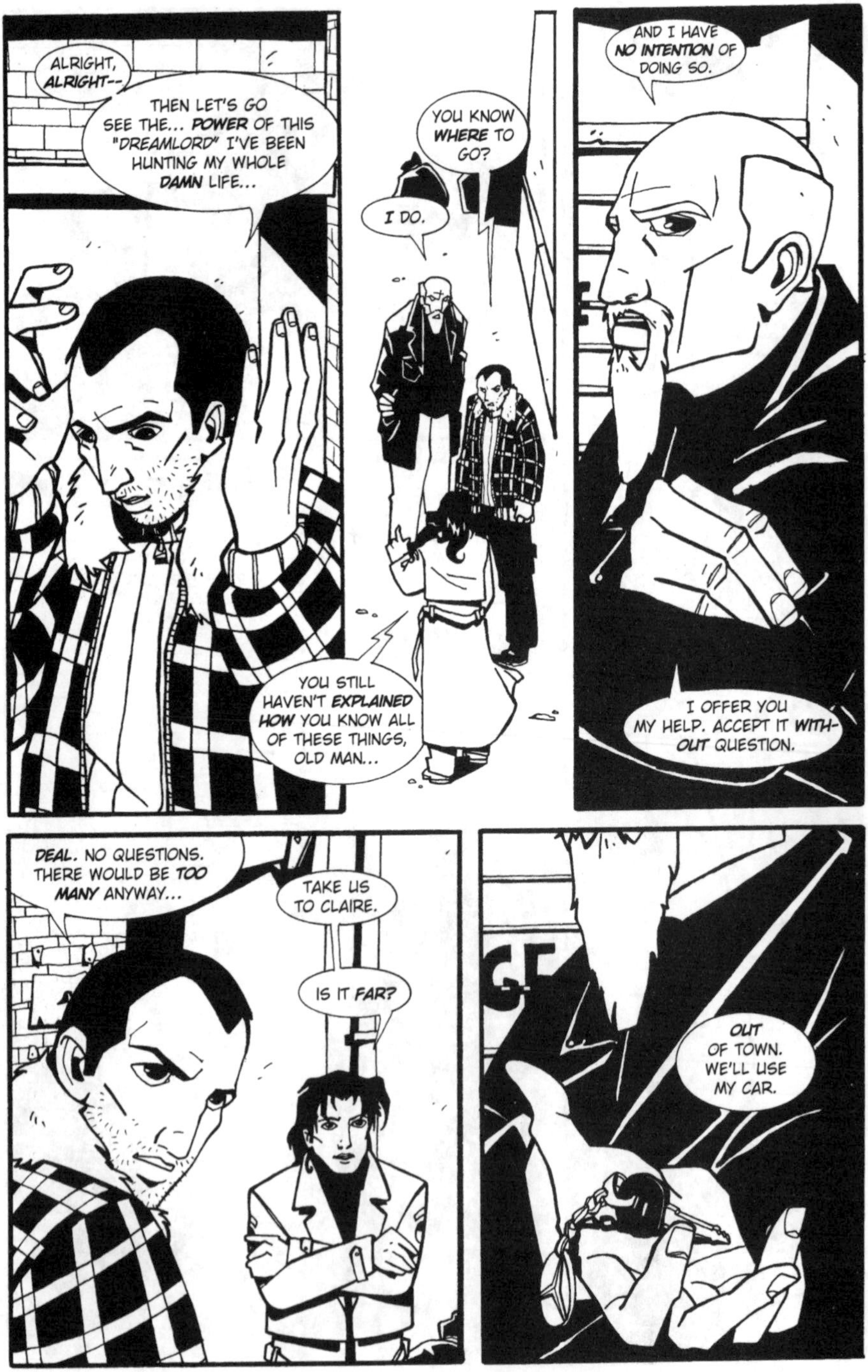
ALRIGHT, ALRIGHT--
THEN LET'S GO SEE THE... POWER OF THIS "DREAMLORD" I'VE BEEN HUNTING MY WHOLE DAMN LIFE...
YOU KNOW WHERE TO GO?
I DO.
YOU STILL HAVEN'T EXPLAINED HOW YOU KNOW ALL OF THESE THINGS, OLD MAN...
AND I HAVE NO INTENTION OF DOING SO.
I OFFER YOU MY HELP. ACCEPT IT WITH-OUT QUESTION.
DEAL. NO QUESTIONS. THERE WOULD BE TOO MANY ANYWAY...
TAKE US TO CLAIRE.
IS IT FAR?
OUT OF TOWN. WE'LL USE MY CAR.

I DON'T TRUST THIS MAN, HECTOR--

I DON'T CARE WHAT *YOU* THINK. I'M GOING.

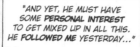

"AND YET, HE MUST HAVE SOME *PERSONAL INTEREST* TO GET MIXED UP IN ALL THIS. HE *FOLLOWED ME* YESTERDAY..."

"HE FOLLOWED *ME* TOO... BUT I DON'T WANT TO THINK ABOUT IT..."

...WHAT MATTERS *NOW*, IS CLAIRE--

AREN'T YOU FORGETTING *SOMETHING*, MYDLAR?

HECTOR--

CAN WE HAVE *LUNCH* NOW...?

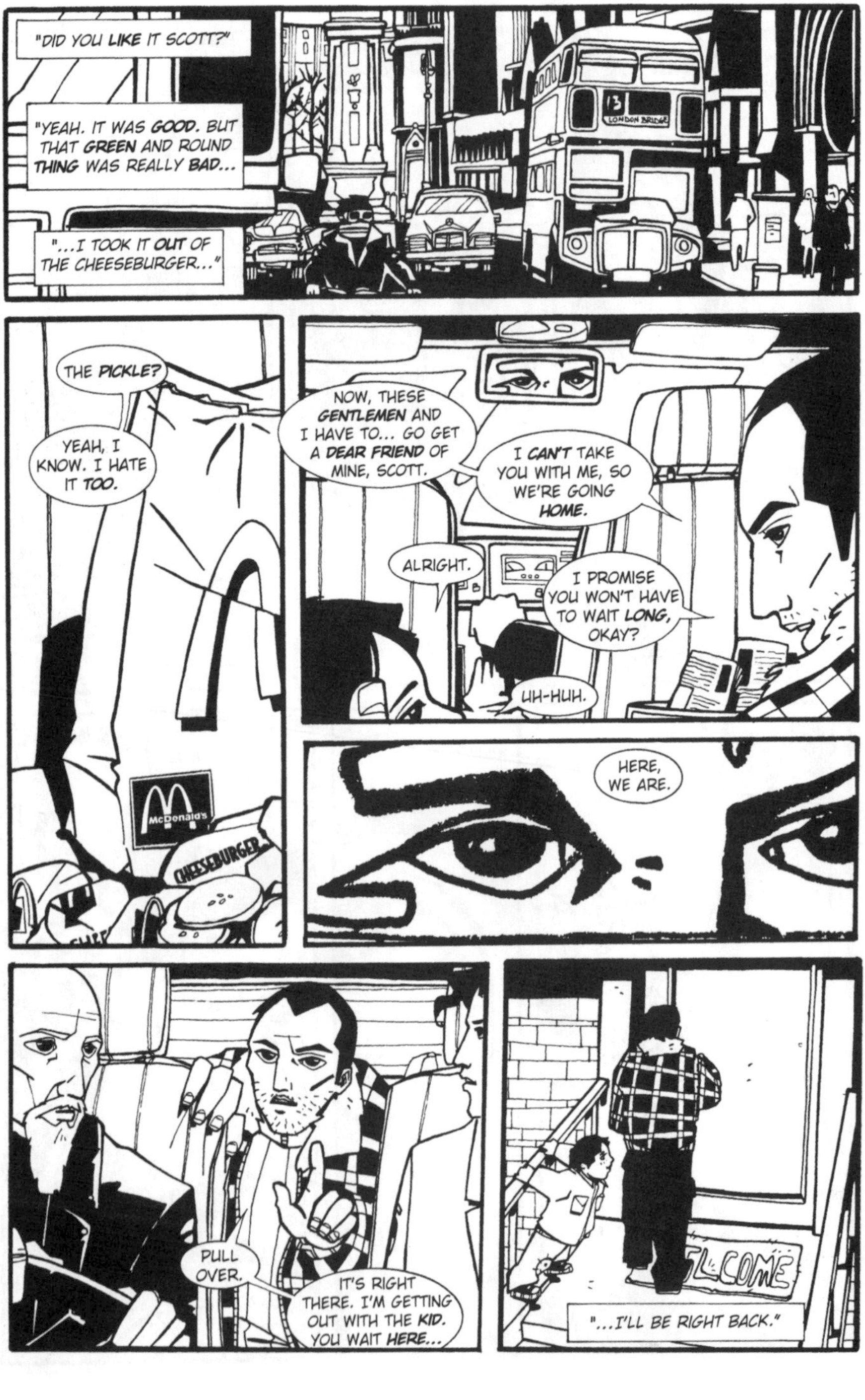
"DID YOU LIKE IT SCOTT?"
"YEAH. IT WAS GOOD. BUT THAT GREEN AND ROUND THING WAS REALLY BAD...
"...I TOOK IT OUT OF THE CHEESEBURGER..."
13
LONDON BRIDGE
THE PICKLE?
YEAH, I KNOW. I HATE IT TOO.
McDonald's
CHEESEBURGER
NOW, THESE GENTLEMEN AND I HAVE TO... GO GET A DEAR FRIEND OF MINE, SCOTT.
I CAN'T TAKE YOU WITH ME, SO WE'RE GOING HOME.
ALRIGHT.
I PROMISE YOU WON'T HAVE TO WAIT LONG, OKAY?
UH-HUH.
HERE, WE ARE.
PULL OVER.
IT'S RIGHT THERE. I'M GETTING OUT WITH THE KID. YOU WAIT HERE...
LCOME
"...I'LL BE RIGHT BACK."

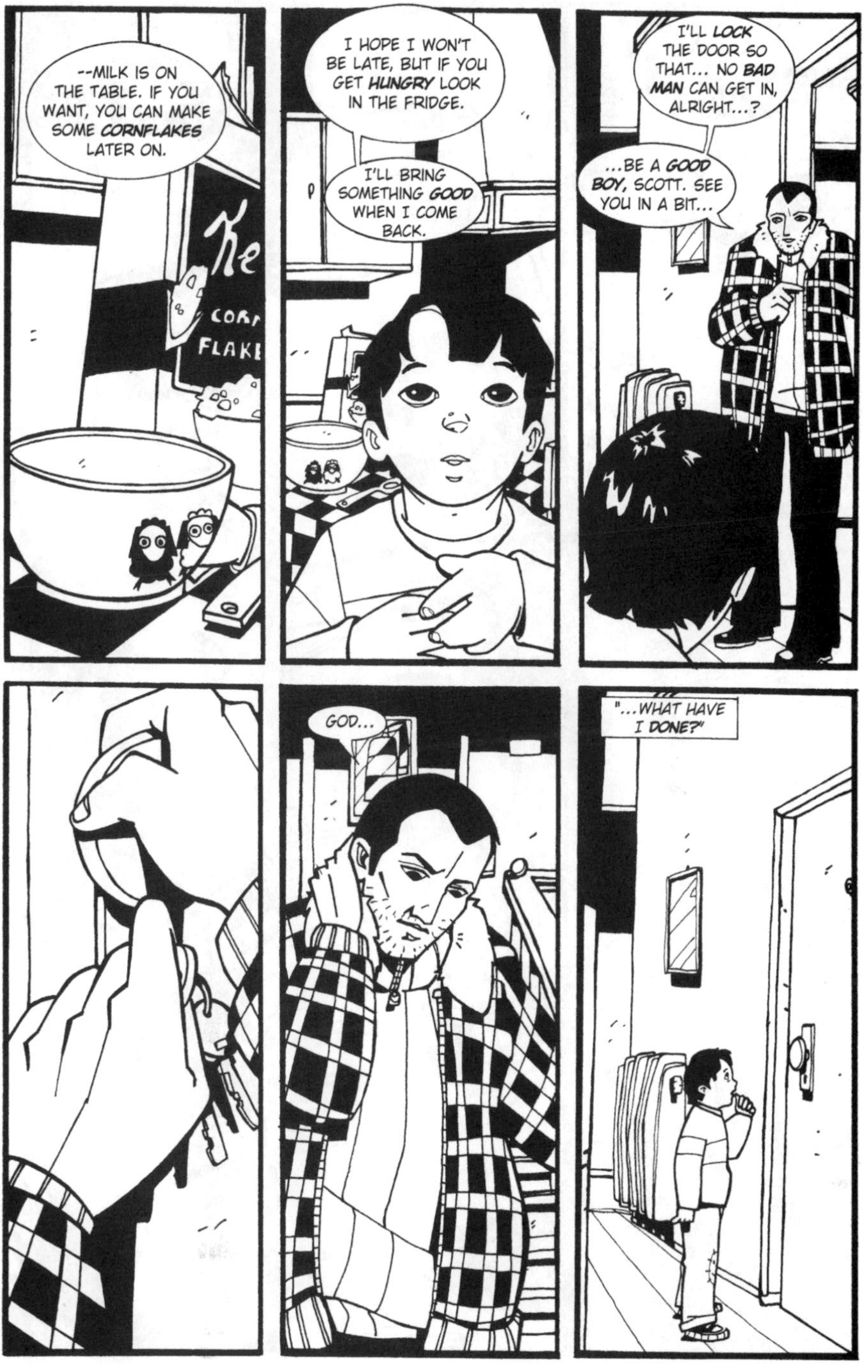
--MILK IS ON THE TABLE. IF YOU WANT, YOU CAN MAKE SOME CORNFLAKES LATER ON.
I HOPE I WON'T BE LATE, BUT IF YOU GET HUNGRY LOOK IN THE FRIDGE.
I'LL BRING SOMETHING GOOD WHEN I COME BACK.
I'LL LOCK THE DOOR SO THAT... NO BAD MAN CAN GET IN, ALRIGHT...?
...BE A GOOD BOY, SCOTT. SEE YOU IN A BIT...
GOD...
"...WHAT HAVE I DONE?"

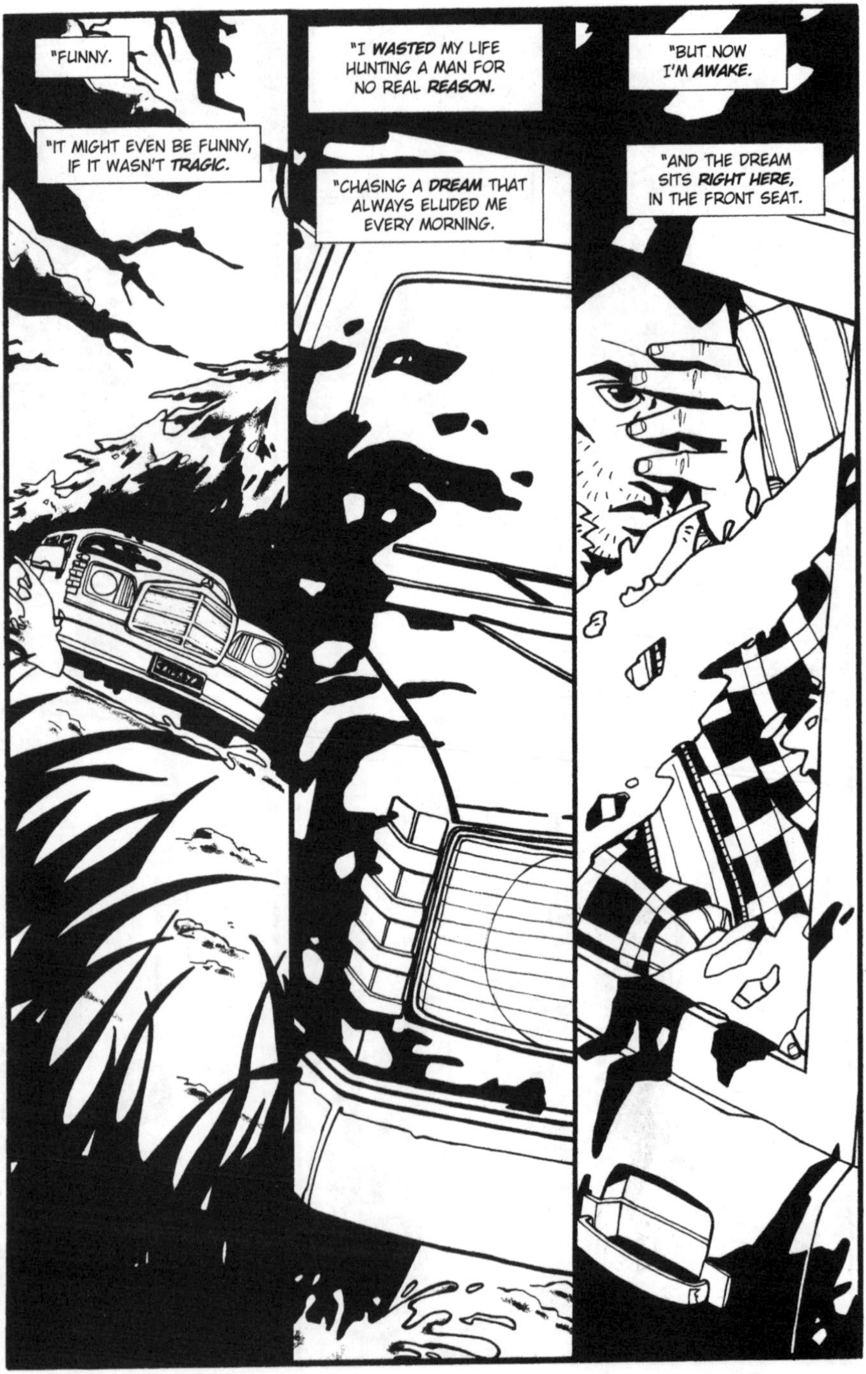
"FUNNY.
"IT MIGHT EVEN BE FUNNY, IF IT WASN'T TRAGIC.
"I WASTED MY LIFE HUNTING A MAN FOR NO REAL REASON.
"CHASING A DREAM THAT ALWAYS ELUDED ME EVERY MORNING.
"BUT NOW I'M AWAKE.
"AND THE DREAM SITS RIGHT HERE, IN THE FRONT SEAT.

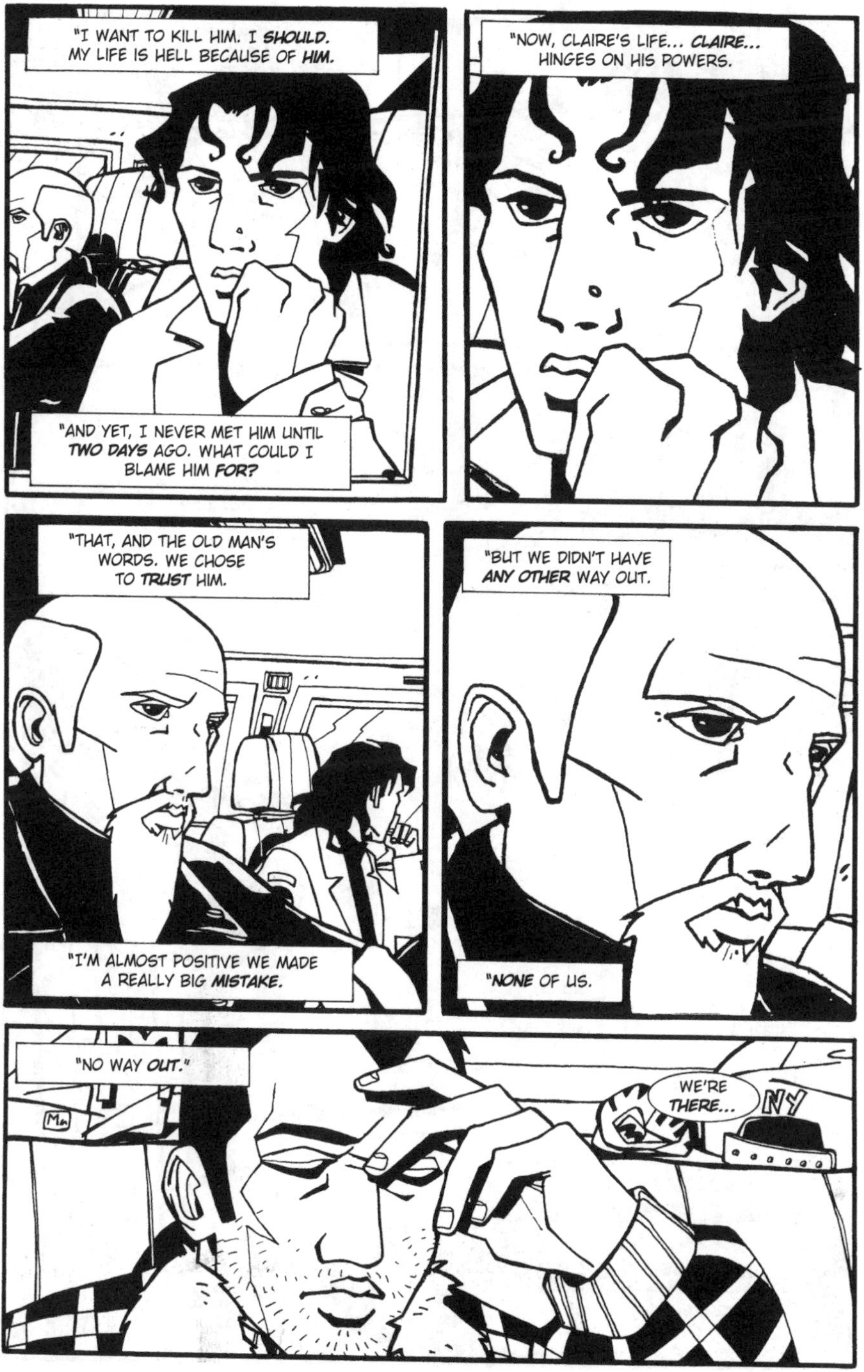
"I WANT TO KILL HIM. I SHOULD. MY LIFE IS HELL BECAUSE OF HIM.
"AND YET, I NEVER MET HIM UNTIL TWO DAYS AGO. WHAT COULD I BLAME HIM FOR?
"NOW, CLAIRE'S LIFE... CLAIRE... HINGES ON HIS POWERS.
"THAT, AND THE OLD MAN'S WORDS. WE CHOSE TO TRUST HIM.
"I'M ALMOST POSITIVE WE MADE A REALLY BIG MISTAKE.
"BUT WE DIDN'T HAVE ANY OTHER WAY OUT.
"NONE OF US.
"NO WAY OUT."
WE'RE THERE...
NY

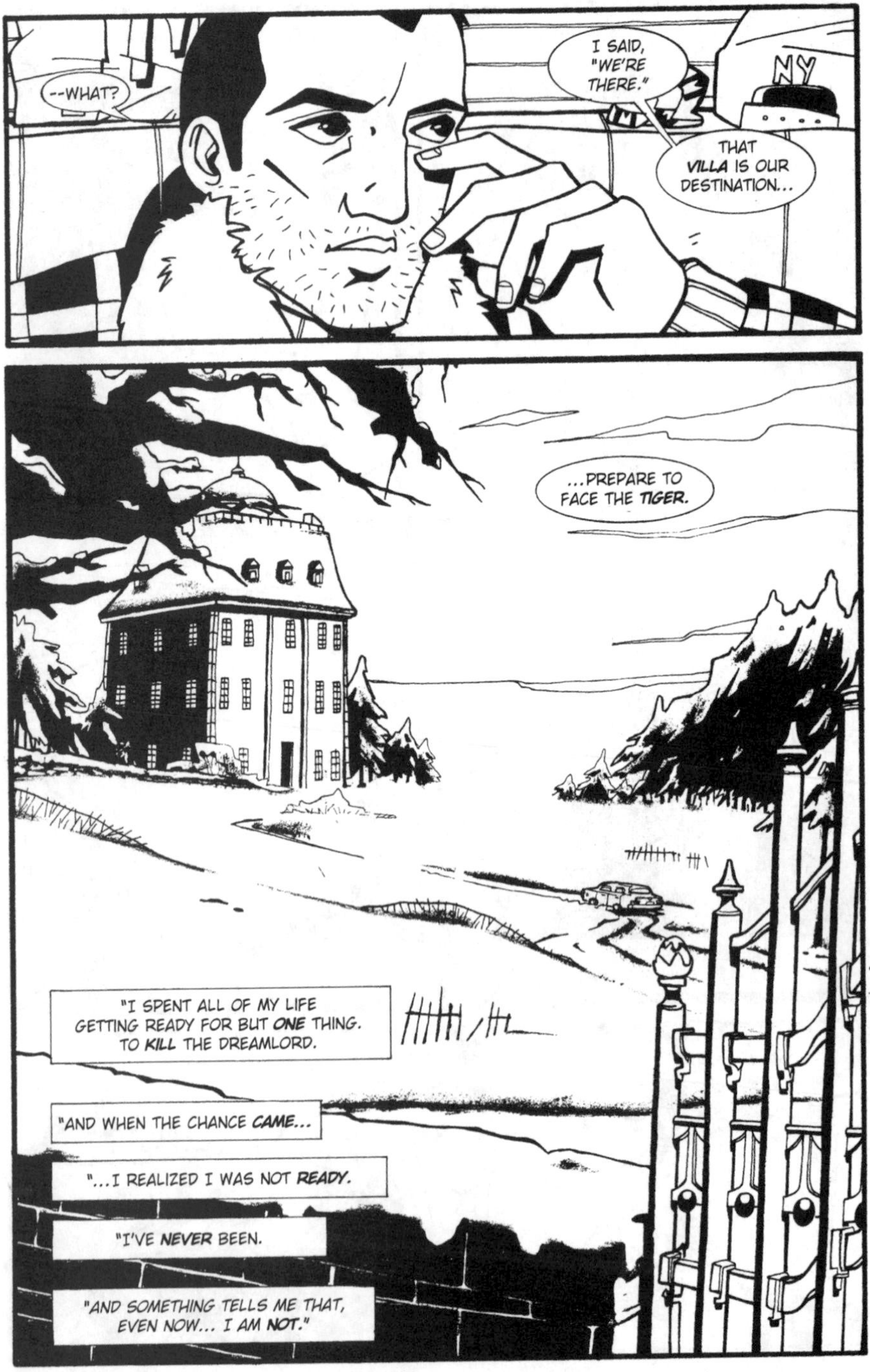
--WHAT?
I SAID, "WE'RE THERE."
THAT VILLA IS OUR DESTINATION...
...PREPARE TO FACE THE TIGER.
"I SPENT ALL OF MY LIFE GETTING READY FOR BUT ONE THING. TO KILL THE DREAMLORD.
"AND WHEN THE CHANCE CAME...
"...I REALIZED I WAS NOT READY.
"I'VE NEVER BEEN.
"AND SOMETHING TELLS ME THAT, EVEN NOW... I AM NOT."

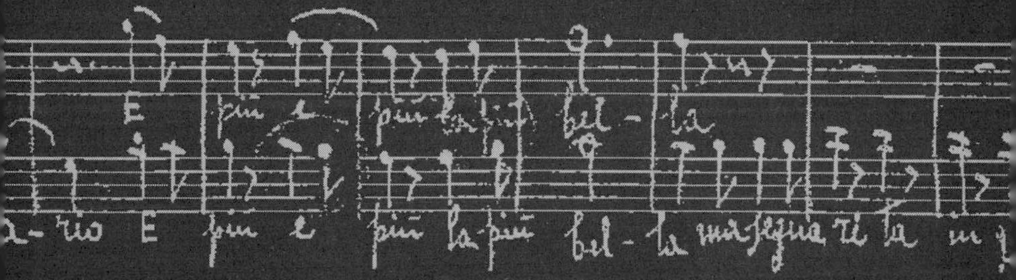

chapter five

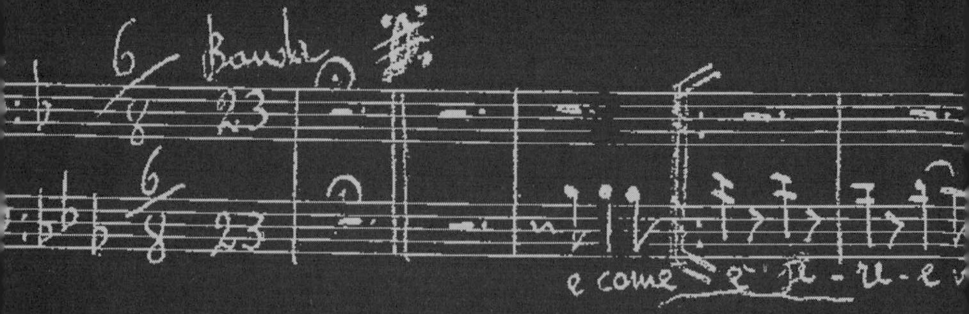
e come

Story
MATTEO CASALI

Art
ALESSANDRO DeANGELIS

TWENTY MINUTES AGO.

SHE SPOKE, **SOFTLY.**
HE BREATHED, **HEAVILY.**

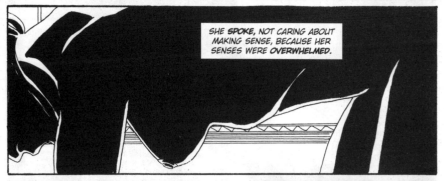

SHE **SPOKE,** NOT CARING ABOUT MAKING SENSE, BECAUSE HER SENSES WERE **OVERWHELMED.**

COMPLETELY OVERWHELMED.

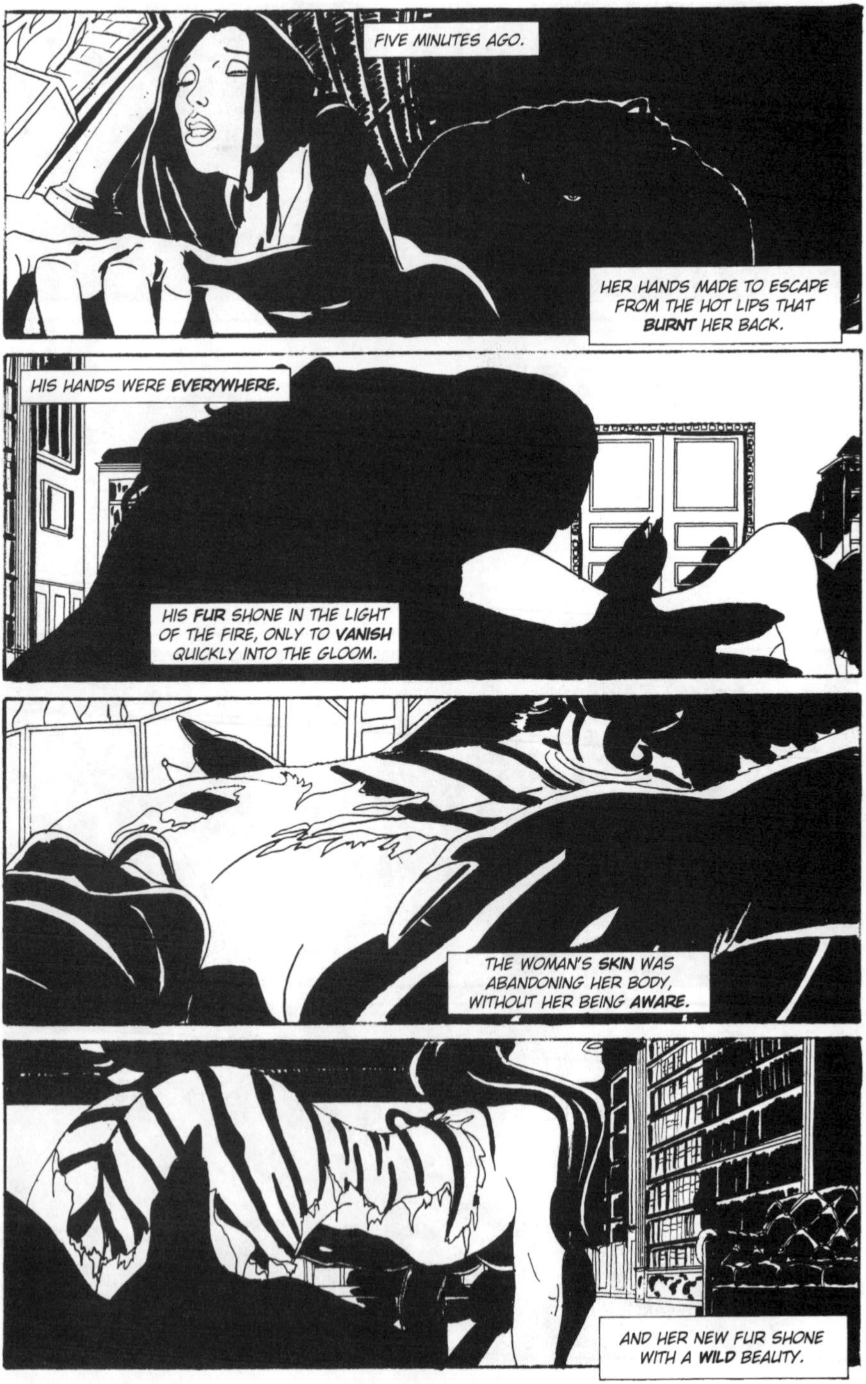
FIVE MINUTES AGO.
HER HANDS MADE TO ESCAPE FROM THE HOT LIPS THAT **BURNT** HER BACK.
HIS HANDS WERE **EVERYWHERE.**
HIS **FUR** SHONE IN THE LIGHT OF THE FIRE, ONLY TO **VANISH** QUICKLY INTO THE GLOOM.
THE WOMAN'S **SKIN** WAS ABANDONING HER BODY, WITHOUT HER BEING **AWARE.**
AND HER NEW FUR SHONE WITH A **WILD** BEAUTY.

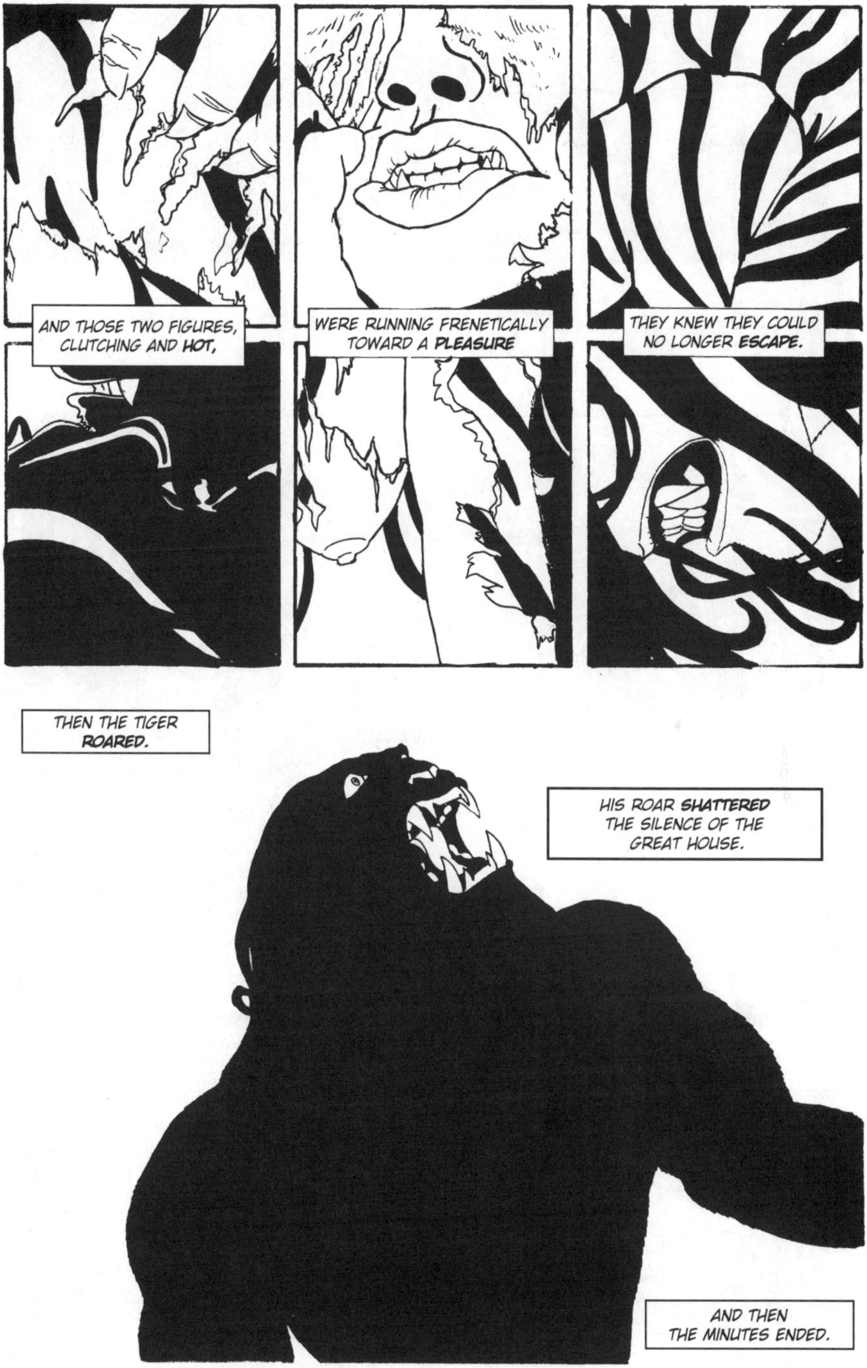
AND THOSE TWO FIGURES, CLUTCHING AND HOT,
WERE RUNNING FRENETICALLY TOWARD A PLEASURE
THEY KNEW THEY COULD NO LONGER ESCAPE.
THEN THE TIGER ROARED.
HIS ROAR SHATTERED THE SILENCE OF THE GREAT HOUSE.
AND THEN THE MINUTES ENDED.

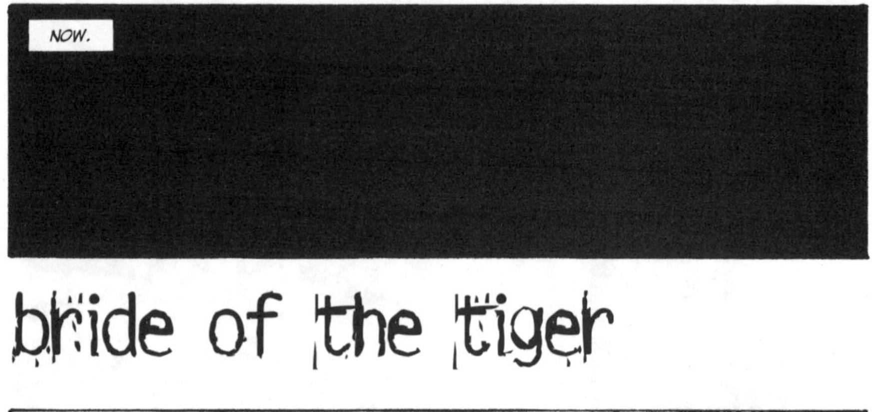
NOW.

bride of the tiger

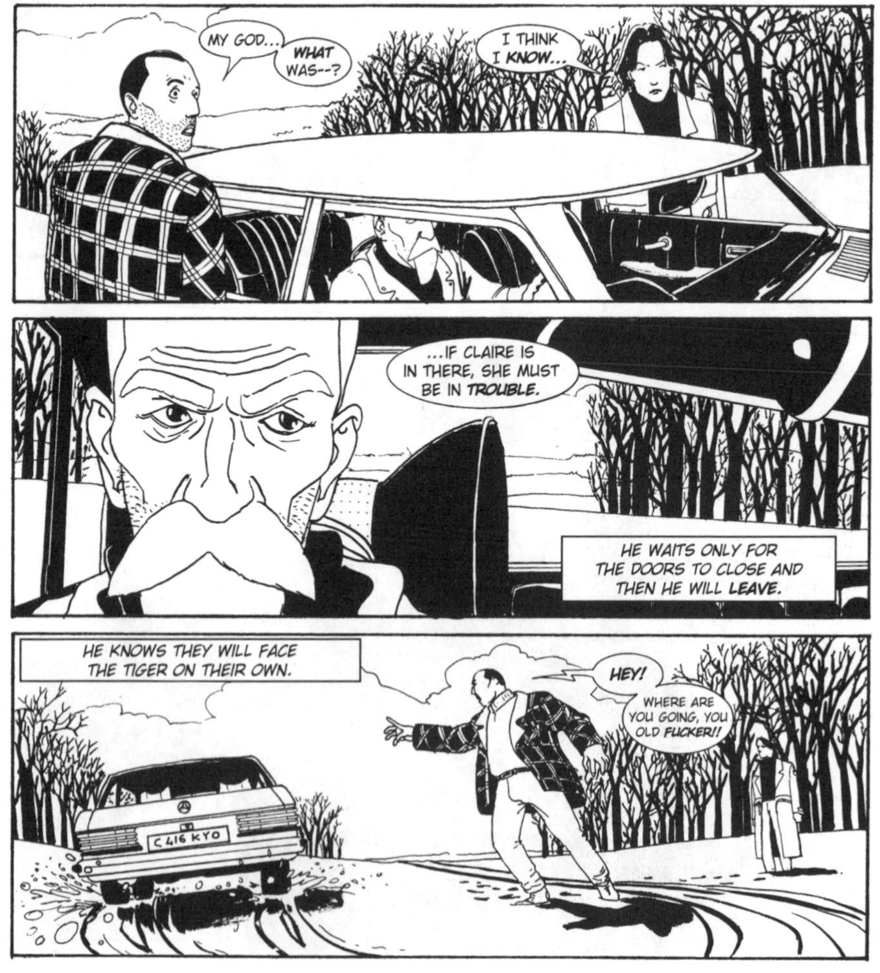
MY GOD... WHAT WAS--?
I THINK I KNOW...
...IF CLAIRE IS IN THERE, SHE MUST BE IN TROUBLE.
HE WAITS ONLY FOR THE DOORS TO CLOSE AND THEN HE WILL LEAVE.
HE KNOWS THEY WILL FACE THE TIGER ON THEIR OWN.
HEY!
WHERE ARE YOU GOING, YOU OLD FUCKER!!
C 416 KYO

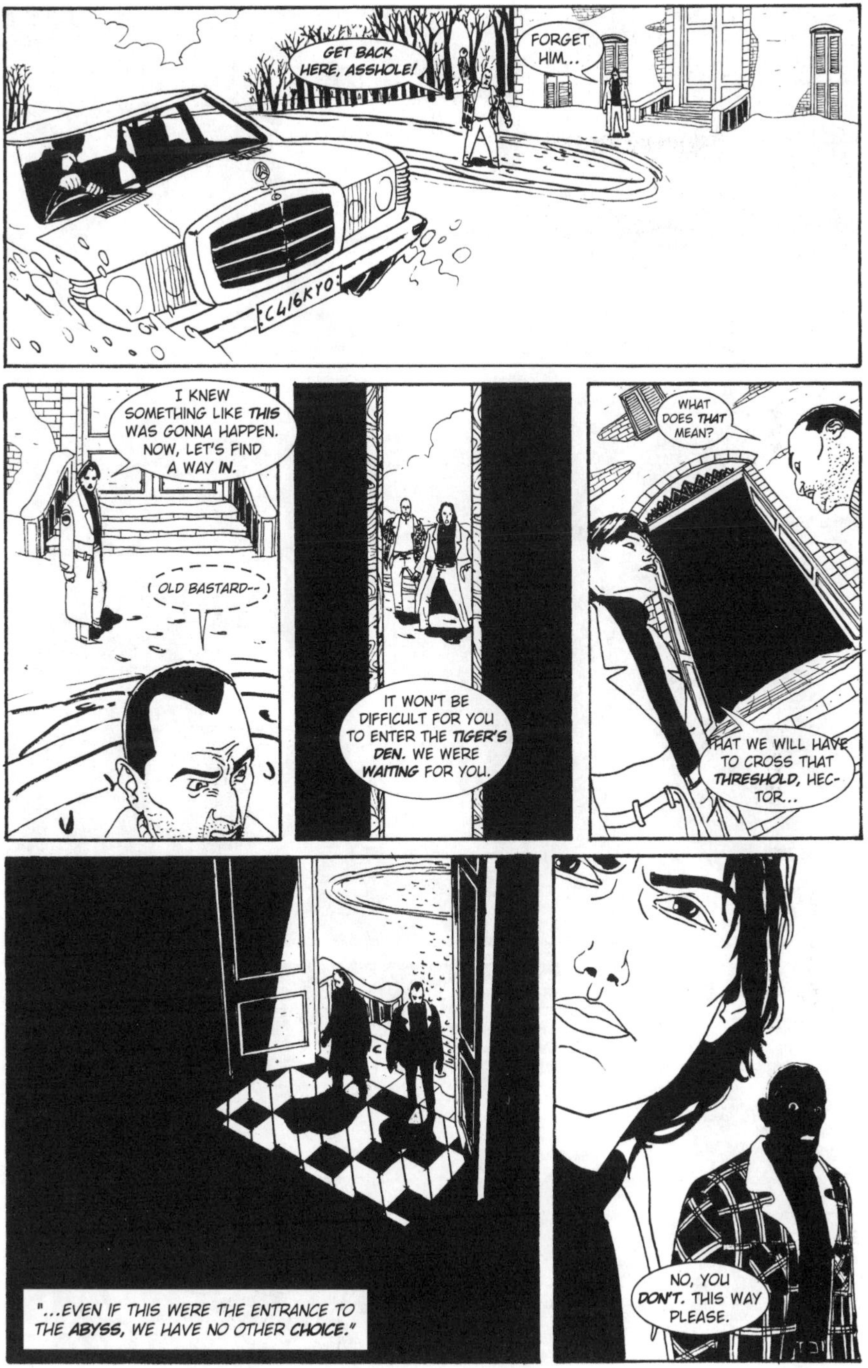
GET BACK HERE, ASSHOLE!
FORGET HIM...
C416KYO
I KNEW SOMETHING LIKE THIS WAS GONNA HAPPEN. NOW, LET'S FIND A WAY IN.
OLD BASTARD--
IT WON'T BE DIFFICULT FOR YOU TO ENTER THE TIGER'S DEN. WE WERE WAITING FOR YOU.
WHAT DOES THAT MEAN?
THAT WE WILL HAVE TO CROSS THAT THRESHOLD, HEC-TOR...
"...EVEN IF THIS WERE THE ENTRANCE TO THE ABYSS, WE HAVE NO OTHER CHOICE."
NO, YOU DON'T. THIS WAY PLEASE.

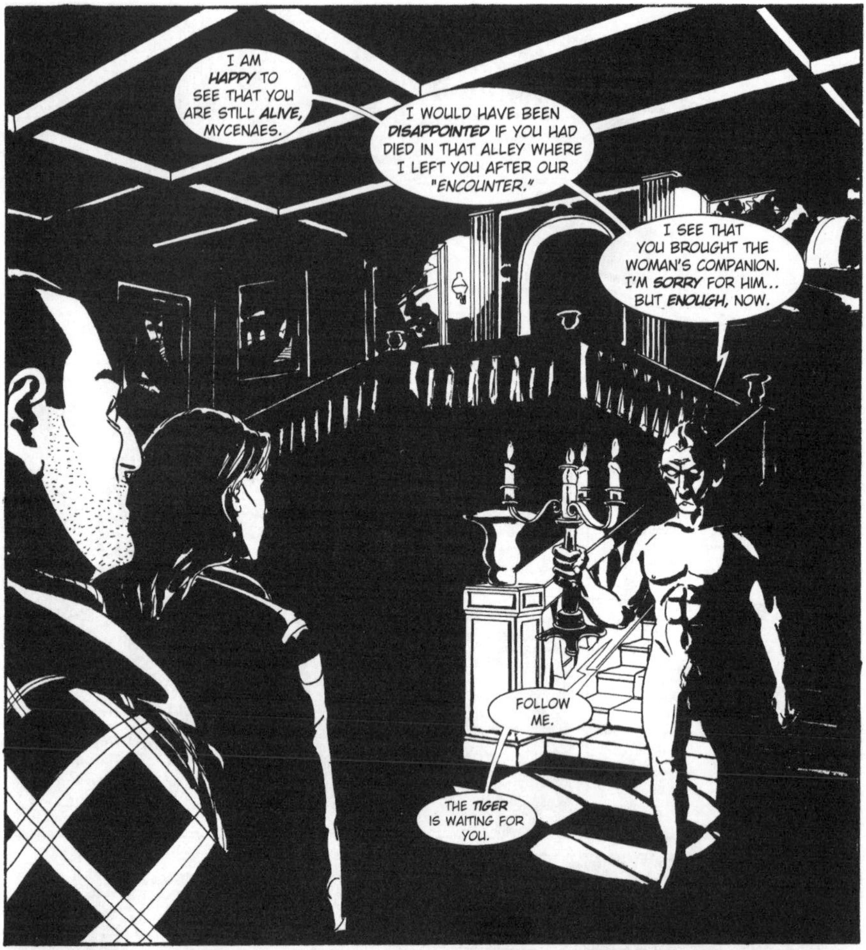
I AM HAPPY TO SEE THAT YOU ARE STILL ALIVE, MYCENAES.
I WOULD HAVE BEEN DISAPPOINTED IF YOU HAD DIED IN THAT ALLEY WHERE I LEFT YOU AFTER OUR "ENCOUNTER."
I SEE THAT YOU BROUGHT THE WOMAN'S COMPANION. I'M SORRY FOR HIM... BUT ENOUGH, NOW.
FOLLOW ME.
THE TIGER IS WAITING FOR YOU.

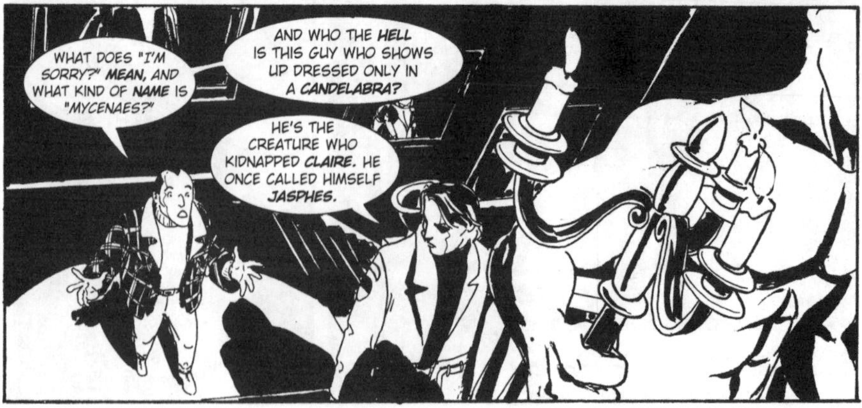
WHAT DOES "I'M SORRY?" MEAN, AND WHAT KIND OF NAME IS "MYCENAES?"
AND WHO THE HELL IS THIS GUY WHO SHOWS UP DRESSED ONLY IN A CANDELABRA?
HE'S THE CREATURE WHO KIDNAPPED CLAIRE. HE ONCE CALLED HIMSELF JASPHES.

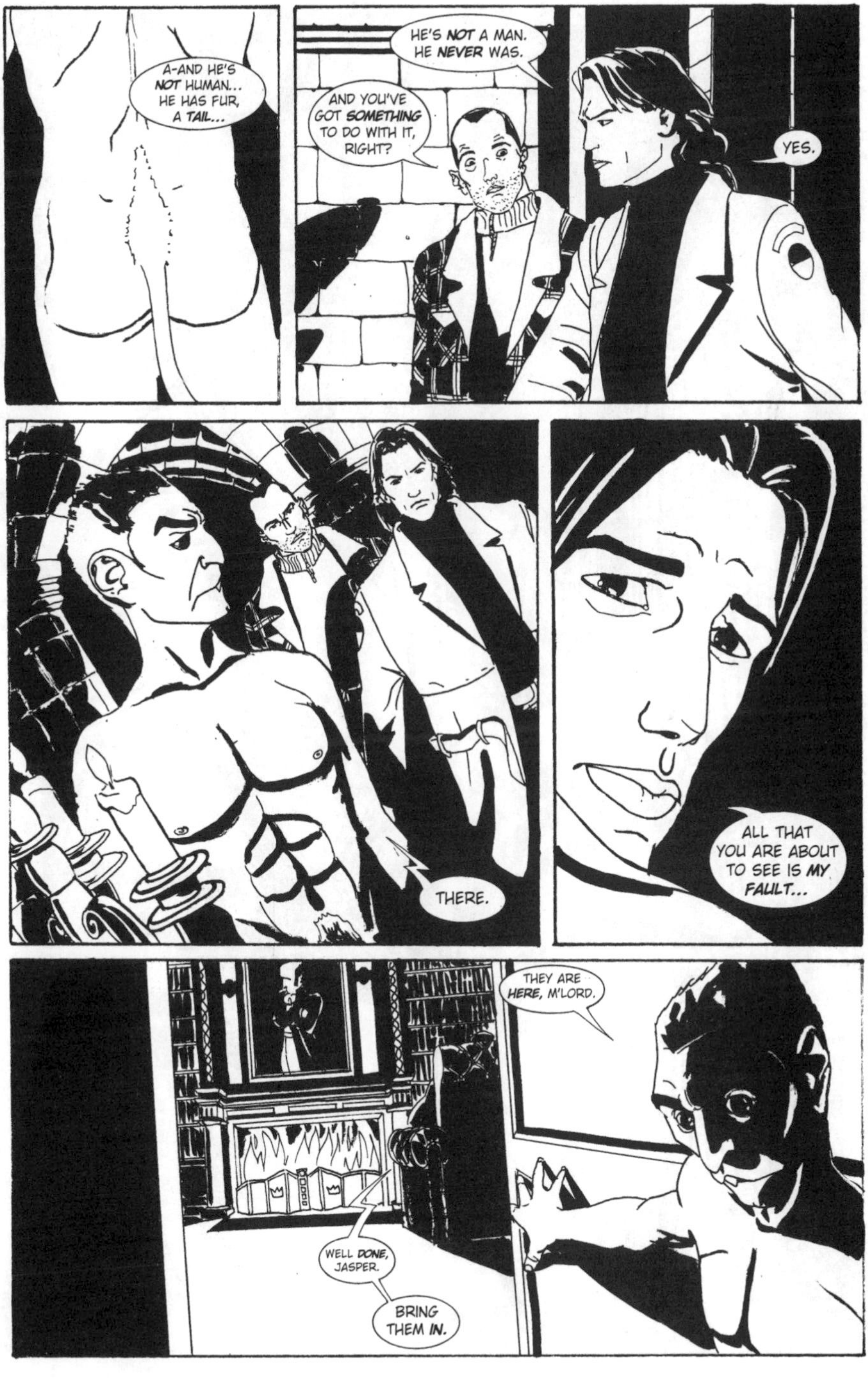
A-AND HE'S **NOT** HUMAN... HE HAS FUR, A **TAIL...**
HE'S **NOT** A MAN. HE **NEVER** WAS.
AND YOU'VE GOT **SOMETHING** TO DO WITH IT, RIGHT?
YES.
THERE.
ALL THAT YOU ARE ABOUT TO SEE IS **MY FAULT...**
THEY ARE **HERE,** M'LORD.
WELL **DONE,** JASPER.
BRING THEM **IN.**

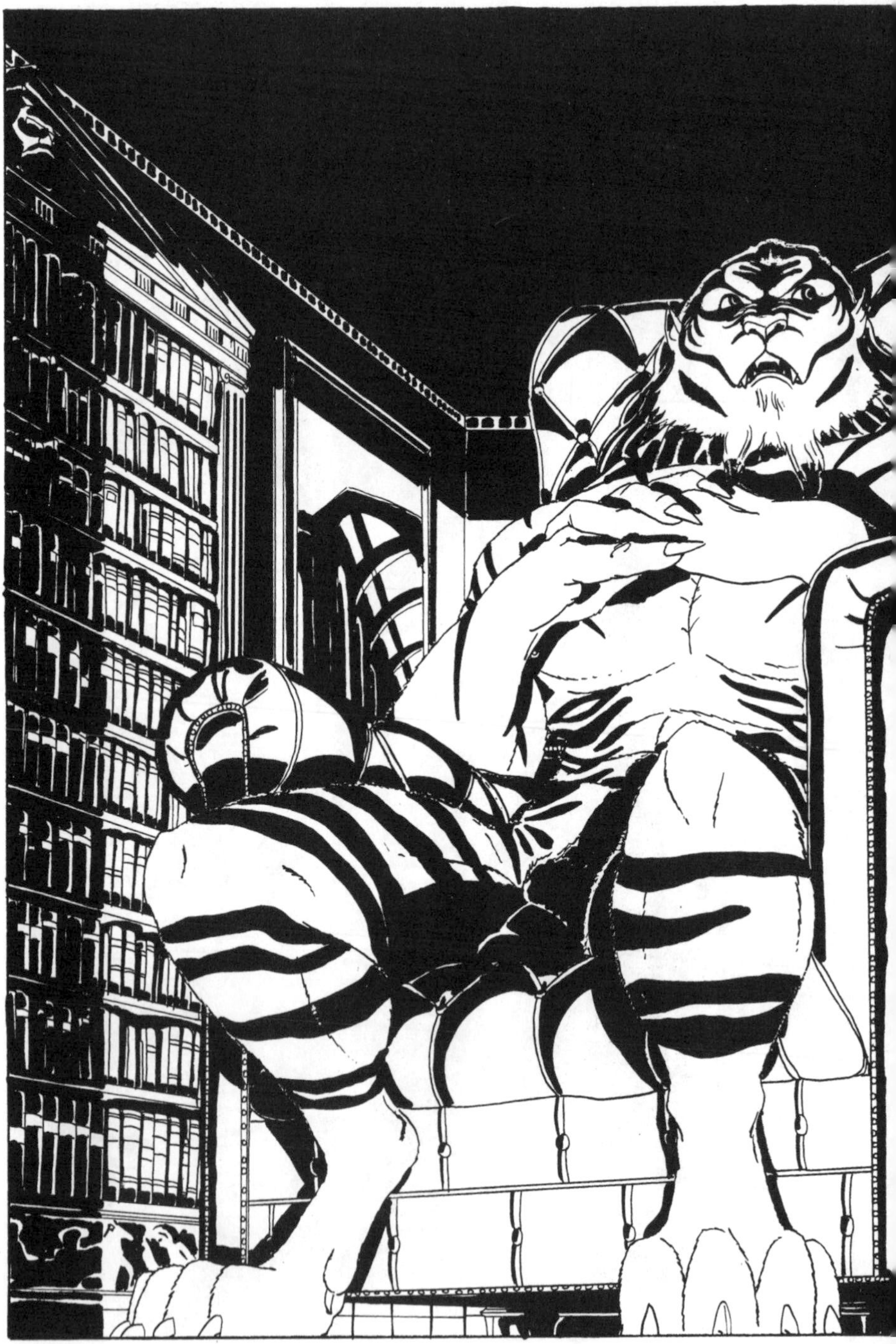

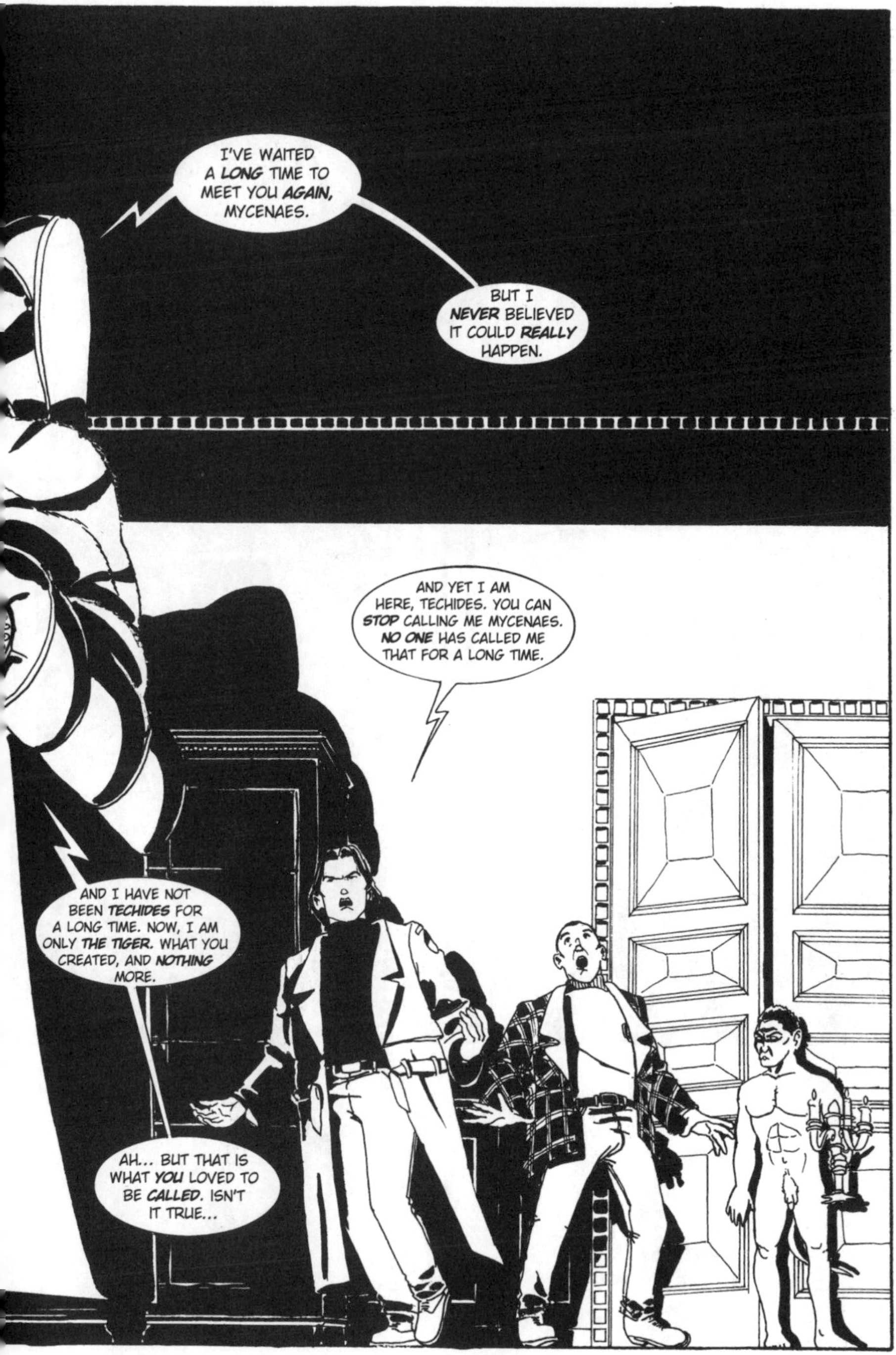

I'VE WAITED A LONG TIME TO MEET YOU AGAIN, MYCENAES.
BUT I NEVER BELIEVED IT COULD REALLY HAPPEN.
AND YET I AM HERE, TECHIDES. YOU CAN STOP CALLING ME MYCENAES. NO ONE HAS CALLED ME THAT FOR A LONG TIME.
AND I HAVE NOT BEEN TECHIDES FOR A LONG TIME. NOW, I AM ONLY THE TIGER. WHAT YOU CREATED, AND NOTHING MORE.
AH... BUT THAT IS WHAT YOU LOVED TO BE CALLED. ISN'T IT TRUE...

...CREATOR?

CREATOR? HOLD IT...

...WHAT THE *HELL* DOES THIS MEAN? WHERE IS *CLAIRE*?

I AM *HERE*, HECTOR. BEHIND YOU.

I AM *ALMOST* HAPPY TO SEE YOU HERE. THIS *CLUMSY* ATTEMPT TO *SAVE ME* WOULD HAVE MADE ME HAPPY, *ONCE*.

BUT IT'S *TOO* LATE.

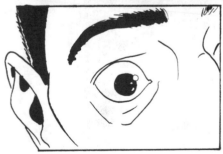

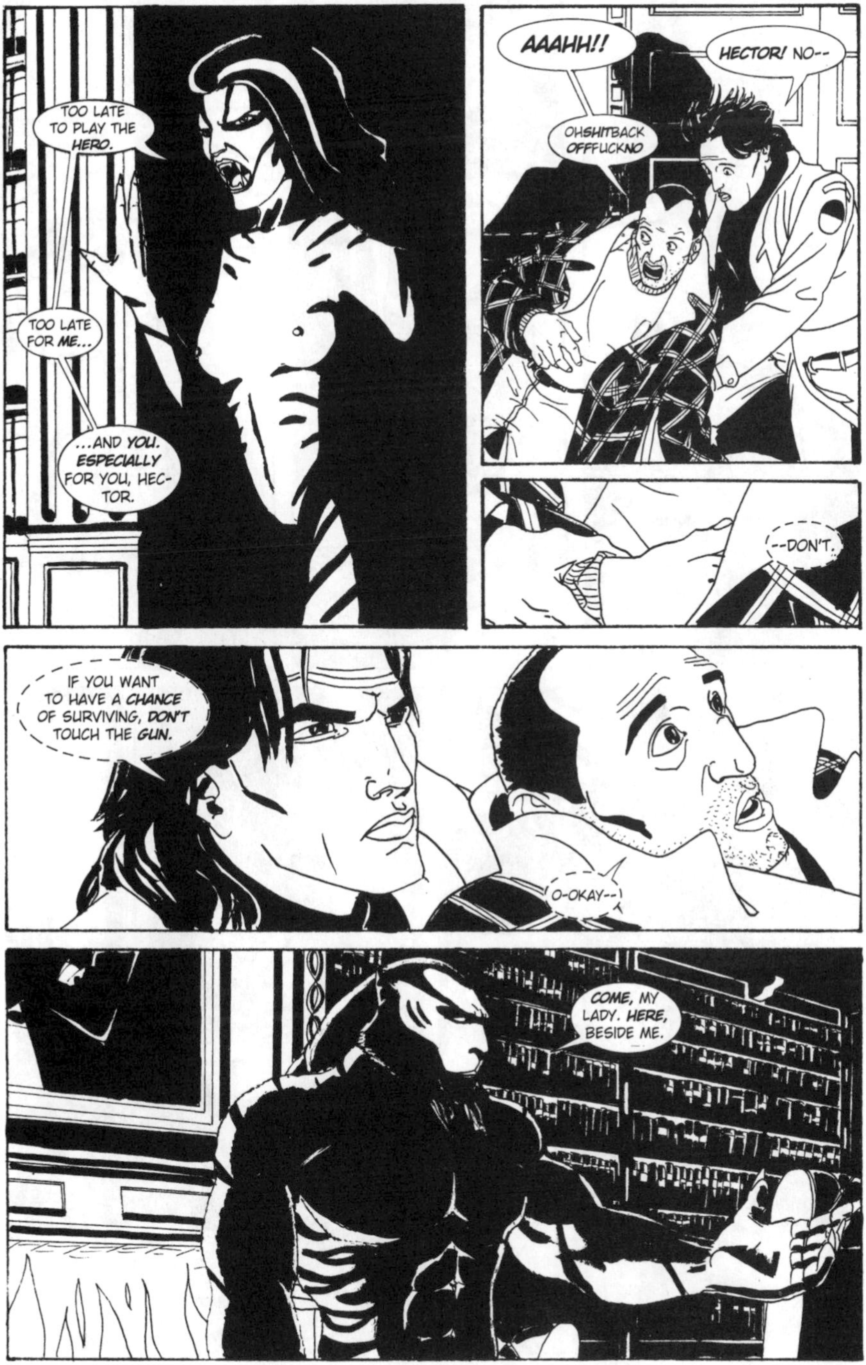
TOO LATE TO PLAY THE HERO.
TOO LATE FOR ME...
...AND YOU. ESPECIALLY FOR YOU, HECTOR.
AAAHH!!
HECTOR! NO--
OHSHITBACK OFFFUCKNO
--DON'T.
IF YOU WANT TO HAVE A CHANCE OF SURVIVING, DON'T TOUCH THE GUN.
O-OKAY--
COME, MY LADY. HERE, BESIDE ME.

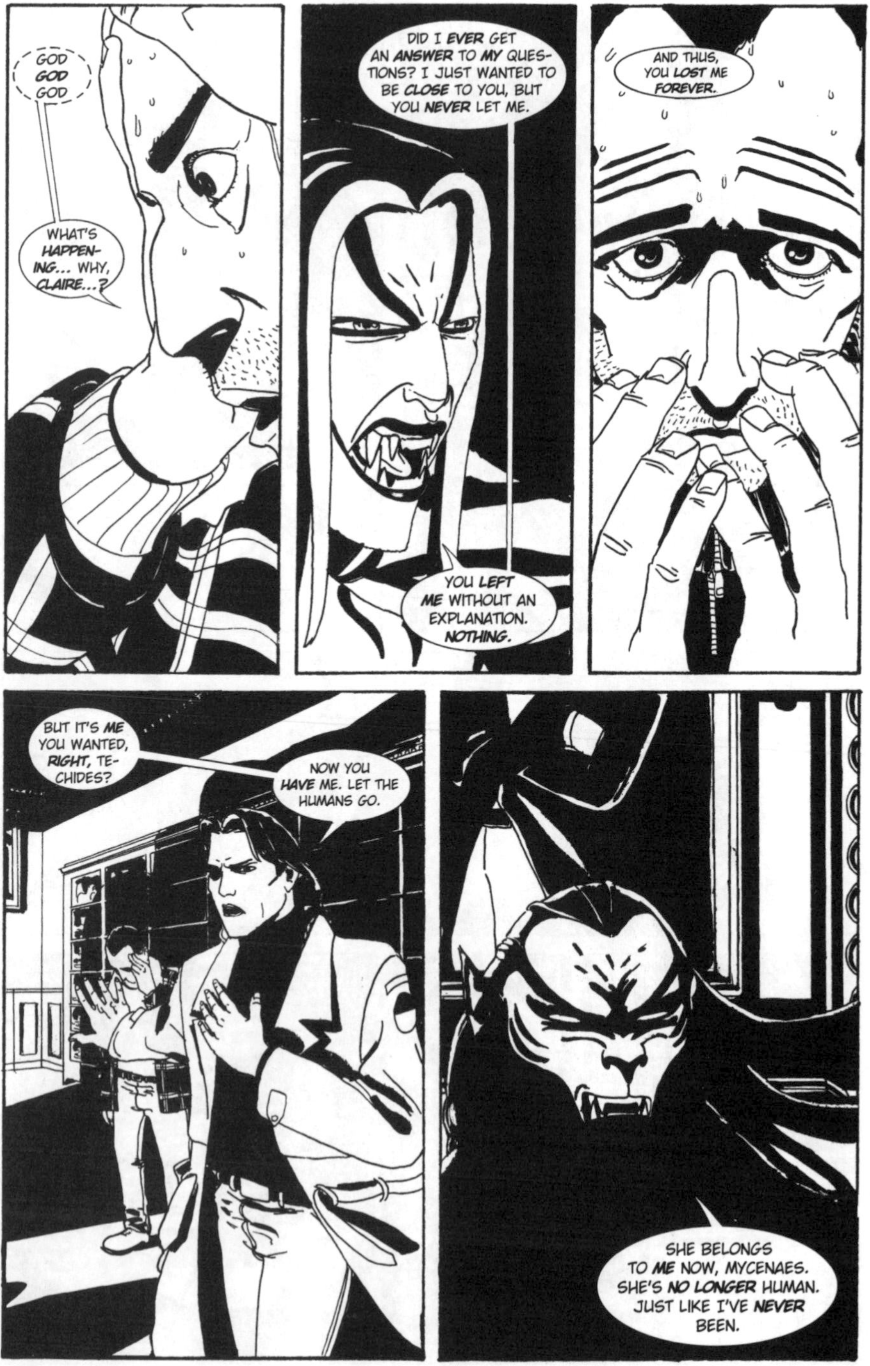
GOD GOD GOD
WHAT'S HAPPENING... WHY, CLAIRE...?
DID I EVER GET AN ANSWER TO MY QUESTIONS? I JUST WANTED TO BE CLOSE TO YOU, BUT YOU NEVER LET ME.
YOU LEFT ME WITHOUT AN EXPLANATION. NOTHING.
AND THUS, YOU LOST ME FOREVER.
BUT IT'S ME YOU WANTED, RIGHT, TECHIDES?
NOW YOU HAVE ME. LET THE HUMANS GO.
SHE BELONGS TO ME NOW, MYCENAES. SHE'S NO LONGER HUMAN. JUST LIKE I'VE NEVER BEEN.

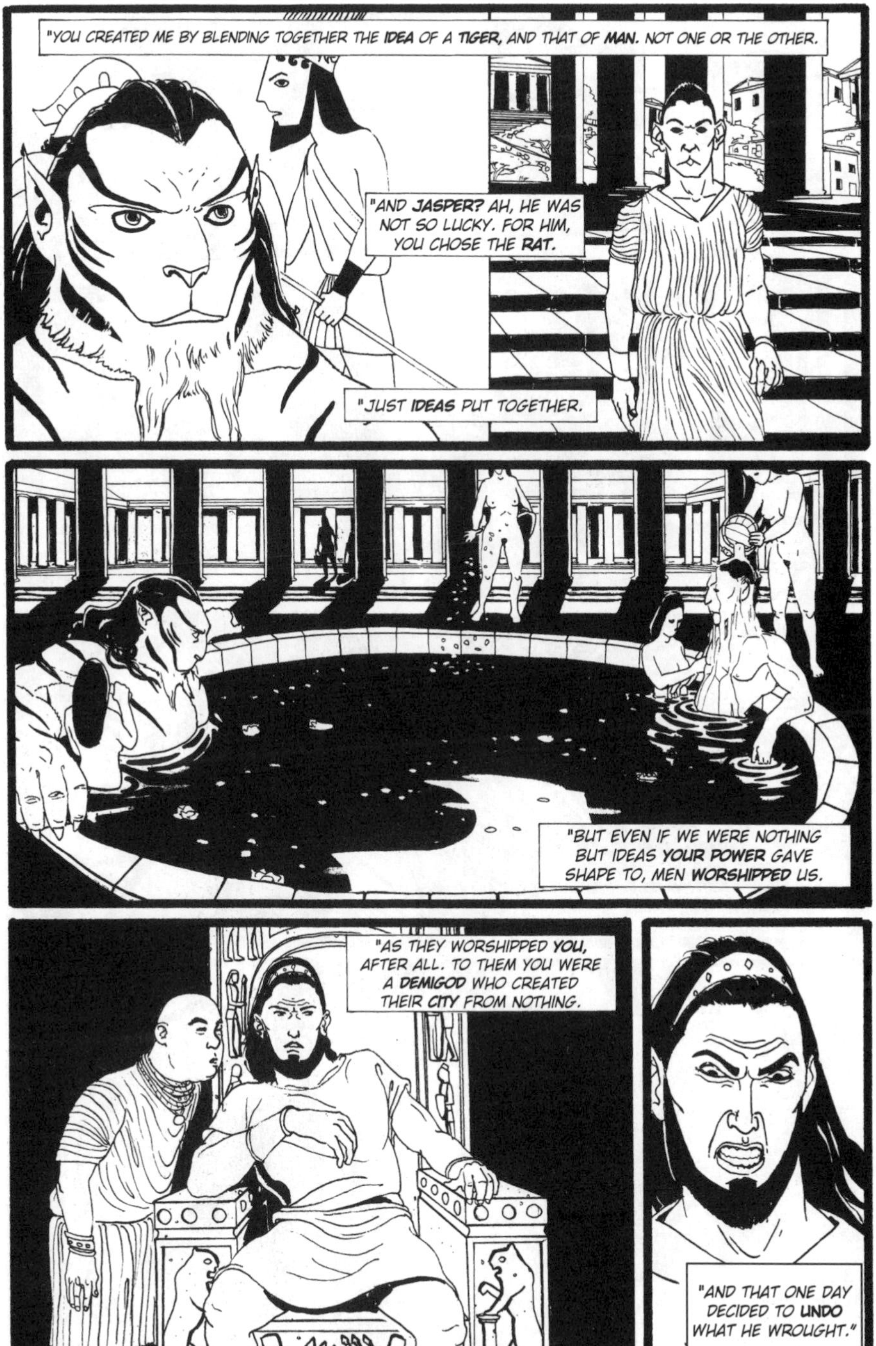
"YOU CREATED ME BY BLENDING TOGETHER THE IDEA OF A TIGER, AND THAT OF MAN. NOT ONE OR THE OTHER.
"AND JASPER? AH, HE WAS NOT SO LUCKY. FOR HIM, YOU CHOSE THE RAT.
"JUST IDEAS PUT TOGETHER.
"BUT EVEN IF WE WERE NOTHING BUT IDEAS YOUR POWER GAVE SHAPE TO, MEN WORSHIPPED US.
"AS THEY WORSHIPPED YOU, AFTER ALL. TO THEM YOU WERE A DEMIGOD WHO CREATED THEIR CITY FROM NOTHING.
"AND THAT ONE DAY DECIDED TO UNDO WHAT HE WROUGHT."

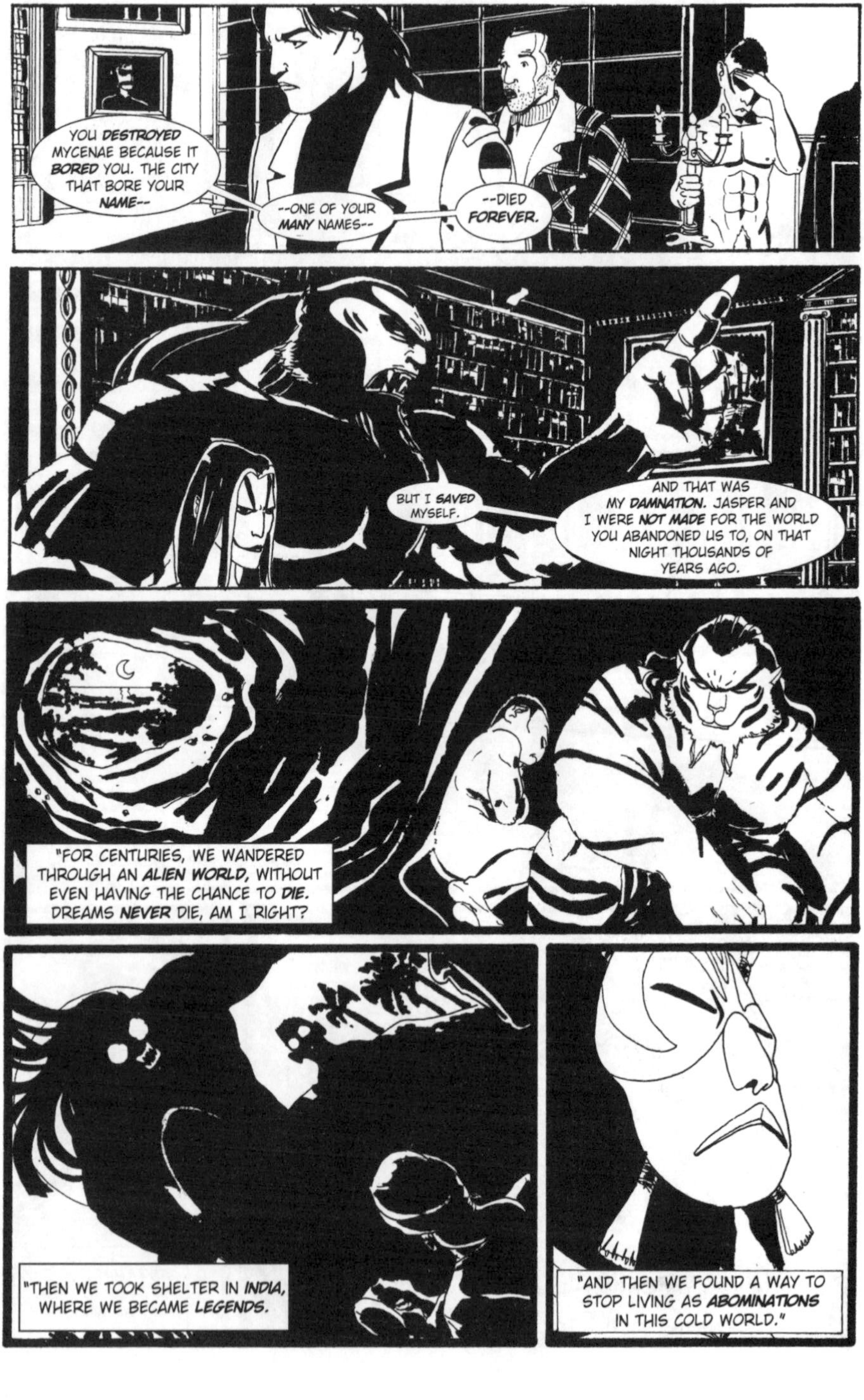

YOU DESTROYED MYCENAE BECAUSE IT BORED YOU. THE CITY THAT BORE YOUR NAME--
--ONE OF YOUR MANY NAMES--
--DIED FOREVER.
BUT I SAVED MYSELF.
AND THAT WAS MY DAMNATION. JASPER AND I WERE NOT MADE FOR THE WORLD YOU ABANDONED US TO, ON THAT NIGHT THOUSANDS OF YEARS AGO.
"FOR CENTURIES, WE WANDERED THROUGH AN ALIEN WORLD, WITHOUT EVEN HAVING THE CHANCE TO DIE. DREAMS NEVER DIE, AM I RIGHT?
"THEN WE TOOK SHELTER IN INDIA, WHERE WE BECAME LEGENDS.
"AND THEN WE FOUND A WAY TO STOP LIVING AS ABOMINATIONS IN THIS COLD WORLD."

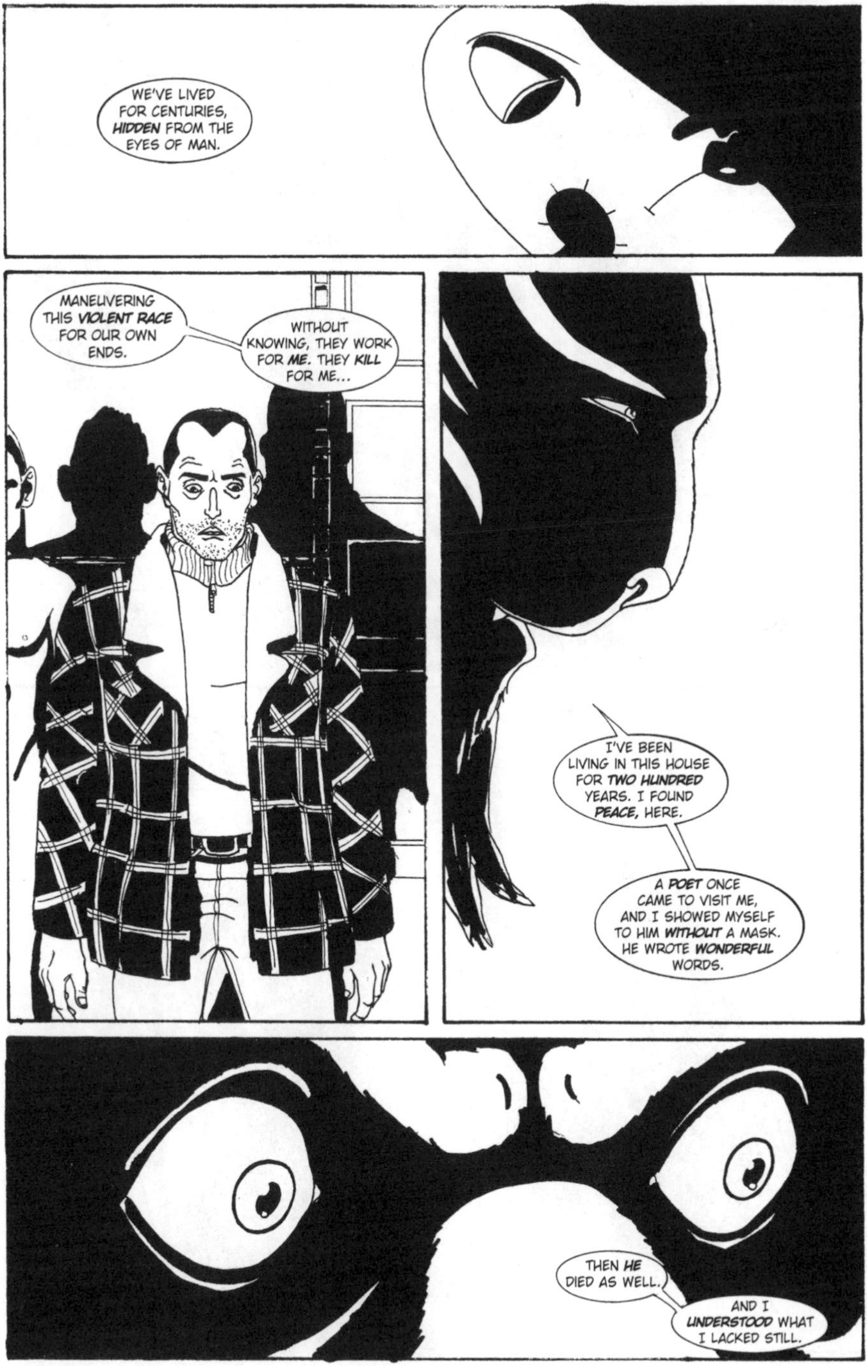

WE'VE LIVED FOR CENTURIES, HIDDEN FROM THE EYES OF MAN.
MANEUVERING THIS VIOLENT RACE FOR OUR OWN ENDS.
WITHOUT KNOWING, THEY WORK FOR ME. THEY KILL FOR ME...
I'VE BEEN LIVING IN THIS HOUSE FOR TWO HUNDRED YEARS. I FOUND PEACE, HERE.
A POET ONCE CAME TO VISIT ME, AND I SHOWED MYSELF TO HIM WITHOUT A MASK. HE WROTE WONDERFUL WORDS.
THEN HE DIED AS WELL.
AND I UNDERSTOOD WHAT I LACKED STILL.

I THOUGHT ONLY THE *CREATOR* COULD GIVE ME WHAT I *ALWAYS* WANTED.

A PARTNER. A *BRIDE*.

I SEARCHED FOR YOU FOR *AGES*.

AND I *HATED* YOU BECAUSE I COULDN'T FIND YOU. AND NOW THAT YOU'RE *HERE*...

...I *DON'T* NEED YOU ANYMORE.

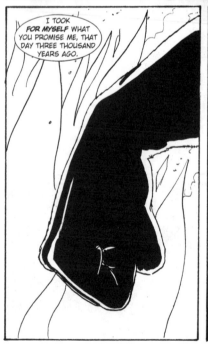

I TOOK *FOR MYSELF* WHAT YOU PROMISE ME, THAT DAY THREE THOUSAND YEARS AGO.

NOW YOU CAN... *MUST* DIE...

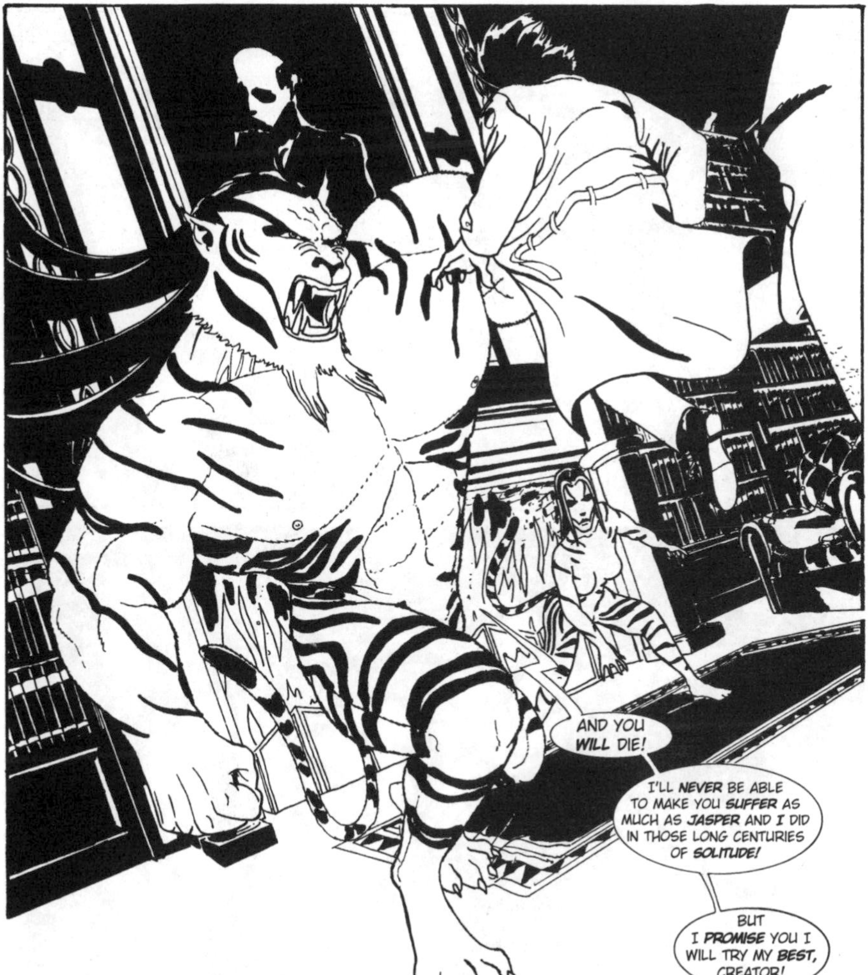
AND YOU WILL DIE!
I'LL NEVER BE ABLE TO MAKE YOU SUFFER AS MUCH AS JASPER AND I DID IN THOSE LONG CENTURIES OF SOLITUDE!
BUT I PROMISE YOU I WILL TRY MY BEST, CREATOR!

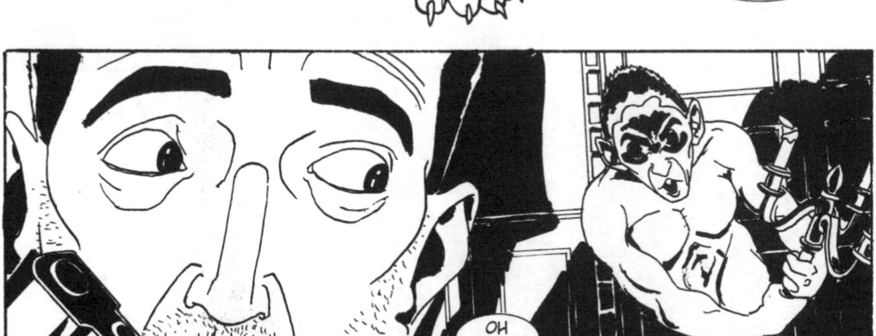
OH SHIT--

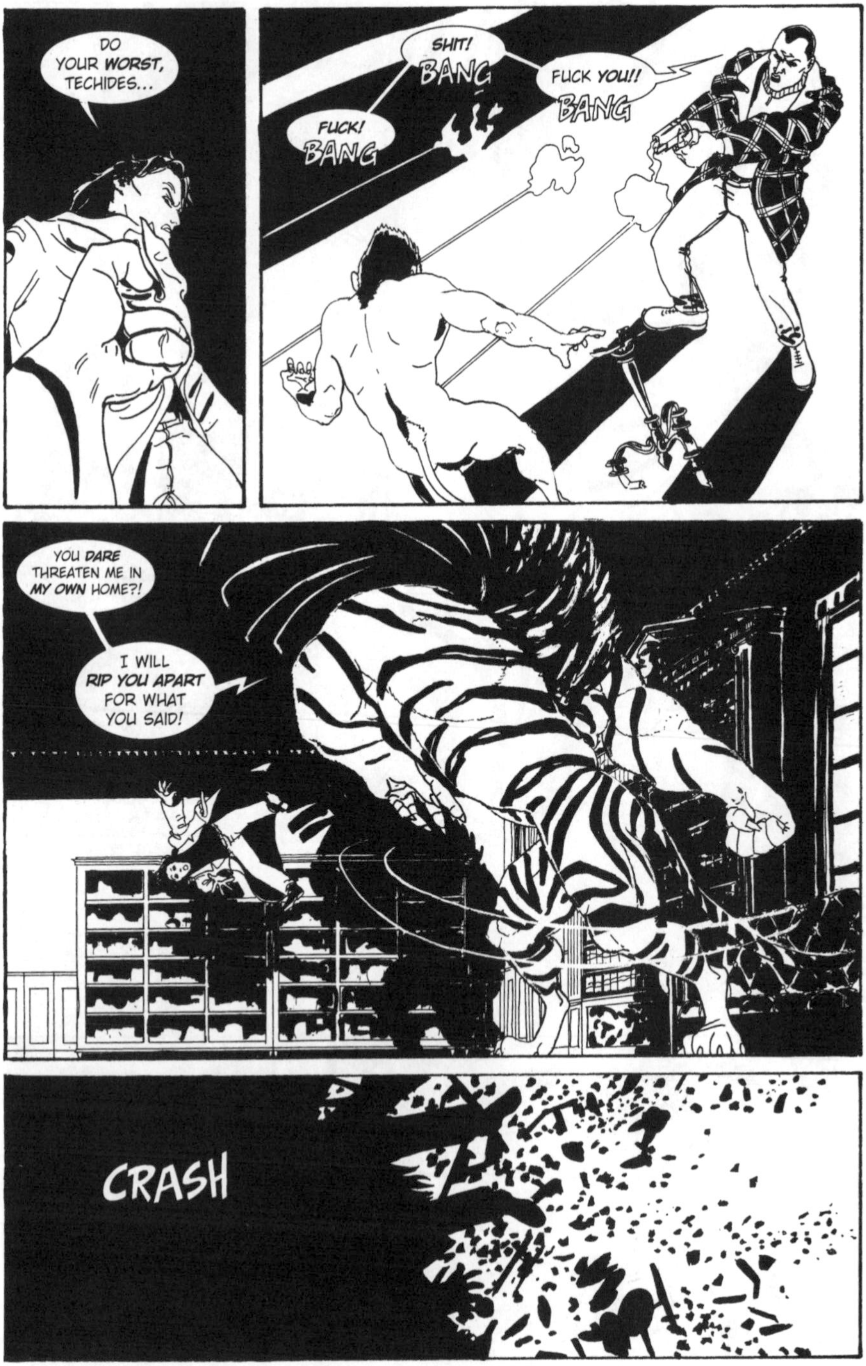
DO YOUR WORST, TECHIDES...
SHIT!
BANG
FUCK!
BANG
FUCK YOU!!
BANG
YOU DARE THREATEN ME IN MY OWN HOME?!
I WILL RIP YOU APART FOR WHAT YOU SAID!
CRASH

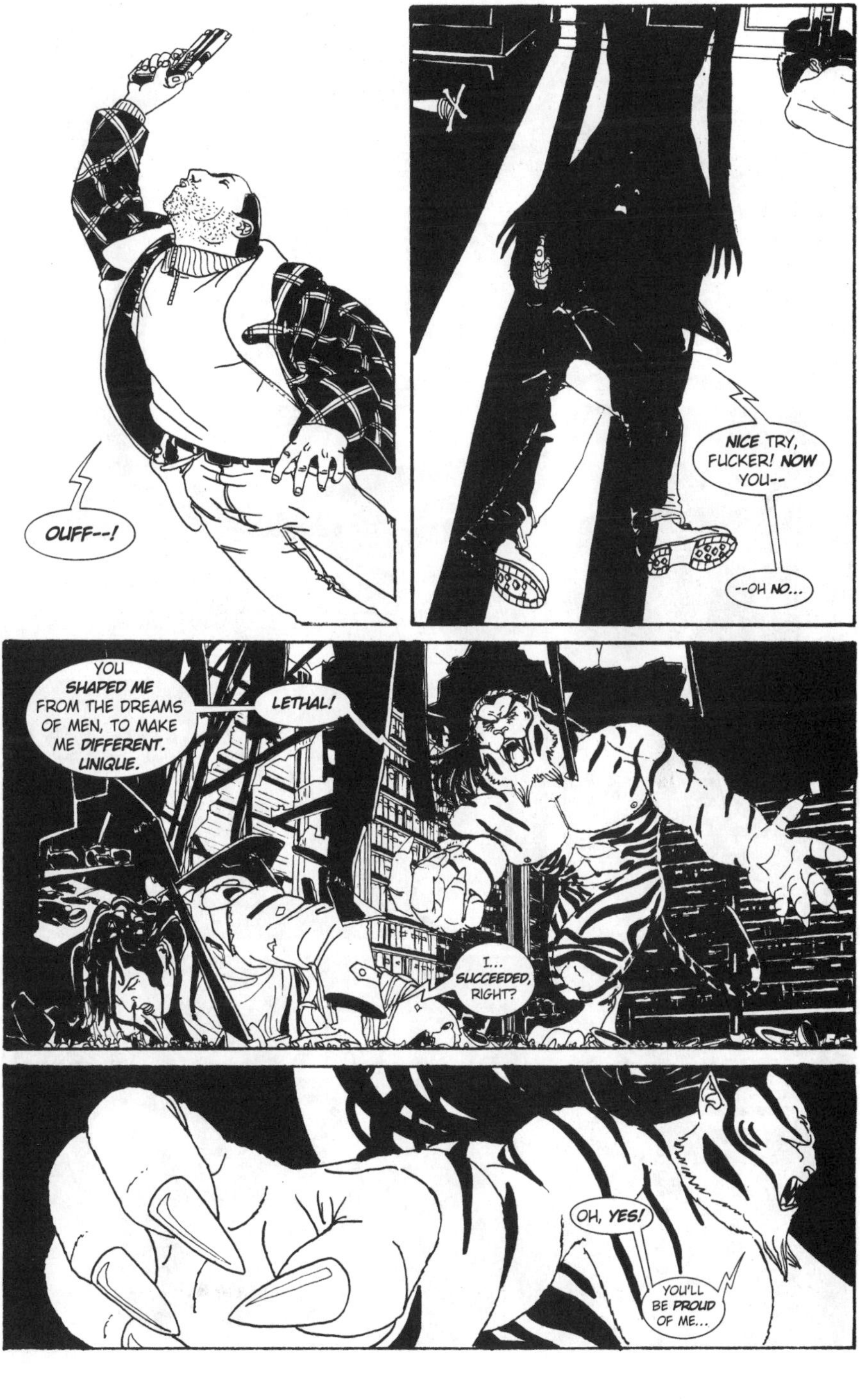
OUFF--!
NICE TRY, FUCKER! NOW YOU--
--OH NO...
YOU SHAPED ME FROM THE DREAMS OF MEN, TO MAKE ME DIFFERENT. UNIQUE.
LETHAL!
I... SUCCEEDED, RIGHT?
OH, YES!
YOU'LL BE PROUD OF ME...

UORGH--!
CHKK

PLEASE...

DON'T MAKE ME... I--

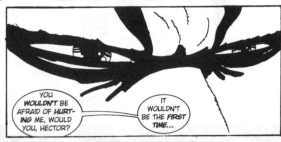

YOU *WOULDN'T* BE AFRAID OF *HURT-ING* ME, WOULD YOU, HECTOR?

IT WOULDN'T BE THE *FIRST TIME*...

CLAIRE... I'M *SORRY,* I--

NO!

I *DON'T* WANT TO HEAR MORE *EXCUSES, MORE* WORDS! *ENOUGH!*

AH!

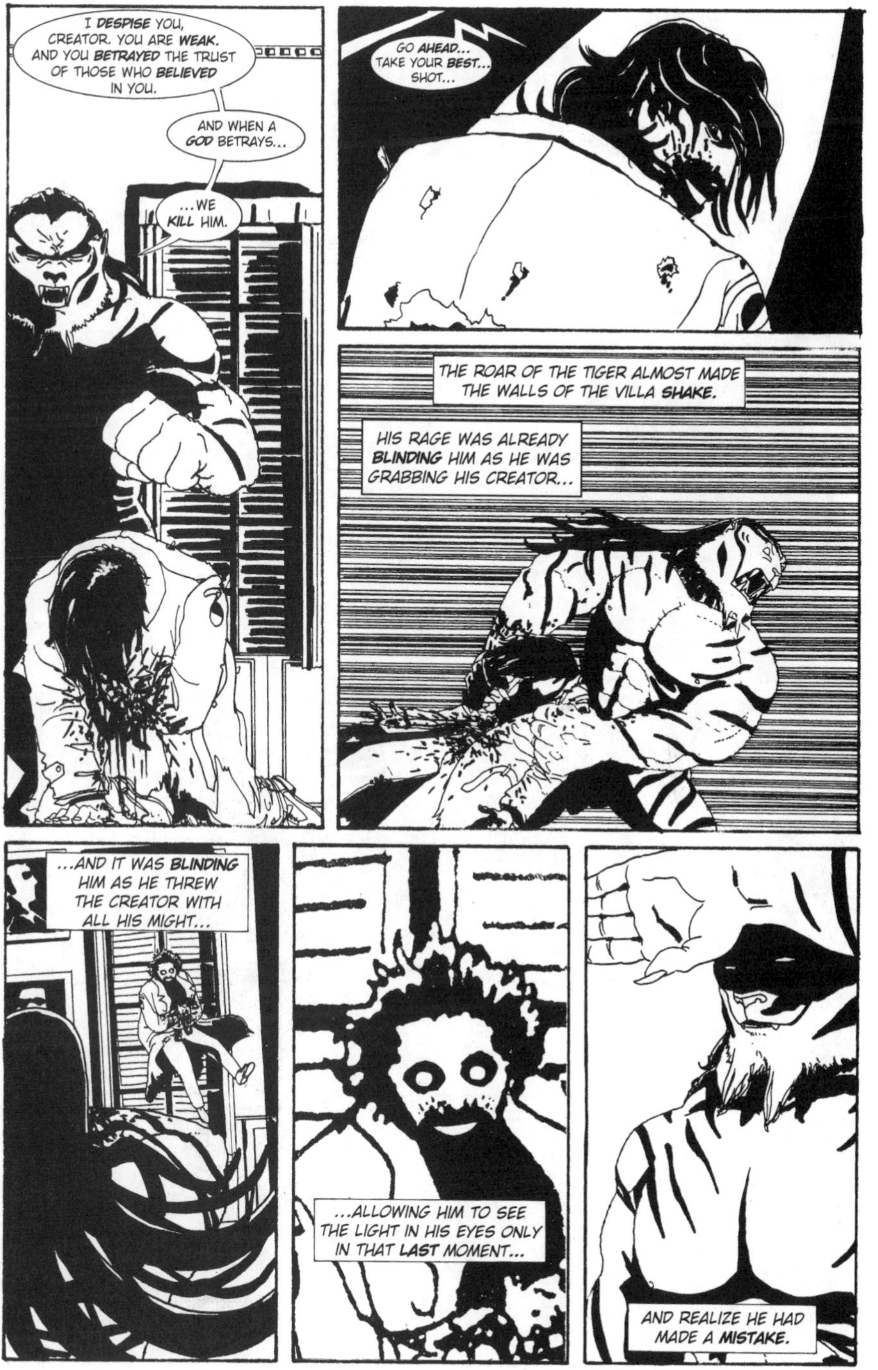
I DESPISE YOU, CREATOR. YOU ARE WEAK. AND YOU BETRAYED THE TRUST OF THOSE WHO BELIEVED IN YOU.
AND WHEN A GOD BETRAYS...
...WE KILL HIM.
GO AHEAD... TAKE YOUR BEST... SHOT...
THE ROAR OF THE TIGER ALMOST MADE THE WALLS OF THE VILLA SHAKE.
HIS RAGE WAS ALREADY BLINDING HIM AS HE WAS GRABBING HIS CREATOR...
...AND IT WAS BLINDING HIM AS HE THREW THE CREATOR WITH ALL HIS MIGHT...
...ALLOWING HIM TO SEE THE LIGHT IN HIS EYES ONLY IN THAT LAST MOMENT...
AND REALIZE HE HAD MADE A MISTAKE.

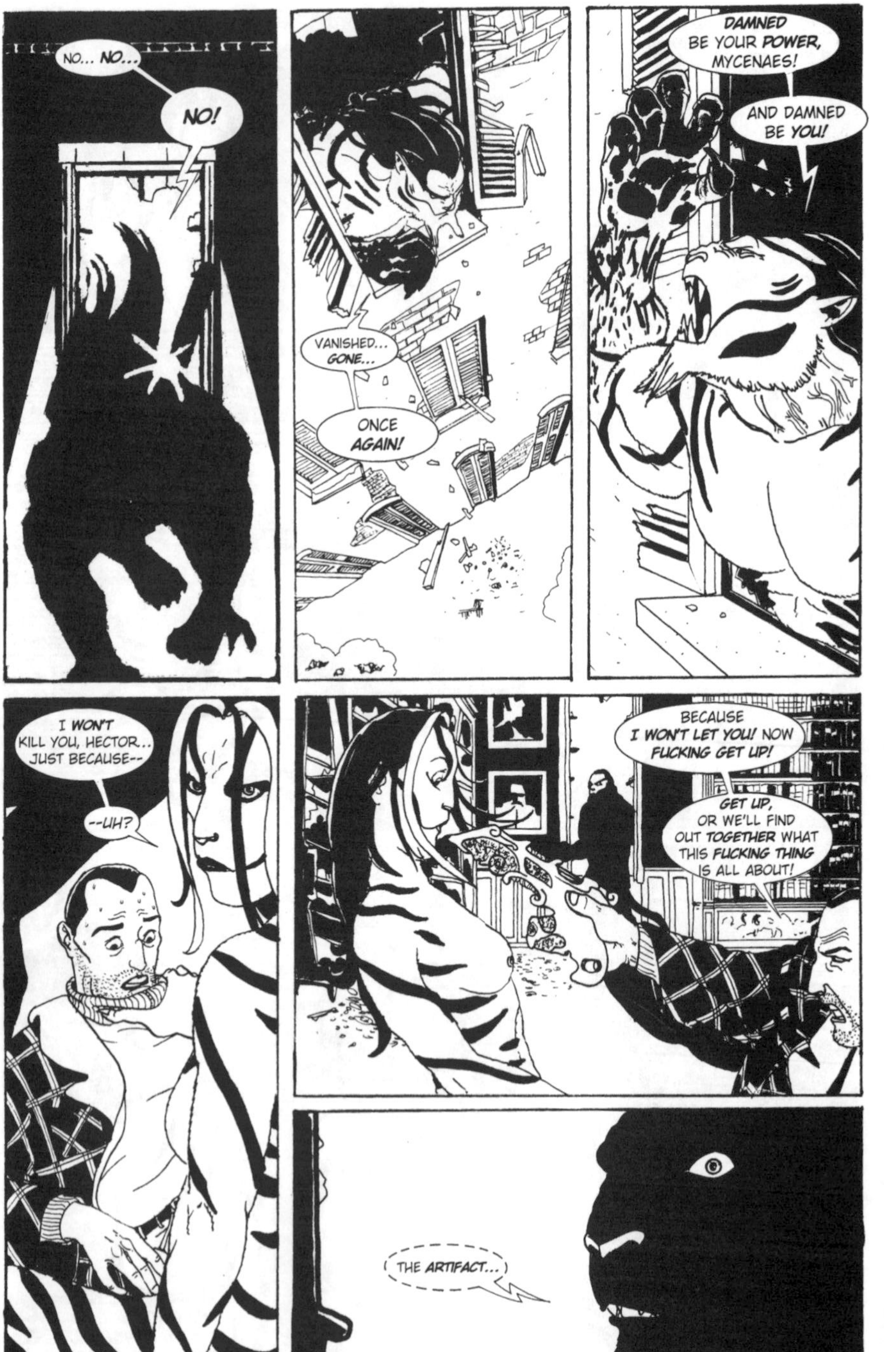
NO... NO...
NO!
VANISHED... GONE...
ONCE AGAIN!
DAMNED BE YOUR POWER, MYCENAES!
AND DAMNED BE YOU!
I WON'T KILL YOU, HECTOR... JUST BECAUSE--
--UH?
BECAUSE I WON'T LET YOU! NOW FUCKING GET UP!
GET UP, OR WE'LL FIND OUT TOGETHER WHAT THIS FUCKING THING IS ALL ABOUT!
THE ARTIFACT...

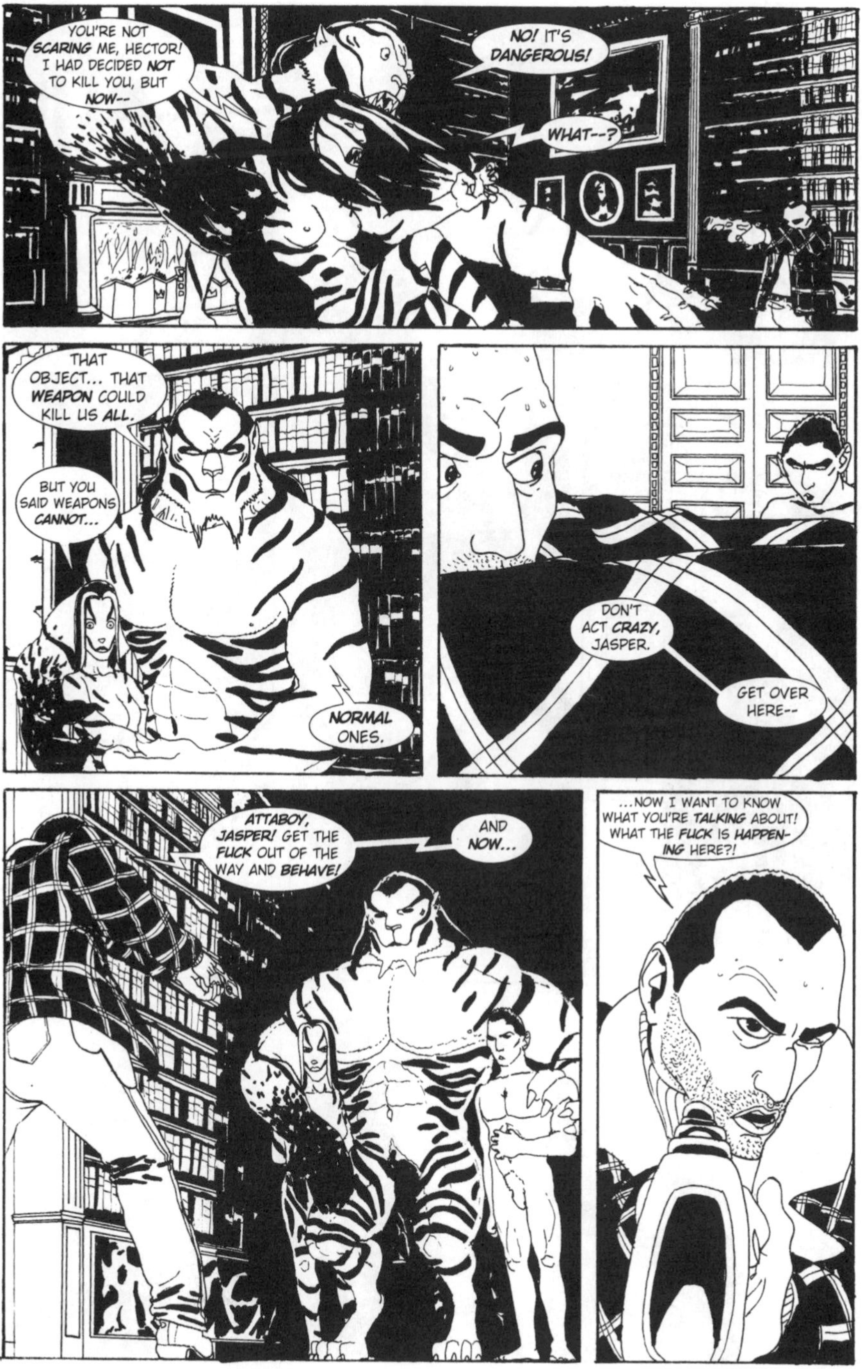
YOU'RE NOT SCARING ME, HECTOR! I HAD DECIDED NOT TO KILL YOU, BUT NOW--
NO! IT'S DANGEROUS!
WHAT--?
THAT OBJECT... THAT WEAPON COULD KILL US ALL.
BUT YOU SAID WEAPONS CANNOT...
NORMAL ONES.
DON'T ACT CRAZY, JASPER.
GET OVER HERE--
ATTABOY, JASPER! GET THE FUCK OUT OF THE WAY AND BEHAVE!
AND NOW...
...NOW I WANT TO KNOW WHAT YOU'RE TALKING ABOUT! WHAT THE FUCK IS HAPPEN-ING HERE?!

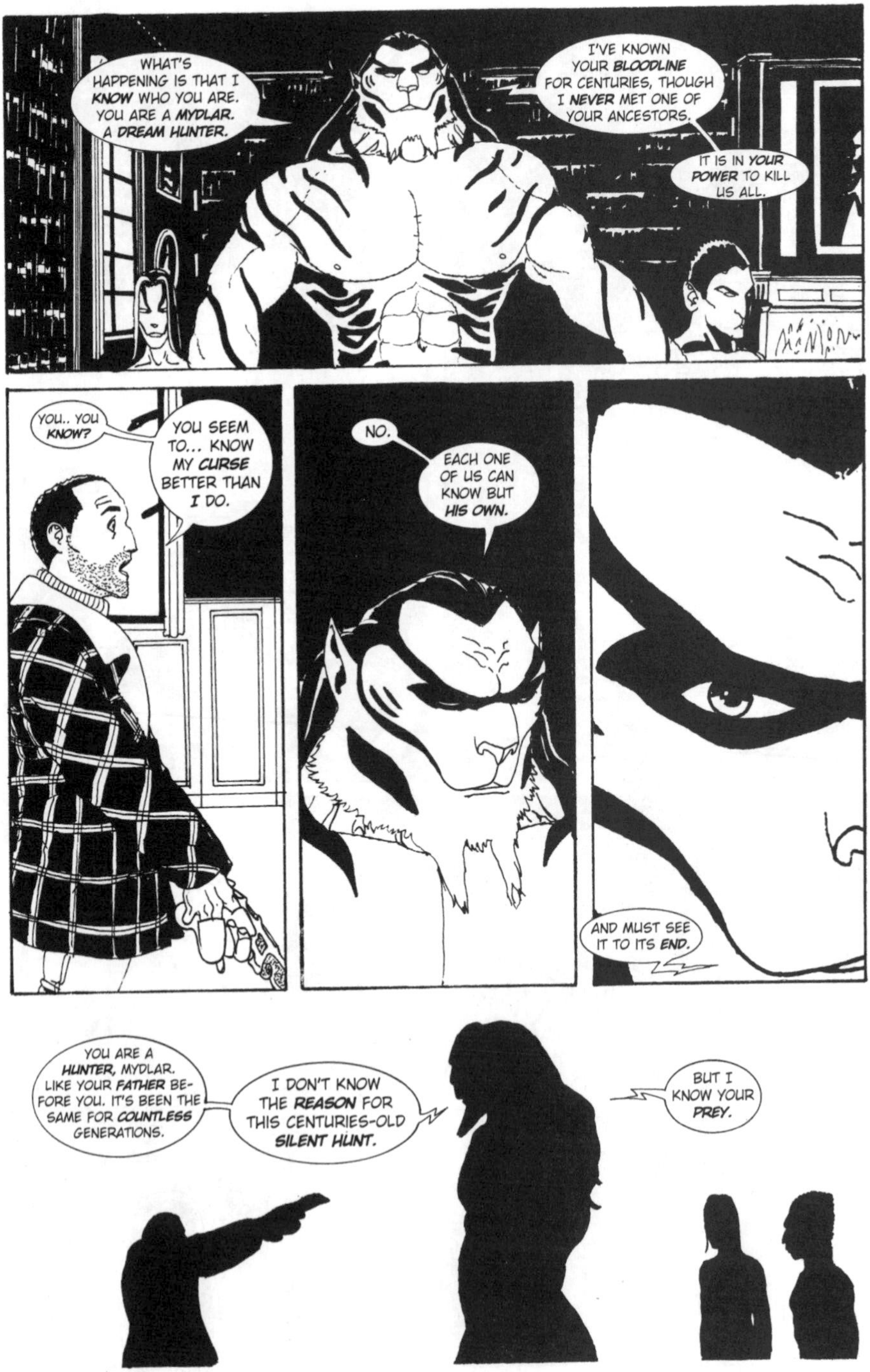

WHAT'S HAPPENING IS THAT I KNOW WHO YOU ARE. YOU ARE A MYDLAR. A DREAM HUNTER.
I'VE KNOWN YOUR BLOODLINE FOR CENTURIES, THOUGH I NEVER MET ONE OF YOUR ANCESTORS.
IT IS IN YOUR POWER TO KILL US ALL.
YOU.. YOU KNOW?
YOU SEEM TO... KNOW MY CURSE BETTER THAN I DO.
NO.
EACH ONE OF US CAN KNOW BUT HIS OWN.
AND MUST SEE IT TO ITS END.
YOU ARE A HUNTER, MYDLAR. LIKE YOUR FATHER BEFORE YOU. IT'S BEEN THE SAME FOR COUNTLESS GENERATIONS.
I DON'T KNOW THE REASON FOR THIS CENTURIES-OLD SILENT HUNT.
BUT I KNOW YOUR PREY.

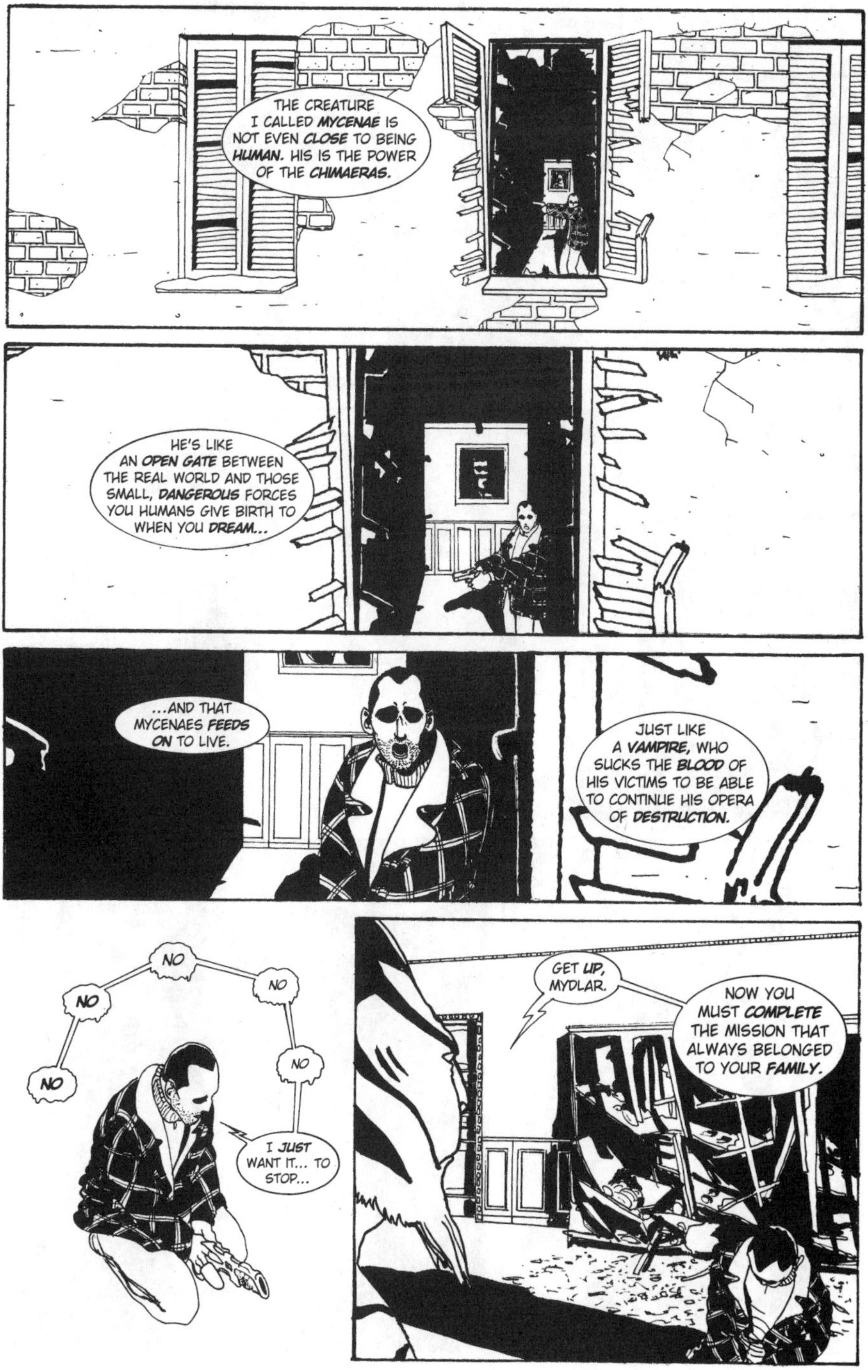
THE CREATURE I CALLED MYCENAE IS NOT EVEN CLOSE TO BEING HUMAN. HIS IS THE POWER OF THE CHIMAERAS.
HE'S LIKE AN OPEN GATE BETWEEN THE REAL WORLD AND THOSE SMALL, DANGEROUS FORCES YOU HUMANS GIVE BIRTH TO WHEN YOU DREAM...
...AND THAT MYCENAES FEEDS ON TO LIVE.
JUST LIKE A VAMPIRE, WHO SUCKS THE BLOOD OF HIS VICTIMS TO BE ABLE TO CONTINUE HIS OPERA OF DESTRUCTION.
NO
NO
NO
NO
NO
I JUST WANT IT... TO STOP...
GET UP, MYDLAR.
NOW YOU MUST COMPLETE THE MISSION THAT ALWAYS BELONGED TO YOUR FAMILY.

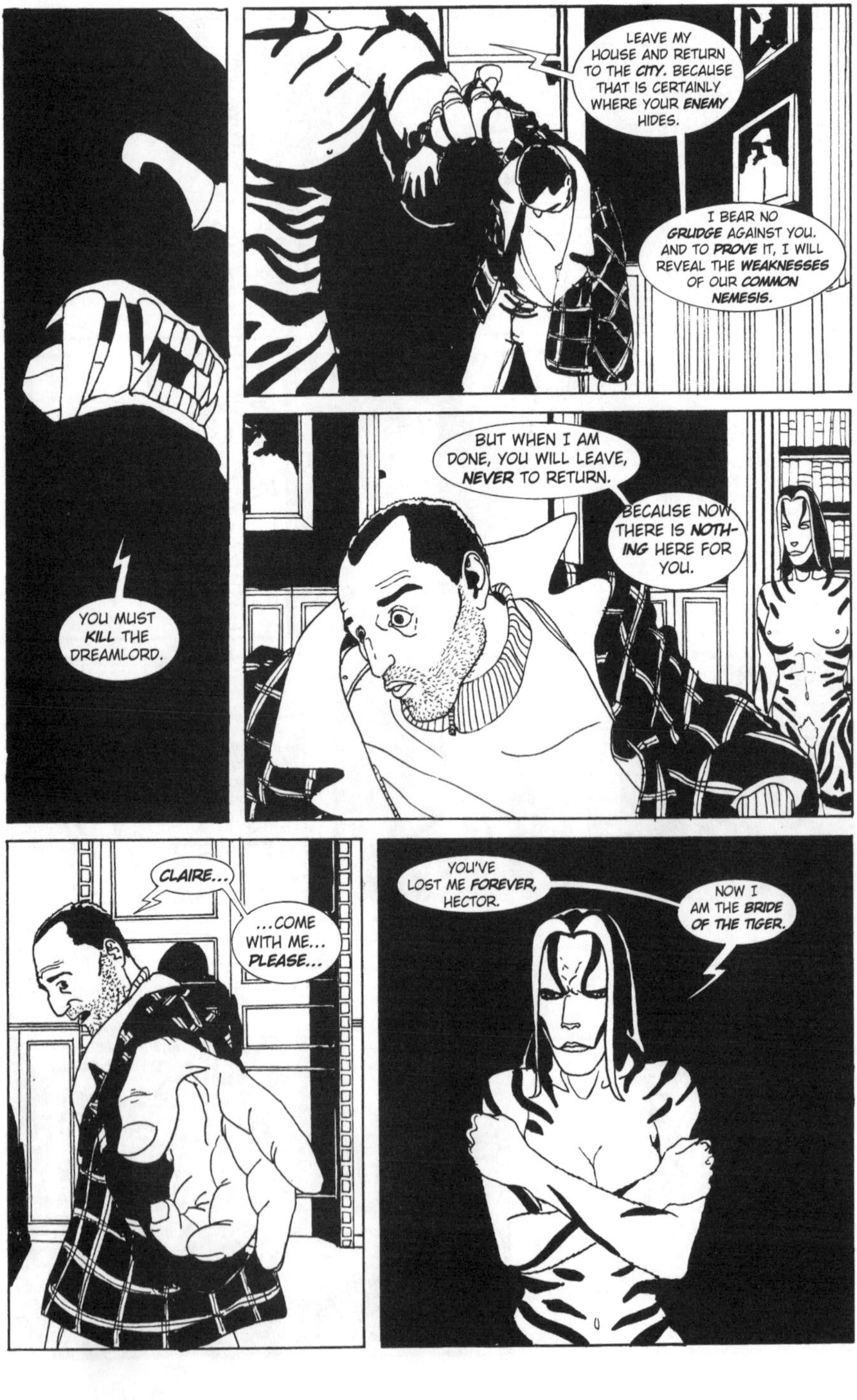
LEAVE MY HOUSE AND RETURN TO THE CITY. BECAUSE THAT IS CERTAINLY WHERE YOUR ENEMY HIDES.
I BEAR NO GRUDGE AGAINST YOU. AND TO PROVE IT, I WILL REVEAL THE WEAKNESSES OF OUR COMMON NEMESIS.
YOU MUST KILL THE DREAMLORD.
BUT WHEN I AM DONE, YOU WILL LEAVE, NEVER TO RETURN.
BECAUSE NOW THERE IS NOTHING HERE FOR YOU.
CLAIRE...
...COME WITH ME... PLEASE...
YOU'VE LOST ME FOREVER, HECTOR.
NOW I AM THE BRIDE OF THE TIGER.

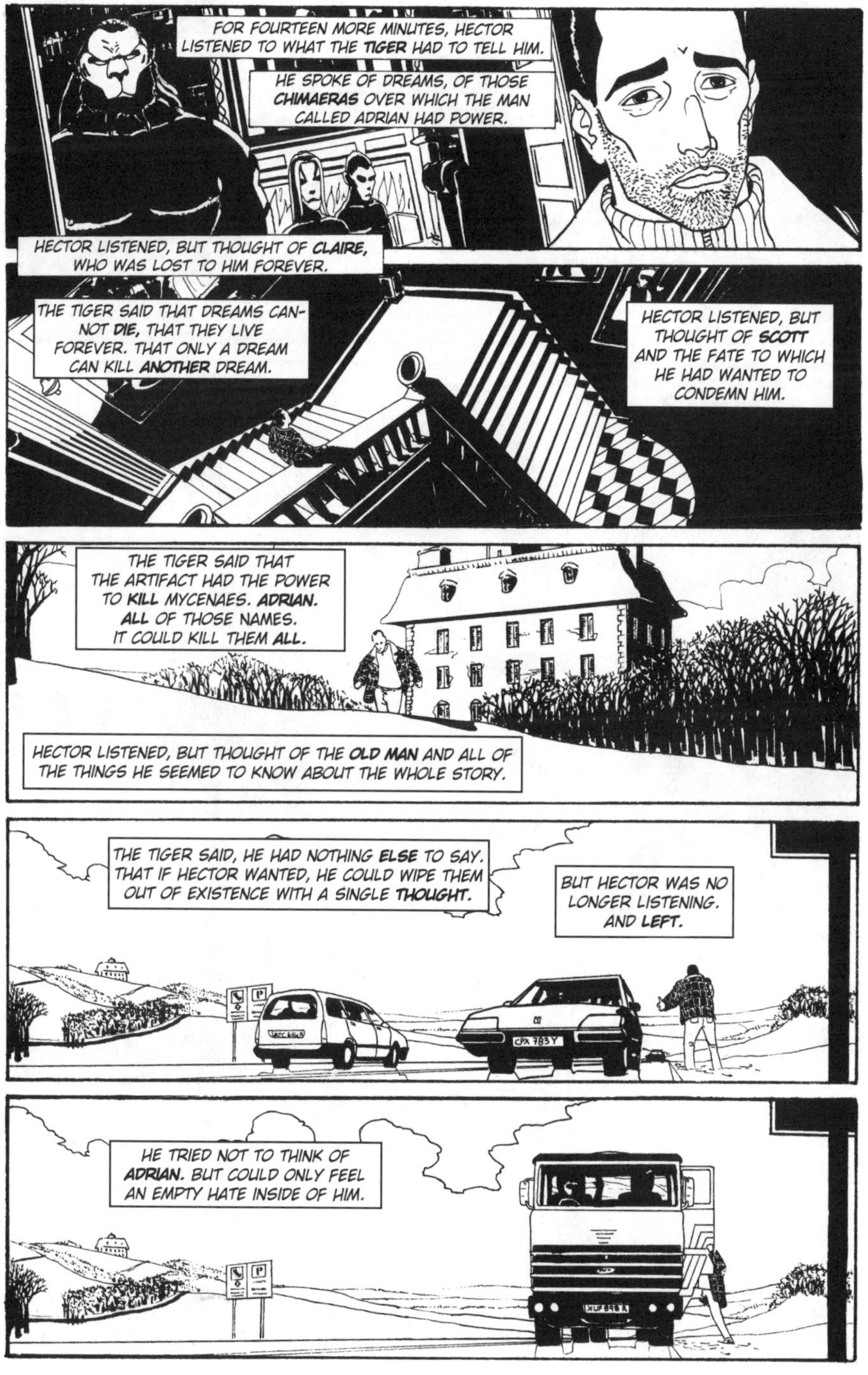
FOR FOURTEEN MORE MINUTES, HECTOR LISTENED TO WHAT THE TIGER HAD TO TELL HIM.
HE SPOKE OF DREAMS, OF THOSE CHIMAERAS OVER WHICH THE MAN CALLED ADRIAN HAD POWER.
HECTOR LISTENED, BUT THOUGHT OF CLAIRE, WHO WAS LOST TO HIM FOREVER.
THE TIGER SAID THAT DREAMS CANNOT DIE, THAT THEY LIVE FOREVER. THAT ONLY A DREAM CAN KILL ANOTHER DREAM.
HECTOR LISTENED, BUT THOUGHT OF SCOTT AND THE FATE TO WHICH HE HAD WANTED TO CONDEMN HIM.
THE TIGER SAID THAT THE ARTIFACT HAD THE POWER TO KILL MYCENAES. ADRIAN. ALL OF THOSE NAMES. IT COULD KILL THEM ALL.
HECTOR LISTENED, BUT THOUGHT OF THE OLD MAN AND ALL OF THE THINGS HE SEEMED TO KNOW ABOUT THE WHOLE STORY.
THE TIGER SAID, HE HAD NOTHING ELSE TO SAY. THAT IF HECTOR WANTED, HE COULD WIPE THEM OUT OF EXISTENCE WITH A SINGLE THOUGHT.
BUT HECTOR WAS NO LONGER LISTENING. AND LEFT.
CPX 783Y
HE TRIED NOT TO THINK OF ADRIAN. BUT COULD ONLY FEEL AN EMPTY HATE INSIDE OF HIM.

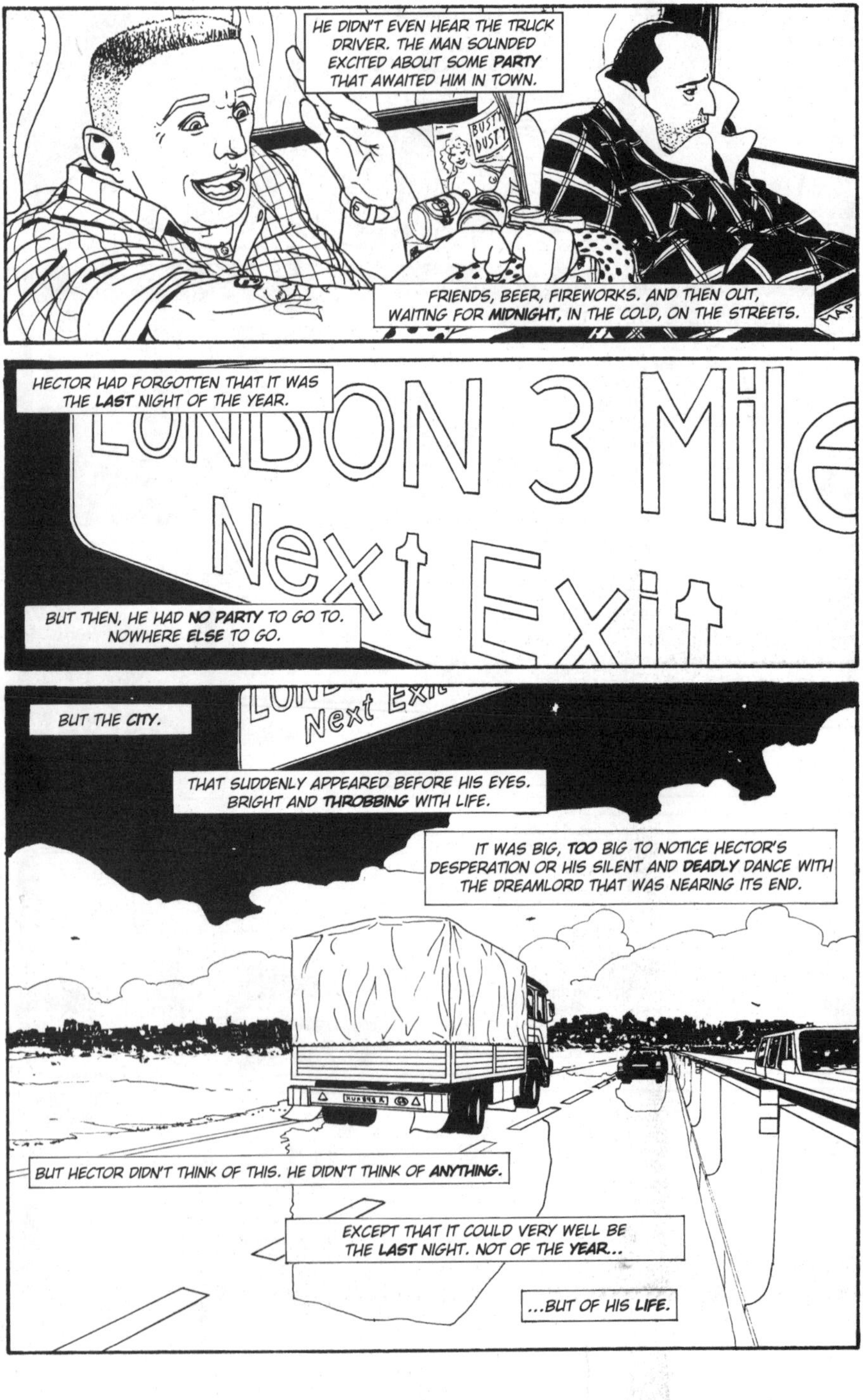

HE DIDN'T EVEN HEAR THE TRUCK DRIVER. THE MAN SOUNDED EXCITED ABOUT SOME PARTY THAT AWAITED HIM IN TOWN.
BUSTY DUSTY
FRIENDS, BEER, FIREWORKS. AND THEN OUT, WAITING FOR MIDNIGHT, IN THE COLD, ON THE STREETS.
MAP
HECTOR HAD FORGOTTEN THAT IT WAS THE LAST NIGHT OF THE YEAR.
LONDON 3 Mile
Next Exit
BUT THEN, HE HAD NO PARTY TO GO TO. NOWHERE ELSE TO GO.
BUT THE CITY.
Next Exit
THAT SUDDENLY APPEARED BEFORE HIS EYES. BRIGHT AND THROBBING WITH LIFE.
IT WAS BIG, TOO BIG TO NOTICE HECTOR'S DESPERATION OR HIS SILENT AND DEADLY DANCE WITH THE DREAMLORD THAT WAS NEARING ITS END.
BUT HECTOR DIDN'T THINK OF THIS. HE DIDN'T THINK OF ANYTHING.
EXCEPT THAT IT COULD VERY WELL BE THE LAST NIGHT. NOT OF THE YEAR...
...BUT OF HIS LIFE.

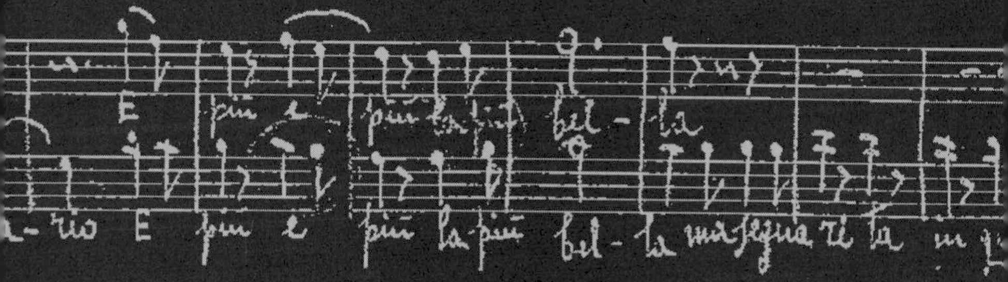
E più è più la più bel - la

chapter six

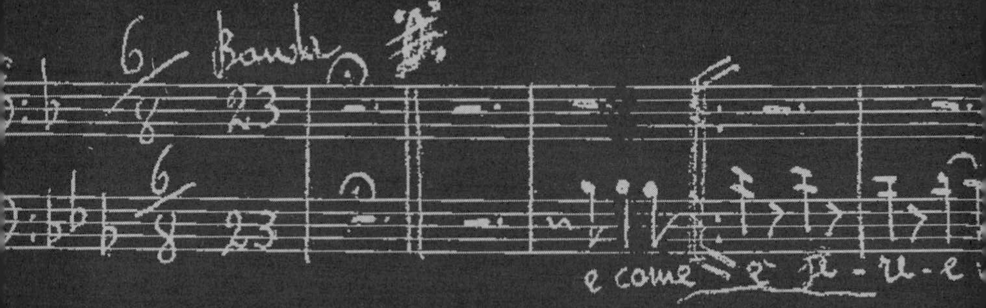
e come

Story
MATTEO CASALI

Art
ALESSANDRO DeANGELIS

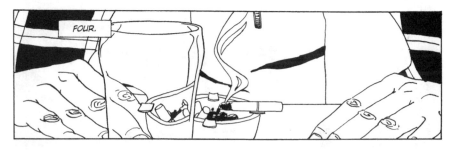

FOUR.

OWEN--?

HMM-- ADRI-AN?

ADRIAN! MY GOD, WHERE HAVE YOU BEEN? I WAS AFRAID THAT--

CALM DOWN, OWEN. I'M HERE, NOW.

JESUS...

...WHAT HAPPENED TO YOU?

ADRIAN? **WHO** DID THIS TO YOU?

WHAT HAPPENED?

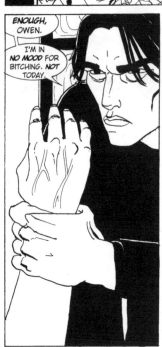

ENOUGH, OWEN. I'M IN **NO MOOD** FOR BITCHING. **NOT** TODAY.

ADRIAN... YOU'RE **HURT** **-IN'** ME...

LET MY HAND... **ADRIAN...?**

LISTEN--

SOMETHING REALLY **BAD** HAS HAPPENED. I KNEW IT WOULD SOONER OR LATER. ONLY, I HOPED "LATER" WAS... **FURTHER** AWAY.

I'M IN **DANGER.** AND YOU ARE **TOO,** AS LONG AS YOU'RE WITH **ME.**

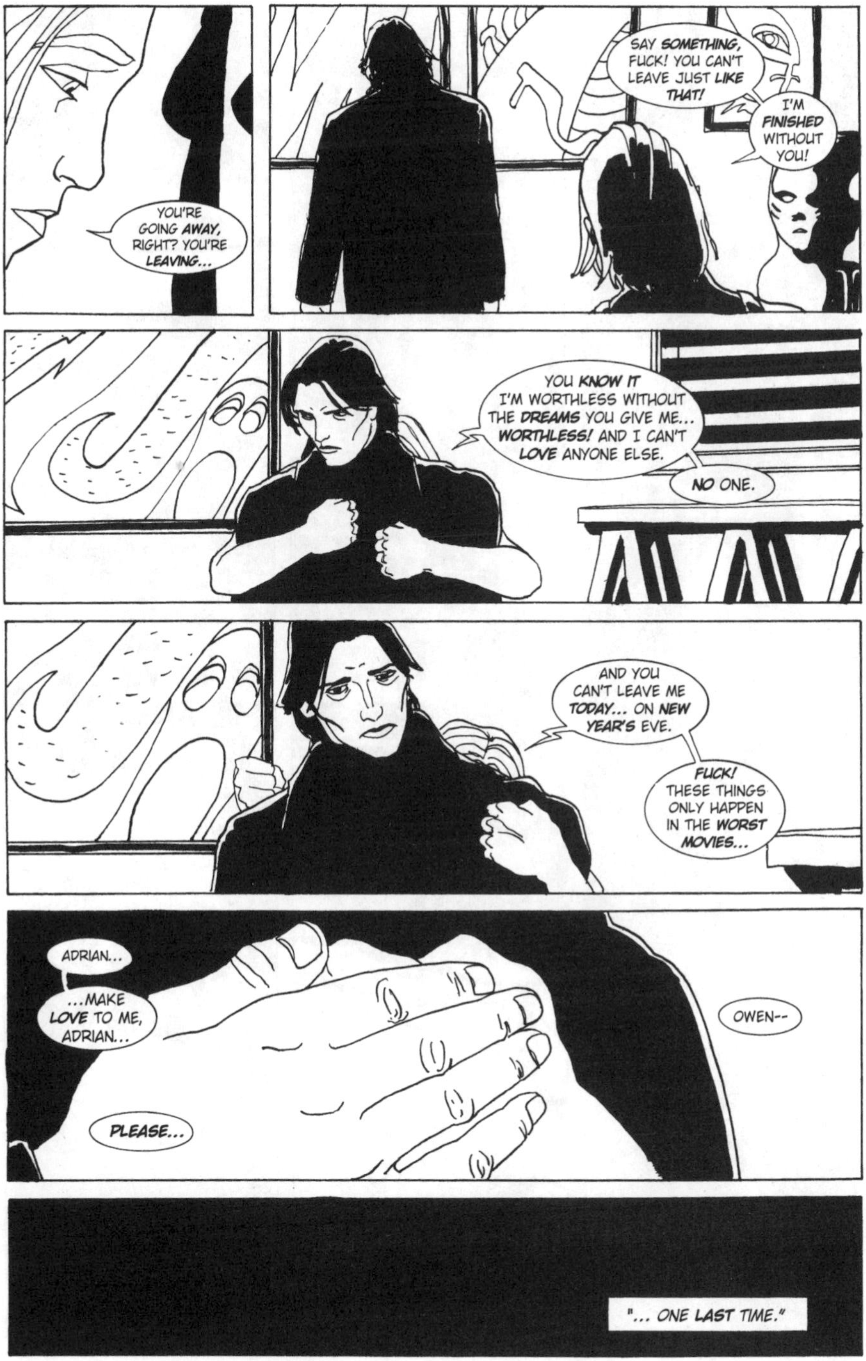
YOU'RE GOING AWAY, RIGHT? YOU'RE LEAVING...
SAY SOMETHING, FUCK! YOU CAN'T LEAVE JUST LIKE THAT!
I'M FINISHED WITHOUT YOU!
YOU KNOW IT I'M WORTHLESS WITHOUT THE DREAMS YOU GIVE ME... WORTHLESS! AND I CAN'T LOVE ANYONE ELSE.
NO ONE.
AND YOU CAN'T LEAVE ME TODAY... ON NEW YEAR'S EVE.
FUCK! THESE THINGS ONLY HAPPEN IN THE WORST MOVIES...
ADRIAN...
...MAKE LOVE TO ME, ADRIAN...
PLEASE...
OWEN--
"... ONE LAST TIME."

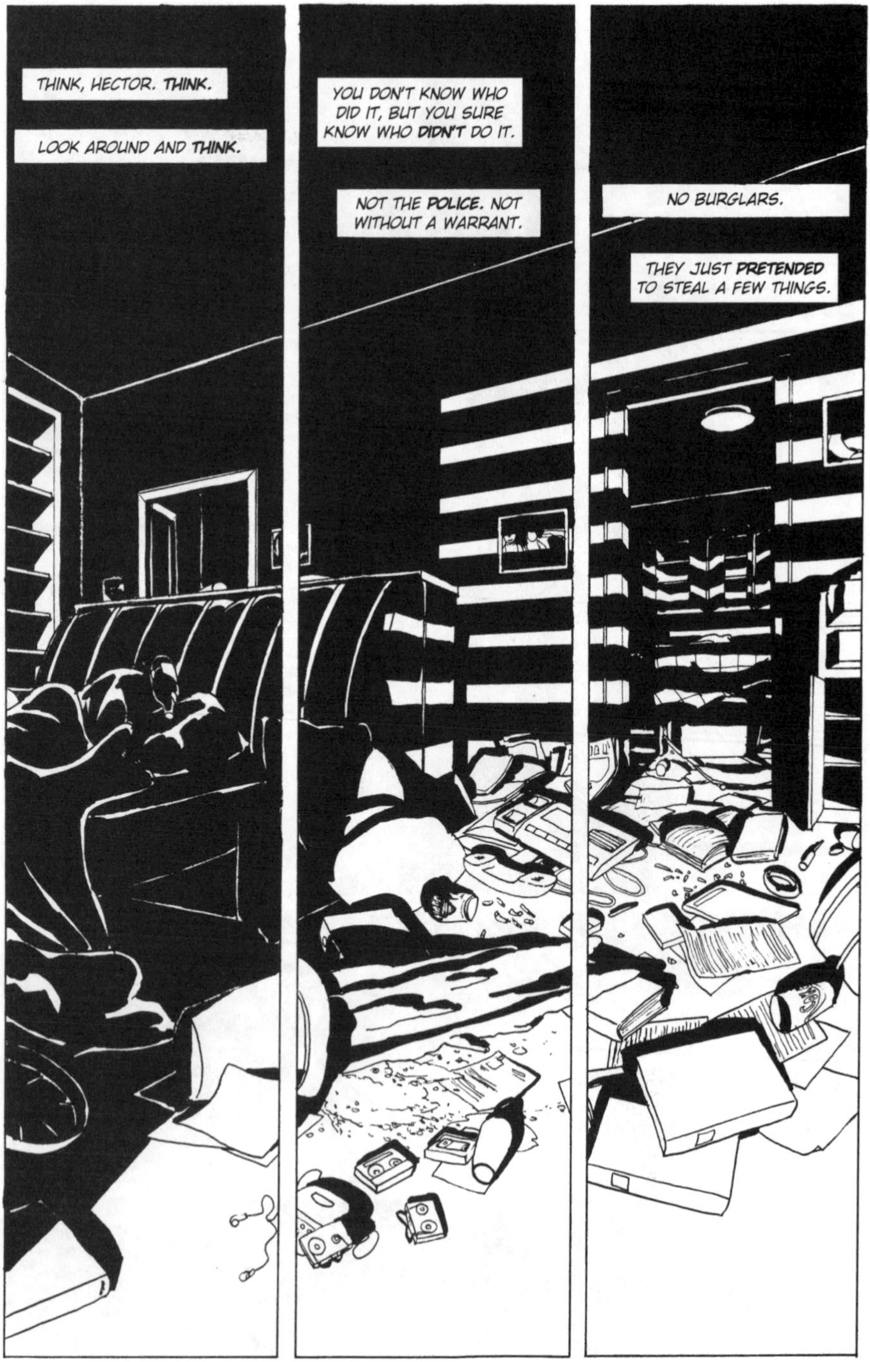
THINK, HECTOR. THINK.
LOOK AROUND AND THINK.
YOU DON'T KNOW WHO DID IT, BUT YOU SURE KNOW WHO DIDN'T DO IT.
NOT THE POLICE. NOT WITHOUT A WARRANT.
NO BURGLARS.
THEY JUST PRETENDED TO STEAL A FEW THINGS.

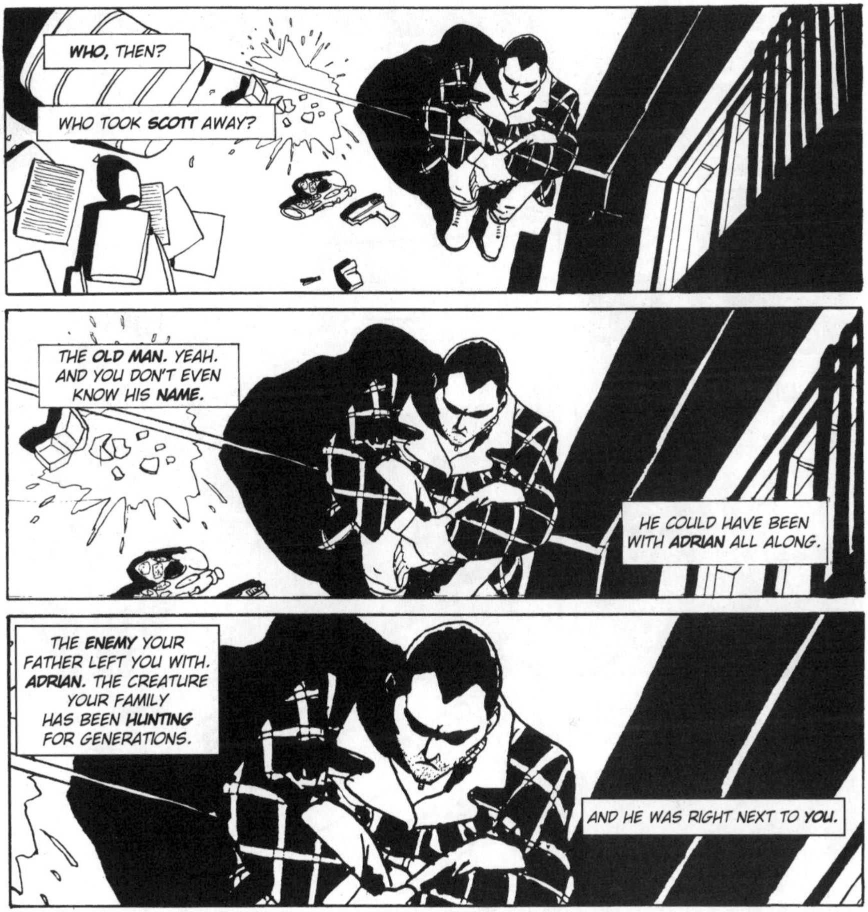
WHO, THEN?
WHO TOOK SCOTT AWAY?
THE OLD MAN. YEAH. AND YOU DON'T EVEN KNOW HIS NAME.
HE COULD HAVE BEEN WITH ADRIAN ALL ALONG.
THE ENEMY YOUR FATHER LEFT YOU WITH. ADRIAN. THE CREATURE YOUR FAMILY HAS BEEN HUNTING FOR GENERATIONS.
AND HE WAS RIGHT NEXT TO YOU.

final round

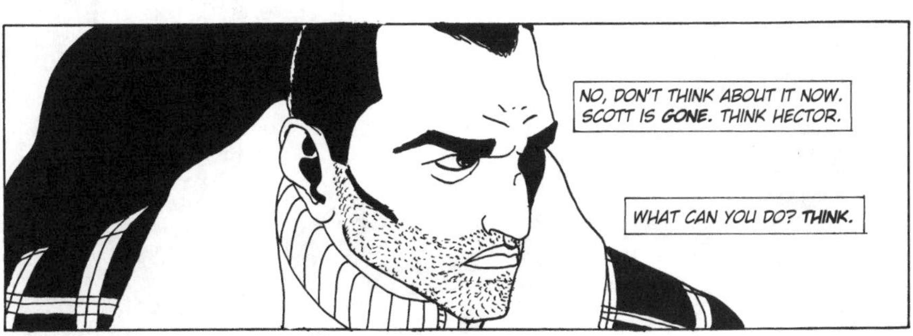
NO, DON'T THINK ABOUT IT NOW. SCOTT IS GONE. THINK HECTOR.
WHAT CAN YOU DO? THINK.

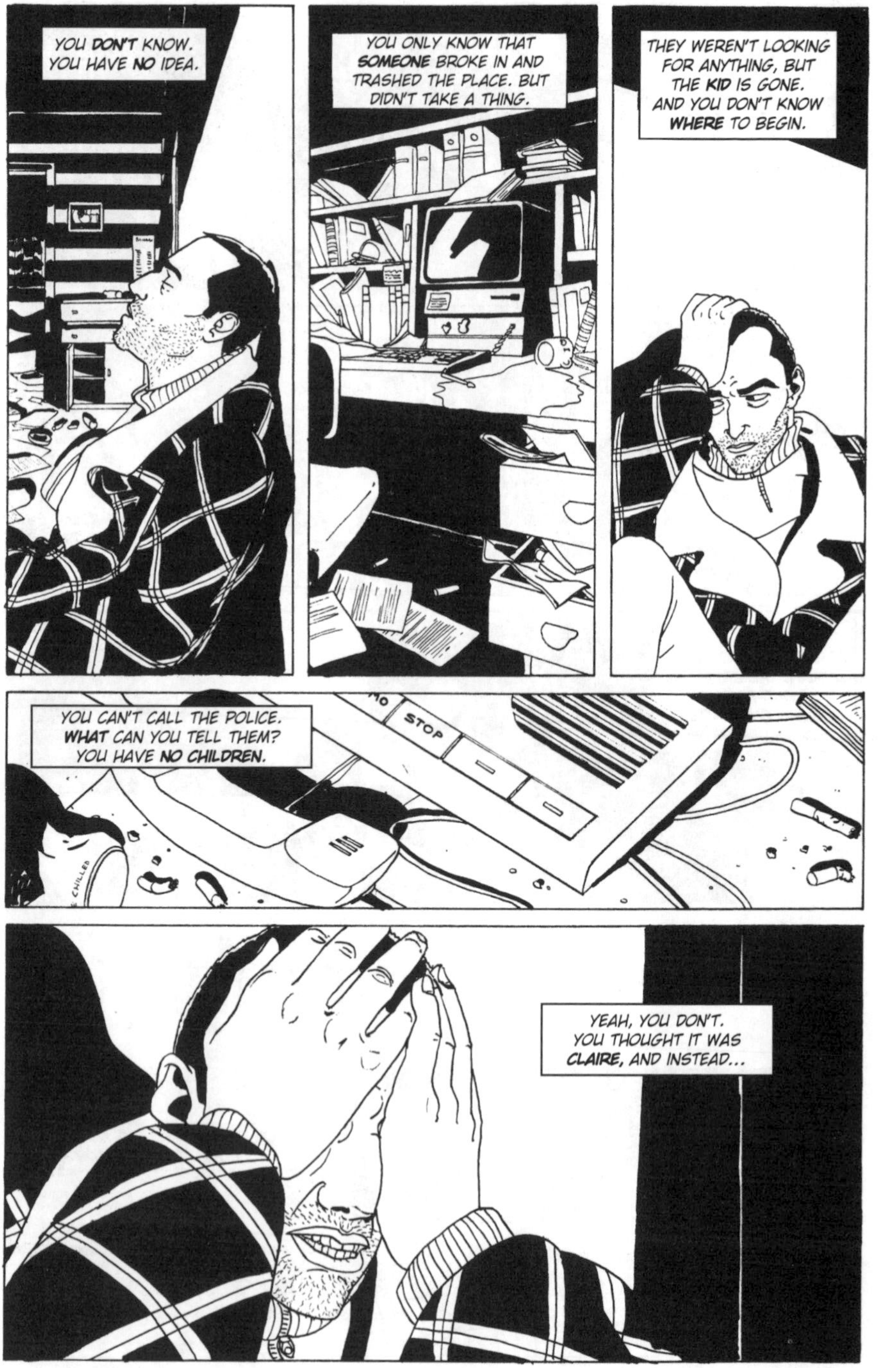
YOU DON'T KNOW. YOU HAVE NO IDEA.
YOU ONLY KNOW THAT SOMEONE BROKE IN AND TRASHED THE PLACE. BUT DIDN'T TAKE A THING.
THEY WEREN'T LOOKING FOR ANYTHING, BUT THE KID IS GONE. AND YOU DON'T KNOW WHERE TO BEGIN.
YOU CAN'T CALL THE POLICE. WHAT CAN YOU TELL THEM? YOU HAVE NO CHILDREN.
STOP
YEAH, YOU DON'T. YOU THOUGHT IT WAS CLAIRE, AND INSTEAD...

NO! DON'T THINK OF CLAIRE!

STOP!

...CLAIRE--

EVERYTHING.

CLAIRE SCOTT
THE OLD MAN
THE BLOOD
YOUR LIFE
EVERYTHING.

IT'S ALL
ADRIAN'S FAULT.

IT'S TIME TO **END IT.** THIS STORY,
THIS ABSURD DEADLY **DANCE.**

END IT ONCE
AND **FOR ALL.**

IT'S THE LAST NIGHT OF THE YEAR.

AND IT WILL HAVE TO BE
FOR THE DREAMLORD AS
WELL. THE **LAST NIGHT.**

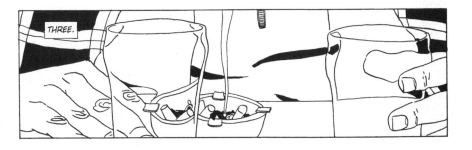

THREE.

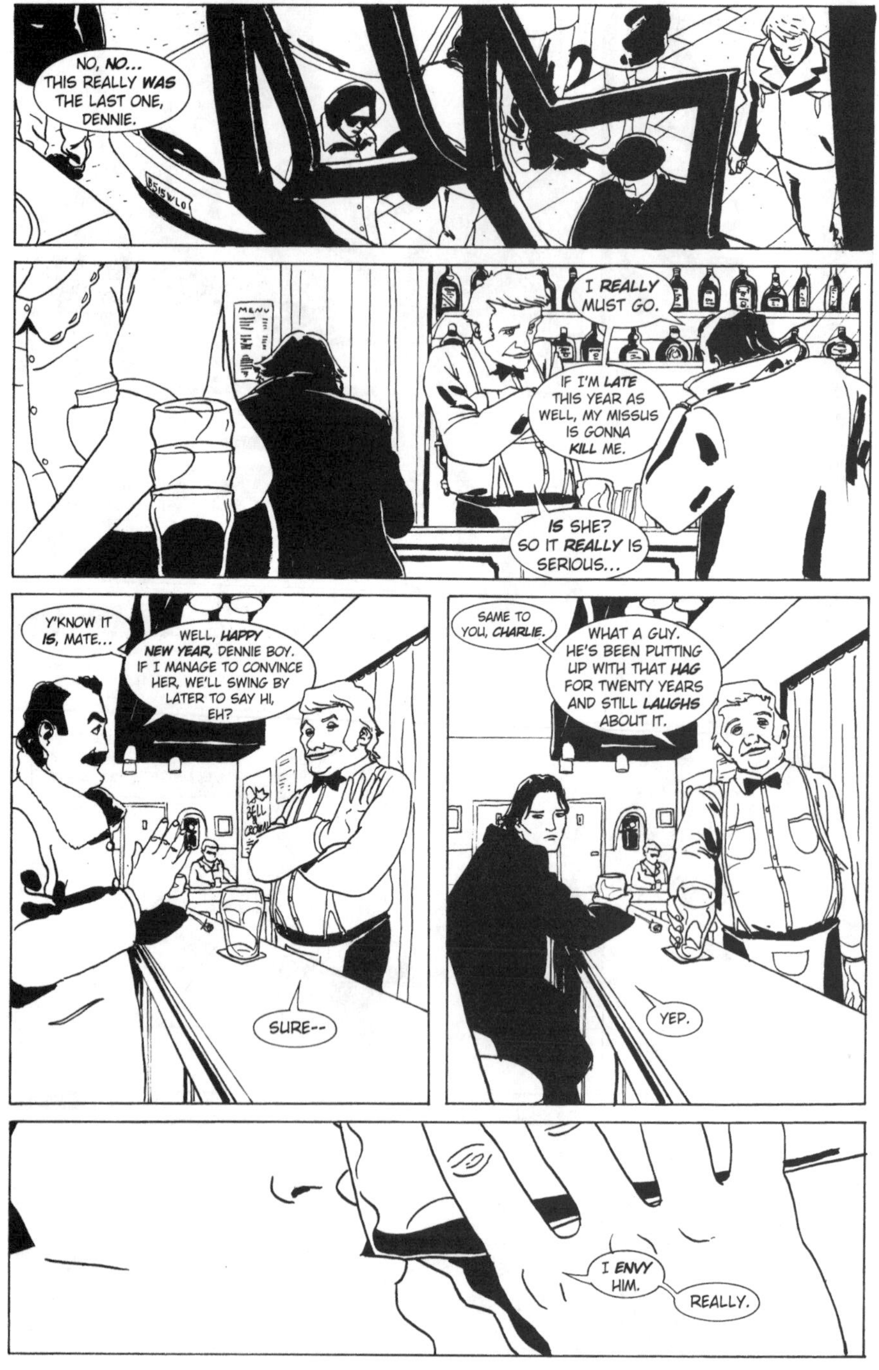
NO, NO... THIS REALLY WAS THE LAST ONE, DENNIE.
I REALLY MUST GO.
IF I'M LATE THIS YEAR AS WELL, MY MISSUS IS GONNA KILL ME.
IS SHE? SO IT REALLY IS SERIOUS...
Y'KNOW IT IS, MATE...
WELL, HAPPY NEW YEAR, DENNIE BOY. IF I MANAGE TO CONVINCE HER, WE'LL SWING BY LATER TO SAY HI, EH?
SURE--
SAME TO YOU, CHARLIE.
WHAT A GUY. HE'S BEEN PUTTING UP WITH THAT HAG FOR TWENTY YEARS AND STILL LAUGHS ABOUT IT.
YEP.
I ENVY HIM.
REALLY.

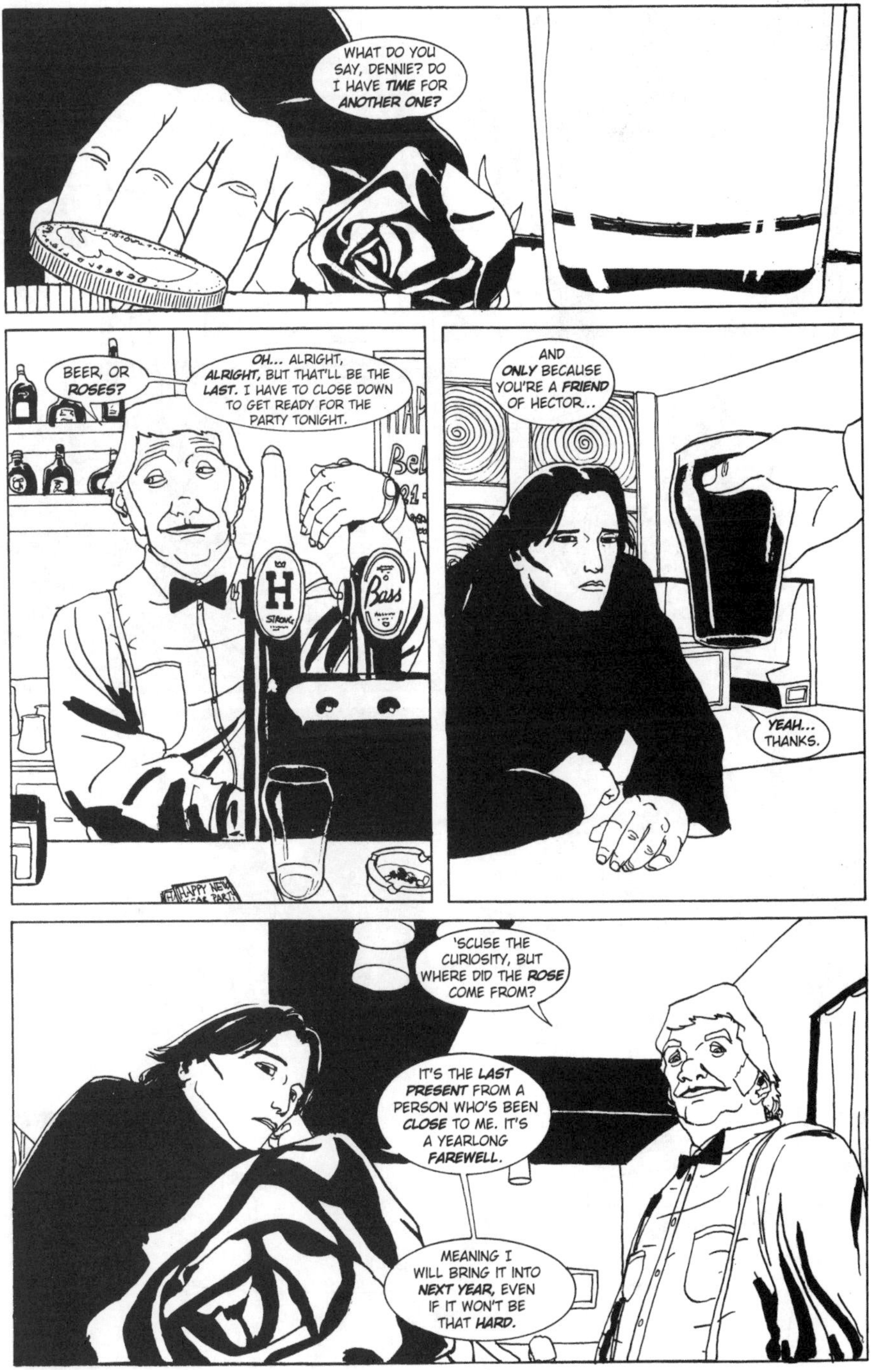
WHAT DO YOU SAY, DENNIE? DO I HAVE TIME FOR ANOTHER ONE?
BEER, OR ROSES?
OH... ALRIGHT, ALRIGHT, BUT THAT'LL BE THE LAST. I HAVE TO CLOSE DOWN TO GET READY FOR THE PARTY TONIGHT.
AND ONLY BECAUSE YOU'RE A FRIEND OF HECTOR...
YEAH... THANKS.
'SCUSE THE CURIOSITY, BUT WHERE DID THE ROSE COME FROM?
IT'S THE LAST PRESENT FROM A PERSON WHO'S BEEN CLOSE TO ME. IT'S A YEARLONG FAREWELL.
MEANING I WILL BRING IT INTO NEXT YEAR, EVEN IF IT WON'T BE THAT HARD.

ITS LIFE, SO *BRIEF* AND WONDERFUL... I *ENVY* IT.

IT MUST REALLY BE *INTENSE.*

ALL BRIEF LIVES ARE. WITH THEIR *BROKEN DREAMS* THAT HAVE NO TIME TO GROW *OLD...*

...NO DREAM CAN EVER HAVE THE INTENSE FLAVOR *ONE* LIFE HAS.

I SHOULD HAVE UNDERSTOOD THAT A *LONG* TIME AGO...

I'M *SORRY,* OLD MATE. I DON'T KNOW *ABOUT WHAT,* BUT I'M *REALLY* SORRY.

AND NOW, I *REALLY* HAVE TO CLOSE UP SHOP.

YEAH, *SURE...* YOU HAVE TONIGHT'S PARTY TO ARRANGE--

MAYBE YOU CAN *COME* 'ROUND?

MAYBE I *WILL--*

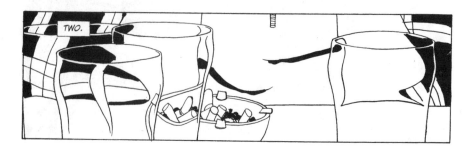

TWO.

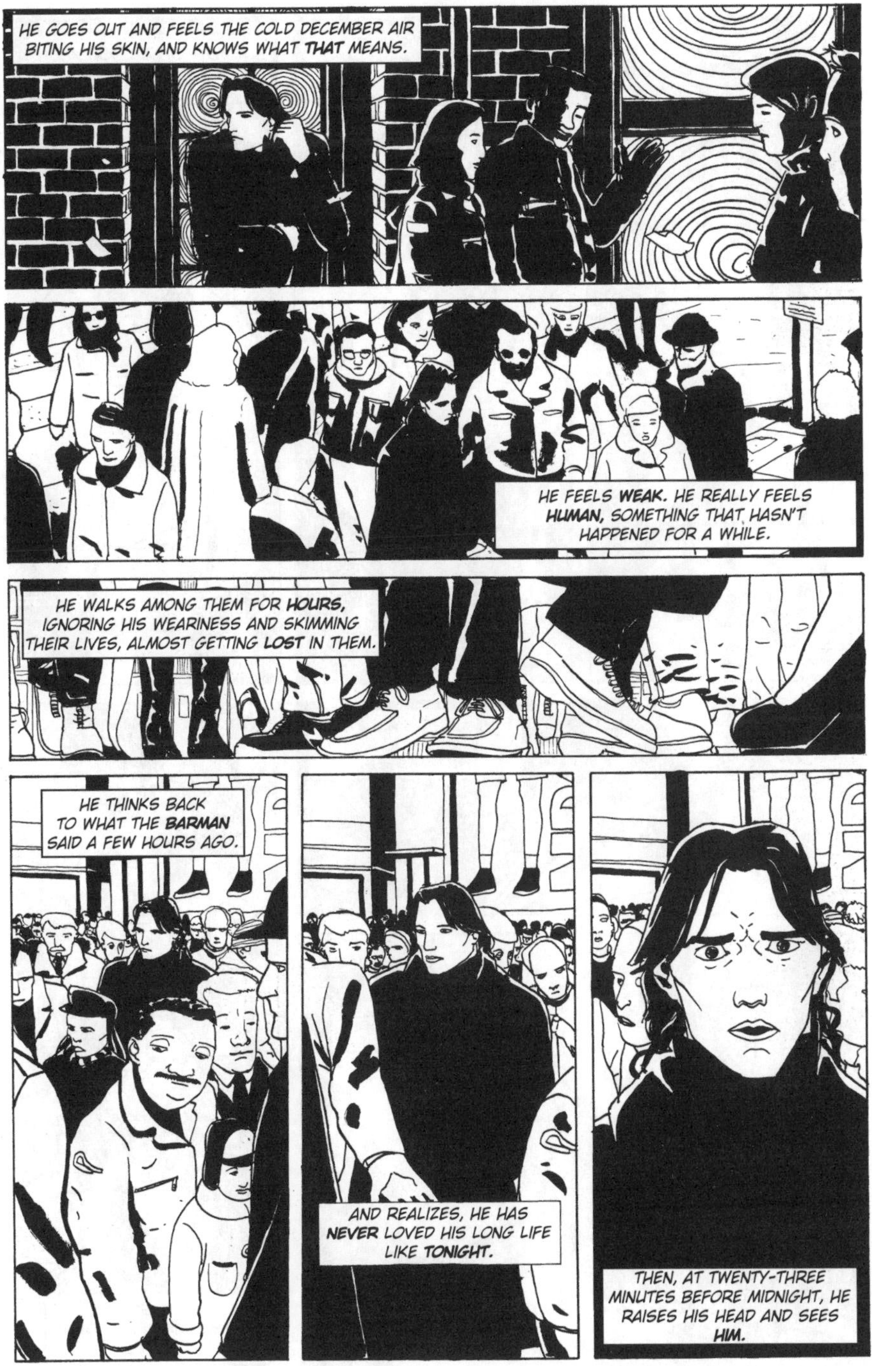

HE GOES OUT AND FEELS THE COLD DECEMBER AIR BITING HIS SKIN, AND KNOWS WHAT **THAT** MEANS.
HE FEELS **WEAK**. HE REALLY FEELS **HUMAN,** SOMETHING THAT HASN'T HAPPENED FOR A WHILE.
HE WALKS AMONG THEM FOR **HOURS,** IGNORING HIS WEARINESS AND SKIMMING THEIR LIVES, ALMOST GETTING **LOST** IN THEM.
HE THINKS BACK TO WHAT THE **BARMAN** SAID A FEW HOURS AGO.
AND REALIZES, HE HAS **NEVER** LOVED HIS LONG LIFE LIKE **TONIGHT.**
THEN, AT TWENTY-THREE MINUTES BEFORE MIDNIGHT, HE RAISES HIS HEAD AND SEES **HIM.**

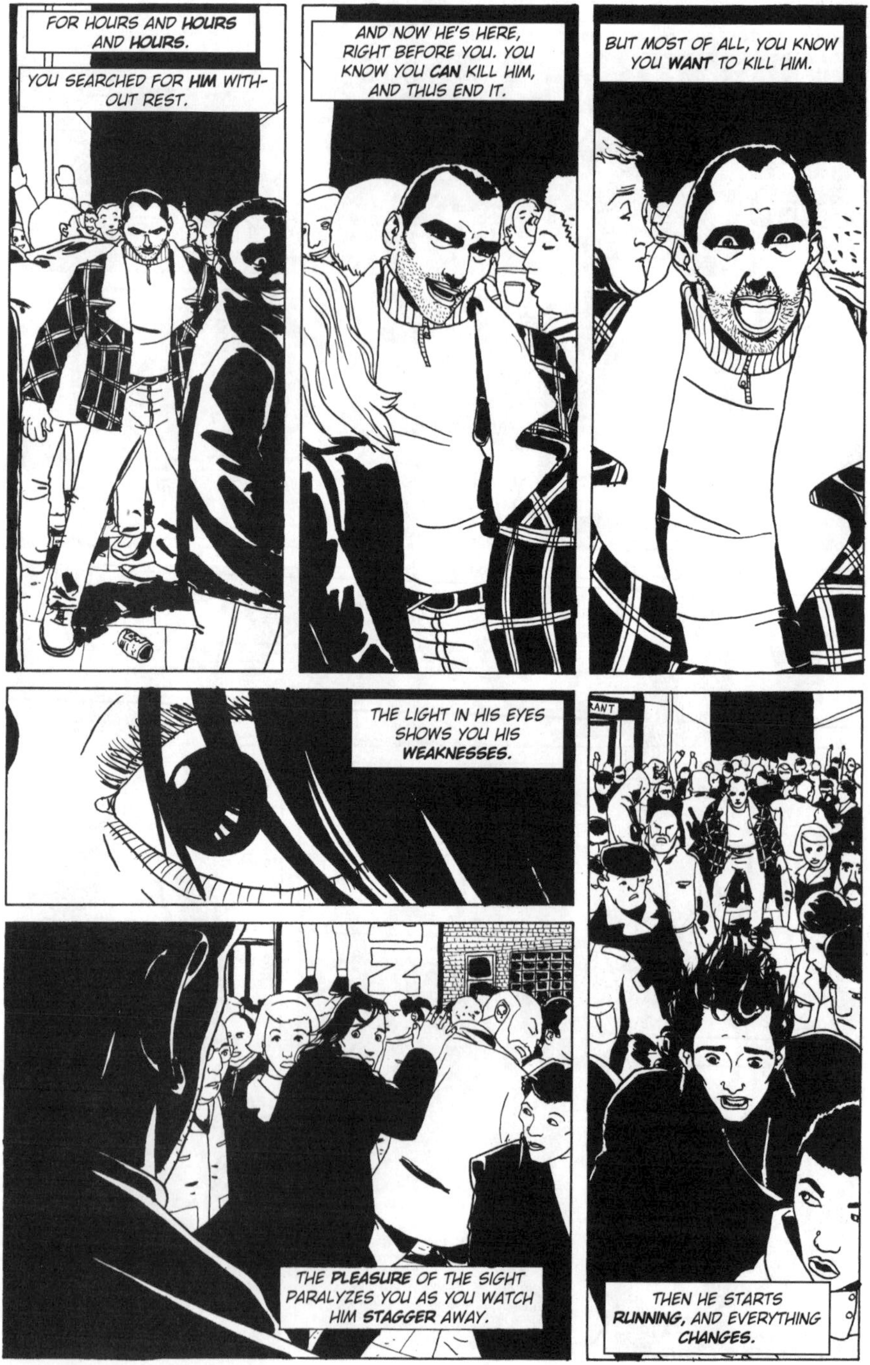
FOR HOURS AND HOURS AND HOURS.
YOU SEARCHED FOR HIM WITH-OUT REST.
AND NOW HE'S HERE, RIGHT BEFORE YOU. YOU KNOW YOU CAN KILL HIM, AND THUS END IT.
BUT MOST OF ALL, YOU KNOW YOU WANT TO KILL HIM.
THE LIGHT IN HIS EYES SHOWS YOU HIS WEAKNESSES.
RANT
THE PLEASURE OF THE SIGHT PARALYZES YOU AS YOU WATCH HIM STAGGER AWAY.
THEN HE STARTS RUNNING, AND EVERYTHING CHANGES.

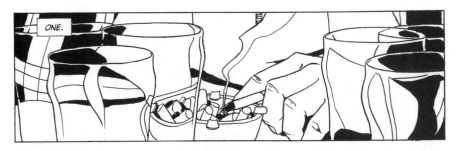

ONE.

YOU FEEL A **RUSH** YOU'VE **NEVER** FELT BEFORE, BUT NOW **EXACTLY** WHAT IT MEANS.

SUDDENLY, WITHOUT WARNING, YOUR HAND SLIDES INTO **RESHU-IZAD** AND THE HUNT ENTERS ITS MOST **BEAUTIFUL** AND **FERAL** PHASE.

THE ONE IN WHICH THE **PREY** FEELS THE **PREDATOR'S** BREATH ON HIS NECK.

THE **LAST** ONE.

NOW YOU **REALLY** FEEL LIKE A **HUNTER**, DON'T YOU HECTOR?

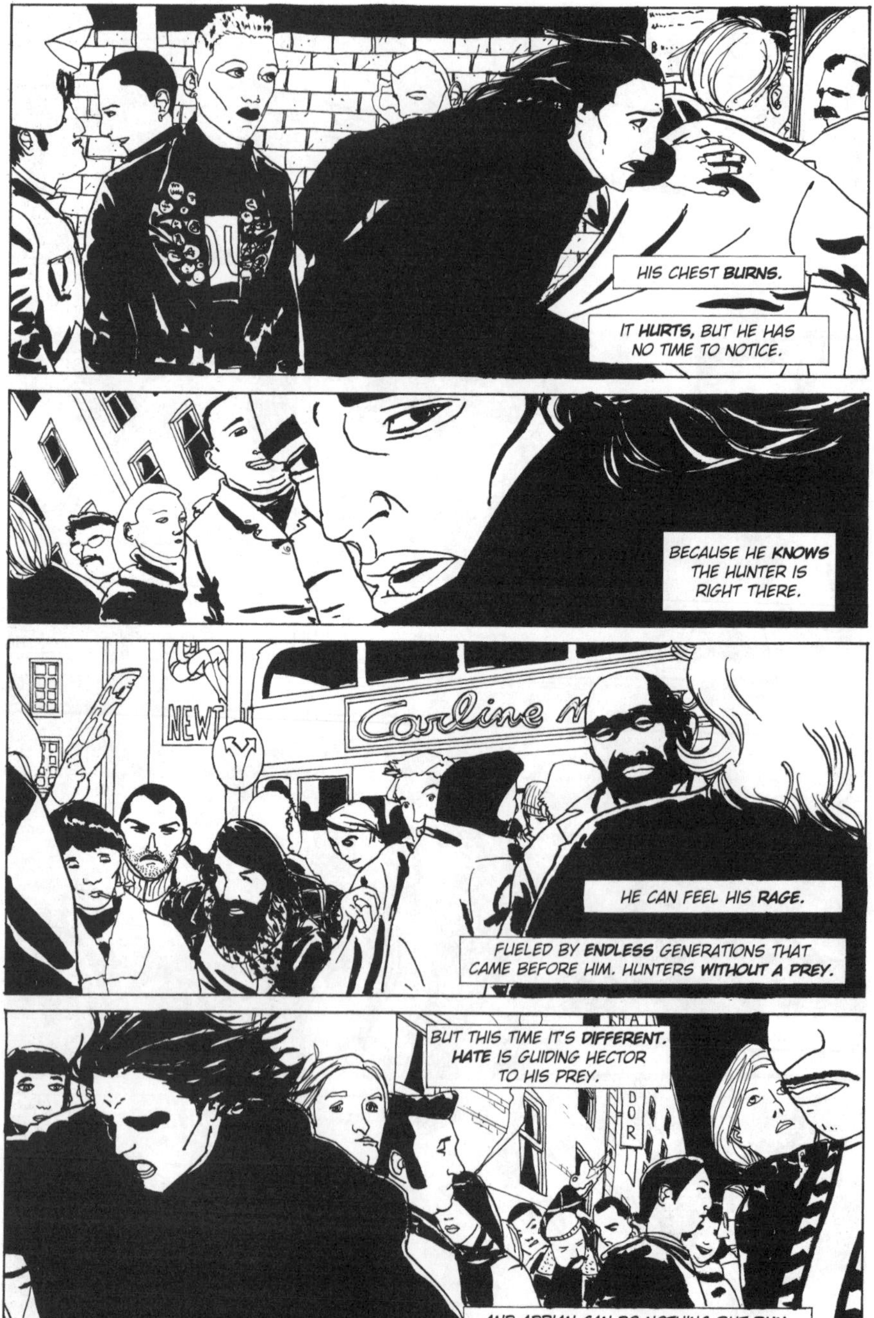
HIS CHEST BURNS.
IT HURTS, BUT HE HAS NO TIME TO NOTICE.
BECAUSE HE KNOWS THE HUNTER IS RIGHT THERE.
NEWT
Carline
HE CAN FEEL HIS RAGE.
FUELED BY ENDLESS GENERATIONS THAT CAME BEFORE HIM. HUNTERS WITHOUT A PREY.
BUT THIS TIME IT'S DIFFERENT. HATE IS GUIDING HECTOR TO HIS PREY.
DOR
AND ADRIAN CAN DO NOTHING BUT RUN, WITHOUT KNOWING WHERE TO GO.

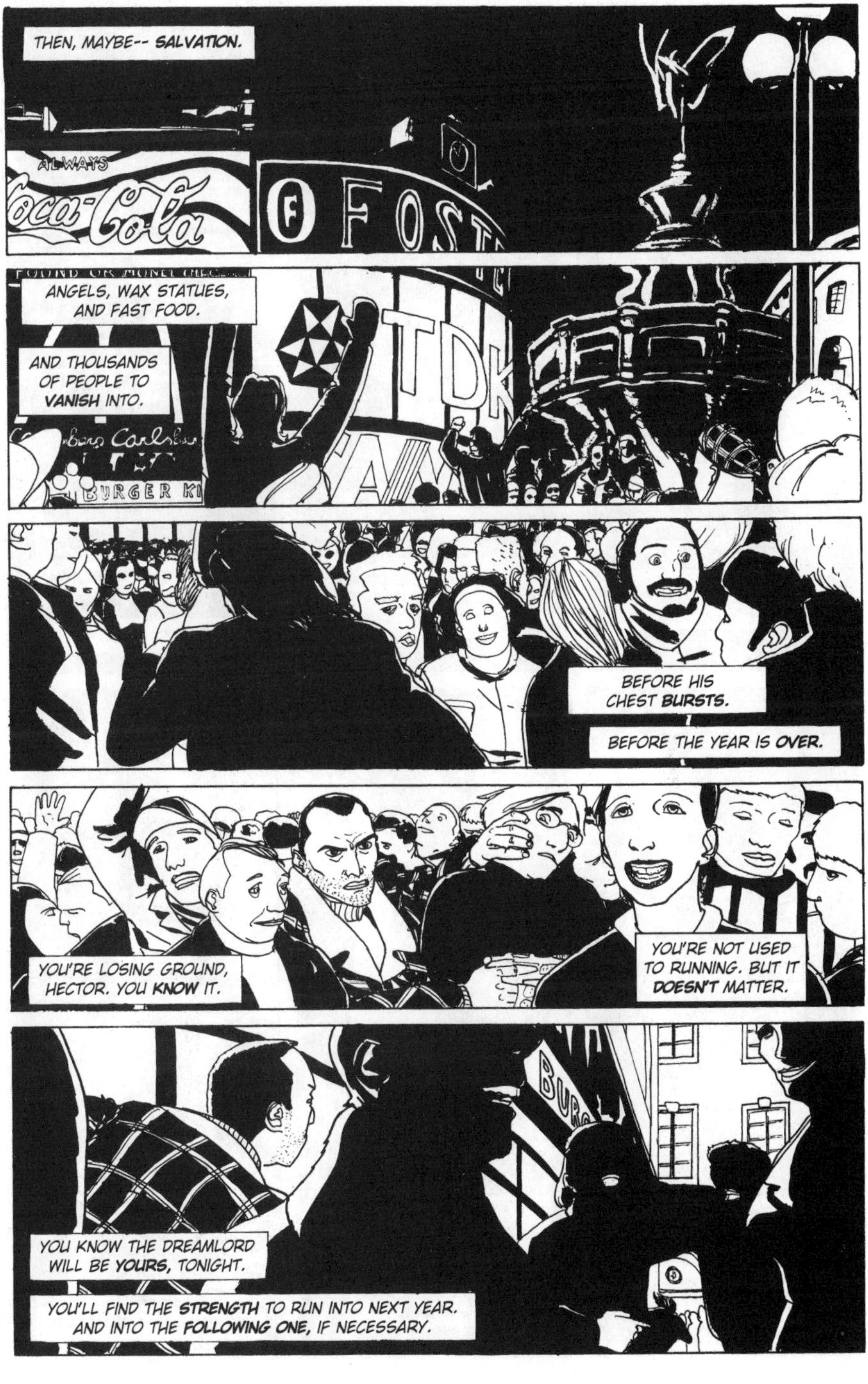
THEN, MAYBE-- SALVATION.
ALWAYS
Coca-Cola
FOSTE
ANGELS, WAX STATUES, AND FAST FOOD.
AND THOUSANDS OF PEOPLE TO VANISH INTO.
TDK
BURGER KI
BEFORE HIS CHEST BURSTS.
BEFORE THE YEAR IS OVER.
YOU'RE LOSING GROUND, HECTOR. YOU KNOW IT.
YOU'RE NOT USED TO RUNNING. BUT IT DOESN'T MATTER.
YOU KNOW THE DREAMLORD WILL BE YOURS, TONIGHT.
YOU'LL FIND THE STRENGTH TO RUN INTO NEXT YEAR. AND INTO THE FOLLOWING ONE, IF NECESSARY.

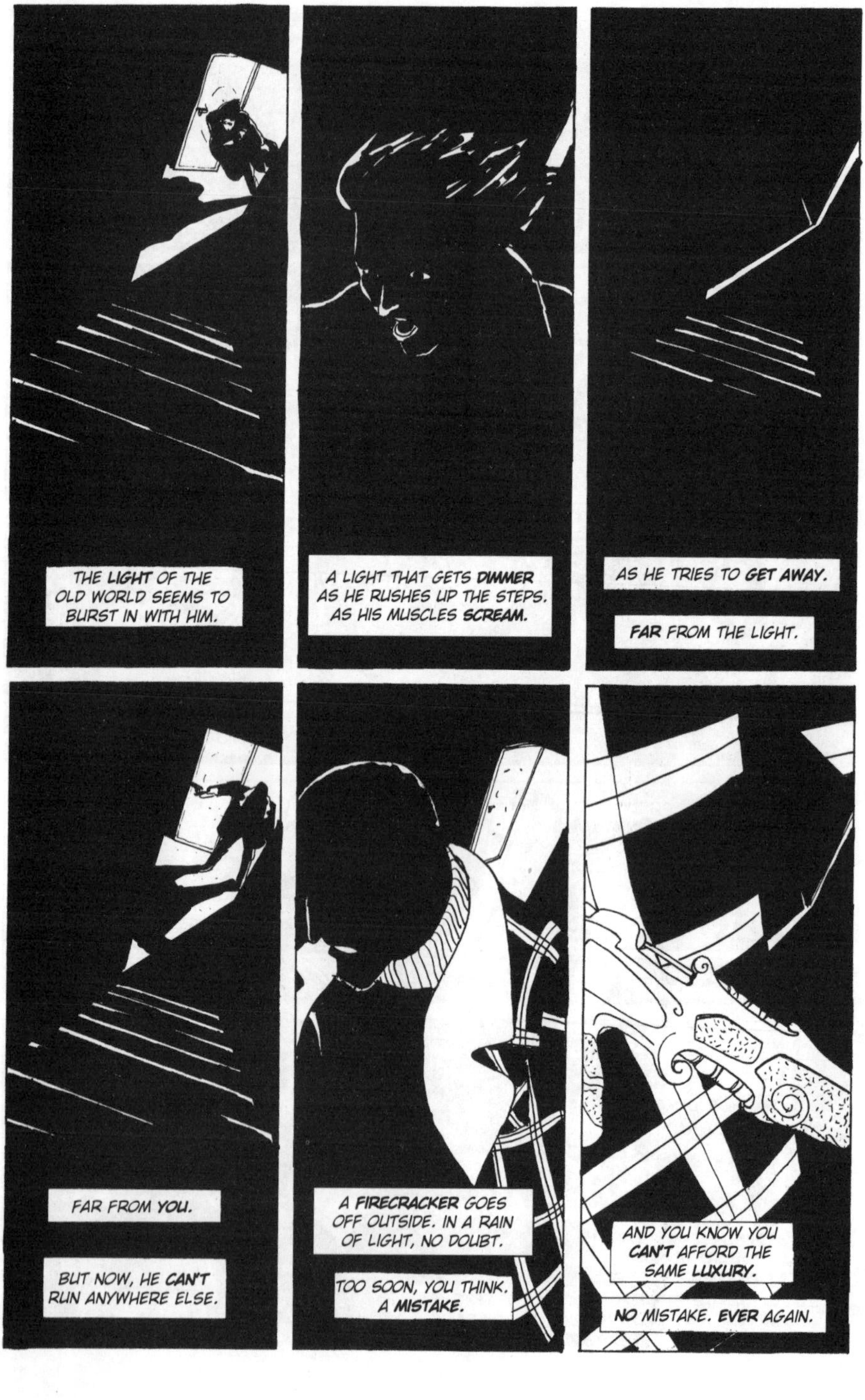
THE LIGHT OF THE OLD WORLD SEEMS TO BURST IN WITH HIM.
A LIGHT THAT GETS DIMMER AS HE RUSHES UP THE STEPS. AS HIS MUSCLES SCREAM.
AS HE TRIES TO GET AWAY.
FAR FROM THE LIGHT.
FAR FROM YOU.
BUT NOW, HE CAN'T RUN ANYWHERE ELSE.
A FIRECRACKER GOES OFF OUTSIDE. IN A RAIN OF LIGHT, NO DOUBT.
TOO SOON, YOU THINK. A MISTAKE.
AND YOU KNOW YOU CAN'T AFFORD THE SAME LUXURY.
NO MISTAKE. EVER AGAIN.

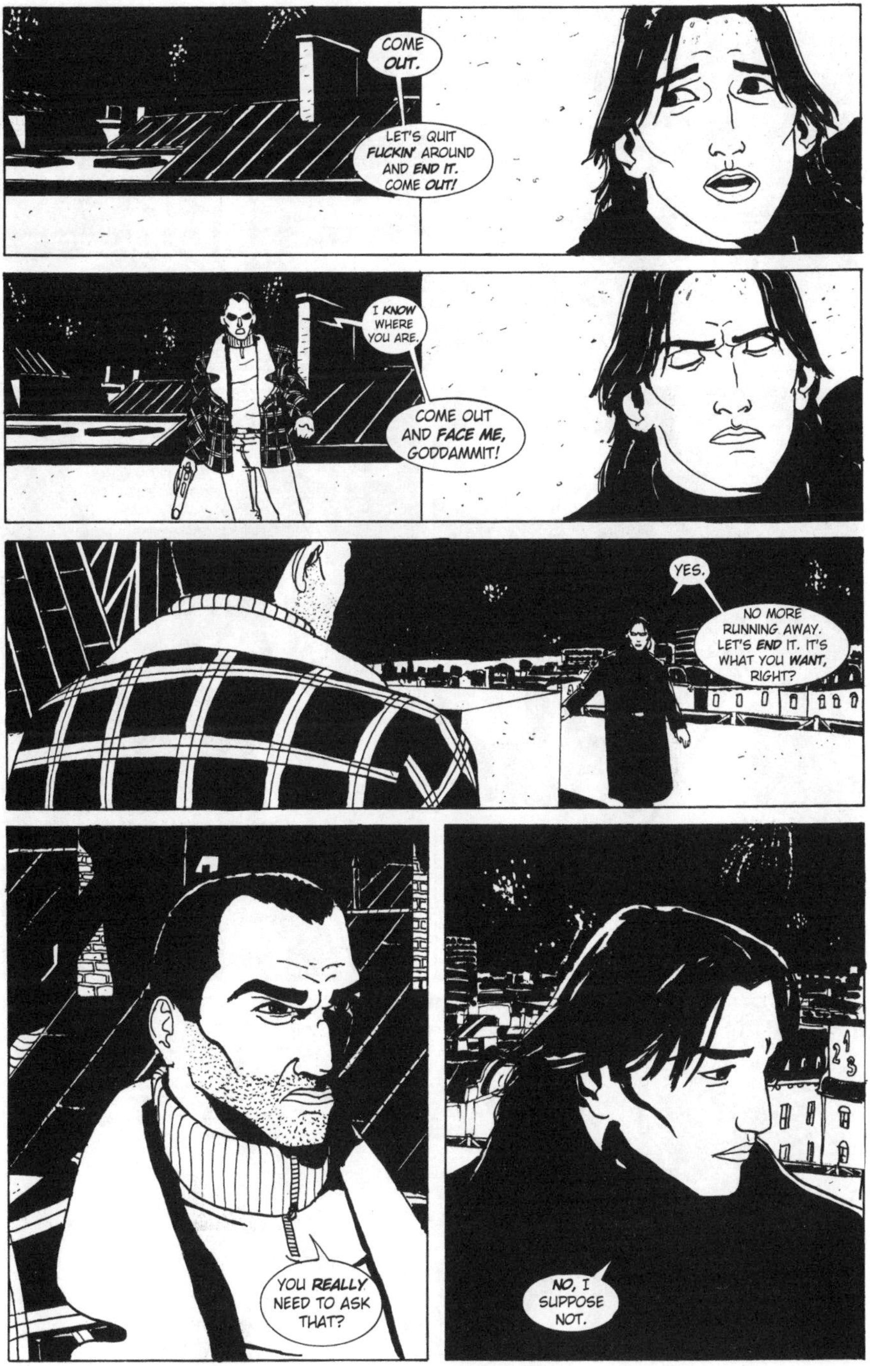
COME OUT.
LET'S QUIT FUCKIN' AROUND AND END IT. COME OUT!
I KNOW WHERE YOU ARE.
COME OUT AND FACE ME, GODDAMMIT!
YES.
NO MORE RUNNING AWAY. LET'S END IT. IT'S WHAT YOU WANT, RIGHT?
YOU REALLY NEED TO ASK THAT?
NO, I SUPPOSE NOT.

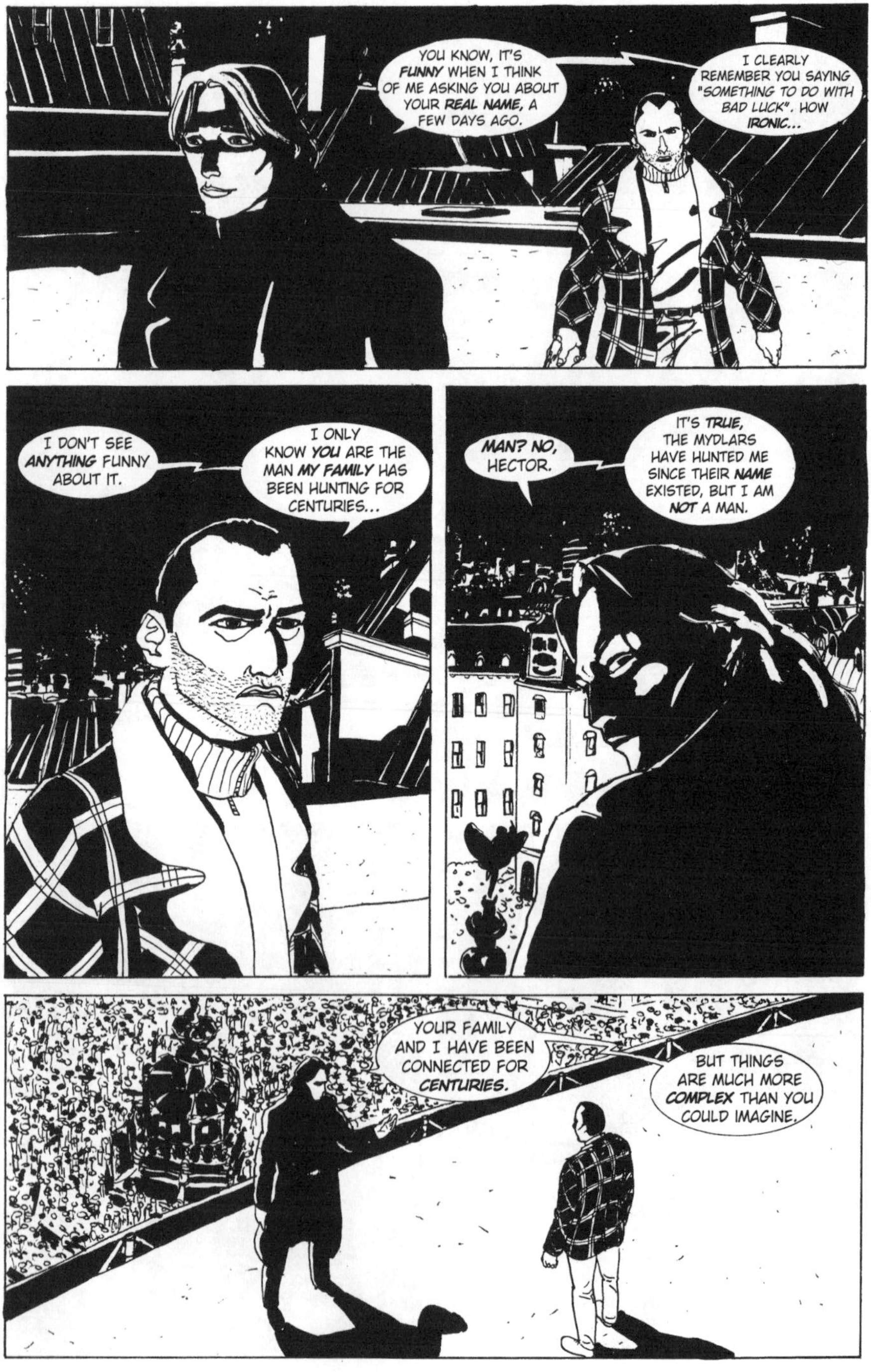
YOU KNOW, IT'S FUNNY WHEN I THINK OF ME ASKING YOU ABOUT YOUR REAL NAME, A FEW DAYS AGO.
I CLEARLY REMEMBER YOU SAYING "SOMETHING TO DO WITH BAD LUCK". HOW IRONIC...
I DON'T SEE ANYTHING FUNNY ABOUT IT.
I ONLY KNOW YOU ARE THE MAN MY FAMILY HAS BEEN HUNTING FOR CENTURIES...
MAN? NO, HECTOR.
IT'S TRUE, THE MYDLARS HAVE HUNTED ME SINCE THEIR NAME EXISTED, BUT I AM NOT A MAN.
YOUR FAMILY AND I HAVE BEEN CONNECTED FOR CENTURIES.
BUT THINGS ARE MUCH MORE COMPLEX THAN YOU COULD IMAGINE.

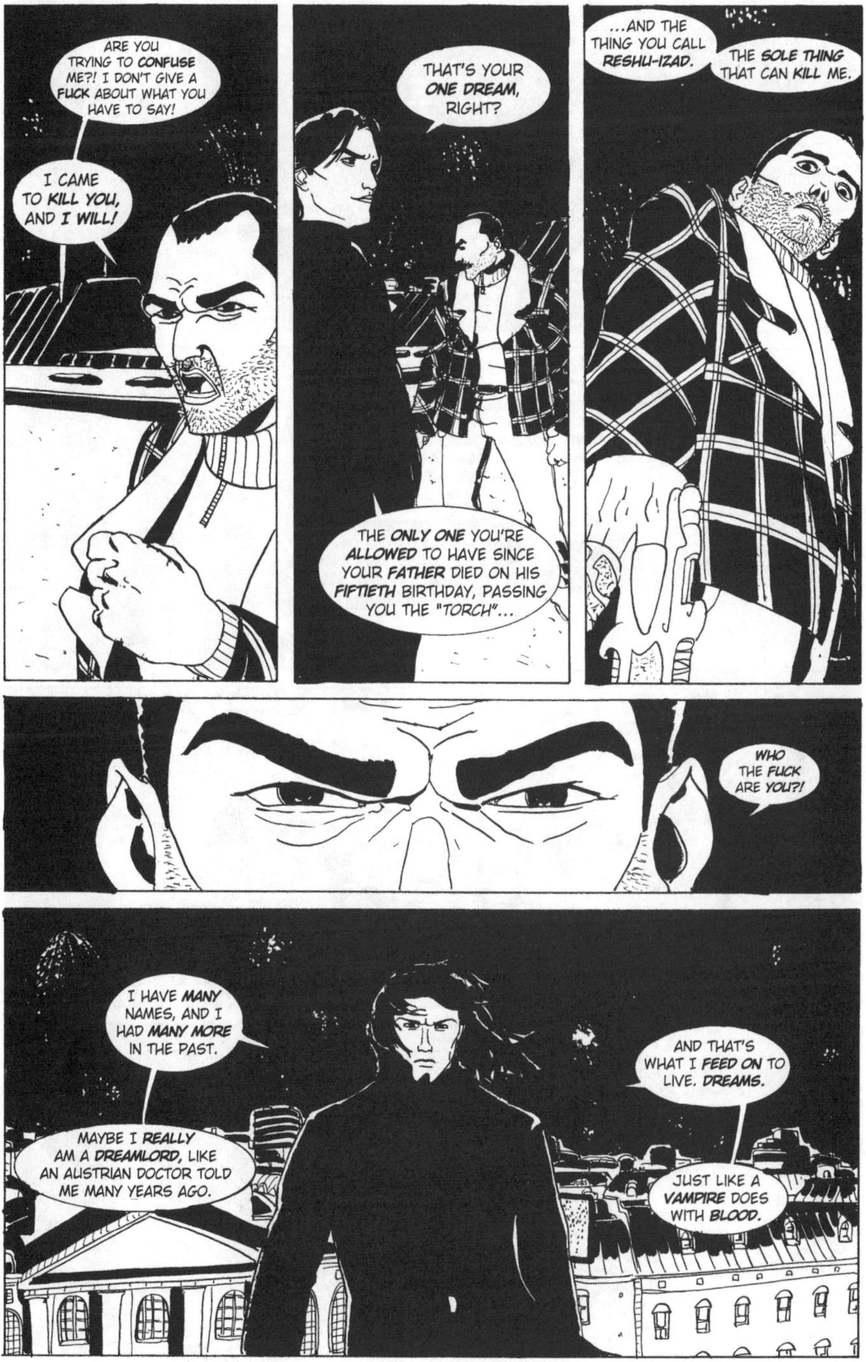
ARE YOU TRYING TO CONFUSE ME?! I DON'T GIVE A FUCK ABOUT WHAT YOU HAVE TO SAY!
I CAME TO KILL YOU, AND I WILL!
THAT'S YOUR ONE DREAM, RIGHT?
THE ONLY ONE YOU'RE ALLOWED TO HAVE SINCE YOUR FATHER DIED ON HIS FIFTIETH BIRTHDAY, PASSING YOU THE "TORCH"...
...AND THE THING YOU CALL RESHU-IZAD.
THE SOLE THING THAT CAN KILL ME.
WHO THE FUCK ARE YOU?!
I HAVE MANY NAMES, AND I HAD MANY MORE IN THE PAST.
MAYBE I REALLY AM A DREAMLORD, LIKE AN AUSTRIAN DOCTOR TOLD ME MANY YEARS AGO.
AND THAT'S WHAT I FEED ON TO LIVE. DREAMS.
JUST LIKE A VAMPIRE DOES WITH BLOOD.

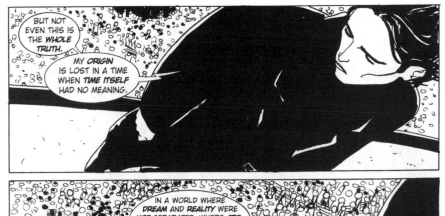

BUT NOT EVEN THIS IS THE *WHOLE TRUTH.*

MY *ORIGIN* IS LOST IN A TIME WHEN *TIME ITSELF* HAD NO MEANING.

IN A WORLD WHERE *DREAM* AND *REALITY* WERE *NOT* SEPARATED, WHERE *CREATORS* AND *CREATURES* WERE ONE AND THE *SAME.* AND THUS... *INSIGNIFICANT.*

THEN, *ONE* DECIDED TO *DESIRE* SOMETHING DIFFERENT. AND EVERYTHING WAS *SHATTERED.*

THE WORLD OF DREAMS, OF THE *CHIMAERAS,* WAS SEPARATED FROM THE *MATERIAL WORLD.* AND HUMAN HISTORY *BEGAN.*

ALL THAT EXISTS, *DOES* EXIST BECAUSE THE *WILL OF ONE* WAS ABLE TO *CHANGE* HIS REALITY.

I WAS THAT *ONE.*

AND I WAS LEFT *ALONE.* IN A WORLD I COULD *NEVER* HAVE IMAGINED. *FOREVER.*

DO YOU NOW WHAT IT MEANS TO *LIVE FOREVER,* HECTOR? WITHOUT

IT MEANS. *LONELINESS.* A LONELINESS YOU CAN *NEVER* ESCAPE.

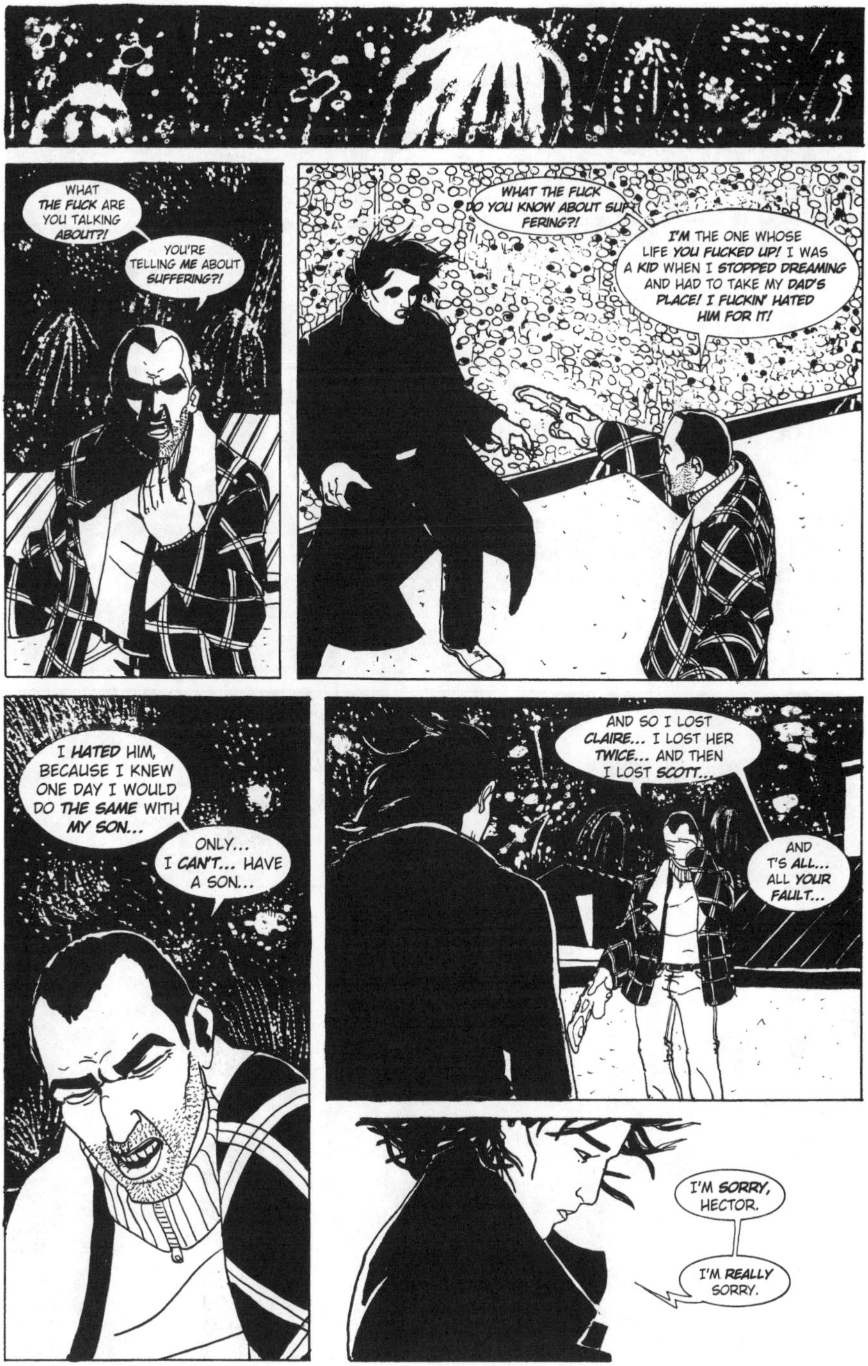
WHAT THE FUCK ARE YOU TALKING ABOUT?!
YOU'RE TELLING ME ABOUT SUFFERING?!
WHAT THE FUCK DO YOU KNOW ABOUT SUF FERING?!
I'M THE ONE WHOSE LIFE YOU FUCKED UP! I WAS A KID WHEN I STOPPED DREAMING AND HAD TO TAKE MY DAD'S PLACE! I FUCKIN' HATED HIM FOR IT!
I HATED HIM, BECAUSE I KNEW ONE DAY I WOULD DO THE SAME WITH MY SON...
ONLY... I CAN'T... HAVE A SON...
AND SO I LOST CLAIRE... I LOST HER TWICE... AND THEN I LOST SCOTT...
AND T'S ALL... ALL YOUR FAULT...
I'M SORRY, HECTOR.
I'M REALLY SORRY.

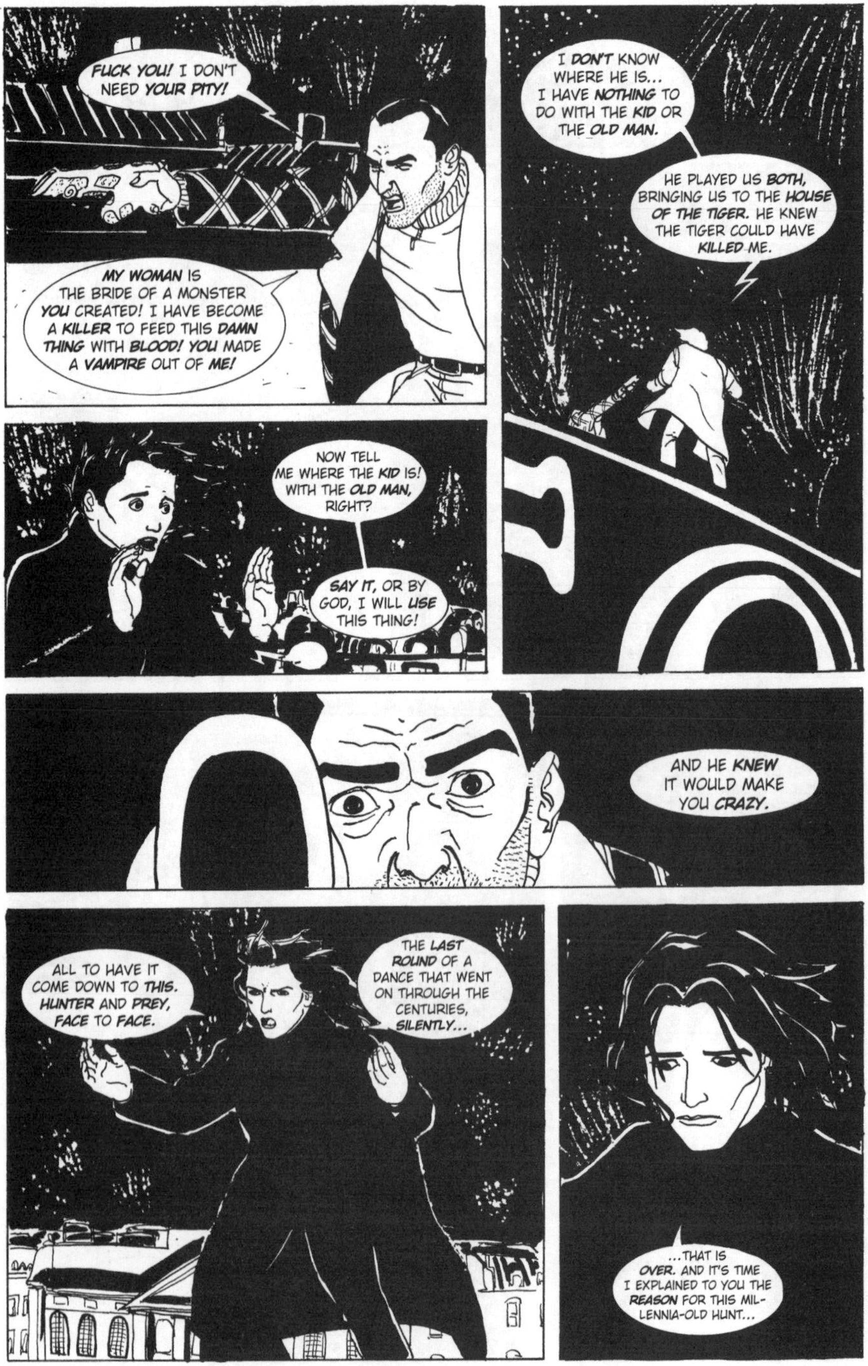
FUCK YOU! I DON'T NEED YOUR PITY!
MY WOMAN IS THE BRIDE OF A MONSTER YOU CREATED! I HAVE BECOME A KILLER TO FEED THIS DAMN THING WITH BLOOD! YOU MADE A VAMPIRE OUT OF ME!
I DON'T KNOW WHERE HE IS... I HAVE NOTHING TO DO WITH THE KID OR THE OLD MAN.
HE PLAYED US BOTH, BRINGING US TO THE HOUSE OF THE TIGER. HE KNEW THE TIGER COULD HAVE KILLED ME.
NOW TELL ME WHERE THE KID IS! WITH THE OLD MAN, RIGHT?
SAY IT, OR BY GOD, I WILL USE THIS THING!
AND HE KNEW IT WOULD MAKE YOU CRAZY.
ALL TO HAVE IT COME DOWN TO THIS. HUNTER AND PREY, FACE TO FACE.
THE LAST ROUND OF A DANCE THAT WENT ON THROUGH THE CENTURIES, SILENTLY...
...THAT IS OVER. AND IT'S TIME I EXPLAINED TO YOU THE REASON FOR THIS MIL-LENNIA-OLD HUNT...

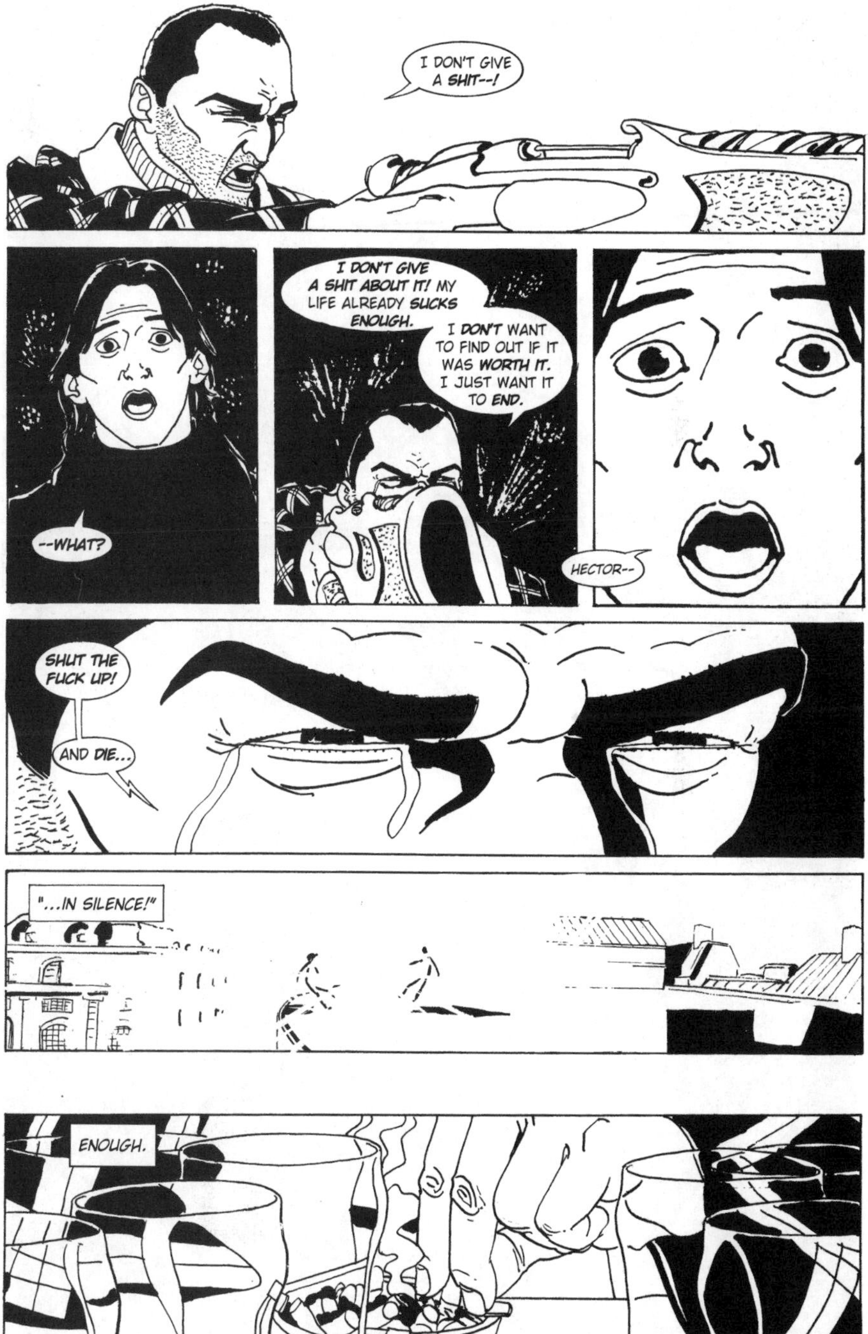
I DON'T GIVE A SHIT--!
--WHAT?
I DON'T GIVE A SHIT ABOUT IT! MY LIFE ALREADY SUCKS ENOUGH.
I DON'T WANT TO FIND OUT IF IT WAS WORTH IT. I JUST WANT IT TO END.
HECTOR--
SHUT THE FUCK UP!
AND DIE...
"...IN SILENCE!"
ENOUGH.

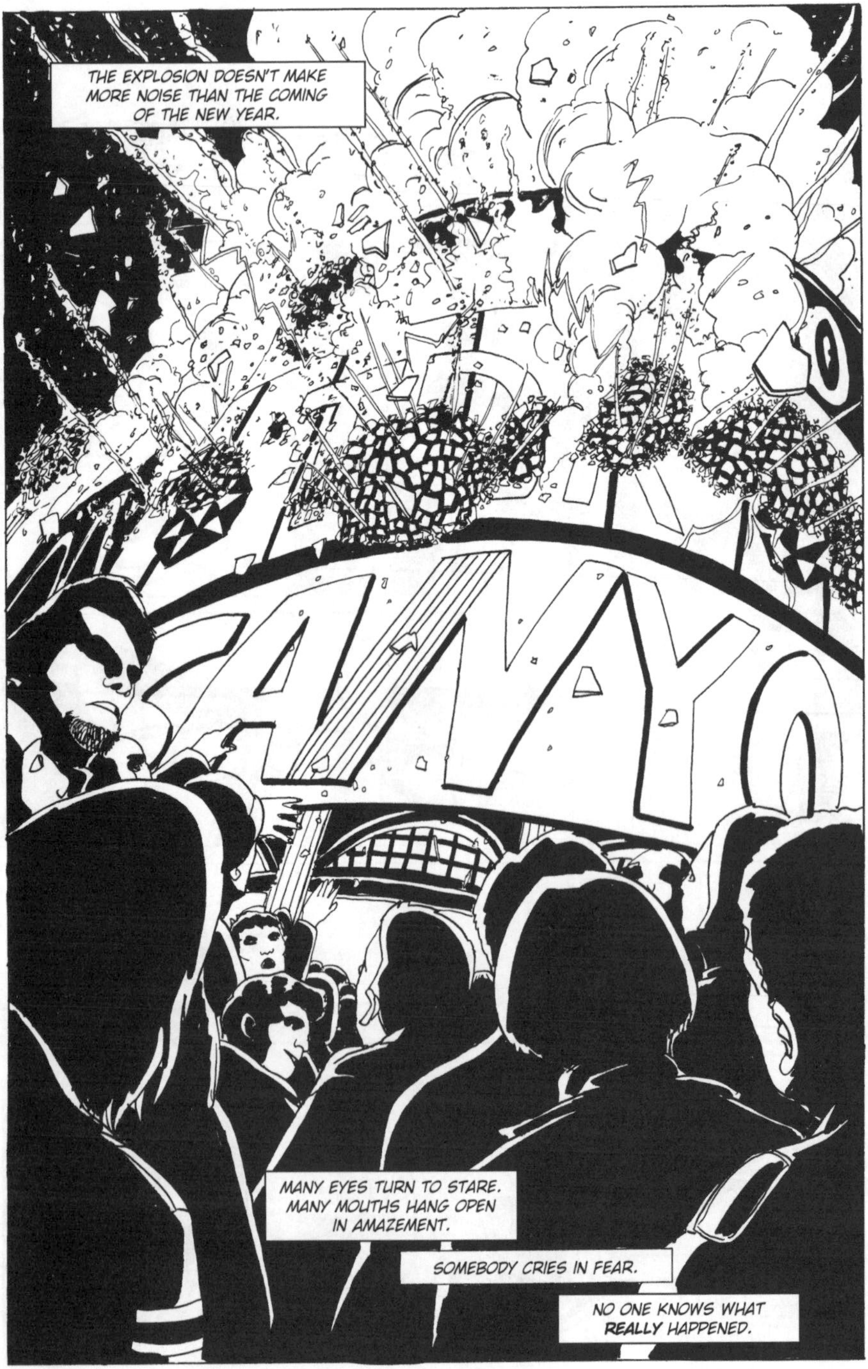
THE EXPLOSION DOESN'T MAKE MORE NOISE THAN THE COMING OF THE NEW YEAR.
MANY EYES TURN TO STARE. MANY MOUTHS HANG OPEN IN AMAZEMENT.
SOMEBODY CRIES IN FEAR.
NO ONE KNOWS WHAT **REALLY** HAPPENED.

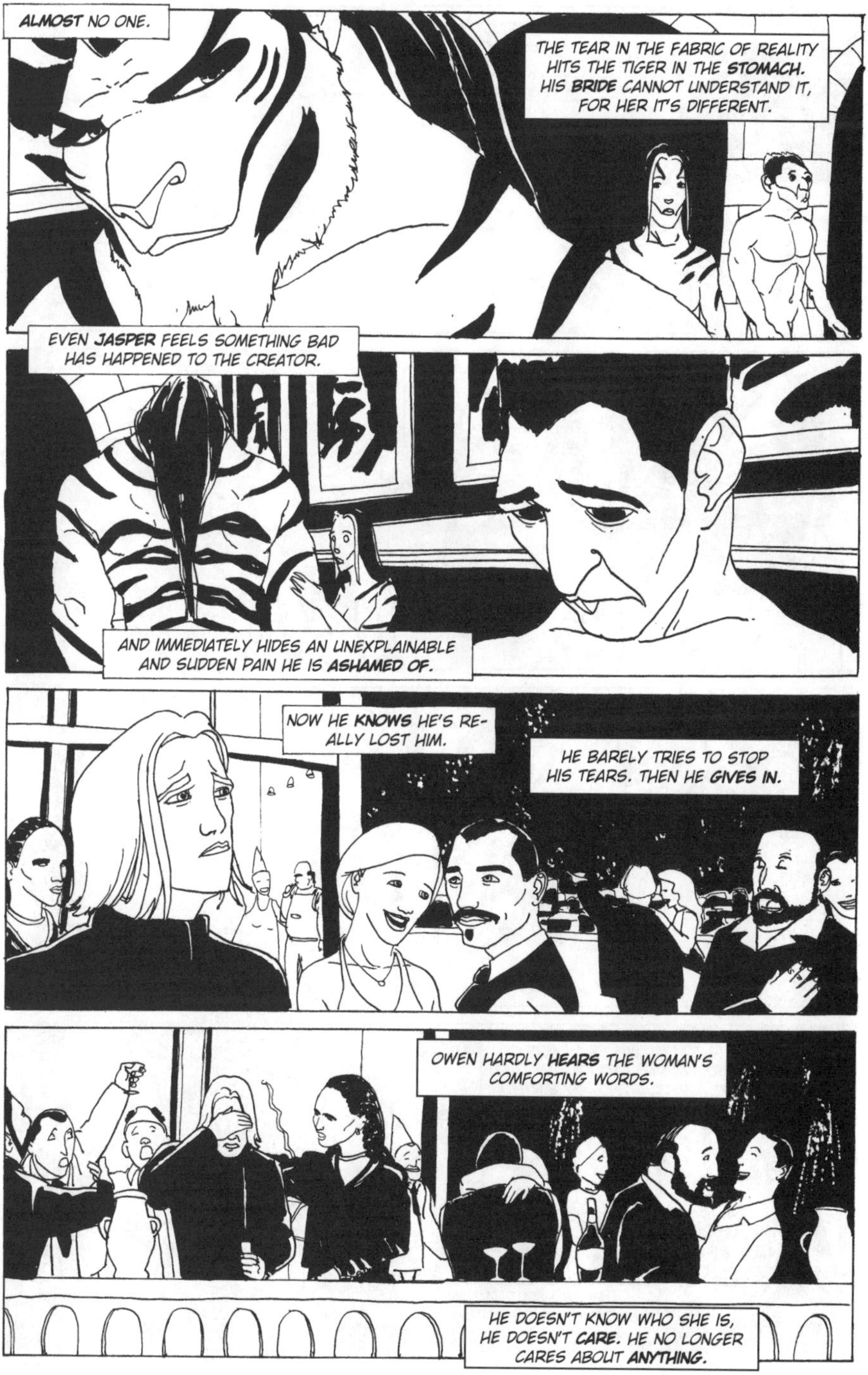

ALMOST NO ONE.
THE TEAR IN THE FABRIC OF REALITY HITS THE TIGER IN THE STOMACH. HIS BRIDE CANNOT UNDERSTAND IT, FOR HER IT'S DIFFERENT.
EVEN JASPER FEELS SOMETHING BAD HAS HAPPENED TO THE CREATOR.
AND IMMEDIATELY HIDES AN UNEXPLAINABLE AND SUDDEN PAIN HE IS ASHAMED OF.
NOW HE KNOWS HE'S REALLY LOST HIM.
HE BARELY TRIES TO STOP HIS TEARS. THEN HE GIVES IN.
OWEN HARDLY HEARS THE WOMAN'S COMFORTING WORDS.
HE DOESN'T KNOW WHO SHE IS, HE DOESN'T CARE. HE NO LONGER CARES ABOUT ANYTHING.

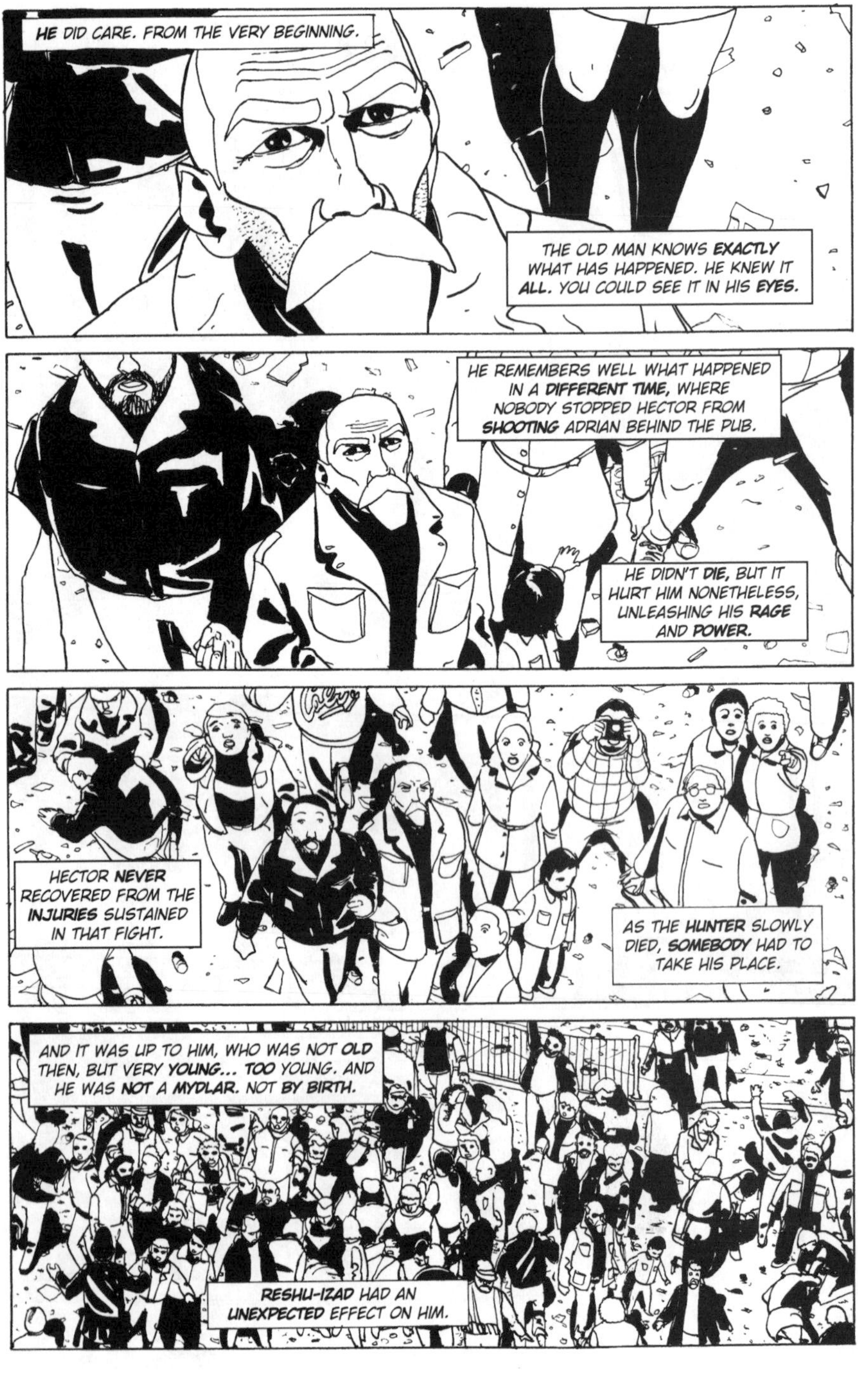
HE DID CARE. FROM THE VERY BEGINNING.
THE OLD MAN KNOWS EXACTLY WHAT HAS HAPPENED. HE KNEW IT ALL. YOU COULD SEE IT IN HIS EYES.
HE REMEMBERS WELL WHAT HAPPENED IN A DIFFERENT TIME, WHERE NOBODY STOPPED HECTOR FROM SHOOTING ADRIAN BEHIND THE PUB.
HE DIDN'T DIE, BUT IT HURT HIM NONETHELESS, UNLEASHING HIS RAGE AND POWER.
HECTOR NEVER RECOVERED FROM THE INJURIES SUSTAINED IN THAT FIGHT.
AS THE HUNTER SLOWLY DIED, SOMEBODY HAD TO TAKE HIS PLACE.
AND IT WAS UP TO HIM, WHO WAS NOT OLD THEN, BUT VERY YOUNG... TOO YOUNG. AND HE WAS NOT A MYDLAR. NOT BY BIRTH.
RESHU-IZAD HAD AN UNEXPECTED EFFECT ON HIM.

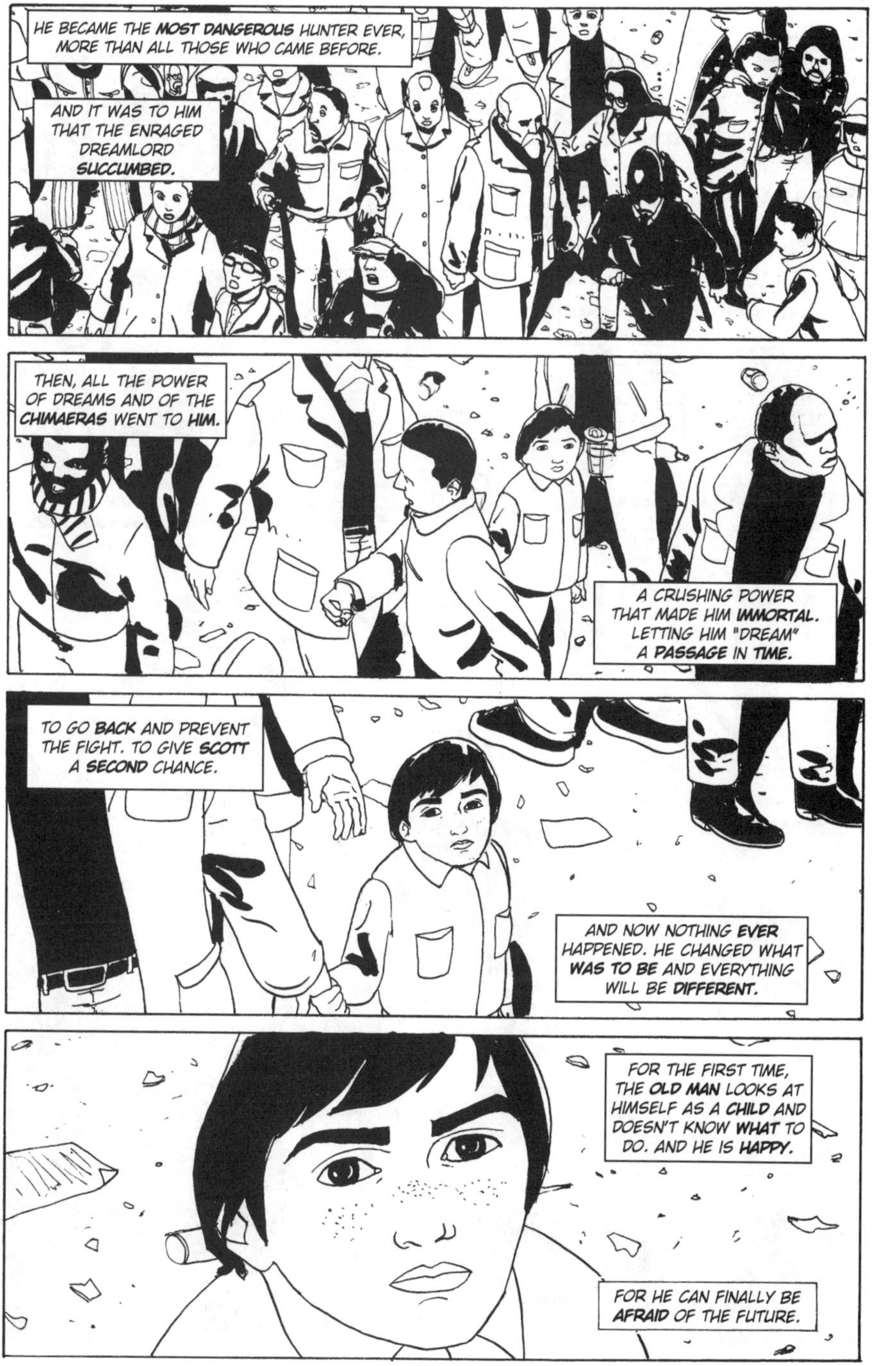
HE BECAME THE MOST DANGEROUS HUNTER EVER, MORE THAN ALL THOSE WHO CAME BEFORE.
AND IT WAS TO HIM THAT THE ENRAGED DREAMLORD SUCCUMBED.
THEN, ALL THE POWER OF DREAMS AND OF THE CHIMAERAS WENT TO HIM.
A CRUSHING POWER THAT MADE HIM IMMORTAL. LETTING HIM "DREAM" A PASSAGE IN TIME.
TO GO BACK AND PREVENT THE FIGHT. TO GIVE SCOTT A SECOND CHANCE.
AND NOW NOTHING EVER HAPPENED. HE CHANGED WHAT WAS TO BE AND EVERYTHING WILL BE DIFFERENT.
FOR THE FIRST TIME, THE OLD MAN LOOKS AT HIMSELF AS A CHILD AND DOESN'T KNOW WHAT TO DO. AND HE IS HAPPY.
FOR HE CAN FINALLY BE AFRAID OF THE FUTURE.

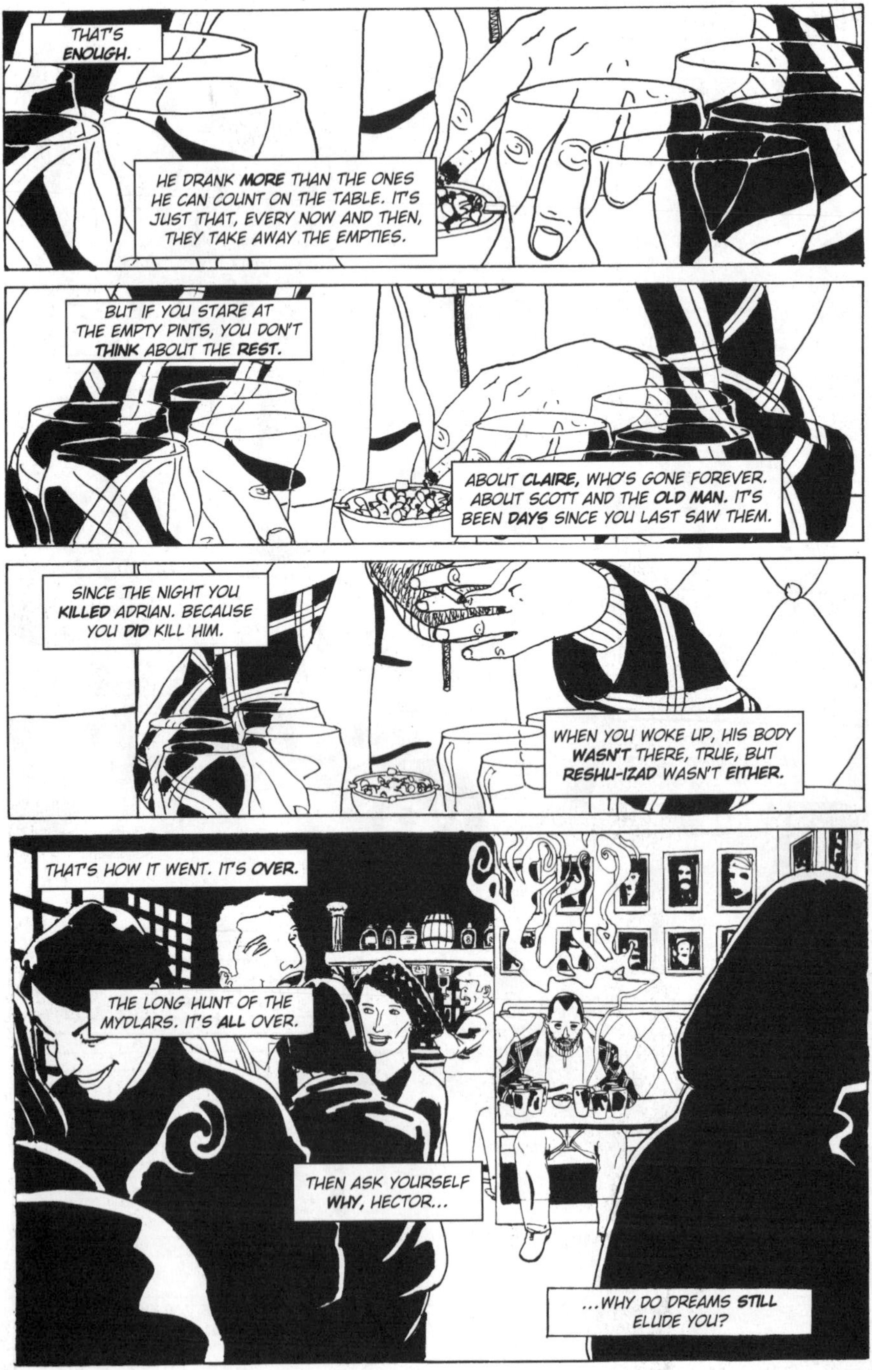
THAT'S ENOUGH.
HE DRANK MORE THAN THE ONES HE CAN COUNT ON THE TABLE. IT'S JUST THAT, EVERY NOW AND THEN, THEY TAKE AWAY THE EMPTIES.
BUT IF YOU STARE AT THE EMPTY PINTS, YOU DON'T THINK ABOUT THE REST.
ABOUT CLAIRE, WHO'S GONE FOREVER. ABOUT SCOTT AND THE OLD MAN. IT'S BEEN DAYS SINCE YOU LAST SAW THEM.
SINCE THE NIGHT YOU KILLED ADRIAN. BECAUSE YOU DID KILL HIM.
WHEN YOU WOKE UP, HIS BODY WASN'T THERE, TRUE, BUT RESHU-IZAD WASN'T EITHER.
THAT'S HOW IT WENT. IT'S OVER.
THE LONG HUNT OF THE MYDLARS. IT'S ALL OVER.
THEN ASK YOURSELF WHY, HECTOR...
...WHY DO DREAMS STILL ELUDE YOU?

MATTEO CASALI started writing professionally in 1997 and is one of the founders of the *Innocent Victim* comics studio, based in Italy. His first work, *Bonerest*, has been published in Italy, Germany, France and recently in the US (by Image Comics). He created and wrote *Quebrada* (Innocent Victim) and *Under a Vicious Sky* (Magic Press) and has been published in books and magazines such as *Vertigo Presenta*, *Sni:z*, *Ragno*, *Kerosene* and *Black*. He also works as an editor and translator for various Italian publishers. His latest projects include writing a story arc for *Catwoman* and the mini-series *Batman: Europa* for DC Comics. In his spare time, he's the frontman for *two* industrial-hardcore bands.

GRAZIA LOBACCARO got her start in comics by attending the *Comic Book Academy* in Milan and going on to win the *2nd National ANAFI New Talents Competition* in 1997. In 1999 she made her professional debut in Italy with the *Silent Dance* trilogy and joined the *Innocent Victim* comics lab. She also contributed to *Quebrada* (Innocent Victim) and had her work published in the anthologies *Mondo Naif* and *Mangazine 100* (Kappa Edizioni, 2001). She collaborates with Eura Editoriale, drawing short stories for their long-standing *Lanciostory* magazine and is currently working on the second and final chapter of the prestige miniseries *Under a Vicious Sky* (Magic Press).

ALESSANDRO DeANGELIS attended the *Comic Book Academy* in Milan before making his pro debut by drawing *Silent Dance* (Esseffe Edizioni) and illustrating one episode of the *Quebrada* series (Innocent Victim). He currently works as graphic-designer in Parma.

THANKS TO
Dan Vado, Jennifer de Guzman and SLG Publishing, Joel Bermejo for his priceless help, Jim Lee and Studio Giocoduro, Beppe Calzolari who believed in us at the beginning, Diego Cajelli, Mauro Muroni and Luca Bertelè, our families and of course, the whole Innocent Victim crew.

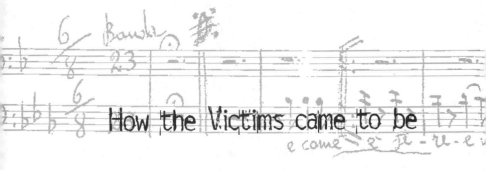

How the Victims came to be

The work of fiction of Matteo Casali, Grazia Lobaccaro and Alessandro DeAngelis you are holding in your hands originated in Italy some time ago. It was published by Innocent Victim (www.innocentvictim.com), a comics studio based in Italy founded in 1997 by writer Matteo Casali and artist Giuseppe Camuncoli.

SOTTO UN
CIELO CATTIVO
MATTEO CASALI - GRAZIA LOBACCARO

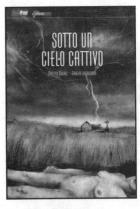

With this then-newborn label, the two authors started self-producing their own comic series, *Bonerest*, quickly gaining attention from readers and critics alike. As interest in the studio's work grew, the original founders were joined by other writers and artists, creating a unique blend of styles that, to this day still produces comics for the national and international comics market.

BONE REST
LA FINE DI UN MONDO
SECONDO AVVENTO
Matteo Casali
Giuseppe Camuncoli
Lorenzo Ruggiero

Starting in 1999, Innocent Victim released various new projects such as the *Silent Dance* trilogy (with Esseffe Editions) two collections of the lucha-noir series *Quebrada* by Casali and various artists, the prestige mini-series *Road's End* by Giuseppe Bazzani and Werther Dell'Edera, Michele Petrucci's first three graphic novels *Keires*, *Silver Salts* and *Numbers* and Casali and Lobaccaro's *Under A Vicious Sky* (Magic Press).

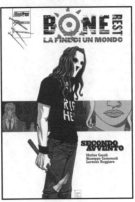

At the time of this writing, many Innocent Victim books have been published in different European countries and in the US, and its creators have been collaborating with various American publishers. Michele Petrucci's works, collected by SLG Publishing in the DUE trade

paperback, were also released in France by Vertige Graphic in 2003. The first two paperbacks of *Bonerest* saw print in Germany (Speed & Panini Comics), France (Panini France), while Image Comics is bringing the series to the United States in the Spring of 2005. Artist Giuseppe Camuncoli contributed to Vertigo's *Swamp Thing*, *Hellblazer* (with *Bonerest* inker Lorenzo Ruggiero), *Bangkok* and Wildstorm's *The Intimates* and *Robin* for DC Comics and also drew an issue of *Spiderman's Tangled Web* for Marvel. Writer Matteo Casali worked on DC Comics' *Catwoman* and *Batman: Europa* (co-written with Brian Azzarello) in addition to this SILENT DANCE release.

Innocent Victim certainly has many more stories to tell, and its creators can do nothing but tell them, one way or another. Stay tuned and keep an eye on the mighty SLG Publishing to catch any future collaboration between the edgy Italian comics lab and the innovative American publisher.

- the Innocent Victim staff
January 2005

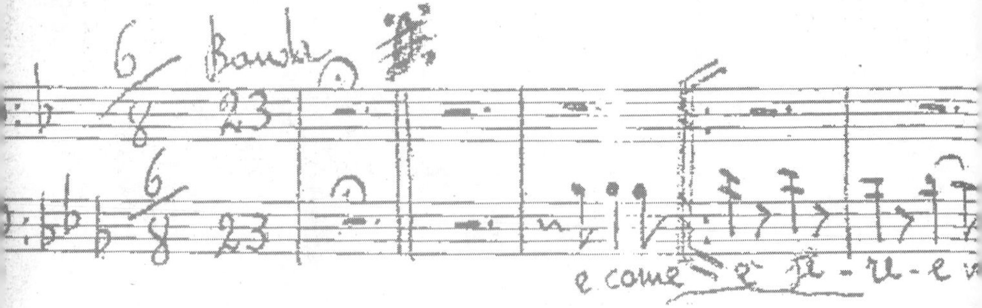
Banda
e come è pi - u - e